Generalized Blockmodeling

This book provides an integrated treatment of blockmodeling, the most frequently used technique in social network analysis. It secures its mathematical foundations and then generalizes blockmodeling for analyzing many types of network structures. Examples are used throughout the text and include small group structures, little league baseball teams, intra-organizational networks, inter-organizational networks, baboon grooming networks, marriage ties of noble families, trust networks, signed networks, Supreme Court decisions, journal citation networks, and alliance networks. Also provided is an integrated treatment of algebraic and graph theoretic concepts for network analysis and a broad introduction to cluster analysis. These formal ideas are the foundations for the authors' proposal for direct optimizational approaches to blockmodeling, which yield blockmodels that best fit the data – a measure of fit that is integral to the establishment of blockmodels – and creates the potential for many generalizations and a deductive use of blockmodeling.

Patrick Doreian is a professor of sociology and statistics at the University of Pittsburgh and is chair of the Department of Sociology. He has edited the *Journal of Mathematical Sociology* since 1982 and has been a member of the editorial board for *Social Networks* since 2003. He was a Centennial professor at The London School of Economics during 2002. He has been a visiting professor at the University of California-Irvine and the University of Ljubljana. His interests include social networks, mathematical sociology, interorganizational networks environmental sociology, and social movements.

Vladimir Batagelj is a professor of discrete and computational mathematics at the University of Ljubljana and is chair of the Department of Theoretical Computer Science at IMFM, Ljubljana. He is a member of editorial boards of *Informatica* and *Journal of Social Structure*. He was visiting professor at University of Pittsburgh in 1990 to 1991 and at University of Konstanz (Germany) in 2002. His main research interests are in graph theory, algorithms on graphs and networks, combinatorial optimization, data analysis, and applications of information technology in education. He is coauthor (with Andrej Mrvar) of Pajek – a program for analysis and visualization of large networks.

Anuška Ferligoj is a professor of statistics at the University of Ljubljana and is dean of the Faculty of Social Sciences. She is editor of the series *Metodoloski zvezki* since 1987 and is a member of the editorial boards of the *Journal of Mathematical Sociology*, *Journal of Classification*, *Social Networks*, and *Statistics in Transition*. She was a Fulbright scholar in 1990 and visiting professor at the University of Pittsburgh. She was awarded the title of Ambassador of Science of the Republic of Slovenia in 1997. Her interests include multivariate analysis (constrained and multicriteria clustering), social networks (measurement quality and blockmodeling), and survey methodology (reliability and validity of measurement).

Structural Analysis in the Social Sciences

The series *Structural Analysis in the Social Sciences* presents approaches that explain social behavior and institutions by reference to relations among such concrete entities as persons and organizations. This contrasts with at least four other popular strategies used in social science analysis: (1) reductionist attempts to explain a focus solely in terms of individuals; (2) explanations stressing the causal primacy of such abstract concepts as ideas, values, mental harmonies, and cognitive maps (thus, "structuralism" on the Continent should be distinguished from structural analysis in the present sense); (3) technological and material determination; (4) the use of "variables" as the main analytical concept (as in the "structural equation" models that dominated much of the sociology of the 1970s), where the structure connects variables rather than actual social entities.

The social network approach is an important example of the strategy of structural analysis. The series also draws on social science theory and research that is not framed explicitly in network terms but rather stresses the importance of relations over the atomization of reduction or the determination of ideas, technology, or material conditions. Although the structural perspective has become extremely popular and influential in all the social sciences, it does not have a coherent identity, and no series yet pulls together such work under a single rubric. By bringing the achievements of structurally oriented scholars to a wider public, the *Structural Analysis* series hopes to encourage the use of this very fruitful approach.

Mark Granovetter

Other Books in the Series:

1. Mark S. Mizruchi & Michael Schwartz, eds., *Intercorporate Relations: The Structural Analysis of Business*.
2. Barry Wellman & S. D. Berkowitz, eds., *Social Structures: A Network Approach*.
3. Ronald L. Brieger, ed., *Social Mobility and Social Structure*.
4. David Knoke, *Political Networks: The Structural Perspective*.
5. John L. Campbell, J. Rogers Hollingsworth, & Leon N. Lindberg, eds., *Governance of the American Economy*.
6. Kyriakos Kontopoulos, *The Logics of Social Structure*.
7. Philippa Pattison, *Algebraic Models for Social Structure*.
8. Stanley Wasserman & Katherine Faust, *Social Network Analysis: Methods and Applications*.
9. Gary Herrigel, *Industrial Constructions: The Sources of German Industrial Power*.
10. Philippe Bourgois, *In Search of Respect: Selling Crack in El Barrio*.
11. Per Hage & Frank Harary, *Island Networks: Communication, Kinship, and Classification Structures in Oceana*.
12. Thomas Schweizer & Douglas R. White, eds., *Kinship, Networks and Exchange*.
13. Noah E. Friedkin, *A Structural Theory of Social Influence*.
14. David Wank, *Commodifying Communism: Business, Trust, and Politics in a Chinese City*.
15. Rebecca Adams & Graham Allan, *Placing Friendship in Context*.
16. Robert L. Nelson & William P. Bridges, *Legalizing Gender Inequality: Courts, Markets and Unequal Pay for Women in America*.
17. Robert Freeland, *The Struggle for Control of the Modern Corporation: Organizational Change at General Motors, 1924–1970*.
18. Yi-min Lin, *Between Politics and Markets: Firms, Competition, and Institutional Change in Post-Mao China*.
19. Nan Lin, *Social Capital: A Theory of Social Structure and Action*.
20. Christopher Ansell, *Schism and Solidarity in Social Movements: The Politics of Labor in the French Third Republic*.

Continued after Index

Generalized Blockmodeling

Patrick Doreian
University of Pittsburgh

Vladimir Batagelj
University of Ljubljana

Anuška Ferligoj
University of Ljubljana

PUBLISHED BY THE PRESS SYNDICATE OF THE UNIVERSITY OF CAMBRIDGE
The Pitt Building, Trumpington Street, Cambridge, United Kingdom

CAMBRIDGE UNIVERSITY PRESS
The Edinburgh Building, Cambridge CB2 2RU, UK
40 West 20th Street, New York, NY 10011-4211, USA
477 Williamstown Road, Port Melbourne, VIC 3207, Australia
Ruiz de Alarcón 13, 28014 Madrid, Spain
Dock House, The Waterfront, Cape Town 8001, South Africa

http://www.cambridge.org

First published 2005

Printed in the United States of America

Typeface Times Roman 10/12 pt.   *System* LᴬTEX 2_ε [TB]

A catalog record for this book is available from the British Library.

Library of Congress Cataloging in Publication Data
Doreian, Patrick.
Generalized blockmodeling / Patrick Doreian, Vladimir Batagelj, Anuška Ferligoj.
p.   cm. – (Structural analysis in the social sciences)
Includes bibliographical references and indexes.
ISBN 0-521-84085-6
1. Social networks – Mathematical models.   2. Sociometry.
I. Title: Blockmodeling.   II. Batagelj, Vladimir, 1948–
III. Ferligoj, Anuska.   IV. Title.   V. Series.
HM741.D67   2004
302′.01′5195 – dc22   2004040784

ISBN 0 521 84085 6 hardback

CONTENTS

PREFACE

Once upon a time, in 1974 to be precise, three youngsters met during the ECPR workshop at the University of Essex in England. We knew nothing of what would unfold beyond liking each other's company and sharing a commitment to using mathematical ideas to advance social science research. We stayed in contact and next met at the SOECO conference in Ljubljana in 1976. Over the years since that meeting, we got together when we could, but it was not until the Social Science Methodology conference at Dubrovnik in 1988 that the idea formed for a collaboration. At that time, Vlado and Nuša saw themselves as cluster analysts and Pat was a social network analyst. As we talked, it became clear that the two fields could be joined to mutual benefit. A shared passion and dream was born: form a synthesis of cluster analytic ideas and social network ideas. This book is a result of pursuing that passion and dream.

We owe many debts and we will try to acknowledge them here. Institutional support of various forms was critical. A Fulbright fellowship allowed Nuša to visit Pittsburgh for seven months in 1990–91, and we thank the Fulbright Commission for their support. The Universities of Ljubljana and Pittsburgh have an exchange agreement. Under that agreement, Vlado came to Pittsburgh in 1991, and we worked on our joint project. This period marked the true beginning of our professional collaboration, and we presented some results at the Sunbelt XI conference in Tampa in 1991. The University of Ljubljana supported Pat as a visiting professor for a two-month stay in 1993, and our first statement on generalized blockmodeling was presented during the International Social Network Conference in Munich later that year. A grant from the National Academy of Science/National Research Council Collaboration in Basic Science and Engineering (COBASE) allowed Pat to return to Ljubljana for another two months in 1994. Under the exchange agreement between our universities, Nuša was able to visit Pittsburgh again in 1996. We thank conference organizers, our funders, and especially our universities for the support that made our joint work possible.

Besides the formal support, Nuša and Vlado made several visits to Pittsburgh and Pat visited Ljubljana in 1998, 1999, 2002 (twice), and 2003. The visits in 2002 were facilitated by Pat's having a Centennial Professorship at the London School of Economics, and we appreciate that piece of institutional support greatly. Critical as the institutional support has been, our greatest debt is to Esther Sales. Married to Pat, she accepted, supported, and most importantly, encouraged his frequent visits to Slovenia knowing full well that "the block" seemed no more than a pretext for him to go to one of his most favored places on the planet. Socially, we became a quartet and the work of "the triad" could never have proceeded without Esther's love and support.

We are most appreciative of Mark Granovetter's encouragement and recommendation that this book be a part of the Cambridge Structural Analysis series that he edits. Katie Faust reviewed the book for Cambridge and made many wonderful recommendations for changes and restructuring of some of the arguments. (Of course, we did not know who reviewed the manuscript at that time, but by living in the same network, we came to know her identity well before learning it formally.) Peter Marsden generously agreed to read through the manuscript and offered us many helpful suggestions. Although we are convinced of our arguments, it is always nice to receive positive feedback from other scholars, and we appreciate the expressive support as much as the instrumental support. We are also grateful for the contributions of Andrej Mrvar through programming of the 1996 version of the balance partitioning and his part in the creation of PAJEK. He has also been a wonderful supportive colleague over the years. We also value the comments of students in our classes at the Universities of Pittsburgh and Ljubljana, as well as their frankness in telling us when we indulged in havers (Old English for "foolish talk").

There are some less obvious things that made the book possible. We consumed much dvojna kava, temno pivo, refošk, teran, shiraz, and Newcastle Brown. We thank many brewers, wine makers, and coffee producers for fueling our endeavors – so much so that we do not envy them their profits from our liquid consumption patterns. We also thank publishers, notably Elsevier and Springer-Verlag, for their permission to use some of the materials that we published in their journals. And we do not envy their profits from our labors either.

Some authors are quite forthright in declaring why they write their books and why the world will benefit from someone's paying attention. We are less ambitious. We wrote this book primarily to have fun, enjoy each other's company, collect our thoughts in one place, and build upon them. Certainly, our objective was not to become rich and famous! The book is a product of having fun, glorious fun. But we think that we did achieve some worthwhile things. We have produced a synthesis between cluster analysis and network analysis. However, it is for others to judge whether or not this truly has merit. We think that we have secured the mathematical foundations for generalized blockmodeling and have opened the way for many further generalizations. Although the book can be viewed as very technical and mathematical, we do emphasize that substance comes first. This is especially clear in the analysis of role systems, structural balance, and ranked systems. We have a particularly soft spot for the materials in the chapter on the symmetric–acyclic decomposition of networks because for us, the underlying concepts started in sociological substance. The mathematics and methods that we created came in response to substantive concerns instead of groping for something on the shelves. Finally, we like to emphasize the use of "deductive" blockmodeling through the prespecification of generalized blockmodels. Often, researchers know more than they think they do, and this knowledge can be mobilized fruitfully.

Much remains to be done, and we point to some of this in our final chapter. For us, the future concerns us most, and we hope that others will, so to speak, put their shoulders to this wheel. We will continue to work in this area, and the tools we create will be located in PAJEK. Above all, we will continue to have fun and to enjoy the love and affection that we share.

Piran, Slovenia

1

SOCIAL NETWORKS AND BLOCKMODELS

These are exciting times for social network analysts. As Hummon and Carley (1993) observed, their area has emerged as an integrated social scientific specialty. Some (e.g., Berkowitz 1982:150 and Rogers 1987:308) have declared that social network analysis is revolutionary for the social sciences. Doreian (1995) argued that this is a premature judgment. It was not clear then – nor is it clear now – that there is a network paradigm in the sense of "a set of shared methods, standards, modes of explanation, or theories or a body of shared knowledge" (Cohen 1985:26) adhered to by all network analysts. In part, this can be attributed to the field's having its historical origins in a wide variety of disciplines. Fields such as anthropology, business administration, communication, history, mathematics, political science, and sociology have scholars whose research, at least in part, includes network analytic ideas. Even though some network analysts view social networks as *their* field, they do not share *all* of the features of a specialty listed by Cohen. However, network analysts do agree that social networks are important – even crucial – and that network-based explanations of social phenomena have a distinctive character. Wellman (1988) is most persuasive in arguing that network accounts of social phenomena, in addition to being distinctive, are also more potent. Even so, network analysts differ on some of the specifics. In our view, this is a positive feature of the specialty given a commitment to using network tools of some sort.

Certainly the trappings of a coherent social science specialty are in place: The International Association of Social Network Analysts (INSNA) was formed in 1976. Members of INSNA have received *Connections*, a professional newsletter – now available online – that has linked their invisible college since 1977, and a specialty journal (*Social Networks*) was created in 1978 specifically for the emerging field. There is an annual (International Sunbelt Social Network) conference. Within this institutionalized forum, network analysts have pursued a wide variety of topics with regard to substance and the development of network analytic tools.

The so-called knowledge generated by scientists working within a particular discipline or sets of disciplines is conditioned by the technology they use. For our purposes here, we view technology (both hardware and software) as the means by which sets of tools can be fashioned. Even though it is far too early to know if social network analysis is in the vanguard of a scientific revolution for the social sciences, it is useful to examine the first stage of a scientific revolution. Cohen (1985) characterized it as an intellectual revolution that "occurs whenever a scientist (or a group of scientists) devises a radical solution to some major problem or problems, finds a new method of using information . . . sets forth a new framework for knowledge into which existing information can be put in a wholly new way . . . [and] introduces a set of concepts that change the character of existing knowledge or proposes a revolutionary new theory" (1985:28). We believe that social network analysis in general, and blockmodeling in particular, has this character.

Lorrain and White's (1971) paper on structural equivalence was dramatically different and changed[1] the way many social network analysts viewed their field. Work on *blockmodeling* and *positional analysis* blossomed. In Hummon and Carley's citation study of the articles in the first 12 volumes of *Social Networks*, positional analysis was identified as one of the dominant interests.

There are two broad rationales for considering blockmodeling as an important set of network analytic tools. One is substantive and concerns the delineation of role structures. In general, there are well-defined places in social structures. We call these places *positions* and provide an intuitive description of this term later in this chapter and a much fuller characterization in Chapter 6. A social role is a set of expectations that are coupled to the positions. *Parent* is a position, and there are expectations as to what parents should do. *Child* is another position with (age-graded) expectations of what children should do. These positions and roles form a *coupled system* in which parents and children have expectations of each other.[2] *Chief Executive Officer* (CEO) is another position defined in a corporation, as is the position of *Vice President* (VP). There are coupled expectations of how CEOs and VPs should behave with regard to each other and to other actors inside (and outside) the corporation. These roles include and, more importantly, generate social relations with observed network behavior, especially interaction, providing indicators of the fundamental social structure in which social actors are located (see Figure 1.3 and Table 1.8 in the paragraphs that follow). Actors in those roles will share some common features. As Schwartz and Sprinzen (1984) put it, "the occupants of a common position will exhibit a common pattern of relations, across multiple relations, consistently tending to have certain relations with occupants of particular other positions and to not have the same type of relation with occupants of yet other positions" (1984:104). Using the network in Figure 1.3 (shown in the paragraphs that follow) as an example, we find that informal social interactions are more likely to occur at each level of the hierarchy rather than to involve people from different levels. In this example of a network, the idea of positions and roles

---

1 This language is chosen to emphasize that the potential for a revolution was there.
2 These expectations need not agree and, indeed, they tend to diverge as children grow older – at least in Western societies.

is built into the organizational structure. Blockmodeling tools provide ways of describing these structures in a theoretically informed way.

The second rationale is more pragmatic in the sense of discerning the fundamental (basic) structure of social networks. Most, if not all, social networks have a nonrandom structure. Put differently, they have systematic features that characterize their social structures. For small networks, be they formal roles systems or generated empirical networks, these structures are relatively straightforward to discern. However, once networks are large or complex, identifying their basic structure becomes a difficult task. We note that the structure of the small Kansas Search and Rescue network that is described in Section 2.2.4 with just 20 organizations is such an example, for it has a structure that is nonobvious upon visual inspection. On the basis of our experience of fitting many blockmodels, we also note that a perceived obvious structure need not be fundamental and that blockmodeling can suggest alternative structures to analysts. Blockmodeling provides a coherent approach to identifying fundamental structures of social networks, and generalized blockmodeling provides a much expanded set of blockmodeling tools.

The following treatment of generalized blockmodeling is offered in the hope that such an integrated presentation will secure its intellectual foundations and establish a fruitful methodological basis for the analysis of a wide range of relational structures and network processes. In short, *our goal here is to present an integrated and generalized treatment of blockmodeling.* We do not present a chronological history of blockmodeling. Readers who are familiar with network analysis and with conventional blockmodeling can skip ahead to Section 1.6 for a concise statement of generalized blockmodeling and some of the ways in which it can be done.

We use the rest of this chapter to provide an intuitive statement of social network analytic ideas (Section 1.1), a description of blocks as parts of networks (Section 1.2), a listing of some block types (Section 1.3), a discussion of specifying blockmodels with some concrete examples (Section 1.4), a preliminary characterization of blockmodeling that starts with conventional blockmodeling (Section 1.5), and a general statement about generalized blockmodeling, including a description of how it generalizes and greatly extends conventional blockmodeling (Section 1.6). In section 1.7 we provide an outline map of the book that is represented in Figure 1.5. Sections marked with ⊙ contain more techanical materials and can be skipped on a first reading.

1.1   AN INTUITIVE STATEMENT OF NETWORK IDEAS

We start with an intuitive statement of some social network issues, problems, and ideas. Our intent is to provide an overview of some key network analytic terms as they relate to blockmodeling. These ideas help provide motivation for the formal tools we begin to develop in Chapter 3 and use throughout the subsequent chapters.

Social networks consist of social actors with one or more social relations defined over those actors. Social actors and social relations are everywhere – so much so that is impossible to think of social life without also thinking of social relations.

Most people, at many points in their lives, belong to small groups. There have been an extraordinary number of definitions of this concept. Because we do not want to get into a protracted terminological debate, we consider a group to be *two or more individuals who are interdependent through sustained interaction.*[3] Groups can be found in workplaces, in religious organizations, in dormitories, and so on. Terms such as *support groups* and *friendship groups* acknowledge the widespread existence of relatively small collections of individuals sharing some kind of salient identity. People's relations with each other in their groups are crucial for understanding their actions within those groups. Indeed, there is a large literature devoted to the study of the structure of social relations in groups.[4] We note its existence here, in passing, but we return to it in Chapters 6–12. These relations help determine the ways in which human groups evolve through time. See, for example, some of the contributions to Doreian and Stokman's (1997) edited volume on social network evolution.[5] Affective relations or sentiments (Homans 1950) having positive and negative values (such as like or dislike) are particularly relevant. We consider signed relations in detail in Chapter 10.

Network analytic techniques are not confined to small-group applications, and, as a first step away from a small-group focus, we note that there can be social relations between groups. Two bowling teams can have a friendly rivalry, or two support groups can provide mutual support. For these two examples, it is unlikely that a group constrains the activities of its members with regard to between-group behavior. However, intergroup relations can be negative. Some people belong to gangs, and there are important social relations between gangs, notably being allied with, or an enemy of, other gangs. Relations between the gangs set both the permitted and proscribed behaviors for individuals belonging to them. So too for families: The drama of Shakespeare's Romeo and Juliet is driven by the enmity between the houses of Capulet and Montague.

Many people work in organizations in which there are social relations such as "has authority over" or "receives orders from" as well as some of the interpersonal relations that are created when people work and necessarily interact with each other. Homans (1950) made a distinction between the external and internal systems of small human groups. The external system is part of the wider organizational environment, including the physical layout of work areas such as the Bank Wiring Room (BWR; Roethlisberger and Dickson, 1939). We describe some of the classic BWR data in Chapter 2 and report analyses of them in Chapters 6,

---

3 We leave to one side the issue of whether characteristics such as size, sentiment ties, group identity, goals, identification, solidarity, conformity, or support are used to help define a group, or whether they are variables that can be used to characterize groups – or both.

4 See, for example, Forsyth (1990).

5 There have been two subsequent special issues of the *Journal of Mathematical Sociology* that have extended this line of work. Part II of *Evolution of Social Networks* appeared in Volume 25(1) in 2001, and Part III appeared in Volume 27(1–2) in 2003.

7, and 10. There are relations between different departments of an organization. In an organization manufacturing some durable product, minimally, raw resources and partially finished goods move between different organizational units. There can be relations between organizations also. Organizations shipping goods back and forth have social relations such as "transports to" and "communicates with." The sets of agencies providing social services to a population in some geographical location are linked by a rich set of social relations that include referrals (of clients) between agencies, the provision of services for other agencies, and money flows.

Cities are linked by a variety of infrastructures – roads, railways, optical fibers, and satellite links – that permit people to travel between places, make telephone calls, and fax messages to one another. Economic goods can be moved between areas even if they are far apart. We can think of countries as being linked by many of the social relations that also link cities. Certainly, they have trading ties, can recognize each other diplomatically, form alliances, and go to war – all of which are social relations.

The foregoing discussion makes it clear that we do not confine the term *social actor* to individuals. Any human collectivity with a clear identity is a potential social actor: groups, organizations, cities, and nations have the potential to act. At a minimum, interaction involves outputs from actors that are coupled to inputs from other actors. According to Olsen (1968:32), social interaction "occurs whenever one social actor *affects* the thoughts or *actions* of another social actor in some fashion" (emphasis added). Furthermore, we regard a social relationship as enduring social interaction.[6] In this sense, then, we can talk of relationships between organizations or any well-defined collectivities. We recognize that the words *organizations interact* can be expressed in terms of the behavior of specific individuals within these organizations. We can take the statement about organizations interacting as a shorthand expression for the actions of all of the human actors involved in that transaction. However, we want to use the term *interact* in a much more general sense. *The key concept is to identify social actors as socially defined units.* Transactions can occur between any social collectivities that are identified as meaningful, well-defined social units.

1.1.1   Fundamental types of social relations

In each of the examples described thus far, the social actors are individuals, groups, organizations, and the like. They are social and they can act. We use *social actor* as a generic term. If the focus is on one type of social actor, people for instance, then in terms of our narrative thus far, attention will be focused on the relations between people. If the focus is on organizations, attention is confined to relations between

---

6   Although we are mindful that transient events can have important structural consequences (Doreian 2002), our concern is with discerning structures, and we take them to be reasonably stable.

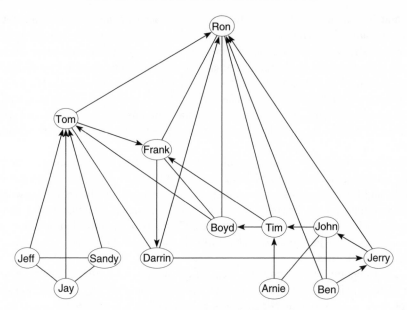

Figure 1.1. Transatlantic industries friendship ties.

these organizations.[7] A specific network analysis can have multiple types of social actors. For a particular discussion, the relevant social actors can also be referred to as the *units (of analysis)* consistent with both the idea of socially defined units and most discussions of research methods.

One-mode social relations. For this type of relation, a one-mode social network is defined as the set of social actors and the relations defined only between them. In most discussions of social networks, this is the meaning of the term *network*, and we also adopt this usage of the term. The units are all of a single type. For a small group, this will be the people and their social ties – for example, "likes" or "is my best friend." As an example, consider the diagram[8] in Figure 1.1 for a Little League baseball team (Transatlantic Industries) with 13 boys (Fine 1987). Each boy was asked to name his three best friends.[9] The social actors are the boys and the relation is "my best friend." The lines represent the presence of the social ties from one boy to another. The line from Tom to Ron shows Tom's choice of Ron as someone he likes well enough to be among his top three choices. Ron does not view Tom in the same way. In a similar fashion, Tim and Boyd have a tie in one direction but

7   Of course, the relations among the organizations can have implications for the relations among the people in the organizations.

8   In our diagrams we use a solid line without arrowheads for reciprocated ties.

9   The relations "likes the most" and "my best friend" need not be the same. The structure of the network in Figure 1.1 may be an amalgam of the two types of ties. For this example, we use "likes the most" and "is one of my best friends" as the same.

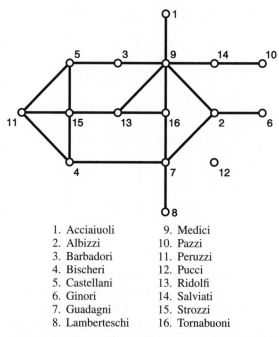

1. Acciaiuoli
2. Albizzi
3. Barbadori
4. Bischeri
5. Castellani
6. Ginori
7. Guadagni
8. Lamberteschi
9. Medici
10. Pazzi
11. Peruzzi
12. Pucci
13. Ridolfi
14. Salviati
15. Strozzi
16. Tornabuoni

Figure 1.2. Elite families in Florence in the 15th century.

not in the other. Ron and Frank have a reciprocal tie whereas Darrin and Tim have no tie between them. The rest of the figure can be read in the same fashion. All of the information concerning this social relation is contained in the diagram. Such figures were called sociograms by Moreno (1934), which is a term still in use today.

Figure 1.1 illustrates the concept of a graph in a pictorial representation of the set of social actors and the relation defined over them. The relation is the set of pairs of boys (as actors) that are linked by the social ties. The graph is the display of the boys and the pairs of boys where one is chosen by the other. This and related concepts are defined in Chapter 4. When our attention is on a graph as a representation of a social network, we will use the term *vertex* for a represented social actor. For the ties among the social actors, we will use the term *lines* (in a graph).

As a second example, consider the elite Florentine families in the 15th century as shown in Figure 1.2. Here the social relation is "linked by marriage" with the lines showing the existence of a marriage tie between families. This graph can be read in the same way as Figure 1.1. For example, the Medici family has marriage ties to six other families. The Bischeri family is not among those linked directly by marriage to the Medici family. However, it is linked with the Peruzzi family by marriage. Again, all of the information concerning the incidence of marriage linkages is contained in the graph.

We note one difference between the relations depicted in Figures 1.1 and 1.2. For the boys in the Little League baseball team the social relation has a direction

Table 1.1. Matrix with the Ties of the Transatlantic Industries Team

		1	2	3	4	5	6	7	8	9	10	11	12	13
Ron	1	0	0	1	1	1	0	0	0	0	0	0	0	0
Tom	2	1	0	1	0	0	0	0	0	0	0	1	0	0
Frank	3	1	0	0	1	0	0	0	0	0	0	1	0	0
Boyd	4	1	1	1	0	0	0	0	0	0	0	0	0	0
Tim	5	1	0	1	1	0	0	0	0	0	0	0	0	0
John	6	0	0	0	0	1	0	0	0	0	0	0	1	1
Jeff	7	0	1	0	0	0	0	0	1	1	0	0	0	0
Jay	8	0	1	0	0	0	0	1	0	1	0	0	0	0
Sandy	9	0	1	0	0	0	0	1	1	0	0	0	0	0
Jerry	10	1	0	0	0	0	1	0	0	0	0	0	0	0
Darrin	11	1	1	0	0	0	0	0	0	0	1	0	0	0
Ben	12	1	0	0	0	0	1	0	0	0	1	0	0	0
Arnie	13	0	0	0	0	1	1	0	0	0	0	0	0	0

(from the chooser to the chosen), while the relation for the Florentine families does not. If we preserved the distinction of men marrying women and women marrying men, then the marriage tie between families would be directed also.[10] Two types of lines in the graph are distinguished: edges (undirected lines) and arcs (directed lines). Generically, we use the term lines, and the context will make clear the specific type of tie.

Using a visual version of a graph is one way of representing a social relation. An alternative form for representing the same information about the presence of a social relation is a square array or matrix. Table 1.1 provides the same information that is contained in Figure 1.1. Here the numeral 1 represents the presence of a tie between two actors, and the numeral 0 represents the absence of a tie between actors.

Table 1.2 shows *exactly* the same marriage data contained in Figure 1.2. Both the rows and columns are coordinated by the family names, and the presence of a 1 indicates a marriage tie between the two families and 0 represents the absence of such a tie. The matrix representation of ties is known also as a sociomatrix. It is possible, and often desirable, to examine multiple relations defined over the same collection of social actors.

It should be clear that any social relation, as defined above, can be represented either by a graph or an array (a matrix). These representations take the same abstract forms, regardless of the nature of the units and the relations between them. We make extensive use of both throughout this volume. While pictures do have a visual immediacy and have value because of this, matrix representations have greater relevance for blockmodeling. In essence, the technical core of what we propose throughout this book is a sophisticated form of row and column permutation to

10   We provide an example of such ties for families in Ragusa (Dubrovnik) in the 16th century and again in the early 19th century in Chapters 2 and 11.

Table 1.2. Padgett's Florentine Families Marriage Data

		1	2	3	4	5	6	7	8	9	10	11	12	13	14	15	16
Acciaiuoli	1	0	0	0	0	0	0	0	0	1	0	0	0	0	0	0	0
Albizzi	2	0	0	0	0	0	1	1	0	1	0	0	0	0	0	0	0
Barbadori	3	0	0	0	0	1	0	0	0	1	0	0	0	0	0	0	0
Bischeri	4	0	0	0	0	0	0	1	0	0	0	1	0	0	0	1	0
Castellani	5	0	0	1	0	0	0	0	0	0	0	1	0	0	0	1	0
Ginori	6	0	1	0	0	0	0	0	0	0	0	0	0	0	0	0	0
Guadagni	7	0	1	0	1	0	0	0	1	0	0	0	0	0	0	0	1
Lamberteschi	8	0	0	0	0	0	0	1	0	0	0	0	0	0	0	0	0
Medici	9	1	1	1	0	0	0	0	0	0	0	0	0	1	1	0	1
Pazzi	10	0	0	0	0	0	0	0	0	0	0	0	0	0	1	0	0
Peruzzi	11	0	0	0	1	1	0	0	0	0	0	0	0	0	0	1	0
Pucci	12	0	0	0	0	0	0	0	0	0	0	0	0	0	0	0	0
Ridolfi	13	0	0	0	0	0	0	0	0	1	0	0	0	0	0	1	1
Salviati	14	0	0	0	0	0	0	0	0	1	1	0	0	0	0	0	0
Strozzi	15	0	0	0	1	1	0	0	0	0	0	1	0	1	0	0	0
Tornabuoni	16	0	0	0	0	0	0	1	0	1	0	0	0	1	0	0	0

reveal structure. Of course, once we have the fundamenal form of a network, graphical methods are again important for displaying this form.

Membership social relations. The second fundamental network relation is membership or affiliation. Although it was not described explicitly in our discussion thus far, it was acknowledged implicitly. Gang members belong to gangs, people are employed by organizations, and individuals belong to families. For membership ties, there are two types of units – and the data for such a relation are often referred to as two-mode data. (See Wasserman and Faust 1994:29–30 and 291–298, for a discussion of two-mode data.) One of the classic membership data sets is shown in Table 1.3 (Davis, Gardner, and Gardner 1941).

The data represent the attendance patterns of 18 women for 14 events. Typically, such two-mode data are represented in rectangular arrays. In this case, the array is coordinated by women for the rows and by events for the columns. It is straightforward to construct Table 1.4, which contains counts (off the main diagonal) of the number of times each pair of women was at the same event. For example, Eleanor and Brenda jointly attended events E_2, E_4, E_8, and E_{12}. The values in the diagonal contain counts of the number of events each woman attended. Eleanor attended just four events while Brenda attended seven events. In addition to the events attended by Eleanor, Brenda was also present at events E_7, E_{10}, and E_{13}. These two-mode data will be analyzed with our blockmodeling tools for two-mode data in Chapter 8.

In a specific network study, both one-mode and two-mode relations can be observed. It may well be the case that one of the relations has some importance for the other. If we look at people belonging to gangs, their memberships will constrain their choices of friends. Although employees work for organizations, they

Table 1.3. Membership Relation for Women and Events

	E_1	E_2	E_3	E_4	E_5	E_6	E_7	E_8	E_9	E_{10}	E_{11}	E_{12}	E_{13}	E_{14}
Eleanor	0	1	0	1	0	0	0	1	0	0	0	1	0	0
Brenda	0	1	0	1	0	0	1	1	0	1	0	1	1	0
Dorothy	0	0	0	0	0	1	0	0	0	0	0	1	0	0
Verne	0	0	0	1	1	1	0	0	0	0	0	1	0	0
Flora	1	0	0	0	0	1	0	0	0	0	0	0	0	0
Olivia	1	0	0	0	0	1	0	0	0	0	0	0	0	0
Laura	0	1	1	1	0	0	1	1	0	1	0	1	0	0
Evelyn	0	1	1	0	0	1	1	1	0	1	0	1	1	0
Pearl	0	0	0	0	0	1	0	1	0	0	0	1	0	0
Ruth	0	1	0	1	0	1	0	0	0	0	0	1	0	0
Sylvia	0	0	0	1	1	1	0	0	1	0	1	1	0	1
Katherine	0	0	0	0	1	1	0	0	1	0	1	1	0	1
Myrna	0	0	0	0	1	1	0	0	1	0	0	1	0	0
Theresa	0	1	1	1	0	1	1	1	0	0	0	1	1	0
Charlotte	0	1	0	1	0	0	1	0	0	0	0	0	1	0
Frances	0	1	0	0	0	0	1	1	0	0	0	1	0	0
Helen	1	0	0	1	1	0	0	0	1	0	0	1	0	0
Nora	1	0	0	1	1	1	0	1	1	0	1	0	0	1

do this in distinct organizational units, and their locations in these units constrain their interactions with other organizational members. Although the linkage of these relations will not be perfect, we will say that one relation constrains the other. We expand these ideas formally in Chapter 3 (Section 3.2.2).

Table 1.4. Woman-by-Woman Joint Attendance of Events Relation

		1	2	3	4	5	6	7	8	9	10	11	12	13	14	15	16	17	18
Eleanor	1	4																	
Brenda	2	4	7																
Dorothy	3	1	1	2															
Verne	4	2	2	2	4														
Flora	5	0	0	1	1	2													
Olivia	6	0	0	1	1	2	2												
Laura	7	4	6	1	2	0	0	7											
Evelyn	8	3	6	2	2	1	1	6	8										
Pearl	9	2	2	2	2	1	1	2	3	3									
Ruth	10	3	3	2	3	1	1	3	3	2	4								
Sylvia	11	2	2	2	4	1	1	2	2	2	3	7							
Katherine	12	1	1	2	3	1	1	1	2	2	2	6	6						
Myrna	13	1	1	2	3	1	1	1	2	2	2	4	4	4					
Theresa	14	4	6	2	3	1	1	6	7	3	4	3	2	2	8				
Charlotte	15	2	4	0	1	0	0	3	3	0	1	1	0	0	4	4			
Frances	16	3	4	1	1	0	0	4	4	2	2	1	1	1	4	2	4		
Helen	17	2	2	1	3	1	1	2	1	1	2	4	3	3	2	1	1	5	
Nora	18	2	2	1	3	2	2	2	2	2	2	6	5	3	3	1	1	4	8

Table 1.5. Types of Data Arrays

		Directed Ties	
		No	Yes
Type of Link	Binary	Simple Binary	Directed Binary
	Valued	Simple Valued	Directed Valued

1.1.2   Types of relational data arrays

The relational data arrays of Section 1.1.1 can be expressed in terms of two characteristics. One specifies whether the relation is symmetric or nonsymmetric. Alternatively, we can describe the graph as being directed or nondirected. The second characteristic is whether the ties are valued or not. Together, these two features – direction and type – define the four cells shown in Table 1.5.

All that we intend by using the term "valued" is to allow for cases in which there is some magnitude beyond the existence of the tie. If the boys in the Little League baseball team had been asked to name their best friends in order, then we could assume that "best friend" has greater magnitude than "second best friend" (although we would not be able to say by how much with only this information). The relation "number of clients referred" from one social services agency to another defines a network with valued ties. Most network analyses feature binary networks, and we follow this practice in much of this volume. This is changing quite rapidly among network analysts, and increasing attention will be given to valued networks. However, special care is needed in dealing with them. To focus on the fundamental aspects of blockmodeling, we primarily consider binary networks.

The ties shown in Figure 1.2 are undirected, and if all ties take this form we are dealing with an undirected graph. The ties in Figure 1.1 are directed, and such graphs are called directed graphs or, simply, digraphs. Many empirical networks have pairs of actors linked by undirected (mutual) ties and pairs of actors linked by directed ties. The distinction between directed and undirected ties is particularly important in Chapter 11.

1.2   BLOCKS AS PARTS OF NETWORKS

The two networks shown in Figure 1.1 and Figure 1.2 are quite simple, but even for these uncomplicated networks there are many structural features that are not obvious (as we show in Chapters 6 and 7). For larger and more complex networks, it is often impossible to discern the real structure(s) present in the data. One of the main goals of network analysis is to identify, in a given network, clusters of actors that share structural characteristics in terms of some relation(s). The actors within a cluster should have the same (or similar) pattern of ties, and actors in different clusters should be also connected through specific patterns of ties. If we present a relation by using a matrix, we can rearrange the matrix in such a way that the actors belonging to the first cluster are given first (by rows and by columns), then the actors of the second cluster, and so on. The relational matrix can then be partitioned by the clusters into several blocks. Blockmodeling provides a method and rationale for distilling the clusters of actors that share as much, as possible, common patterns of ties within and between the clusters. In essence, (generalized) blockmodeling is nothing more that assembling a set of blocks into a blockmodel. Our whole approach to generalized blockmodeling can be seen as selecting block types, assembling them into a blockmodel, and then fitting the resulting blockmodel to network data. The characterizations of the blocks of a blockmodel are constructed from the network ties they contain.

1.2.1   Blocks

For simplicity, we start by having two clusters of actors: $\{a, b, c\}$ and $\{d, e, f, g\}$. A block is defined as the relation between two clusters of actors. If we first consider only the ties within a cluster, our attention is confined only to the actors in that cluster. This defines a *diagonal block*, which is in this matrix form:

	a	b	c
a	0	–	–
b	–	0	–
c	–	–	0

The dashes denote a location where empirical information about a relational tie would be recorded. By convention, in most cases, the diagonal entries (marked 0) are defined as null ties, although this need not be the case (see Section 6.1.1). If we confine our attention to ties between the two different clusters of actors, we are dealing with *off-diagonal blocks*, in the following form:

	d	e	f	g
a	–	–	–	–
b	–	–	–	–
c	–	–	–	–

Here, every element in the matrix array is a location where network data can be recorded. A blockmodel is built by using diagonal and off-diagonal blocks in a systematic fashion.

Two block types. One type of diagonal block is the complete block in which all of the actors are linked in reciprocal ties as follows:

	a	b	c
a	0	1	1
b	1	0	1
c	1	1	0

The off-diagonal complete block has 1s everywhere:

	d	e	f	g
a	1	1	1	1
b	1	1	1	1
c	1	1	1	1

At the other extreme, a null block is one with 0s everywhere in the block – for both diagonal and off-diagonal blocks. We show only the off-diagonal block:

	d	e	f	g
a	0	0	0	0
b	0	0	0	0
c	0	0	0	0

A simple blockmodel. Suppose we had a set of social actors, $\{a, b, c, d, e, f, g\}$, whose matrix of ties is

	a	b	c	d	e	f	g
a	0	1	1	0	0	0	0
b	1	0	1	0	0	0	0
c	1	1	0	0	0	0	0
d	1	1	1	0	0	0	0
e	1	1	1	0	0	0	0
f	1	1	1	0	0	0	0
g	1	1	1	0	0	0	0

If we look closely at these ties, we see the following: (i) $\{a, b, c\}$ all have ties with each other; (ii) these actors send no ties to $\{d, e, f, g\}$; (iii) in the second cluster, the actors have no ties to each other; and (iv) $\{d, e, f, g\}$ have ties directed to $\{a, b, c\}$. With these descriptions, we can partition the relational matrix into four blocks:

	a	b	c	d	e	f	g
a	0	1	1	0	0	0	0
b	1	0	1	0	0	0	0
c	1	1	0	0	0	0	0
d	1	1	1	0	0	0	0
e	1	1	1	0	0	0	0
f	1	1	1	0	0	0	0
g	1	1	1	0	0	0	0

This representation makes it clear that the four blocks obtained can be described by the following block types:

$$\begin{array}{ll} \text{complete} & \text{null} \\ \text{complete} & \text{null} \end{array}$$

The words in this array carry their obvious meaning, but if we write 1 for complete and 0 for null, the network information is stated in an even more compact form:

$$\begin{array}{ll} 1 & 0 \\ 1 & 0 \end{array}$$

Later, we will come to characterize this as one form of a center–periphery model. This compact form is viewed as an *image* of the original network. For this representation of the network, we use the term *model* and say that it is a *blockmodel*. The image can be used as a description of the essential structure of the network. All we need are the ideas that actors (as vertices) can be grouped into clusters. These clusters, which form *positions*, become the (new) units of the blockmodel. The ties between the actors within a cluster are used to describe the diagonal blocks, whereas the ties between actors in pairs of distinct clusters are used to construct the off-diagonal blocks. These off-diagonal blocks characterize the ties between positions. If there are k positions, there are k^2 blocks in the blockmodel with k diagonal blocks and $k(k-1)$ off-diagonal blocks.

To build more appropriate and interesting blockmodels, we need the following: (i) a more extensive collection of types of blocks, (ii) substantive reasons for specifying blocks, and (iii) a compelling reason for combining these blocks into a blockmodel. We start by outlining some block types. In doing so, we use the format of an off-diagonal block.

1.3   SOME BLOCK TYPES

We define the following types of blocks in addition to the two defined in the previous section.

1. Null blocks (in which there are no ties between any pair of actors in the two clusters):

$$\begin{array}{llll} 0 & 0 & 0 & 0 \\ 0 & 0 & 0 & 0 \\ 0 & 0 & 0 & 0 \end{array}$$

2. Complete blocks (in which there is a tie between all pairs of actors in the two clusters):

```
1  1  1  1
1  1  1  1
1  1  1  1
```

3. Regular blocks (in which there is a least one 1 in every row and column):

```
1  0  1  1
0  1  1  0
1  0  1  1
```

4. Row-regular blocks (in which there is at least one 1 in each row):

```
0  1  1  0
1  0  1  0
0  1  1  0
```

5. Column-regular blocks (in which there is one 1 in every column):

```
0  1  1  1
0  0  0  0
1  1  0  0
```

Because the regular blocks are defined as blocks with at least one 1 in every row and at least one 1 in every column, there are many potential regular blocks. It does not matter how many 1s are in each row or in each column. All that matters is that there is at least one 1 in all rows and columns. Of course, a complete block is also a regular block. A row-regular block has at least one 1 in each row. As shown in the example used in Item 4, there is always at least one column of 0s in this kind of block. A regular block is also row regular, but a row-regular block need not be a regular block – as is the case in these examples. Similarly, a column-regular block requires a 1 in each column. As shown in Item 5, this type of block will have null rows. A regular block is also column regular. If a block is both row regular and column regular, then it is regular.

The final block type that we introduce here is the symmetric diagonal block. For this block type, any tie that is present must be reciprocated.

```
0  1  0  1
1  0  1  0
0  1  0  1
1  0  1  0
```

Table 1.6. A Small Network of Parents
and Children

	p_1	p_2	c_1	c_2	c_3	c_4	c_5
p_1	0	0	1	1	0	0	0
p_2	0	0	0	0	1	1	1
c_1	1	0	0	0	0	0	0
c_2	1	0	0	0	0	0	0
c_3	0	1	0	0	0	0	0
c_4	0	1	0	0	0	0	0
c_5	0	1	0	0	0	0	0

1.4   SPECIFYING BLOCKMODELS

Blockmodels are specified in terms of intuition, substance, or some insight into the nature of a studied network. We explore some examples here.

1.4.1   Parent–child role systems

Imagine we had some network data for two parents $\{p_1, p_2\}$ and five children $\{c_1, c_2, c_3, c_4, c_5\}$. Suppose that p_1 is the parent of c_1 and c_2, and p_2 is the parent of c_3, c_4, and c_5. The parent–child ties are shown in Table 1.6. We have described a bond between a parent and a child as a symmetric tie.

In this table, p_1 and p_2 are each singletons. The children c_1 and c_2 belong to a cluster, and children c_3, c_4, and c_5 are in another cluster. The blocks in the blockmodel are either complete or null, and the blockmodel could be written as

null	null	complete	null		0	0	1	0
null	null	null	complete	or	0	0	0	1
complete	null	null	null		1	0	0	0
null	complete	null	null		0	1	0	0

One of the fundamental motivations behind blockmodeling is to learn about role systems and represent them. From this vantage point, the partition in Table 1.6 seems flawed. If there are parent–child role systems, then parents occupy one position, whereas children occupy another. Separating actors in terms of specific role ties for specific other individuals is problematic. What if we group parents together into a position and put the children into a second position? This is shown in Table 1.7. There are just two positions and only four blocks. There are two null

Table 1.7. *Another Model of the*
Parent–Child Network

	p_1	p_2	c_1	c_2	c_3	c_4	c_5
p_1	0	0	1	1	0	0	0
p_2	0	0	0	0	1	1	1
c_1	1	0	0	0	0	0	0
c_2	1	0	0	0	0	0	0
c_3	0	1	0	0	0	0	0
c_4	0	1	0	0	0	0	0
c_5	0	1	0	0	0	0	0

blocks and two regular blocks:

null	regular
regular	null

or

0	1
1	0

For the image, we use 1 for regular and 0 for null. This seems a simpler and more general model.

1.4.2 *Organizational hierarchies*

Next we consider the organizational hierarchy shown in matrix form in Table 1.8. There are 24 actors in the structure with four levels. The network structure shown on the left of Figure 1.3 represents the simple organizational chart in Table 1.8. There are 24 actors and the relation is "has authority over." Imagine being asked to characterize the essence of its structure. One workable – and most reasonable – response is that the organization is viewed best as hierarchical with four levels. Consistent with this, the picture on the left of Figure 1.3 has been reduced to, or is represented by, the structure on the right side of the figure. The corresponding blockmodel is

	A	B	C	D
A	null	complete	null	null
B	null	null	regular	null
C	null	null	null	regular
D	null	null	null	null

or

	A	B	C	D
A	0	1	0	0
B	0	0	1	0
C	0	0	0	1
D	0	0	0	0

In constructing this alternative picture, we kept *a* as a singleton, *A*; grouped *b*, *c*, and *d* into *B*; grouped actors *e* through *l* into *C*; and put actors *m* through *x* into *D*. In this new reduced structure, *A* is the CEO, *B* is made up of the VPs, *C* can

Table 1.8. An Idealized Organizational Hierarchy

	a	b	c	d	e	f	g	h	i	j	k	l	m	n	o	p	q	r	s	t	u	v	w	x
a	0	1	1	1	0	0	0	0	0	0	0	0	0	0	0	0	0	0	0	0	0	0	0	0
b	0	0	0	0	1	1	1	0	0	0	0	0	0	0	0	0	0	0	0	0	0	0	0	0
c	0	0	0	0	0	0	0	1	1	0	0	0	0	0	0	0	0	0	0	0	0	0	0	0
d	0	0	0	0	0	0	0	0	0	1	1	1	0	0	0	0	0	0	0	0	0	0	0	0
e	0	0	0	0	0	0	0	0	0	0	0	0	1	1	0	0	0	0	0	0	0	0	0	0
f	0	0	0	0	0	0	0	0	0	0	0	0	0	0	1	1	0	0	0	0	0	0	0	0
g	0	0	0	0	0	0	0	0	0	0	0	0	0	0	0	0	1	0	0	0	0	0	0	0
h	0	0	0	0	0	0	0	0	0	0	0	0	0	0	0	0	0	1	0	0	0	0	0	0
i	0	0	0	0	0	0	0	0	0	0	0	0	0	0	0	0	0	0	1	1	0	0	0	0
j	0	0	0	0	0	0	0	0	0	0	0	0	0	0	0	0	0	0	0	0	1	0	0	0
k	0	0	0	0	0	0	0	0	0	0	0	0	0	0	0	0	0	0	0	0	0	1	0	0
l	0	0	0	0	0	0	0	0	0	0	0	0	0	0	0	0	0	0	0	0	0	0	1	1
m	0	0	0	0	0	0	0	0	0	0	0	0	0	0	0	0	0	0	0	0	0	0	0	0
n	0	0	0	0	0	0	0	0	0	0	0	0	0	0	0	0	0	0	0	0	0	0	0	0
o	0	0	0	0	0	0	0	0	0	0	0	0	0	0	0	0	0	0	0	0	0	0	0	0
p	0	0	0	0	0	0	0	0	0	0	0	0	0	0	0	0	0	0	0	0	0	0	0	0
q	0	0	0	0	0	0	0	0	0	0	0	0	0	0	0	0	0	0	0	0	0	0	0	0
r	0	0	0	0	0	0	0	0	0	0	0	0	0	0	0	0	0	0	0	0	0	0	0	0
s	0	0	0	0	0	0	0	0	0	0	0	0	0	0	0	0	0	0	0	0	0	0	0	0
t	0	0	0	0	0	0	0	0	0	0	0	0	0	0	0	0	0	0	0	0	0	0	0	0
u	0	0	0	0	0	0	0	0	0	0	0	0	0	0	0	0	0	0	0	0	0	0	0	0
v	0	0	0	0	0	0	0	0	0	0	0	0	0	0	0	0	0	0	0	0	0	0	0	0
w	0	0	0	0	0	0	0	0	0	0	0	0	0	0	0	0	0	0	0	0	0	0	0	0
x	0	0	0	0	0	0	0	0	0	0	0	0	0	0	0	0	0	0	0	0	0	0	0	0

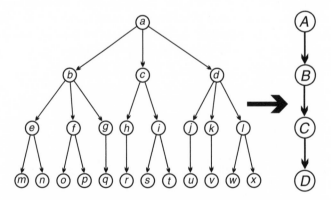

Figure 1.3. A picture of the organizational hierarchy in Table 1.8.

be viewed as middle management, and *D* is made up of those at the bottom of the organizational hierarchy. The single member of *A* has authority directly over the members of *B*. Each member of *B* has direct authority over at least one member of the middle management level, *C*. In a similar way, each member of *C* has authority over at least one member of the bottom level. The directed tie from *A* to *B* in the new graph (image) is constructed from the authority ties of *a* over *b*, *c*, and *d*. The directed tie from *B* to *C* is an aggregation of the ties from *b*, *c*, and *d* to their direct subordinates. We establish the tie from *C* to *D* in the same way, using the authority ties from middle management to members at the bottom level. The image structure of the blockmodel, as represented in tabular form, with *A*, *B*, *C*, and *D* as units, and in pictorial form on the right of Figure 1.3, captures the essential structure of the hierarchy. The image provides a blockmodel of the network.

The construction of the new representation can be viewed in two ways. First, all actors at a given level of the hierarchy are linked essentially in the same way to the rest of the structure. Clearly, *A* is unique. Each actor in *B* is a direct subordinate of *a*, and any tie one of them has to a subordinate in *C* is matched by a tie from another member of *B* to a member of *C*. For example, the tie from *b* to *e* corresponds to the tie from *c* to *h* and the tie from *d* to *k*. Similarly, each member of *C* has a subordinate in *D* as well as a superordinant in *B*. In making this description, we see that the similarity of the patterns of relational ties is primary. The elements {*A*, *B*, *C*, *D*} are the positions of the network.[11]

The second idea related to Figure 1.3 concerns the expectations that members in any one category of actors may have concerning their behavior toward members of other categories (and the expected behaviors from members of the other categories). These expectations define social roles, and role similarity is primary. The two are linked: roles are coupled to the positions in the network. Occupants of the same position have the same social roles. Of course, in the organizational image of this example, actors in the same roles, by virtue of those roles, also have similar linkage patterns.

1.4.3 Systems of ranked clusters

Distilling some essential ideas from Homans (1950), Davis and Leinhardt (1972) formulated two distinct structural features as general descriptions of small-group structures for affect ties. One is the differentiation of these groups into cliques in which all actors are reciprocally linked. The other feature is the elaboration of ranks. They argued that the social processes generating these two structural features reinforce each other. As a result, cliques are found at distinct levels. A single clique may exist as the sole occupant of a level, or multiple cliques can do so. In the latter case, there are only null ties between members of the two cliques.

With regard to cliques at distinct levels, the hypothesized structure is one in which there are asymmetric ties directed up from lower-ranked cliques to

---

11   See Borgatti and Everett (1992a) for a lucid treatment of the position concept.

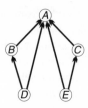

Figure 1.4. A three-level ranked-clusters model.

higher-ranked cliques. No asymmetric ties are directed down from higher-ranked cliques to lower-level cliques (and there are no mutual ties between units at different levels), hence the label of ranked clusters. For the relation "likes," this labeling of "up" is appropriate. If the relation is "liked by" then the relation is "down" the levels. The ranking requirement is that the asymmetric ties between levels all have the same direction. An idealized model of Davis and Leinhardt's concept is shown in Figure 1.4 with five positions (as clusters) and three levels. The highest ranking position is A, with two positions, B and C, in the second level and two positions, D and E, in the third level.

Requiring full reciprocity in the cliques is a very stringent condition. However, we can generalize this idea in the following way. Instead of having complete blocks (i.e., cliques) on the diagonal, we can specify symmetric diagonal blocks. Of course, the complete block is symmetric (and is consistent with the specification of the symmetric block type). We note that the null block is symmetric also. The "no ties up" condition is retained in full. Table 1.9 provides an example of such a structure. We have used a dot to represent 0 in this matrix for visual clarity.

To construct a blockmodel from the network presented in the matrix form in Table 1.9, we group $\{a, b, c, d, e\}$ into A; $\{f, g, h\}$ into B; $\{i, j, k, l\}$ into C; $\{m, n, o, p, q\}$ into D; and $\{r, s, t, u, v\}$ into E. We denote symmetric as sym, complete as com, and null as nul. Additionally, we define a one block as any block below the mail diagonal that contains at least a 1. The blockmodel of the network is contained in Table 1.10.

1.4.4 Baboon grooming networks

We now consider a real empirical example. Table 1.11 contains network of grooming ties for a group of baboons. There are seven females (f_1–f_7) and five males (m_1–m_5) in the group.[12]

Our goal here is to describe the structure of this network. There is a strong clue as to how to partition this network: Males do not groom other males. This suggests that the grooming structure is centered on the females and is a first step in constructing a blockmodel as a center–periphery structure.[13]

---

12   These data are for the first of two time points. We return to these data in Chapter 7, where we also consider the second time point.

13   We provide some definitions of center–periphery structures in Chapter 7 (Section 7.5).

Table 1.9. A Ranked-Clusters Blockmodel

a	. 1 1 1 .	. . .	. . . .	. . . . .	. . . . .
b	1 . 1 1 1	. . .	. . . .	. . . . .	. . . . .
c	1 1 . 1 1	. . .	. . . .	. . . . .	. . . . .
d	1 1 1 . 1	. . .	. . . .	. . . . .	. . . . .
e	. 1 1 1 .	. . .	. . . .	. . . . .	. . . . .
f	1 1 . 1 1	. 1 1	. . . .	. . . . .	. . . . .
g	. 1 1 1 .	1 . 1	. . . .	. . . . .	. . . . .
h	1 1 . 1 1	1 1 .	. . . .	. . . . .	. . . . .
i	1 . 1 1 1	. . .	. 1 1 1	. . . . .	. . . . .
j	1 1 1 1 1	. . .	1 . . .	. . . . .	. . . . .
k	1 1 1 . 1	. . .	1 . . 1	. . . . .	. . . . .
l	. 1 1 1 .	. . .	1 . 1 .	. . . . .	. . . . .
m	. 1 1 1 .	. 1 .	. . . .	. 1 1 1 1	. . . . .
n	1 1 . . 1	1 . .	. . . .	1 . 1 1 1	. . . . .
o	1 . 1 1 .	1 . 1	. . . .	1 1 . 1 1	. . . . .
p	. 1 1 . 1	. 1 .	. . . .	1 1 1 . 1	. . . . .
q	. 1 . 1 1	. 1 .	. . . .	1 1 1 1 .	. . . . .
r	. 1 . . .	. . .	1 1 1 .	. . . . .	. 1 1 . 1
s	1 1 . . 1	. . .	1 1 1 1	. . . . .	1 . . 1 1
t	1 . 1 1 .	. . .	1 . 1 .	. . . . .	1 . . 1 1
u	1 1 1 . 1	. . .	1 1 . 1	. . . . .	. 1 1 . 1
v	1 1 . 1 1	. . .	. 1 1 1	. . . . .	1 1 1 1 .

Specifications of the center and the periphery together with a statement about the content of the blocks are required. One concept of a center is one in which they are densely connected. One operationalization of this is that diagonal blocks are complete. This may be too stringent if a coherent center does not require that all actors be mutually linked. However, for social cohesion in the center, enough pairs need to be in mutual ties. Another possible specification is that the center block is regular – in the sense of regular equivalence – so that each member in the center is (mutually) linked to at least one other unit in the center. For these baboons, this specification implies that each female is groomed by at least one other female.

Table 1.10. A Blockmodel of the Ranked-Clusters Network in Table 1.9

	A	*B*	*C*	*D*	*E*
A	sym	nul	nul	nul	nul
B	one	com	nul	nul	nul
C	one	nul	sym	nul	nul
D	one	one	nul	com	nul
E	one	nul	one	nul	sym

or

	A	*B*	*C*	*D*	*E*
A	1	0	0	0	0
B	1	1	0	0	0
C	1	0	1	0	0
D	1	1	0	1	0
E	1	0	1	0	1

Table 1.11. Permuted Grooming Ties for a Two-Cluster Model

		1	3	4	6	8	10	11	2	5	7	9	12
f_1	1	.	.	1	.	.	.	1	1	1	.	.	1
f_2	3	.	.	1	1	.	1	1	.	1	1	.	1
f_3	4	1	1	.	1	.	1	.	.	1	1	.	1
f_4	6	.	1	1	.	.	1	.	.	1	.	.	1
f_5	8	.	.	.	.	.	1	.	.	1	1	1	.
f_6	10	.	1	1	1	1	.	.	.	.	.	.	.
f_7	11	1	1	.	.	.	.	.	.	.	.	.	.
m_1	2	1	.	.	.	.	.	.	.	.	.	.	.
m_2	5	1	1	1	1	1	.	.	.	.	.	.	.
m_3	7	.	1	1	.	1	.	.	.	.	.	.	.
m_4	9	.	.	.	.	1	.	.	.	.	.	.	.
m_5	12	1	1	1	1	.	.	.	.	.	.	.	.

In many instances of using center–periphery ideas, there is the conception in which the center is organized and cohesive whereas the periphery is disorganized. This can be translated into there being too few ties among peripheral units. The most stringent version is that there are no ties among units in the periphery. The corresponding diagonal block would be null. In the baboon example, in which males (in the periphery) do not groom males, this seems an appropriate specification.

Next, the links between a center and its periphery need to be specified. If the center is really different from the periphery, the pattern of ties toward the periphery from the center will differ from those from the periphery to the center. In the baboon example, we can reason that if the periphery is linked to the center, each male has to be groomed, which implies that each male has to be groomed by at least one female baboon. However, not all females need to be involved in grooming males. The block of the periphery to the center can be specified as row regular. The corresponding center to periphery block is specified as column regular. The specified model is

regular or complete	column regular
row regular	null

Thus far, our attention in this chapter has focused on the blocks and their construction. In specifying a blockmodel, we can also pay attention to the nature of the actors occupying a position. We can express this in terms of an additional constraint. In this example, the constraint specifies that positions are either occupied by males or by females. When this blockmodel is specified, and fitted, we get the result presented in Table 1.11. It is readily apparent that this model fits the data exactly for a center that is regular. We note that if we were to specify a complete block as the center, the null ties in that block would not be consistent with its being complete.

Table 1.12. A Four-Position Model Fitted to a Baboon Network

		3	4	10	1	6	8	11	5	7	12	2	9
f_2	3	.	1	1	.	1	.	1	1	1	1	.	.
f_3	4	1	.	1	1	1	.	.	1	1	1	.	.
f_6	10	1	1	.	.	1	1	.	.	.	.	.	.
f_1	1	.	1	.	.	.	.	1	1	.	1	1	.
f_4	6	1	1	1	.	.	.	.	1	.	1	.	.
f_5	8	.	.	1	.	.	.	.	1	1	.	.	1
f_7	11	1	.	.	1	.	.	.	.	.	.	.	.
m_2	5	1	1	.	1	1	1	.	.	.	.	.	.
m_3	7	1	1	.	.	.	1	.	.	.	.	.	.
m_5	12	1	1	.	1	1	.	.	.	.	.	.	.
m_1	2	.	.	.	1	.	.	.	.	.	.	.	.
m_4	9	.	.	.	.	.	1	.	.	.	.	.	.

Before we become too self-congratulatory, we note a potentially serious problem with this result: There are many other partitions of these baboons into two clusters in which there are no inconsistencies with the type of blockmodel we specified above. However, it is the only such partition into two clusters in which the clusters have either females or males but not both.

We can put some bite into the model by considering four clusters. The primary reason for doing this is that two gender groups each show internal variation. A second blockmodel is one in which the diagonal blocks can be null, complete, or regular. Continuing the logic of the two-position model, we state that above the diagonal (in the image matrix) the blocks are specified as column regular or null, and below the diagonal the blocks are specified as row regular or null. Again, each cluster is constrained to be homogeneous with regard to gender. This fitted blockmodel is shown in Table 1.12.

The fitted four-position prespecified model is

complete	col regular	col regular	null
row regular	null	col regular	col regular
row regular	row regular	null	null
null	row regular	null	null

Before interpreting this partition, we point to a specific feature of this fitted blockmodel: The tie between f_1 and f_7 is located in a block that we specified as a null. Its presence indicates that the blockmodel does not fit exactly. For most empirical networks, blockmodels need not and very often do not fit exactly. We refer to these as *instances in which an empirical blockmodel is inconsistent with the specified blockmodel*. This is a cumbersome phrase, and so we use the term *inconsistency* for it. So, in this case, the baboon network was fitted with two inconsistencies. Throughout this volume we present methods for fitting block-models with the smallest number of inconsistencies between a fitted blockmodel and the empirical network data.[14]

The interpretation of this baboon grooming blockmodel seems straightforward. The core of the network is f_2, f_3, and f_6, who all groom many other baboons. The three males involved in multiple grooming ties are m_2, m_3, and m_5. These are two of the clusters shown in Table 1.12. The female baboons f_1, f_4, f_5, and f_7 form the other female baboon cluster. With the exception of f_1, these females are less involved in grooming. Indeed, f_7 (and f_6) groom no males. The two males, m_1 and m_4, are each groomed by only one female and form the last identified cluster.

1.5   CONVENTIONAL BLOCKMODELING

We have described blockmodeling in terms of specifying the blocks, combining them into a blockmodel, and then interpreting the resulting blockmodel. Thus far, we have said very little about how these models are used empirically. Given that the overall purpose of this book is to provide an integrated treatment of generalized blockmodeling, we first describe what we call conventional blockmodeling before going on to describe the ways in which we generalize this idea.

1.5.1   Equivalence and blockmodeling

Apart from noting the foundational paper of Lorrain and White (1971), we have remained silent on the topic of equivalence. As noted above, the location of an actor in a network is defined as the set of ties of that actor to the others in the network. This includes the absence of ties as well as the presence of ties. The key initial step in blockmodeling is to define some notion of equivalence. One option is to define social actors as *structurally equivalent* if they have exactly the same set of ties to the rest of the social actors. It is straightforward to prove that if an empirical network is fully consistent with regard to this type of equivalence, all blocks must be either complete or null. (See also Chapter 6, especially Section 6.4.1.) Another popular definition of equivalence is regular equivalence. If two actors are *regularly equivalent*, they are equivalently connected to equivalent others. This notion is illustrated in Figure 1.3, where the partition of the actors in the hypothetical organization is consistent with regular equivalence. We prove in Chapter 6 – see also Batagelj, Doreian, and Ferligoj (1992) and Borgatti (1989) – that if a network is fully consistent with this type of equivalence, the only permitted block types for regular equivalence are regular and null.

In the chronological development of blockmodeling, the concept of structural equivalence came first as proposed by Lorrain and White (1971). Regular equivalence was proposed in 1983 by White and Reitz (1983). As described by Everett

---

14   Throughout this volume we do not use the term *error* for an inconsistency or *errors* for multiple inconsistencies.

and Borgatti (1994), there are a variety of other equivalences that are special cases of regular equivalence, including structural equivalence. For our purposes, conventional blockmodeling has three features: (i) an indirect approach is used; (ii) attention is restricted to structural and regular equivalence (in which much more of the empirical work utilizes structural equivalence[15]); and (iii) there is little or no attention to how well an established blockmodel fits the network data that have been blockmodeled.[16]

All of our examples thus far have been couched in terms of the ties in the network data. The indirect approach of conventional blockmodeling does not deal with the data directly. Instead, the data are transformed in some fashion and then clustered. We describe some of these transformations in Chapter 5 and simply note here that Euclidean distance and the product moment correlation are the two most frequently used transformations in the conventional blockmodeling approach. Chapter 5 also describes some of the clustering procedures that could be used to cluster the transformed network data. The indirect approach, which is based on using (dis)similarities and cluster analytic methods, is described more fully in Section 6.3 (see especially Figure 6.5).

The second component of conventional blockmodeling is the restriction of attention to null, regular, or complete blocks. In fact, this restriction is the entire specification of a blockmodel in the conventional blockmodeling approach: These are the only possible block types, and they can appear anywhere in the blockmodel. Finally, the clustering produced from the use of a clustering algorithm is accepted as is by the analyst. If a measure of fit is used, seldom is it a part of the procedure of actually fitting the blockmodel. How then does generalized blockmodeling differ?

1.6 GENERALIZED BLOCKMODELING

The first difference is that, with generalized blockmodeling, we use (and advocate) a *direct approach* in which we work only with the network data. Transformations to (dis)similarities introduce the properties of these measures into the partitioned methods that are chosen. As shown in Chapter 6, if an indirect approach is taken, the (dis)similarity measure used needs to be compatible with the type of equivalence that has been selected. Working directly with the data is much cleaner.

Another difference is that we introduce a much broader set of block types. In conventional blockmodeling, certain types of equivalences are introduced, and later the permitted block types consistent with the equivalence type are identified. The generalization by specifying permitted block types is much more straightforward

---

15 Strictly speaking, we could say, simply, that attention is restricted to regular equivalence given that structural equivalence is a special case of regular equivalence. However, because the preponderance of the empirical work has focused on structural equivalence, we keep both regular and structural equivalence in our statement.

16 There has been some attention to measuring the fit of blockmodels, for example, by Carrington, Heil, and Berkowitz (1980) and Panning (1982), but such efforts are not systematically a part of the fitting process and occur after a blockmodel has been established.

than starting with additional definitions of equivalence types.[17] We introduced some of these new block types in Section 1.3, and others are introduced throughout Chapters 7–11.

A third difference comes, in principle, with the way that a blockmodel is specified beyond just permitting certain block types. Conventional blockmodeling is inductive because neither the clusters nor the location of block types is specified. Clusters and blocks are simply found in the (transformed) data and then interpreted in some fashion. We use the term *prespecification* to label the process in which knowledge is used to specify the *location* of at least one block with regard to its type. A completely prespecified blockmodel is one in which all of the block types are specified by location in the blockmodel. A prespecified blockmodel can be constrained by specifying, in part or in total, the membership of the clusters. In the baboon network, for example, having clusters composed of only females or only males is a constraint. When blockmodels are prespecified in some fashion (i.e., to some extent up to a complete prespecification), the blockmodeling procedure can be seen as *deductive*. We think that it is important to realize that analysts often have more knowledge about the network being studied beyond thinking that certain block types might occur. This knowledge can be incorporated into prespecifying blockmodels prior to a blockmodeling analysis.

Yet another difference comes with the fitting procedure of generalized blockmodeling. Given a permitted (ideal) block type, it is straightforward to define departures from the block type. For example, a 1 in a null block is inconsistent with the nature of a null block, and we can count the number of 1s in (what should be) a null block as a simple measure of the total inconsistency between an empirical block and an ideal null block type. Having 0s in a complete-block type is treated in a similar fashion. As another example, suppose we are considering regular equivalence. One of the permitted block types is the regular block. If there is a row or column in a block that has only 0s, this is inconsistent with a regular block. We could count the number of rows or columns having only 0s as a measure of the inconsistency between an empirical block and an ideal regular block. Alternatively, we could count the number of 0s in rows and columns as a measure of the inconsistency. In general, a measure of fit – called a criterion function – can be specified and a fitting method sought that makes the number of inconsistencies as small as possible (or, in the alternative language, minimizes the criterion function). In this sense, a measure of fit is built into the fitting procedure. Methods for doing this are presented throughout Chapters 6–11.

In summary, our approach is to specify block types, assemble them into a blockmodel, and then fit this blockmodel to data. This can range from prespecifying everything about a blockmodel to prespecifying only some of the blockmodel. If we know nothing about a blockmodel beyond the idea that permitted blocks types might occur, then the use of blockmodeling is an exploratory tool. In short, conventional blockmodeling is exploratory. Characterizing confirmatory blockmodeling

---

17   Of course, every partition specifies an equivalence relation.

is not so straightforward. If, prior to a blockmodeling analysis, we do prespecify everything about the blockmodel and then fit that specific model, it is reasonable to call this a confirmatory blockmodeling procedure. However, much of the time, we are caught between these two extremes. We know something but not everything about a potential blockmodel. We might know some of the clusters or the location of some of the block types. *Partially confirmatory* is a possible label for this usage. A generalized blockmodel can be established in stages as we build up our knowledge about a particular network by fitting blockmodels to it. In a sense, this combines both exploratory and confirmatory aspects of blockmodeling.

1.7 AN OUTLINE MAP OF THE TOPICS CONSIDERED

The remainder of this book is devoted to specifying blockmodels – both conventional and generalized – in terms of block types and fitting them. The original foundations of blockmodeling were rigorous and founded in category theory. In practice, however, a variety of empirical procedures were devised to promote the establishment of blockmodels given network data. Breiger, Boorman, and Arabie (1975) proposed the use of iterated correlations in CONCOR, the first general-purpose algorithm for conventional blockmodeling. Burt (1976) presented STRUCTURE as another program for doing conventional blockmodeling in which Euclidean distance was used as a dissimilarity measure. Both programs are decidedly ad hoc in their operation. One of our goals is to return to specifying the foundations of blockmodeling rigorously and, on this basis, to develop algorithms for solving the corresponding blockmodeling problems. All analyses presented in this book were done with the PAJEK program (Batagelj and Mrvar 2003).[18] An introduction to PAJEK and a description of how to use it for several blockmodeling procedures discussed in this book can be found in de Nooy, Mrvar, and Batagelj (2003).

Chapter 2 presents some classic data sets as well as newer data sets. The former are important because blockmodeling methods have been applied to them. So, in addition to presenting these data sets, we present some of the partitions that were reached by means of conventional blockmodeling.

Given our focus on providing a sound rigorous foundation for blockmodeling methods, we present a variety of mathematical and clustering tools that form the core of this foundation. Chapters 3 and 4 along with 9 provide the mathematical basis for blockmodeling. Chapter 3 presents the general mathematical background, especially Section 3.2, in which the relations are elaborated. Chapter 4 discusses aspects of graph theory and relations that are used for social network analysis. The essential sections are those discussing graphs (Section 4.1), partitions (Section 4.3), and equivalence relations (Section 4.3). Some of the sections discuss topics that

---

18 The program PAJEK and information about it can be found at its home page (http://vlado.fmf. uni-lj.si/pub/networks/pajek/).

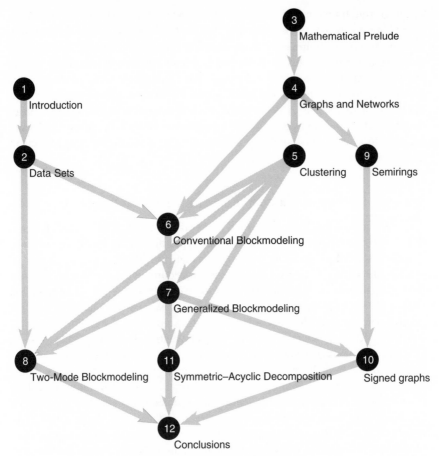

Figure 1.5. Ordering of chapters.

are used for more advanced applications (e.g., transitive closure in Section 4.2.2, orders in Section 4.5, and factorization in Section 4.5.1). Chapter 9 extends some ideas from Chapters 3 and 4 and describes semirings and lattices. Some of the materials in Chapters 3, 4, and 9 are standard mathematical results, and some are re-presentations of network analytic results. However, some of the materials are genuinely new. All have been brought together and organized to emphasize their relevance for blockmodeling.

At its core, blockmodeling is a form of cluster analysis – a feature made clear by Burt's (1976) explicit incorporation of cluster analytic methods in STRUCTURE. Chapter 5 presents some essential material on cluster analysis, including the general relocation algorithm that forms the core of our methods for fitting blockmodels to data. Chapter 6 presents conventional blockmodeling (in Section 6.1) and then a view of conventional blockmodeling through the lens of using optimizational methods in the generalized blockmodeling framework (in Section 6.2). Although we discuss indirect methods, the main procedural point is that direct methods are vastly superior in terms of the conceptual features and foundations for block-modeling. Chapter 7 moves fully into the generalized blockmodeling approach and includes the presentation on new block types, new types of blockmodels, and fitting generalized blockmodels.

Blockmodeling was first developed for one-mode data. However, generalized blockmodeling is also a way of looking at network structures and is an open-ended activity insofar as new block types can be defined and different data structures can be incorporated. We introduced two-mode data earlier in this chapter, and the obvious question is this: Why not think about extending generalized blockmodeling to two-mode data? We respond to this question in Chapter 8, and we present some new formal materials for blockmodeling two-mode data and provide some new empirical results.

Structural balance theory, starting with Heider's (1946) classic discussion, is often viewed as a separate domain because it is concerned with signed networks. It turns out that it, too, can be viewed as a form of generalized blockmodeling. We introduce some further mathematical foundations on semirings and lattices in Chapter 9 and then bring balance theory – as far as delineating the structure of signed networks – into the generalized blockmodeling framework in Chapter 10.

Chapter 11 deals with what we call symmetric–acyclic blockmodels and has as its point of departure the ranked-clusters model introduced informally earlier in this chapter. There are some new mathematical results – first presented in Doreian, Batagelj, and Ferligoj (2000) – that were created to analyze systems of ranked clusters. In this case, we started with substantive concerns and ended up defining a new block type and a new type of blockmodel. Fitting this generalized blockmodel demanded the construction of new formal tools. Again, new empirical results are presented.

Chapters 10 and 11 make clear the open-ended nature of generalized block-modeling in which new block types, new types of blockmodels, and new criterion functions can all be defined and mobilized within the generalized blockmodeling framework. Chapter 12 provides some summary remarks on generalized block-modeling and some suggestions as to where we can head in the future. Above all, Chapter 12 extends an invitation for others to create extensions that we have not considered.

Figure 1.5 presents the ordering of chapters that facilitates the reading of this book. A line in this figure connects two chapters if the earlier chapter discusses topics that are necessary for reading the later chapter.

2

NETWORK DATA SETS

Generalized blockmodeling is both an approach to the analysis of network data and an expanding set of data analytic procedures. Data are crucially important. For any substantive problem, it is useful to combine the results of different analyses. This is true also for network analysis, and all analyses have the potential to inform subsequent studies of relevant network data. We mirror this by making repeated use of specific data sets in the chapters that follow. As a result, the interpretation of our analyses cumulates with each use of a specific data set. We use this chapter to provide descriptions of the data sets we use most often. Some of these are classic data sets that have been used repeatedly as test beds[1] for assessing new tools, whereas other data sets we use have seen little utilization beyond their first report.

These data sets have been chosen to represent a variety of network data structures that include the following: (i) a binary relation at one point in time, (ii) a binary relation at multiple points in time, (iii) a valued relation at one point in time, (iv) a valued relation at multiple points in time, (v) multiple binary relations, (vi) multiple valued relations, and (vi) signed graphs. Each data set is accompanied by a description of some earlier analyses of these data. We use a specific capitalized label for each data set, and the first use of each label is enclosed in parentheses. Our focus is on partitioning social actors involved in these networks into clusters and partitioning of the social ties into blocks.

2.1 CLASSIC DATA SETS

The classic data sets we use are the Sampson monastery (SM) data, the Bank Wiring Room (BWR) data, and the Newcomb fraternity (NF) data. The BWR data are viewed as cross-sectional even though they are the result of continuous observation at a specific workplace over a six-month period. Some workers were moved into a special observation room, and the data represent social action once

---

1 These are among the data sets distributed as a part of UCINET (VI Borgatti et al. 2004).

things had settled down. They can be viewed as highly reliable but static data consistent with Homans' (1950) use of them as describing an equilibrium state. These data are used in Chapters 3–10.

Both the SM and the NF data are longitudinal. There are three waves of data in SM, as described in the next section, for a group of 18 monks in training. We use these data primarily in Chapter 10, where we consider structural and generalized balance in signed graphs. The NF data were obtained at 15 weekly[2] points in time. These data are used primarily in Chapter 10.

2.1.1 Sampson monastery data

Sampson (1968) reported data at five points in time among a group of trainee monks[3] at a New England monastery. Of interest here are the 18 trainee monks present at three points in time (labeled as T_2, T_3, and T_4, consistent with Sampson's labeling). The 18 actors at T_2 formed two aggregates: the Cloisterville group (who were present at T_1 and remained after others of their group had graduated) and a new group of actors who entered the monastery at T_2.[4]

Sampson collected data for four relations: affect, esteem, influence, and sanctioning. Affective ties were "various forms of cathectic orientation relationships in which the object of ego's orientation is an alter" (1968:314). This includes both positive and negative ties, which, for affect, we label like and dislike.[5] Esteem ties are "composed of forms of cognitive orientations of alters, based upon judgments made in terms of relevant evaluative orientations" (1968:314–315). Influence ties were cognitive orientations defined in terms of an "alter's impact on ego's experience or behavior" (1968:315). Sampson noted that the trainee monks assumed that those other trainee monks they disliked (or who disliked them) could not exert any influence, positive or negative, on them. Finally, there is the sanctioning relationship. The positive pole of these ties was defined in terms of going "out of your way to support, praise and/or help because their behavior was consistent with your view," whereas the negative pole was defined in terms of going "out of your way to correct, encourage and/or help because their behavior was not consistent with your view" (1968:318). For both poles, the view of an actor was defined in terms of the Order of Mystical Union to which they all belonged.

The Cloisterville set of six trainee monks were Peter, Bonaventure, Berthold, Ambrose, Victor, and Mark. Of these, Peter was the best liked, the most influential,

---

2 With one exception: no data were reported for Week 9.

3 We use this term to cover both postulants (candidates for admission to a religious order) and novices (people accepted into a religious order who have not taken final vows).

4 Sampson also obtained data for a fifth time point for the seven actors remaining after a series of expulsions and voluntary withdrawals. We ignore these data, as well as those collected for the so-called first time point, because the detailed structure at these times is not relevant for the dynamics among the 18 actors that start at T_2.

5 In the questionnaire described by Sampson, the affect tie was operationalized explicitly as like–dislike.

Table 2.1. Sampson Affect Data at T_2

		1	2	3	4	5	6	7	8	9	10	11	12	13	14	15	16	17	18
John Bosco	1	0	0	2	0	3	-2	-1	0	0	-3	0	0	0	1	0	0	0	0
Gregory	2	3	0	0	0	0	0	2	0	0	-1	0	0	-3	1	0	0	-2	0
Basil	3	2	3	0	-1	0	0	0	-3	-2	0	0	0	0	0	0	0	1	0
Peter	4	0	0	-2	0	3	1	-3	0	0	2	0	0	0	0	0	0	0	-1
Bonaventure	5	0	0	0	3	0	0	0	0	0	0	2	0	1	0	0	0	0	0
Berthold	6	1	0	0	3	0	0	-3	-1	2	0	-2	0	0	0	0	0	0	0
Mark	7	0	2	0	-3	-1	-2	0	1	0	0	0	0	0	0	0	3	0	0
Victor	8	3	2	-3	0	0	0	0	0	1	0	0	0	0	-2	0	0	-1	0
Ambrose	9	0	0	-3	0	2	0	0	3	0	0	0	0	0	0	0	1	-2	-1
Romuald	10	0	0	0	3	0	0	0	1	0	0	0	0	0	2	0	0	0	0
Louis	11	0	0	-1	0	3	0	0	1	0	0	0	0	-3	2	0	0	-2	0
Winifrid	12	3	2	-1	-3	0	0	0	0	0	0	-2	0	0	1	0	0	0	0
Amand	13	0	-3	0	0	2	-2	1	0	0	0	0	-1	0	0	0	0	0	3
Hugh	14	3	0	0	0	0	0	0	-2	0	0	1	2	-3	0	2	0	-1	0
Boniface	15	3	2	-2	0	0	0	0	0	0	0	0	0	-3	1	0	0	-1	-1
Albert	16	1	2	0	0	0	0	3	0	0	0	0	0	-1	0	0	0	-3	-2
Elias	17	0	0	3	-3	-2	0	0	0	0	0	-1	0	2	0	0	0	0	1
Simplicius	18	2	3	0	-3	0	-2	1	0	0	0	0	0	0	0	0	-1	0	0

the most esteemed, and the most positively sanctioned. He was their leader. Bonaventure and Berthold joined him as the core of this set of actors. Both Ambrose and Victor were peripheral to, but linked with, this core. Mark, at the opposite extreme to Peter on all four of the relational ties, was an isolate within the Cloisterville set of trainee monks. The 12 members of the new class entering the monastery at T_2 were John Bosco, Gregory, Basil, Romuald, Louis, Winifrid, Amand, Hugh, Boniface, Albert, Elias, and Simplicius. Of these, John Bosco and Gregory emerged as leaders. Bonaventure was ranked third in the liking ties. Basil was rejected by everyone, whereas both Simplicius and Elias were identified as "needing help." Sampson asked his respondents to distinguish the top three positive choices and the bottom three negative choices. Here, +3 represents "likes the most" while +2 is the second positive choice and +1 is the third positive choice. Similarly, −3 represents the tie to the "most disliked" alter, −2 represents the tie to the second most disliked alter, and −1 is for the third most disliked alter. Most, but not all, of the respondents used these tie labels. Table 2.1 displays the affect ties for T_2.

Sampson identified a period of subgroup differentiation and polarization. Increasingly, all but one of the members of the new class of trainee monks became alienated from the Cloisterville group. At T_3, when a meeting was called to discuss theological and organizational problems surfacing in the monastery, there were clear lines of division. In the main, they were between the old and the new members of the class with two exceptions: Mark, the disliked and isolated member of the Cloisterville set, had allied himself with members of the new class and, among the new class, only Louis was able to relate to, and be accepted by, members

Table 2.2. Sampson Affect Data at T_3

		1	2	3	4	5	6	7	8	9	10	11	12	13	14	15	16	17	18
John Bosco	1	0	2	0	−2	1	0	0	3	0	−3	−1	0	0	0	0	0	0	0
Gregory	2	3	0	0	−3	0	0	1	−2	0	0	0	2	−1	0	1	0	0	0
Basil	3	3	−1	0	0	0	−2	0	−3	0	0	0	0	0	0	0	0	1	2
Peter	4	−2	−3	0	0	3	2	0	0	0	0	1	0	0	0	0	0	0	0
Bonaventure	5	2	0	0	3	0	0	0	0	0	0	1	0	0	0	0	0	0	0
Berthold	6	1	0	−3	3	0	0	0	−1	2	0	0	−2	0	0	0	0	0	0
Mark	7	1	2	0	−3	0	−2	0	−1	0	0	0	0	0	0	0	3	0	0
Victor	8	−2	−3	−1	3	0	1	0	0	0	2	0	0	0	0	0	0	0	0
Ambrose	9	0	0	−3	0	1	0	0	3	0	0	0	2	0	0	0	0	−2	−1
Romuald	10	0	0	0	3	1	0	0	0	0	0	0	0	2	0	0	0	0	0
Louis	11	−1	−3	−2	2	3	0	0	0	0	0	0	0	0	0	0	1	0	0
Winifrid	12	3	1	−3	0	0	−2	0	0	0	0	0	0	0	2	0	0	−1	0
Amand	13	0	−3	0	0	2	−2	1	0	0	0	0	−1	0	0	0	0	0	3
Hugh	14	3	1	0	−3	0	0	0	0	0	−2	0	1	0	0	2	0	−1	0
Boniface	15	2	3	−2	0	1	0	0	0	0	−1	0	0	−3	1	0	0	−1	0
Albert	16	0	2	−1	−3	0	0	3	0	0	0	0	1	0	0	0	0	−2	0
Elias	17	0	1	2	−2	0	−1	0	0	0	0	−3	0	0	0	0	0	0	3
Simplicius	18	0	1	0	−3	0	−2	0	0	0	0	−1	0	2	0	0	0	3	0

of the Cloisterville group. Basil, Elias, and Simplicius were denied membership in both of the opposed groupings.

The T_3 meeting brought conflicts further into the open. Even the selection of a Chair for the meeting was disputed. Peter (the Cloisterville group's leader) objected to the whole procedure throughout the meeting. Gregory nominated John Bosco, who reciprocated this nomination. Louis nominated Berthold and, perhaps surprisingly given the shared view of Basil, Amand nominated Basil. Sampson (1968:354–355) was able to reconstruct the voting in the secret ballot: Amand voted for Basil; Louis and Berthold voted for Berthold; Gregory, Basil, and Victor voted for John Bosco; and the remaining actors all voted for Gregory. The distribution of the affect ties at T_3 is shown in Table 2.2, where the meaning of the entries is the same as for Table 2.1. Sampson identified four sets of actors. The Young Turks were Gregory (their leader), John Bosco, Winifrid, Hugh, Albert, Boniface, and Mark, whereas the members of the Loyal Opposition were Peter (their leader), Bonaventure, Berthold, Louis, and Ambrose (1968:371). Among the members of this subgroup, only Ambrose was marginal.[6] Both groups were defined by Sampson in terms of agreement with the opinions of their leaders. Sampson also identified an Interstitial group of Romuald, Victor, and Amand (1968:371). The Outcasts were Basil, Simplicius, and Elias. In some discussions, the interstitial group is included with the Loyal Opposition (see the discussion that follows). The affect data for T_4 are displayed in Table 2.3, again with the same meaning for the entries as in Table 2.1.

6 Sampson stated that he was also "very much influenced by the Young Turks" (1968:371).

Table 2.3. Sampson Affect Data at T_4

		1	2	3	4	5	6	7	8	9	10	11	12	13	14	15	16	17	18
John Bosco	1	0	-2	3	0	0	0	-3	0	0	-1	0	1	0	2	0	0	0	0
Gregory	2	3	0	0	-3	0	0	1	-2	0	0	0	2	-1	0	0	0	0	0
Basil	3	3	-2	0	-3	0	-2	0	0	0	0	0	0	2	0	0	-1	1	2
Peter	4	-2	-3	0	0	3	1	0	0	0	0	2	0	0	-1	0	0	0	0
Bonaventure	5	0	0	0	3	0	0	0	0	1	0	2	0	0	0	0	0	0	0
Berthold	6	0	-1	-3	3	1	0	-2	0	2	0	0	0	0	0	0	0	-2	0
Mark	7	0	3	0	-3	0	-2	0	-1	0	0	0	1	0	0	0	2	0	0
Victor	8	0	-3	-2	3	0	2	0	0	1	0	0	0	0	-1	0	0	0	0
Ambrose	9	0	0	-3	0	1	0	0	3	0	0	0	2	0	0	0	0	-2	-1
Romuald	10	0	0	0	3	1	0	0	0	1	0	0	0	2	0	0	0	0	0
Louis	11	-1	-3	-2	0	2	0	0	3	0	0	0	0	0	1	0	0	0	0
Winifrid	12	3	2	0	0	0	0	1	0	0	0	0	0	0	0	0	0	0	0
Amand	13	0	-3	0	0	2	-2	1	0	0	0	0	-1	0	0	0	0	0	3
Hugh	14	3	0	0	-3	0	0	0	-2	0	0	0	1	0	0	2	0	-1	0
Boniface	15	0	3	-2	-1	0	0	1	0	0	0	0	2	-3	0	0	0	0	0
Albert	16	0	3	-1	-3	0	0	2	0	0	0	0	0	0	0	1	0	-2	0
Elias	17	0	1	2	-1	0	-3	0	-2	0	0	0	0	0	0	0	0	0	3
Simplicius	18	0	1	2	-1	0	0	0	-3	0	-2	0	0	0	0	0	0	3	0

Some reanalyses of the SM data. Parts of the Sampson data have been reanalyzed many times. As far as blockmodeling is concerned, the two most consequential analyses are those of Breiger et al. (1975) and of White, Boorman, and Breiger (1976). Both of these studies considered the affect, esteem, influence, and sanction relations *for T_4 only*. For completeness, we include the additional (T_4) data here. The esteem data are in Table 2.4, the influence data are in Table 2.5, and the sanction data are in Table 2.6.

Table 2.4. Sampson Esteem Data at T_4

		1	2	3	4	5	6	7	8	9	10	11	12	13	14	15	16	17	18
John Bosco	1	0	-2	-1	0	1	0	-3	3	0	0	0	2	0	0	0	0	0	0
Gregory	2	3	0	-2	-3	1	0	0	2	0	0	0	0	-1	0	0	0	0	0
Basil	3	3	-1	0	-3	0	-2	0	0	0	0	0	0	2	0	0	0	1	1
Peter	4	-2	-3	0	0	0	1	0	0	0	2	3	0	0	-1	0	0	0	0
Bonaventure	5	0	0	-1	3	0	0	0	0	1	0	2	0	0	0	0	0	-3	-2
Berthold	6	0	0	-2	3	0	0	-3	-1	0	0	2	0	0	0	0	0	-2	0
Mark	7	0	3	-2	-2	0	-3	0	-2	0	0	0	1	0	0	1	2	-1	0
Victor	8	0	0	0	3	1	2	0	0	0	0	0	0	0	-1	0	0	-2	-3
Ambrose	9	1	0	0	3	0	0	0	2	0	0	0	0	-1	0	0	0	-3	-2
Romuald	10	0	0	0	0	0	0	0	0	0	0	0	0	0	0	0	0	0	0
Louis	11	-1	-3	-2	0	2	0	0	0	3	0	0	0	0	0	0	-1	0	0
Winifrid	12	3	2	0	0	0	0	0	0	0	0	0	0	0	1	0	0	0	0
Amand	13	0	-2	-1	0	3	-3	2	0	0	0	1	0	0	0	0	0	0	0
Hugh	14	3	2	0	-2	0	0	0	0	0	0	-2	1	-3	0	2	0	-1	-1
Boniface	15	1	3	-2	-3	0	0	0	0	0	0	-1	0	0	2	0	0	-1	-1
Albert	16	0	3	-2	-3	0	0	2	0	0	0	0	1	0	0	2	0	-2	-1
Elias	17	0	1	2	-2	0	-3	0	-1	0	0	0	0	1	0	0	0	0	3
Simplicius	18	0	2	3	-2	0	-2	0	-3	0	-1	0	0	0	0	0	0	1	0

Table 2.5. Sampson Influence Data at T_4

		1	2	3	4	5	6	7	8	9	10	11	12	13	14	15	16	17	18
John Bosco	1	0	3	0	0	0	0	1	0	0	-2	0	2	0	0	0	-1	0	-3
Gregory	2	3	0	0	-3	0	0	1	0	0	0	0	2	-2	0	0	0	0	0
Basil	3	3	-1	0	-3	0	-2	0	0	0	0	0	0	2	0	0	0	1	0
Peter	4	-2	-3	0	0	0	1	0	0	0	2	3	0	0	-1	0	0	0	0
Bonaventure	5	0	1	-1	3	0	0	0	0	0	0	2	0	0	0	0	0	-3	-2
Berthold	6	0	1	0	3	0	0	-3	0	2	0	0	0	0	0	0	0	-2	-1
Mark	7	0	3	-2	-2	0	-3	0	-2	0	0	0	1	0	0	0	2	-1	0
Victor	8	2	0	0	3	0	0	0	0	1	0	2	-1	-2	0	0	-3	0	0
Ambrose	9	3	2	0	1	0	0	0	0	0	0	0	-1	0	0	0	0	-3	-2
Romuald	10	0	0	0	0	0	0	0	0	0	0	0	0	0	0	0	0	0	0
Louis	11	0	0	0	1	3	0	-3	0	2	0	0	0	0	0	0	0	-1	-2
Winifrid	12	3	2	0	0	0	0	1	0	0	0	0	0	0	0	0	0	0	0
Amand	13	0	-3	0	0	3	-2	2	0	0	0	1	-1	0	0	0	0	0	0
Hugh	14	3	2	0	-2	0	0	0	0	0	0	0	1	-3	0	2	0	-1	-1
Boniface	15	0	3	-1	-3	0	0	1	0	0	0	0	0	-2	2	0	0	0	0
Albert	16	0	3	-1	-3	0	0	2	0	0	0	-2	0	0	0	1	0	0	0
Elias	17	0	1	2	-2	0	-3	0	-1	0	0	0	0	0	0	0	0	0	3
Simplicius	18	0	3	2	-3	0	-1	0	0	0	0	0	-2	0	0	0	0	1	0

Breiger et al. (1975) applied CONCOR to the set of four matrices in their raw form (preserving the ordinal values as reported by Sampson). White et al. (1976) split each matrix into two matrices for the positive and negative ties. For that reanalysis, all eight of the constructed matrices were binarized and stacked as input to CONCOR. The four-cluster partition reported by Breiger et al. (1975:352)

Table 2.6. Sampson Sanction Data at T_4

		1	2	3	4	5	6	7	8	9	10	11	12	13	14	15	16	17	18
John Bosco	1	0	0	-3	0	0	0	0	0	0	0	-2	2	0	3	0	0	1	-1
Gregory	2	3	0	-3	0	0	0	1	0	0	0	0	2	0	0	0	0	0	0
Basil	3	3	-2	0	-3	0	0	0	0	0	0	0	0	2	-1	0	0	1	0
Peter	4	0	-3	0	0	0	1	-1	0	0	2	3	0	0	-2	0	0	0	0
Bonaventure	5	0	0	0	0	0	0	0	0	0	0	0	0	0	0	0	0	0	0
Berthold	6	0	0	0	3	0	0	-3	0	1	0	2	0	-1	0	0	0	-2	-1
Mark	7	0	3	-3	-2	0	-1	0	0	0	0	0	0	0	0	1	2	0	0
Victor	8	0	0	-1	3	0	2	0	0	0	1	0	0	0	0	0	0	-2	-3
Ambrose	9	0	0	0	0	0	0	0	0	0	0	0	0	0	0	0	0	0	0
Romuald	10	0	0	0	0	0	0	0	0	0	0	0	0	0	0	0	0	0	0
Louis	11	0	0	0	3	0	0	0	2	0	0	0	0	0	-1	0	1	-2	-3
Winifrid	12	0	0	0	0	0	0	0	0	0	0	0	0	0	-2	0	0	-1	-3
Amand	13	0	-1	0	0	3	0	0	0	0	0	2	0	0	0	0	0	-2	-3
Hugh	14	3	3	-1	-3	0	0	0	0	0	0	-2	0	0	0	2	1	0	0
Boniface	15	1	3	-2	-1	0	0	0	0	0	0	0	0	-3	2	0	0	0	-1
Albert	16	0	2	-2	-3	0	0	3	0	0	0	0	0	-1	0	1	0	-2	-2
Elias	17	0	0	0	0	0	0	0	0	0	0	0	0	0	0	0	0	0	0
Simplicius	18	1	1	0	0	0	0	0	0	0	0	0	0	0	0	0	0	1	0

is, with the numerical identifiers in parentheses, as follows:

1. John Bosco (1), Gregory (2), Mark (7), Winifrid (12), Hugh (14), Boniface (15), and Albert (16);
2. Basil (3), Elias (17), and Simplicius (18);
3. Peter (4), Berthold (6), Victor (8), Romuald (10), and Louis (11);
4. Bonaventure (5), Ambrose (9), and Amand (13).

The first cluster is exactly the Young Turks identified by Sampson and the second is exactly the Outcasts. The other two clusters are mixtures of the Loyal Opposition and the Interstitial monks.[7] Breiger et al. (1975:354) also reported a three-cluster partition:

1. John Bosco (1), Gregory (2), Mark (7), Winifrid (12), Hugh (14), Boniface (15), and Albert (16);
2. Basil (3), Elias (17), and Simplicius (18);
3. Peter (4), Bonaventure (5), Berthold (6), Victor (8), Ambrose (9), Romuald (10), and Louis (11), and Amand (13).

In a related analysis, White et al. (1976) reported a three-cluster partition that is close to the three-cluster partition of Breiger et al.:

1. John Bosco (1), Gregory (2), Mark (7), Winifrid (12), Hugh (14), Boniface (15), and Albert (16);
2. Basil (3), Amand (13), Elias (17), and Simplicius (18);
3. Peter (4), Bonaventure (5), Berthold (6), Victor (8), Ambrose (9), Romuald (10), and Louis (11).

Some of the ethnographic detail provided by Sampson supports the inclusion of Amand with the Outcasts. White et al. (1976) also reported a five-cluster partition:

1. Bonaventure (5), Ambrose (9), and Romuald (10);
2. Peter (4), Berthold (6), Victor (8), and Louis (11);
3. John Bosco (1), Gregory (2), and Winifrid (12);
4. Mark (7), Hugh (14), Boniface (15), and Albert (16);
5. Basil (3), Amand (13), Elias (17), and Simplicius (18).

Both sets of authors pointed to the close match between their partitions and the groupings reported by Sampson.

Faust (1988) used the binarized (and stacked) matrices for the esteem and disesteem matrices as input to CONCOR.[8] The resulting partition was as follows:

1. John Bosco (1), Gregory (2), Winifrid (12), Hugh (14), and Boniface (15);
2. Basil (3), Amand (13), Elias (17), and Simplicius (18);
3. Peter (4), Berthold (6), Victor (8), Romuald (10), and Louis (11);
4. Bonaventure (5), Mark (7), Ambrose (9), and Albert (16).

---

7   For finer grained partitions, the Young Turks were split into {1, 2, 7, 15} and {12, 14, 16}, together with an interpretation of the internal structure of the cluster. The Outcasts were split into {3} and {17, 18}. Additionally, Cluster 3 was split into {4, 6, 8} and {10, 11} and Cluster 4 into {5, 9} and {13}. Not all of these subsequent splits merit further attention and are not discussed by Breiger et al. in any detail.

8   The version she used was implemented in an early version of UCINET.

Table 2.7. Two Partitions Using Different Equivalence Ideas

Structural Equivalence Clusters	Socioemotional Leaders	Task-Oriented Leaders	Followers	Outcasts
Loyal Opposition	(5, 9)	(4, 8, 11)	(6, 10)	–
Young Turks	(1, 12, 15)	(2)	(7, 14, 16)	–
Outcasts	–	–	–	(3, 13, 17, 18)

The first cluster contains most of the Young Turks; the second cluster has the Outcasts plus Amand (consistent with the clusters reported by White et al. 1976); the third has three members of the Loyal Opposition plus two of the Interstitial monks. The last cluster looks rather odd when viewed through a lens shaped by Sampson's narrative, as it has two members from the Young Turks and two from the Loyal Opposition. In part, this is a result of looking only at the esteem relations. Faust also reported some multidimensional scaling (MDS) plots that were based on (dis)similarity matrices whose elements measured the extent to which actors are structurally equivalent. One used product moment correlations as measures of structural equivalence, while the other used Euclidean distances as measures of nonequivalence. In both plots "the groups of monks identified by Sampson are in clear evidence" (1988:323).

When Faust used a more general notion of equivalence, she obtained very different partitions, as did Pattison (1988) when using an analysis based on local role equivalence. We consider this approach further in Chapter 7. In Pattison's analysis, only the separate like and dislike relations (in binarized form) were considered. When it is compared with the analyses based on structural equivalence, some interesting contrasts emerge. Her role analysis identified four positions: socioemotional leaders, task-oriented leaders, followers, and outcasts. Cross-tabulating this variable with the structural equivalence partitions, Pattison obtained the results shown in the Table 2.7. In presenting a three-cluster partition, we have adopted Pattison's inclusion of the Interstitial monks in these clusters. Trainee monks Victor and Romuald are included in the Loyal Opposition, while Amand is placed with the Outcasts.

Both Pattison's and Faust's reanalyses of the Sampson data provide examples of *partitioning a network in different ways depending on the type of equivalence considered*. These issues are considered further when we discuss blockmodeling (Chapter 6) and generalized blockmodeling (Chapter 7). We reconsider the (signed) Sampson data in Chapter 10 when structural balance theory is expressed in a generalized blockmodel form (also see Doreian and Mrvar 1996).

2.1.2   Bank wiring room data

The data collected in the 'BWR' have become legendary in social network circles. We have taken these data from the report by Homans (1950), who extracted

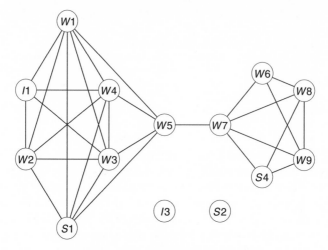

Figure 2.1. Game-playing ties in the BWR.

them from a study conducted by Roethlisberger and Dickson (1939). As a part of a wider study, 14 workers – nine wiremen, three solderers, and two inspectors – were located in a special observation room. Present also was an observer who recorded output and interaction activity over a six-month period (once the room had settled into a period of normalcy following the move). Six of the wiremen {$W1$, $W2$, $W3$, $W4$, $W5$, $W6$} wired connectors and were assigned to two soldering units. Solderer $S1$ soldered the units assembled by $W1$, $W2$, and $W3$, while $S2$ soldered the units wired by $W3$, $W4$, and $W5$. Wiremen $W7$, $W8$, and $W9$ wired selectors and, with solderer $S4$, formed the third soldering unit. Inspector $I1$ inspected the work of $W1$ through $W5$ plus $S1$ and $S2$. The other inspector, $I3$, inspected the work of $W5$ through $W9$ plus the work of $S2$ and $S4$.[9]

The geography of the room was important with the front and back clearly identified. The connector wiremen were at the front (and middle), and the selector wiremen were at the back. The organizational ranked ordering of the occupations was inspectors, connector wiremen, selector wiremen, solderers, and truckers (who brought raw materials into the room and moved completed units out). The truckers played no part in the socioemotional dynamics observed in the wiring room. Roethlisberger and Dickson (RD henceforth) started their account with a discussion of the games played in the room during lulls in the work routine and during breaks. The recorded game-playing interactions are shown in Figure 2.1 and Table 2.8. It is clear that the game-playing activity occurred within two differentiated subgroups. Group A, as described by RD, is made up of $W1$, $W2$, $W3$, $W4$, $W5$, $S1$, and $I1$, whereas Group B is composed of $W6$, $W7$, $W8$, $W9$, and $S4$. There was a report of a $W5$–$W7$ tie. RD (1939:502) stated that this link was activated only once and,

9   Two additional actors, $S3$ and $I2$, were in the room initially but were not there long. Like Homans, and, before him, Roethlisberger and Dickson, we ignore these actors but retain the original identifying labels.

Table 2.8. The BWR – Game-Playing Relation

	I1	I3	W1	W2	W3	W4	W5	W6	W7	W8	W9	S1	S2	S4
I1	0	0	1	1	1	1	0	0	0	0	0	0	0	0
I3	0	0	0	0	0	0	0	0	0	0	0	0	0	0
W1	1	0	0	1	1	1	1	0	0	0	0	1	0	0
W2	1	0	1	0	1	1	0	0	0	0	0	1	0	0
W3	1	0	1	1	0	1	1	0	0	0	0	1	0	0
W4	1	0	1	1	1	0	1	0	0	0	0	1	0	0
W5	0	0	1	0	1	1	0	0	1	0	0	1	0	0
W6	0	0	0	0	0	0	0	0	1	1	1	0	0	0
W7	0	0	0	0	0	0	1	1	0	1	1	0	0	1
W8	0	0	0	0	0	0	0	1	1	0	1	0	0	1
W9	0	0	0	0	0	0	0	1	1	1	0	0	0	1
S1	0	0	1	1	1	1	1	0	0	0	0	0	0	0
S2	0	0	0	0	0	0	0	0	0	0	0	0	0	0
S4	0	0	0	0	0	0	0	0	1	1	1	0	0	0

Table 2.9. The BWR – Positive and Negative Relations

(a) Positive Relation

	I1	I3	W1	W2	W3	W4	W5	W6	W7	W8	W9	S1	S2	S4
I1	0	0	0	0	1	0	0	0	0	0	0	0	0	0
I3	0	0	0	0	0	0	0	0	0	0	0	0	0	0
W1	0	0	0	0	1	1	0	0	0	0	0	1	0	0
W2	0	0	0	0	0	0	0	0	0	0	0	0	0	0
W3	1	0	1	0	0	1	0	0	0	0	0	1	0	0
W4	0	0	1	0	1	0	0	0	0	0	0	1	0	0
W5	0	0	0	0	0	0	0	0	0	0	0	0	0	0
W6	0	0	0	0	0	0	0	0	0	0	0	0	0	0
W7	0	0	0	0	0	0	0	0	0	1	1	1	0	0
W8	0	0	0	0	0	0	0	0	1	0	1	0	0	1
W9	0	0	0	0	0	0	0	0	1	1	0	0	0	1
S1	0	0	1	0	1	1	0	0	1	0	0	0	0	0
S2	0	0	0	0	0	0	0	0	0	0	0	0	0	0
S4	0	0	0	0	0	0	0	0	0	1	1	0	0	0

(b) Negative Relation

	I1	I3	W1	W2	W3	W4	W5	W6	W7	W8	W9	S1	S2	S4
I1	0	1	0	1	0	0	0	0	0	0	0	0	0	0
I3	1	0	0	0	0	0	1	1	1	1	1	0	0	1
W1	0	0	0	0	0	0	0	0	0	0	0	0	0	0
W2	1	0	0	0	0	0	0	0	1	1	1	0	0	0
W3	0	0	0	0	0	0	0	0	0	0	0	0	0	0
W4	0	0	0	0	0	0	1	0	0	0	0	0	0	0
W5	0	1	0	0	0	1	0	1	1	1	1	1	1	0
W6	0	1	0	0	0	0	1	0	1	0	0	0	0	0
W7	0	1	0	1	0	0	1	1	0	0	0	0	0	0
W8	0	1	0	1	0	0	1	0	0	0	0	0	0	0
W9	0	1	0	1	0	0	1	0	0	0	0	0	0	0
S1	0	0	0	0	0	0	1	0	0	0	0	0	0	0
S2	0	0	0	0	0	0	1	0	0	0	0	0	0	0
S4	0	1	0	0	0	0	0	0	0	0	0	0	0	0

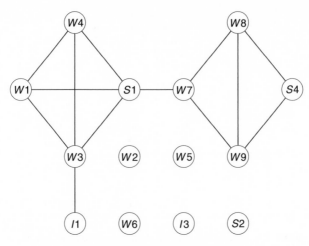

Figure 2.2. Positive ties in the BWR.

as emphasized by Homans (1950:69), it was not a game-playing link through the observation period. Neither $S2$ nor $I3$ take any part in the game-playing activity.

Next, we consider the positive (friendship) ties in Table 2.9(a) and Figure 2.2, and the negative (antagonism) ties in Table 2.9(b) and Figure 2.3, between these men, as recorded by the observer. They are consistent with the identified game-playing subgroups. Actors $W1$, $W3$, $W4$, $S1$, and $I1$, who all belong to Group A, are linked by these ties, as are $W7$, $W8$, $W9$, and $S4$, all of whom belong to Group B. Of interest is the friendship (positive) tie between $S1$ and $W7$ that bridges the two subgroups. None of the remaining actors have friendship ties in the room (see Figure 2.2).

As RD and Homans both emphasized, many of the negative ties are focused on $I3$ and $W5$. The former was the oldest and most disliked person in the room, followed by $W5$. Both were involved in seven antagonistic ties, including their own mutual dislike. Most of the remaining negative ties are between the selector wiremen at the back of the room and the connector wiremen in the middle of the room. There are some negative ties among the men in the middle soldering unit plus an antagonistic tie between $I1$ and $I3$ and one between $S1$ and $W5$. Neither $W1$ nor $W3$ is involved in the antagonistic ties (see Figure 2.3).

On the basis of these relations, RD identified two clear cliques, each of which can be described in relation to the provisionally identified groups. Although $W2$ and $W5$ are in the game-playing (sub)group, A, they are not involved in friendship ties with the other members of A. So, Clique A is identified as $W1$, $W3$, $W4$, $S1$, and $I1$. In a similar fashion, although $W6$ plays games with members of B, he has no friendship ties with them. Clique B is $W7$, $W8$, $W9$, and $S4$. The placement of the remaining five actors was, in RD's term, approximate.[10]

---

10 Note that clique is used in its colloquial sense and not in the sense of the maximal complete subgraph.

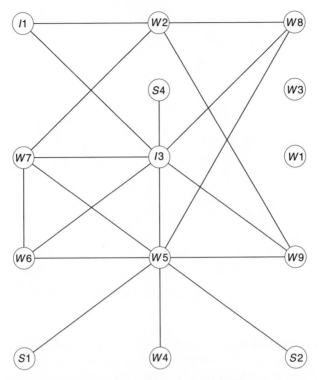

Figure 2.3. Negative ties in the BWR.

RD were clear that *W*5, *S*2, and *I*3 belonged to neither group and saw these workers as isolated, at least in the friendship ties. As noted in the figure, two of them, *W*5 and *I*3, were involved in many antagonistic ties. *W*2 played games with members of A and can be viewed as oriented toward Clique A. As *W*6 played games with members of Clique B, both RD and Homans reported he was oriented toward Clique B. He even sought leadership of that group. In Homans' narrative, his attempts to do this were resisted and he was disliked as a result. It seems, then, that the partition of the members of the network in the BWR, according to RD, is as follows:

1. *W*1, *W*3, *W*4, *S*1, and *I*1;
2. *W*2;
3. *W*7, *W*8, *W*9, and *S*4;
4. *W*6;
5. *W*5, *S*2, and *I*3.

These game-playing and affect ties are clearly part of what Homans called the internal system. They are social relationships that are not dictated solely by the geography of the room. (Of course they are not completely independent of the room layout either.) The sequential nature of the tasks is, for Homans, part of the

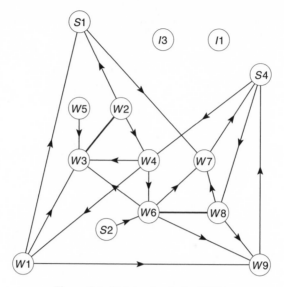

Figure 2.4. Helping ties in the BWR.

external system. Conflict over the room's windows (having them open or closed) is conditioned by the room's layout in terms of the actors' locations in relation to the windows. Helping with regard to work is rooted also in the physical infrastructure. The helping ties are shown in Figure 2.4 and Table 2.10(a).

There were conflictual ties over having the windows of the workroom open or closed. These ties are shown in Table 2.10(b) and displayed in Figure 2.5.

Some reanalyses of the BWR data. There have been many reanalyses of these data also, starting with that of Homans (1950). For our purposes, the most noteworthy are those of Breiger et al. (1975) and White et al. (1976). By stacking and thereby using all five relations as input to CONCOR, Breiger et al. reported a variety of partitions. Of immediate interest is their four-cluster partition:

1. $W1$, $W3$, $W4$, $S1$, and $I1$ (Clique A);
2. $W2$, $W5$, and $I3$;
3. $W7$, $W8$, $W9$, and $S4$ (Clique B);
4. $W6$ and $S2$.

These clusters are portrayed, respectively, as Clique A, hangers-on to Clique A, Clique B, and hangers-on to Clique B. We have some doubt over the characterization of the hangers-on. At best it seems reasonable to view $W2$ as a hanger-on to A and $W6$ as a hanger-on to B given the RD description. Breiger et al. (1975) also describe a six-cluster model obtained by White et al. (1976). White et al. wrote that "Homans' (1950) classic account of the Bank Wiring Room suggested

Table 2.10. The BWR – Helping and Conflict over Windows Relations

(a) Helping														
	*I*1	*I*3	*W*1	*W*2	*W*3	*W*4	*W*5	*W*6	*W*7	*W*8	*W*9	*S*1	*S*2	*S*4
*I*1	0	0	0	0	0	0	0	0	0	0	0	0	0	0
*I*3	0	0	0	0	0	0	0	0	0	0	0	0	0	0
*W*1	0	0	0	0	1	0	0	0	0	0	1	1	0	0
*W*2	0	0	0	0	1	1	0	0	0	0	0	1	0	0
*W*3	0	0	0	1	0	0	0	0	0	0	0	0	0	0
*W*4	0	0	1	0	1	0	0	1	0	0	0	0	0	0
*W*5	0	0	0	0	1	0	0	0	0	0	0	0	0	0
*W*6	0	0	0	0	1	0	0	0	1	1	1	0	0	0
*W*7	0	0	0	0	0	0	0	0	0	0	0	0	0	1
*W*8	0	0	0	0	0	0	0	1	1	0	1	0	0	0
*W*9	0	0	0	0	0	0	0	0	0	0	0	0	0	1
*S*1	0	0	0	0	0	0	0	0	1	0	0	0	0	0
*S*2	0	0	0	0	0	0	0	1	0	0	0	0	0	0
*S*4	0	0	0	0	0	1	0	0	0	1	0	0	0	0
(b) Conflict Ties over Windows														
	*I*1	*I*3	*W*1	*W*2	*W*3	*W*4	*W*5	*W*6	*W*7	*W*8	*W*9	*S*1	*S*2	*S*4
*I*1	0	0	0	0	0	0	0	0	0	0	0	0	0	0
*I*3	0	0	0	0	0	0	0	0	0	0	0	0	0	0
*W*1	0	0	0	0	0	0	0	0	0	0	0	0	0	0
*W*2	0	0	0	0	0	0	0	0	0	0	0	0	0	0
*W*3	0	0	0	0	0	0	0	0	0	0	0	0	0	0
*W*4	0	0	0	0	0	0	1	1	1	0	1	0	0	0
*W*5	0	0	0	0	0	1	0	1	0	0	0	1	0	0
*W*6	0	0	0	0	0	1	1	0	1	1	1	1	0	1
*W*7	0	0	0	0	0	1	0	1	0	1	1	0	0	1
*W*8	0	0	0	0	0	0	0	1	1	0	1	1	0	1
*W*9	0	0	0	0	0	1	0	1	1	1	0	1	0	0
*S*1	0	0	0	0	0	0	1	1	0	1	1	0	0	1
*S*2	0	0	0	0	0	0	0	0	0	0	0	0	0	0
*S*4	0	0	0	0	0	0	0	1	1	1	0	1	0	0

a six-cluster blockmodel."[11] Using only the games, friendship, and antagonism relations as stacked input to CONCOR, they established the following clustering:

1. *W*3, *W*4, and *S*1;
2. *W*1 and *I*1;
3. *W*2, *W*5, and *I*3;
4. *W*8 and *W*9;
5. *W*7 and *S*4;
6. *W*6 and *S*2.

---

11 White et al. wrote of a six-block blockmodel. We prefer to keep the term *cluster* for a grouping of actors and use the term *block* as a set of ties. We note also that they refer to a seven-cluster model with *I*3 in a separate cluster.

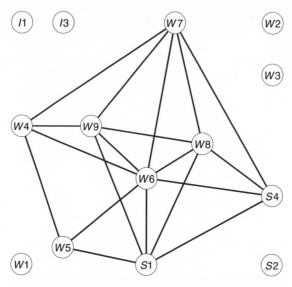

Figure 2.5. Conflict ties over windows in the BWR.

The first two clusters are subsets of A, and the third has the unpopular $W5$ and $I3$ with the ignored (or left alone) $W2$. The next two clusters are subsets of B. We further examine the BWR data in Chapters 4, 6, 7, and 10.

2.1.3   Newcomb fraternity data

Newcomb (1961, 1968) created a pseudofraternity for 17 men who were unacquainted at the beginning of a semester. In exchange for room and board, these men provided, in essence, sociometric data every week throughout the semester.[12] These data are reported in Nordlie (1958) and are also distributed with UCINET. They take a very different form than the data we have described thus far. Each actor was constrained to rank all of the other 16 actors as shown in Table 2.11. Each row of Table 2.11 corresponds to one member of the pseudofraternity and contains his ranking of the other 16 actors at the outset of the study period. Actor A ranks M at the top (the most liked), Q is ranked next, and J is ranked the lowest.

The key feature of the data collected by Newcomb and his associates is that they provide a time series of sociometric relations. Indeed, they are the basis on which Newcomb (1961) studied the acquaintance process. Table 2.12 displays the data for the 10th week, and Table 2.13 shows the comparable data at the end of the study. Clearly, these structures differ, and, with a sequence of such structures, we can examine the evolution of the group structure through time. Newcomb framed his study in terms of structural balance (Heider 1946, 1958; Cartwright and Harary 1956). We focus on the partitions of these structures, staying within the structural balance framework in Chapter 10.

---

12   There is one exception with a two-week gap between a pair of sociometric data sets.

Table 2.11. Rankings Assigned by Each Actor in the First Week

	A	B	C	D	E	F	G	H	I	J	K	L	M	N	O	P	Q
A	0	7	12	11	10	4	13	14	15	16	3	9	1	5	8	6	2
B	8	0	16	1	11	12	2	14	10	13	15	6	7	9	5	3	4
C	13	10	0	7	8	11	9	15	6	5	2	1	16	12	4	14	3
D	13	1	15	0	14	4	3	16	12	7	6	9	8	11	10	5	2
E	14	10	11	7	0	16	12	4	5	6	2	3	13	15	8	9	1
F	7	13	11	3	15	0	10	2	4	16	14	5	1	12	9	8	6
G	15	4	11	3	16	8	0	6	9	10	5	2	14	12	13	7	1
H	9	8	16	7	10	1	14	0	11	3	2	5	4	15	12	13	6
I	6	16	8	14	13	11	4	15	0	7	1	2	9	5	12	10	3
J	2	16	9	14	11	4	3	10	7	0	15	8	12	13	1	6	5
K	12	7	4	8	6	14	9	16	3	13	0	2	10	15	11	5	1
L	15	11	2	6	5	14	7	13	10	4	3	0	16	8	9	12	1
M	1	15	16	7	4	2	12	14	13	8	6	11	0	10	3	9	5
N	14	5	8	6	13	9	2	16	1	3	12	7	15	0	4	11	10
O	16	9	4	8	1	13	11	12	6	2	3	5	10	15	0	14	7
P	8	11	15	3	13	16	14	12	1	9	2	6	10	7	5	0	4
Q	9	15	10	2	4	11	5	12	3	7	8	1	6	16	14	13	0

These (ranked) data are less than ideal and create serious issues over deciding what to do with them. One option is to keep the data as they are and view the ranks as useful quantitative information. Nakao and Romney (1993) adopted this tactic. Another alternative is to work with some transformation of the ranked information, which is a strategy adopted by Doreian et al. (1996). In Chapter 10, we consider

Table 2.12. Rankings Assigned by Each Actor in Week 10

	A	B	C	D	E	F	G	H	I	J	K	L	M	N	O	P	Q
A	0	13	14	8	12	2	7	4	6	16	10	9	1	5	11	15	3
B	9	0	14	3	5	4	10	7	6	13	8	2	11	12	15	16	1
C	12	7	0	8	9	4	3	10	5	16	6	2	13	11	14	15	1
D	10	3	16	0	5	2	8	14	4	15	9	6	7	12	13	11	1
E	2	8	15	7	0	5	9	6	1	13	10	12	3	11	14	16	4
F	1	12	13	5	7	0	11	2	4	15	14	10	3	8	9	16	6
G	12	4	3	10	8	13	0	14	5	11	2	1	7	6	16	15	9
H	1	11	15	8	5	2	13	0	9	14	10	7	4	3	12	16	6
I	12	6	14	4	5	1	9	10	0	16	8	7	11	3	13	15	2
J	5	11	14	15	13	8	4	2	7	0	12	3	10	9	6	16	1
K	11	4	5	6	7	14	8	12	3	13	0	2	9	10	15	16	1
L	11	2	9	6	10	14	1	13	3	16	5	0	8	7	15	12	4
M	1	13	14	10	3	2	7	4	9	16	11	8	0	6	12	15	5
N	2	9	15	5	16	10	4	11	1	12	6	3	7	0	14	13	8
O	10	7	13	2	9	5	11	14	4	15	8	6	12	16	0	1	3
P	14	5	12	4	10	15	9	11	3	16	7	2	13	8	6	0	1
Q	4	5	11	2	3	8	13	12	1	16	6	7	9	14	10	15	0

Table 2.13. Rankings Assigned by Each Actor in the Final Week

	A	B	C	D	E	F	G	H	I	J	K	L	M	N	O	P	Q
A	0	12	15	5	10	11	6	4	7	16	8	9	2	3	13	14	1
B	8	0	13	2	3	6	9	10	5	15	7	4	11	12	14	16	1
C	8	11	0	10	12	3	5	13	4	14	6	2	9	15	7	16	1
D	6	4	15	0	3	2	10	11	5	16	9	8	7	14	12	13	1
E	5	4	13	2	0	8	10	6	1	14	12	11	3	9	15	16	7
F	6	9	14	3	8	0	7	1	2	15	13	11	4	10	12	16	5
G	12	4	8	6	14	10	0	5	9	16	2	1	7	11	13	15	3
H	1	9	15	3	6	4	13	0	11	14	10	8	2	7	12	16	5
I	10	5	13	3	7	1	12	9	0	16	11	6	8	4	14	15	2
J	2	12	14	11	10	6	3	4	7	0	9	1	15	13	5	16	8
K	9	3	6	4	7	13	5	14	8	16	0	2	10	11	12	15	1
L	8	2	12	7	11	14	1	10	3	16	5	0	6	9	15	13	4
M	1	10	14	9	8	5	3	2	7	15	12	11	0	6	13	16	4
N	4	9	16	10	15	2	8	11	1	14	3	7	6	0	12	13	5
O	12	8	11	3	16	7	9	13	4	14	15	5	6	10	0	2	1
P	12	5	16	3	11	8	7	15	2	14	9	1	13	10	6	0	4
Q	4	3	14	2	6	10	9	11	1	16	8	7	5	13	12	15	0

partitioning these networks in terms of structural balance (Doreian and Mrvar 1996), which requires a coding of the ranked ties into positive ties, null ties, and negative ties. The basic intuition here is that actors know whom they like and whom they do not like or, more dramatically, know who their friends and enemies are. Using some of the ethnographic information in Nordlie (1958), Doreian

Table 2.14. Transformed Signed Ties for Each Actor at Week 10

	A	B	C	D	E	F	G	H	I	J	K	L	M	N	O	P	Q
A	0	0	-1	0	0	1	0	0	0	-1	0	0	1	0	0	-1	1
B	0	0	-1	1	0	0	0	0	0	0	0	1	0	0	-1	-1	1
C	0	0	0	0	0	0	1	0	0	-1	0	1	0	0	-1	-1	1
D	0	1	-1	0	0	1	0	-1	0	-1	0	0	0	0	0	0	1
E	1	0	-1	0	0	0	0	0	1	0	0	0	1	0	-1	-1	0
F	1	0	0	0	0	0	0	1	0	-1	-1	0	1	0	0	-1	0
G	0	0	1	0	0	0	0	-1	0	0	1	1	0	0	-1	-1	0
H	1	0	-1	0	0	1	0	0	0	-1	0	0	0	1	0	-1	0
I	0	0	-1	0	0	1	0	0	0	-1	0	0	0	1	0	-1	1
J	0	0	-1	-1	0	0	0	1	0	0	0	1	0	0	0	-1	1
K	0	0	0	0	0	-1	0	0	1	0	0	1	0	0	-1	-1	1
L	0	1	0	0	0	-1	1	0	1	-1	0	0	0	0	-1	0	0
M	1	0	-1	0	1	1	0	0	0	-1	0	0	0	0	0	-1	0
N	1	0	-1	0	-1	0	0	0	1	0	0	1	0	0	-1	0	0
O	0	0	0	1	0	0	0	-1	0	-1	0	0	0	-1	0	1	1
P	-1	0	0	0	0	-1	0	0	1	-1	0	1	0	0	0	0	1
Q	0	0	0	1	1	0	0	0	1	-1	0	0	0	-1	0	-1	0

et al. (1996) recoded the rankings made by the actors. The top four choices were recoded to +1, the lowest three ranks were recoded to −1, and the rest were coded to 0. The partitioned structure at the outset had three subgroups of actors with the positive ties primarily within subgroups and with the negative ties primarily between them. By about Week 10, there was a large group of actors with positive ties among themselves. There were four actors (two singletons and a dyad) who were the objects of over 80% of the negative ties. These four actors also had mutual negative ties. This structure persisted during the remaining weeks, and the imbalance declined through the study period. In Chapter 10, we consider an alternative recoding in which only the top three ranks are recoded to +1 with the other recodes the same. The qualitative results remain robust under this, and similar, recodings. Table 2.14 shows the signed ties in which the bottom three rankings were recoded to −1 and the top three rankings were recoded to 1 for the Week 10 data.

2.2 NEWER DATA SETS

2.2.1 Little league baseball teams

Fine (1987) reported sociometric data for two very successful Little League (LL) baseball teams in the same local league. Fine's primary concern was to examine the creation and elaboration of various forms of idioculture, which he defined as "a system of knowledge, beliefs, behaviors and customs shared by members of an interacting group to which the members can refer and that serve as the basis for further interaction" (1987:125). He contended that the sociometric structure of such teams conditions the formation of their idiocultures.

As described in Chapter 1, Fine asked the boys to list their three best friends on the team.[13] We used the relational data of the Transatlantic Industries (TI) as an illustration of network data in Figure 1.1. Table 2.15 displays these data in matrix form. Fine provided descriptions of only a few team members. Frank is listed as the coach's son, who received preferential treatment from his father in terms of playing time. Four other team members regarded him as one of their three best friends. Tom, "a quiet, mature, responsible twelve year old, was one of TI's best players" (Fine 1987:143), and he was named as a best friend by five other team members. Ron received the most friendship nominations, and Darrin was the best batter on the team. Fine described TI as a decentralized team.

The sociometric data for the Sharpstone Auto (SA) team are shown in Table 2.16. As for the TI team, these data consist of best friendship nominations made by the team members at the end of the season. In describing the structure of this team, Fine mentioned only three of the boys. Justin is characterized as a very talented,[14]

---

13 In one respect, these data are problematic because such a fixed-choice format of asking this question can distort the observed representation of the empirical structure. This is less pressing here given our methodological emphasis on blockmodeling procedures.

14 He was seen by many as the best player in the league.

Table 2.15. Sociometric Data for the TI Team

		1	2	3	4	5	6	7	8	9	10	11	12	13
Ron	1	0	0	1	1	1	0	0	0	0	0	0	0	0
Tom	2	1	0	1	0	0	0	0	0	0	0	1	0	0
Frank	3	1	0	0	1	0	0	0	0	0	0	1	0	0
Boyd	4	1	1	1	0	0	0	0	0	0	0	0	0	0
Tim	5	1	0	1	1	0	0	0	0	0	0	0	0	0
John	6	0	0	0	0	1	0	0	0	0	0	0	1	1
Jeff	7	0	1	0	0	0	0	0	1	1	0	0	0	0
Jay	8	0	1	0	0	0	0	1	0	1	0	0	0	0
Sandy	9	0	1	0	0	0	0	1	1	0	0	0	0	0
Jerry	10	1	0	0	0	0	1	0	0	0	0	0	0	0
Darrin	11	1	1	0	0	0	0	0	0	0	1	0	0	0
Ben	12	1	0	0	0	0	1	0	0	0	1	0	0	0
Arnie	13	0	0	0	0	1	1	0	0	0	0	0	0	0

aggressive, and fearless ballplayer who is the team leader. Harry is listed as another fine player (best pitcher) and Justin's best friend. Whit is a good friend of both Justin and Harry. However, he was a year younger than these players and, although able, was not as good a player. "These three players . . . constituted the heart and soul of Sharpstone Auto" (Fine 1987:140), and Fine saw the team as highly centralized.

Although we have used pictorial displays of networks to help illustrate our arguments, we are mindful that a graph can be drawn in different ways. For example, Figure 2.6 is drawn to display "sociometric standing" with Justin at the top and with Harry and Whit close behind. Figure 2.7 shows an alternative version of this network to emphasize centrality: Justin, Harry, and Whit are the most central

Table 2.16. Sociometric Data for the SA Team

		1	2	3	4	5	6	7	8	9	10	11	12	13
Justin	1	0	1	1	0	0	0	1	0	0	0	0	0	0
Harry	2	1	0	1	0	0	0	1	0	0	0	0	0	0
Whit	3	1	1	0	1	0	0	0	0	0	0	0	0	0
Brian	4	1	1	0	0	1	0	0	0	0	0	0	0	0
Paul	5	1	0	1	0	0	1	0	0	0	0	0	0	0
Ian	6	1	1	1	0	0	0	0	0	0	0	0	0	0
Mike	7	1	1	0	0	0	1	0	0	0	0	0	0	0
Jim	8	1	0	1	1	0	0	0	0	0	0	0	0	0
Dan	9	1	1	1	0	0	0	0	0	0	0	0	0	0
Ray	10	1	1	1	0	0	0	0	0	0	0	0	0	0
Cliff	11	1	1	1	0	0	0	0	0	0	0	0	0	0
Mason	12	1	1	0	1	0	0	0	0	0	0	0	0	0
Roy	13	0	0	1	0	1	0	0	1	0	0	0	0	0

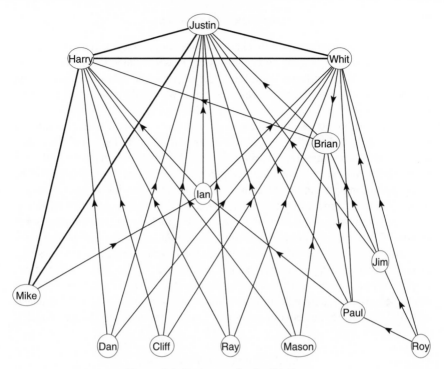

Figure 2.6. Sociogram for the SA Team.

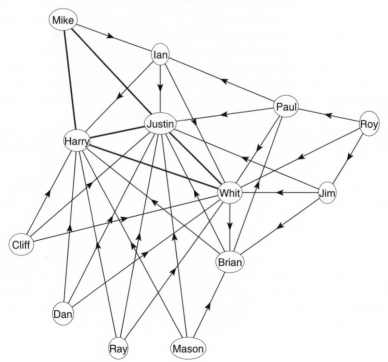

Figure 2.7. An alternative sociogram for the SA Team.

actors. The different versions of that network may suggest quite different structural properties (although standing and centrality are closely related ideas). We suspect that diagrams of networks are useful to convey a particular network narrative, and this, we believe, demands extra care in their use. We consider these issues further in Chapters 6 and 7.

Fine draws two interesting contrasts between these teams. The SA team had a rich idioculture and was highly centralized, whereas the TI team had little idioculture and was decentralized. Justin, Harry, and Whit formed the core of the SA team. Their creation or endorsement of potential idioculture items was one of the forces generating SA's idioculture. In contrast, the TI team "did not have the esprit of many Little League teams, nor was it racked by dissension." In Fine's narrative, "[u]nlike Sharpstone, Transatlantic Industries did not have any true preadolescent leaders. While there was consensus on who were the leaders of Sharpstone, such consensus did not exist on TI ... (it seemed) a team without a clearly defined status hierarchy but with many secondary leaders" (1987:142). "In contrast to Sharpstone, no players epitomized the team. In part, *as a result of this loose structure*, TI never developed a rich idioculture to the extent that Sharpstone did" (1987:145; emphasis added). We analyze the network structure of these two teams in Chapters 6 and 7.

2.2.2 Political actor network

Doreian and Albert (1989) provide network data for a set of prominent political actors (PAs) in a Midwestern city in the U.S. The network tie is "strong political ally," with the relation displayed in Table 2.17. Figure 2.8 displays the PA network. The County Executive (A) and the County Auditor (B) were strong political rivals, each with their own supporters. The substantive issue was the construction of a federally mandated new jail. Each of the protagonists had staked out a position: actor A supported the construction of the jail whereas B opposed this course of action. The County Council (actors D–J) was split over this issue.

Doreian and Albert used blockmodeling tools to partition the actors in Table 2.17. Using both CONCOR and STRUCTURE, they reported the following partition:

1. $\{A, C, D, E, F, G, N\}$;
2. $\{B, H, I, J, M\}$;
3. $\{K, L\}$.

In the Doreian and Albert narrative, the network split into an alliance around the County Executive (A) and an alliance around the County Auditor (B) with a pair of neutral actors. This partition of the network predicted the voting outcomes concerning the construction of the new jail exactly. Given the partition in terms of structural equivalence, Doreian and Albert (1989:287) also reported a partition based on regular[15] equivalence:

---

15   They used REGE as implemented in UCINET.

Table 2.17. PA Network Ties

		A	B	C	D	E	F	G	H	I	J	K	L	M	N
County Executive	A	0	0	1	1	0	0	1	0	0	0	0	0	1	0
County Auditor	B	0	0	0	0	0	0	0	1	1	1	0	1	0	0
Sheriff	C	1	0	0	1	0	1	1	0	0	0	0	0	0	1
Council Member 1	D	1	0	1	0	1	1	1	0	0	0	0	1	0	0
Council Member 2	E	0	0	0	1	0	1	0	0	0	0	0	0	0	0
Council Member 3	F	0	0	1	1	1	0	0	0	0	0	0	1	0	1
Council Member 4	G	1	0	1	1	0	0	0	0	0	0	0	0	0	0
Council President	H	0	1	0	0	0	0	0	0	1	1	0	1	1	0
Council Member 5	I	0	1	0	0	0	0	0	1	0	1	0	0	1	0
Council Member 6	J	0	1	0	0	0	0	0	1	1	0	0	0	1	0
Former Co. Member	K	0	0	0	0	0	0	0	0	0	0	0	1	0	0
Former Co. Pres.	L	0	1	0	1	0	1	0	1	0	0	1	0	1	0
City Mayor	M	1	0	0	0	0	0	0	1	1	1	0	1	0	0
County Prosecutor	N	0	0	1	0	0	1	0	0	0	0	0	0	0	0

1. Central Core: $\{L\}$.
2. Boundary spanning to central core: $\{B, D, F, H, M\}$.
3. Integration inside alliances: $\{A, C, I, J\}$.
4. Completely peripheral actors: $\{E, G, K, N\}$.

While the idea of simultaneously considering partitions based on structural equivalence and regular equivalence is appealing, these two partitions are suboptimal. Using direct partitioning methods we provide in Chapter 6, we obtain so-called better partitions of the PAs based on these two equivalence ideas. In

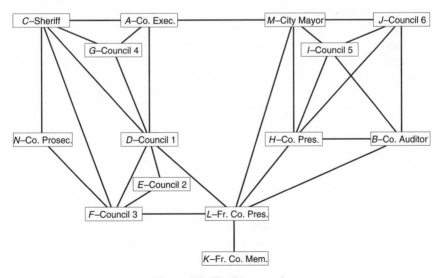

Figure 2.8. The PA network.

Chapter 7 we move to generalized blockmodeling procedures and reconsider this network. Rather than use two equivalence ideas applied to the whole network, we develop procedures in which each block can conform to its own pattern – which can include those blocks consistent with either the structural or regular equivalences.

2.2.3 Student government data

Without doubt, there has been great progress in developing models, methods, and algorithms for the analysis of social network data. Some suggest there is a methodological blind spot with regard to the issue of data quality. For example, Sudman remarked that "[m]any of the theoretical models that have been developed pay little or no attention to response error and simply assume that respondents can and do provide errorless information" (1985:129). The lively debate over informant accuracy (see, e.g., Bernard and Killworth 1977; Killworth and Bernard 1978, 1979; Bernard, Killworth, and Sailer 1982; Bernard et al. 1985) has led to an increased awareness that measuring networks is both important and difficult. However, as noted by Marsden (1990), concern for network measurement has a longer history. Within this, "[m]ost methodological research on network measurement has focused on data obtained through surveys and questionnaires" (Marsden 1990:445). And, within this focus, much of the work has taken the form of experiments. See, for example, Sudman (1985, 1988), Ferligoj and Hlebec (1999), and Hlebec and Ferligoj (2001, 2002), who explored, among other topics, the performance of (unaided) recall and name recognition (from a provided list of other network members) as methods of eliciting network data.

Hlebec (1993) described an experiment in this tradition. Through the use of an interview schedule, network data were obtained for some communication relations among members of the Student Government for a university in Slovenia. Two variables were manipulated: one concerned the wording of the questions asked, and the other focused on whether the respondents used recall or recognition in providing information about their interactions with other members of the governing body. There are 11 actors from whom data were obtained[16] – eight ministers,[17] labeled as M_1 through M_8, and three advisors, labeled A_1 through A_3. The (cognitive) data were elicited through the following three questions:

1. With which of the members and advisors do you (most often) discuss Student Government matters?
2. Which members and advisors of the Student Government do you (most often) ask for an opinion?
3. Which of the members and advisors of the Student Government (most often) ask you for an opinion?

The network data generated by these three questions, together with the recall and recognition variants, are shown in Table 2.18. These data are used first in Chapter 4

---

16 There were 12 members of the Student Government, but one refused to take part in the experiment.
17 One of whom was the Prime Minister.

Table 2.18. Three Ties under Recall and Recognition Formats

(Cognitive) Discussion Ties

		Recall											Recognition										
		1	2	3	4	5	6	7	8	9	10	11	1	2	3	4	5	6	7	8	9	10	11
M_1	1	0	1	1	0	0	1	0	0	0	0	0	0	1	1	0	0	1	0	0	0	1	0
M_2	2	0	0	0	0	0	0	0	1	0	0	0	0	0	0	1	0	1	0	1	0	0	0
M_3	3	1	1	0	1	0	1	1	1	0	0	0	1	1	0	1	1	1	1	1	0	1	0
M_4	4	0	0	0	0	0	0	1	1	0	0	0	0	0	0	0	0	0	1	1	0	0	0
M_5	5	0	1	0	1	0	1	1	1	0	0	0	0	1	0	1	0	1	1	1	0	1	0
M_6	6	0	1	0	1	1	0	1	1	0	0	0	0	1	0	1	1	0	1	1	0	0	0
M_7	7	0	0	0	1	0	0	0	1	1	0	1	0	0	0	1	0	0	0	1	1	0	1
M_8	8	0	1	0	1	0	0	1	0	0	0	1	0	1	0	1	0	0	1	0	0	0	1
A_1	9	0	0	0	1	0	0	1	1	0	0	1	0	1	1	0	0	0	1	1	0	0	1
A_2	10	1	0	1	1	1	0	0	0	0	0	0	1	1	1	0	1	0	0	0	0	0	0
A_3	11	0	0	0	0	0	1	0	1	1	0	0	0	0	0	1	0	1	0	1	0	0	0

Asking for an Opinion Ties

		Recall											Recognition										
M_1	1	0	1	0	0	0	1	0	0	0	0	0	0	1	1	0	0	0	0	0	0	0	0
M_2	2	0	0	0	1	0	0	0	1	0	0	0	0	0	0	1	0	0	0	1	0	0	0
M_3	3	1	1	0	1	0	1	0	1	0	0	0	1	1	0	0	0	0	0	0	0	0	0
M_4	4	0	1	0	0	0	0	0	0	0	0	0	0	0	0	0	0	0	1	1	0	0	0
M_5	5	0	1	0	0	0	1	0	0	0	0	0	0	1	0	0	0	1	0	1	0	1	0
M_6	6	0	1	0	0	0	0	0	0	0	0	0	1	1	1	1	1	0	1	1	0	0	0
M_7	7	0	0	0	1	0	0	0	1	1	0	0	0	0	0	1	0	0	0	1	1	0	0
M_8	8	0	1	0	1	0	0	0	0	0	0	0	0	1	0	1	0	0	0	0	0	0	0
A_1	9	0	0	0	0	0	0	1	1	0	0	1	0	1	0	0	0	0	1	1	0	0	0
A_2	10	1	1	1	0	1	0	0	0	0	0	0	1	1	1	0	1	0	0	0	0	0	0
A_3	11	0	0	1	0	0	1	0	1	0	0	0	0	0	0	1	0	1	0	1	0	0	0

Asked for an Opinion Ties (Transposed)

		Recall											Recognition										
M_1	1	0	1	1	0	0	0	0	0	0	1	1	0	1	1	1	0	0	0	1	0	1	1
M_2	2	1	0	1	1	1	1	1	1	0	1	0	1	0	1	1	0	1	0	1	0	1	0
M_3	3	0	1	0	0	1	0	0	0	0	0	0	1	0	0	0	0	0	0	0	0	0	0
M_4	4	0	1	1	0	0	1	1	1	0	0	1	0	0	1	0	0	1	1	1	1	0	0
M_5	5	0	1	0	0	0	1	1	0	0	1	0	1	1	0	0	0	1	0	0	0	0	0
M_6	6	0	1	0	0	0	0	0	0	0	0	1	1	1	0	0	1	0	0	0	0	0	0
M_7	7	0	0	0	1	0	0	0	1	1	0	1	1	0	0	1	0	1	0	1	1	0	0
M_8	8	0	1	1	1	0	1	1	0	1	0	1	0	1	0	1	0	1	1	0	1	0	1
A_1	9	0	0	0	0	0	0	0	0	0	0	0	0	0	0	0	0	0	1	0	0	0	0
A_2	10	0	1	0	0	1	0	0	0	0	0	0	1	0	1	0	1	0	0	0	0	0	0
A_3	11	0	1	0	0	0	0	0	0	1	0	0	0	0	0	0	0	0	1	0	1	0	0

Table 2.19. Organizations in the Kansas SAR Mission

Label	Organization	Short Name
A	Osage County Sheriff's Department	Sheriff
B	Osage County Civil Defense Office	Civil Def.
C	Osage County Coroner's Office	Coroner
D	Osage County Attorney's Office	Attorney
E	Kansas State Highway Patrol	Highway P
F	Kansas State Parks and Resources Authority	Parks & Res
G	Kansas State Game and Fish Commission	Game & Fish
H	Kansas State Department of Transportation	Kansas DOT
I	U.S. Army Corps of Engineers	Army Corps
J	U.S. Army Reserve	Army Reserve
K	Crable Ambulance	Crable Amb
L	Franklin County Ambulance	Frank Co. Amb
M	Lee's Summit Underwater Rescue Team	Lee Rescue
N	Shawney County Underwater Rescue Team	Shawney
O	Burlingame Police Department	Burl Police
P	Lyndon Police Department	Lynd Police
Q	American Red Cross	Red Cross
R	Topeka Fire Department Rescue #1	Topica FD
S	Carbondale Fire Department	Carb FD
T	Topeka Radiator and Body Works	Topeka RBW

to illustrate centrality measures, and we consider them briefly in Chapter 6 in our discussion of blockmodeling. They are used extensively in our discussion of generalized blockmodeling (Chapter 7).

2.2.4   Kansas search and rescue network

When disasters strike human communities, there will be physical damage, human suffering, and social loss. Both organizations and individuals respond to the needs created by disasters. Their responses are more effective if their actions are co-ordinated in some fashion. In general, this coordination is an interorganizational network that is formed to create an overall Search and Rescue (SAR) Operation mission. Drabek et al. (1981) reported a variety of these networks and discussed their formation through time, the structure(s) generated, and their operation.

An interorganizational SAR network was formed after a small tornado flipped a pleasure boat on Lake Pomona in Kansas. Although many individuals and organizations responded, Drabek et al. argued that the bulk of the SAR effort involved the 20 organizations listed in Table 2.19. They included law enforcement agencies, fire departments, underwater rescue teams, and general emergency agencies, as well as county, state, and federal agencies.

The County Sheriff (A) took control of the SAR effort once the County Attorney (D) assured him of his legal authority to do so. A command post was created in

Table 2.20. Kansas SAR Interorganizational Network

	A	B	C	D	E	F	G	H	I	J	K	L	M	N	O	P	Q	R	S	T
A	–	4	4	0	4	4	4	0	4	0	4	0	0	0	2	2	3	0	0	4
B	4	–	2	0	4	4	4	0	3	0	0	0	0	3	0	2	2	0	0	0
C	4	0	–	1	4	4	0	0	4	0	3	0	0	0	0	0	1	0	0	0
D	4	4	3	–	4	4	4	0	4	0	0	0	0	4	0	0	0	0	0	0
E	4	0	4	4	–	4	4	0	0	0	2	2	4	4	0	4	2	0	0	2
F	4	0	3	1	4	–	3	0	3	0	4	4	0	4	0	0	0	0	0	0
G	4	0	1	1	3	4	–	0	3	1	0	0	0	0	0	1	0	0	0	0
H	1	1	0	0	1	0	0	–	0	1	0	0	0	0	0	0	0	0	0	0
I	4	0	4	0	3	4	4	0	–	0	4	0	0	0	0	0	2	0	0	0
J	4	0	0	0	4	0	0	0	0	–	0	0	0	0	0	0	0	0	0	0
K	4	0	3	0	4	4	3	0	3	0	–	3	0	0	0	0	0	0	0	0
L	2	0	0	0	4	0	4	0	0	0	0	–	0	0	0	0	2	0	0	0
M	3	0	0	0	3	0	0	0	0	0	0	0	–	0	0	0	0	0	0	0
N	4	0	3	0	4	4	4	0	4	0	0	3	1	–	0	0	3	4	0	4
O	4	0	2	1	4	4	1	0	4	1	4	2	1	1	–	4	2	1	0	4
P	4	4	0	0	4	4	4	0	0	0	4	0	0	0	0	–	0	0	0	0
Q	4	4	2	0	4	4	4	0	4	1	0	0	0	2	0	0	–	0	0	0
R	4	0	0	0	4	0	0	0	0	0	0	0	4	4	0	0	0	–	0	0
S	4	4	0	0	4	2	2	0	4	0	0	0	0	0	0	0	2	0	–	0
T	4	0	0	0	4	0	0	0	0	0	0	0	0	3	2	4	0	0	0	–

a Highway Patrol (*E*) facility. Lake Pomona had been created by a dam that was built and operated by the U.S. Army Corps of Engineers (*I*). The State Park that included the lake was under the control of the State Parks and Resources Authority (*F*) with the responsibility shared by the State Game and Fish Commission (*G*). A temporary morgue was established under the control of the County Coroner (*C*) at the offices of the Army Corps. Bodies were brought to this location, and survivors were brought to the office of the state park. There were two ambulance services (*K* and *L*), two fire departments (*R* and *S*), two police departments (*O* and *P*), and three organizations defined in terms of their expertise in underwater rescue (*M*, *N*, and *T*). Additionally, there was the Civil Defense Office (*B*) for the county and the Red Cross (*Q*).

The communication data among these organizations are shown in Table 2.20. The values in the array represent relative magnitudes[18] of communication intensity: (4) continuous, (3) about once an hour, (2) every few hours, (1) about once a day, and (0) no communication. Drabek et al. did provide a diagram of this network, but we find it unintelligible. Our own efforts do not fare well either, and this seems to be a network for which a diagram has little value. One goal of blockmodeling is the establishment of the basic structure of a network. Drabek et al. (1981) presented a

18 They are reverse coded from the original data source so that higher values represent higher rates of communication.

blockmodel analysis of these data. Their partition of the network into five positions (clusters) is this:

1. Authority position: $\{A, E\}$.
2. Primary support: $\{C, F, G, I, K\}$.
3. Critical resources: $\{D, L, N\}$.
4. Secondary support, 1: $\{M, O, P, Q, R, T\}$.
5. Secondary support, 2: $\{B, H, J, S\}$.

This partition is suboptimal, and we provide an alternative, better fitting partition of this network in Chapter 6 – one based on techniques we describe in Chapters 5 and 6.

2.2.5   A Bales-type group dynamics network

We now consider data reported by Schwartz and Sprinzen (SS; 1984) from Bales (1970). After 13 weeks of interaction in a small group dynamics study during a semester, the participants in the group provided ratings of their relations with the other members of the group on three dimensions – positive affect (liking), negative affect (disliking), and similarity. SS recoded the ratings on all three dimensions into binary matrices. The two affect matrices are presented in Table 2.21.

SS reported a blockmodel with three positions; it was established by using all three relations:

1. $\{A, J, K, O, Q, T\}$.
2. $\{B, D, F, M, P, R\}$.
3. $\{C, E, G, H, I, L, N, S\}$.

We consider the SS liking and disliking ties in Chapter 10, where the focus is on balance theoretic partitioning (Doreian and Mrvar 1996) and where a much better partition of these data is provided.

2.2.6   Ragusan families marriage networks

Krivošić (1990) collected interesting data about the population of Ragusa (Dubrovnik), a republic for most of its history. He also constructed two matrices describing the marriage networks of the Ragusan noble families in the 16th century (Table 2.22) and in the 18th century and the beginning of 19th century (Table 2.23). Although these data are similar to the well-known Padgett marriage network for the elite Florentine families in the 15th century (see Section 1.1.1), they are directed and valued. Men marrying women and women marrying men are distinguished.

Ragusa was settled in the seventh century, as reported by Constantine Porphyrogenite, by fugitives from Epidaurum after its destruction. Ragusa was for a time under Byzantine protection, becoming a free commune as early as the 12th century. Ragusa quickly grew into a free city-state. The Ragusan people prospered

Table 2.21. Positive and Negative Ties from a Bales-Type Experiment

Positive Ties

	A	B	C	D	E	F	G	H	I	J	K	L	M	N	O	P	Q	R	S	T
A	0	0	0	0	0	0	0	0	0	0	1	0	0	0	0	1	0	0	0	0
B	0	0	0	0	0	1	0	0	1	0	0	0	0	0	1	0	0	0	1	0
C	1	0	0	0	0	0	1	0	1	1	0	0	0	0	1	0	0	0	0	0
D	0	0	0	0	0	0	0	0	0	1	0	0	0	0	0	0	0	0	0	0
E	0	0	0	0	0	0	1	0	1	0	0	0	1	0	0	0	0	0	0	0
F	0	0	0	0	0	0	0	0	0	0	0	0	0	0	0	0	0	0	0	0
G	1	0	0	0	0	0	0	0	1	1	1	0	0	1	1	0	0	0	0	1
H	0	0	0	0	1	0	1	0	1	1	0	0	0	0	0	0	0	0	0	0
I	1	0	0	0	0	0	0	1	0	0	1	0	0	0	0	0	0	0	1	0
J	0	0	0	0	0	0	0	0	0	0	0	1	0	0	1	0	0	0	0	0
K	0	0	0	0	0	0	0	0	0	1	0	0	0	0	1	0	0	0	0	0
L	0	1	0	0	1	0	0	0	0	0	0	0	0	0	0	1	0	0	0	0
M	0	0	0	0	0	0	0	0	0	0	1	0	0	0	0	0	0	0	0	0
N	0	0	0	0	0	0	1	0	0	0	0	0	0	0	0	0	0	0	0	0
O	1	0	0	0	0	0	0	0	0	1	1	0	0	0	0	0	0	0	0	0
P	0	0	0	0	0	0	0	0	0	1	0	0	0	0	0	0	1	0	1	0
Q	1	0	0	0	0	0	0	0	0	1	0	0	0	0	1	1	0	0	0	0
R	0	0	0	1	0	0	0	0	0	1	0	0	0	0	0	0	0	0	0	1
S	0	0	0	0	0	0	0	0	0	0	0	0	0	0	0	1	0	0	0	0
T	0	0	0	0	0	0	0	0	0	1	0	0	0	0	0	0	0	0	1	0

Negative Ties

	A	B	C	D	E	F	G	H	I	J	K	L	M	N	O	P	Q	R	S	T
A	0	0	0	0	0	1	0	0	0	0	0	0	0	0	0	0	0	0	1	0
B	0	0	0	0	0	0	0	0	0	0	0	0	0	0	0	0	0	0	0	0
C	0	0	0	0	0	0	0	0	0	0	0	0	0	0	0	1	0	1	0	0
D	0	0	0	0	0	1	0	1	0	0	0	0	0	0	1	0	0	0	0	0
E	0	0	0	0	0	0	0	0	0	0	0	0	0	0	0	0	0	0	0	0
F	0	0	0	0	0	0	0	0	0	0	0	0	0	0	0	0	0	0	0	0
G	0	0	0	0	0	0	0	0	0	0	0	0	0	0	0	0	0	1	0	0
H	1	0	0	0	0	1	0	0	0	0	0	0	0	0	1	0	0	1	0	0
I	0	0	0	0	0	0	0	0	0	0	0	0	0	0	0	0	1	1	0	0
J	0	1	0	0	0	0	0	0	0	0	0	0	0	0	0	0	0	0	0	0
K	0	0	0	0	0	0	0	0	0	0	0	0	0	0	0	0	0	1	0	0
L	0	0	0	0	0	0	0	0	0	0	0	0	0	0	0	0	0	0	0	0
M	0	0	1	0	0	1	1	0	0	0	0	0	0	0	0	0	0	1	0	0
N	0	0	0	0	0	1	0	0	0	0	0	0	0	0	0	0	0	1	0	0
O	0	0	0	0	0	0	0	0	0	0	0	0	0	0	0	0	0	0	0	0
P	0	0	0	0	0	0	0	0	0	0	0	0	0	0	0	0	0	1	0	0
Q	0	1	0	0	0	0	0	0	0	0	0	0	1	1	0	0	0	0	0	0
R	0	0	0	0	0	0	0	0	0	0	1	0	0	0	0	0	0	0	0	0
S	0	0	0	0	0	0	0	0	0	0	0	0	1	0	0	0	0	0	0	0
T	0	0	0	0	0	0	0	0	0	0	0	0	1	0	0	0	0	0	0	0

Table 2.22. Ragusan Noble Families Marriage Network, 16th Century

		1	2	3	4	5	6	7	8	9	10	11	12	13	14	15	16	17	18	19	20	21	22	23	24
Babalio	1	·	·	·	·	1	·	·	·	·	·	·	·	·	·	·	·	·	·	·	·	·	2	·	·
Basilio	2	·	·	·	·	·	·	·	·	·	·	·	·	·	·	·	·	·	·	·	·	·	·	·	·
Benessa	3	·	·	·	·	1	·	·	·	·	·	·	·	·	·	·	1	·	·	·	·	·	·	·	1
Bocignolo	4	·	·	·	·	·	·	·	·	·	·	·	·	·	·	·	·	·	·	·	·	·	·	·	·
Bona	5	·	·	2	·	4	·	·	·	1	·	4	1	2	3	1	·	·	·	·	·	·	·	·	1
Bucchia	6	·	·	·	·	·	·	·	·	·	·	·	·	·	·	·	·	·	·	·	·	·	·	·	·
Caboga	7	·	·	·	·	·	1	1	·	·	·	1	·	·	1	·	·	·	·	·	·	·	·	·	·
Crieva	8	·	·	·	·	1	·	·	1	·	1	1	1	·	·	·	·	·	·	1	·	·	·	·	1
Georgio	9	·	·	·	·	1	·	1	·	1	·	·	·	·	·	·	·	·	·	·	1	1	·	·	·
Gondola	10	·	·	·	·	·	·	·	·	·	2	1	·	·	·	·	·	·	·	·	·	·	1	·	·
Goze	11	·	·	1	1	4	·	1	1	·	1	1	·	·	·	·	·	·	1	1	·	·	·	·	·
Gradi	12	·	·	·	·	·	·	·	·	·	1	1	·	·	·	·	·	·	·	·	·	·	5	·	·
Lucari	13	·	·	·	·	·	·	1	·	·	1	1	·	·	·	·	·	·	·	·	·	·	1	·	·
Menze	14	·	1	·	·	1	·	1	·	·	·	1	·	·	·	·	·	·	·	·	·	·	4	·	·
Palmota	15	·	·	·	·	·	·	·	·	·	·	·	·	·	·	·	·	·	·	·	·	·	·	·	·
Poza	16	·	·	·	·	2	·	·	·	1	·	·	·	·	·	·	1	·	·	·	·	·	·	·	·
Proculo	17	·	·	·	·	·	·	·	·	·	·	1	·	·	·	·	·	·	·	·	·	·	·	·	·
Prodanelo	18	·	·	·	·	·	·	·	·	·	1	·	·	·	·	·	·	·	·	·	·	·	·	·	·
Ragnina	19	·	·	·	·	1	·	·	·	·	·	·	·	·	·	·	·	·	1	·	·	·	·	·	·
Resti	20	·	·	·	·	1	1	·	1	1	·	·	·	·	·	·	·	·	1	·	·	·	·	·	·
Saraca	21	·	·	·	·	·	·	·	·	·	·	·	·	·	·	·	·	·	·	·	·	·	·	·	·
Sorgo	22	·	·	1	1	·	·	·	·	·	·	1	2	1	1	·	·	·	·	·	1	·	6	·	·
Tudisio	23	·	·	·	·	·	·	·	·	·	·	·	1	·	1	·	·	·	·	·	·	·	·	·	·
Zamagna	24	·	·	·	·	3	·	·	·	1	2	1	·	·	·	·	·	·	·	·	·	·	1	·	·

unhindered thanks primarily to their clever diplomacy and great skill in balancing the great powers by formally recognizing and paying tribute alternately to one then another. Napoleon, having destroyed the Venetian Republic in 1797, put an end to the Republic of Ragusa in 1806, which subsequently came under Austrian control until the fall of the Austro-Hungarian monarchy in 1918.

The Ragusan nobility evolved in the 12th century through the 14th century and was finally recognized by statute in 1332. After 1332, no new family was accepted until the large earthquake in 1667.

In Ragusa all political power was in the hands of male nobles more than 18 years old. They were members of the Great Council (*Consilium majus*), which had the legislative function. Every year, 11 members of the Small Council (*Consilium minus*) were elected. Together with a duke – who was elected for a period of one month – it had both executive and representative functions. The main power was in the hands of the Senat (*Consilium rogatorum*), which had 45 members elected for one year.

This organization prevented any single family, unlike the Medici in Florence, from prevailing. Nevertheless, the historians agree that the Sorgo family was at all times among the most influential. Note, for example, the following facts:

Table 2.23. Ragusan Noble Families Marriage Network, 18th and 19th Centuries

		1	2	3	4	5	6	7	8	9	10	11	12	13	14	15	16	17	18	19	20	21	22	23
Basilio	1	·	·	·	·	·	·	·	·	·	·	·	·	·	·	·	·	·	·	·	·	1	·	·
Bona	2	·	·	·	·	·	·	1	·	·	·	2	·	2	·	·	·	·	·	·	·	1	·	·
Bonda	3	·	·	·	·	·	·	·	·	·	·	·	·	·	·	·	·	·	·	·	2	·	·	·
Bosdari	4	·	1	·	·	·	·	·	·	·	·	·	·	·	·	·	·	·	·	·	·	·	·	1
Bucchia	5	·	·	·	·	·	·	·	·	·	·	1	·	·	·	·	·	·	·	·	·	·	·	·
Caboga	6	·	·	·	·	·	·	1	·	·	·	·	1	1	·	·	·	·	·	1	·	1	·	·
Cerva	7	·	1	·	·	·	1	·	·	·	·	·	·	1	·	·	·	·	·	·	·	1	·	·
Georgi	8	·	1	2	·	·	1	·	·	·	·	·	·	·	·	·	4	·	·	·	·	·	·	1
Ghetaldi	9	·	1	·	·	·	·	1	·	1	·	·	·	1	·	·	·	1	·	·	·	·	·	·
Gondola	10	·	1	·	·	·	·	·	·	·	·	·	·	·	·	·	·	·	·	·	·	·	·	·
Goze	11	1	2	1	·	·	·	·	·	·	·	2	2	·	·	·	·	·	·	·	·	2	1	·
Gradi	12	·	·	·	·	·	·	·	·	·	·	1	·	·	·	·	·	1	·	·	·	3	·	·
Menze	13	·	·	·	·	·	1	·	·	1	·	·	·	·	·	·	·	·	·	·	·	·	·	1
Natali	14	·	·	·	·	·	·	·	·	·	·	·	·	·	·	·	·	·	·	·	·	·	·	·
Pauli	15	·	1	·	·	·	·	·	·	·	·	·	·	·	·	·	·	·	·	·	·	·	·	·
Poza	16	·	·	2	·	·	·	·	·	·	·	1	·	·	·	·	·	1	·	·	·	1	·	·
Ragnina	17	·	1	1	·	·	·	·	·	·	·	1	·	·	·	·	·	·	·	·	·	1	·	·
Resti	18	·	·	·	·	·	·	·	·	·	·	·	·	1	·	·	·	·	·	·	·	·	·	1
Saraca	19	·	·	·	·	·	·	1	·	·	·	·	·	·	·	·	·	·	·	·	·	·	·	·
Slatarich	20	·	·	·	·	·	·	·	·	·	·	·	·	·	·	·	·	·	·	·	·	·	·	·
Sorgo	21	·	2	1	·	·	·	·	·	·	·	1	·	·	·	·	·	·	·	·	1	1	·	1
Tudisi	22	·	·	·	·	·	·	·	·	·	·	·	·	·	·	·	·	·	·	·	·	1	·	·
Zamagna	23	·	1	·	·	·	·	·	2	·	·	·	·	·	·	·	·	·	·	·	·	1	·	·

- In the 17th century, 50% of the dukes and senators were from the following five families: Bona, Gondola, Goze, Menze, and Sorgo.
- In the 18th century, 56% of the senators were from five families: the Sorgo, Goze, Zamagna, Caboga, and Georgi.
- In the last 8 years of the Republic, 50% of the dukes were from five families: Sorgo, Goze, Gradis, Bona, and Ragnina.

A major problem facing the Ragusan noble families was also that, by a decrease in their numbers and the lack of noble families in the neighboring areas (which were under Turkish control), they became more and more closely related – "*quasi tutti siamo congionti in terzo et in quarto grado di consanguinita et affinita*," Historijski archiv u Dubrovniku, 1566:100–101; that is, the marriages between relatives of only third and fourth removes were frequent.

Previous analyses. Batagelj (1996b) analyzed both marriage networks. First he computed the centrality indices (influence, support, degree, betweenness, and closeness).[19] Indices indicated that the most influential families in the 16th century were the Bona, Goze, and Sorgo as well as the Gradi and Menze. By conventional blockmodeling, Batagelj obtained two basic clusters.

---

19 See Section 4.7 in Chapter 4.

Cluster 1:

Benessa	Bona	Caboga	Crieva	Georgio
Gondola	Goze	Gradi	Lucari	Menze
Poza	Ragnina	Resti	Sorgo	Zamagna

Cluster 2:

Babalio	Basilio	Bocignolo	Bucchia	Palmota
Proculo	Prodanelo	Saraca	Tudisio	

Most marriages are among the families contained in the first cluster; there is no marriage among families of the second cluster; and there are only a few marriages between the two clusters. This structure is an example of a core–periphery model.

Indices calculated for the 18th- and 19th-century marriage network indicated that the most influential families in this period were the Sorgo and Bona as well as the Zamagna, Cerva, and Menze.

Two basic clusters were also found for the second period.

Cluster 1:

Basilio	Bona	Bonda	Caboga	Cerva
Georgi	Ghetaldi	Gondola	Goze	Gradi
Menze	Poza	Saraca	Sorgo	Tudisi
Zamagna				

Cluster 2:

Bosdari	Bucchia	Natali	Pauli	Ragnina
Resti	Slatarich			

The structure of the marriages between families of both clusters is the same as in the first period. Comparing clusterings for both periods, we can see that the main cluster contains almost the same families – the core is Bona, Caboga, Cerva, Gondola, Goze, Gradi, Menze, Poza, Sorgo, and Zamagna. We reanalyze these data in Chapter 11.

2.2.7   Two baboon grooming networks

The final data sets here are taken from Dunbar and Dunbar (1975). Although the original data were valued, we consider only the binarized versions shown in Tables 2.24 and 2.25. The first matrix is for a point of time and features 12 baboons. These ties were discussed in Chapter 1 and shown in blockmodel form in Tables 1.10 and 1.11. Seven baboons are female (f_1-f_7) and five are males (m_1-m_5). Two baboons (f_8 and m_6) were introduced to the group and were accepted by the group. We consider the structure at both time points and see if it changes with the introduction of two new members.

Table 2.24. Binarized Baboon Grooming Network at T_1

		f_1	m_1	f_2	f_3	m_2	f_4	m_3	f_5	m_4	f_6	f_7	m_5
		1	2	3	4	5	6	7	8	9	10	11	12
f_1	1	0	1	0	1	1	0	0	0	0	0	1	1
m_1	2	1	0	0	0	0	0	0	0	0	0	0	0
f_2	3	0	0	0	1	1	1	1	0	0	1	1	1
f_3	4	1	0	1	0	1	1	1	0	0	1	0	1
m_2	5	1	0	1	1	0	1	0	1	0	0	0	0
f_4	6	0	0	1	1	1	0	0	0	0	1	0	1
m_3	7	0	0	1	1	0	0	0	1	0	0	0	0
f_5	8	0	0	0	0	1	0	1	0	1	1	0	0
m_4	9	0	0	0	0	0	0	0	1	0	0	0	0
f_6	10	0	0	1	1	0	1	0	1	0	0	0	0
f_7	11	1	0	1	0	0	0	0	0	0	0	0	0
m_5	12	1	0	1	1	0	1	0	0	0	0	0	0

2.3 DATA SET PROPERTIES

The data sets we have described cover a variety of formats that can be described in terms of four features:

1. Whether or not the relational data are binary (0,1) ties or valued ties;
2. Whether the network has a single relation or multiple relations;
3. Whether the network relation is symmetric (graph) or nonsymmetric (digraph);
4. Whether the network data are cross-sectional or longitudinal.

Table 2.25. Binarized Baboon Grooming Network at T_2

		f_1	m_1	f_2	f_3	m_2	f_4	m_3	f_5	m_4	f_6	f_7	m_5	m_6	f_8
		1	2	3	4	5	6	7	8	9	10	11	12	13	14
f_1	1	0	1	0	1	1	0	1	1	0	0	0	0	0	1
m_1	2	1	0	0	0	0	0	0	0	0	0	0	0	0	0
f_2	3	0	0	0	1	0	1	0	0	0	0	0	1	1	0
f_3	4	1	0	1	0	1	0	0	0	0	1	0	1	0	0
m_2	5	1	0	0	1	0	0	0	0	0	0	0	0	0	1
f_4	6	0	0	1	0	0	0	0	0	0	1	0	1	1	1
m_3	7	1	0	0	0	0	0	0	1	0	0	0	0	0	0
f_5	8	1	0	0	0	0	0	1	0	1	1	1	0	0	1
m_4	9	0	0	0	0	0	0	0	1	0	0	0	0	0	0
f_6	10	0	0	0	1	0	1	0	1	0	0	0	0	0	0
f_7	11	0	0	0	0	0	0	0	1	0	0	0	0	0	0
m_5	12	0	0	1	1	0	1	0	0	0	0	0	0	0	0
m_6	13	0	0	1	0	0	1	0	0	0	0	0	0	0	0
f_8	14	1	0	0	0	1	1	0	1	0	0	0	0	0	0

Table 2.26. Summary of Network Characteristics

Network	Ties	Relations	Direction	Time	Signed
SM	Valued	Multiple (4)	Digraph	Yes (3)	Yes
BWR	Binary	Multiple (5)	Both	No	Both
NF	Valued	Single	Digraph	Yes (15)	Both
LL	Binary	Single	Digraph	No	No
PA	Binary	Single	Graph	No	No
Student Government	Binary	Multiple (6)	Digraph	No	No
Kansas SAR	Valued	Single	Digraph	No	No
SS Bales type	Binary	Multiple (3)	Digraph	No	Both
Ragusa	Valued	Multiple (2)	Digraph	Yes (2)	No
Baboons	Binary	Single	Graph	Yes (2)	No

The classification of the data sets described in this chapter, in terms of these characteristics, is given in Table 2.26. Six of the networks have binary data and four have valued data.[20] The Newcomb fraternity (NF) data have an ambiguous status, for they are recorded as ranks. We regard these as valued but note that the ranks can be recoded to either binary or valued form. Five of the networks have multiple relations, and four have one relation only. The number of relations is given in parentheses in Column 3 of Table 2.26. Four of the networks have longitudinal data: the Sampson monastery (SM) data have three time points, the (NF) data have 15, and the Ragusan data and baboon data both have two.

The final characteristic concerns signed relations. The SM data are clearly signed because they were collected as such.[21] The BWR data contain friendship and antagonistic relations. When viewed together, these can be seen as a signed relation: friendship is positive and antagonism is negative. In Chapter 10 we consider this single (signed) relation in the framework of structural balance and we contrast this with analyses that treat friendship and antagonism as distinct relations. Conflict over the windows is less clear because it is spatially specific and temporally limited. Actors can have disputes over the windows without being in an antagonistic relationship. See, for example, the dyads (W_7, W_9) and (W_8, S_4). The SS Bales-type structure can be viewed either as a single signed relation for one point of time (as in Chapter 10) or as two binary relations (as in Chapters 6 and 7). Under the transformation described in Section 2.1.3, the NF data take the form of a signed relation through time. (Table 2.14 displays the transformed relation for a specific week.) We introduce further signed structures in Chapter 10.

The empirical social ties described briefly in this chapter are used in two ways. Our primary use is to illustrate the partitioning methods we consider throughout the book. They are also used to develop some substantive arguments and motivate further extensions of generalized blockmodeling.

---

20 The BWR data do include a job-trading relation that is valued. However, it is extremely sparse and is excluded here.
21 They are valued also.

2.4 SOME ADDITIONAL REMARKS CONCERNING DATA

Beyond the properties described in Table 2.26, the data sets described in this chapter share two additional features. They are quite small and are drawn from social scientific fields. Small data sets are fine for showing how generalized blockmodeling methods work and for showing clearly the kinds of structures that can be revealed through their use. However, we do not want to convey the impression that only small data sets can be analyzed by means of generalized blockmodeling methods. In principle, data sets of any size can be analyzed. However, moving to large data sets is not quite straightforward. The generalized blockmodeling methods that we describe are computationally demanding, and, as the size of the data sets expands, more efficient algorithms will be required. Generalized blockmodeling tools are very general and, in principle, can also be applied to data sets from fields other than the social sciences. We provide some examples in Chapter 12. The consideration of two-mode data in Chapter 8 opens the way to the consideration of data from other fields such as the physical sciences and engineering.

3

MATHEMATICAL PRELUDE

Relations and graphs are among the technical terms used most often in network analysis. Our discussion of them in Chapter 1 was intuitive and pictorial. Here we take a more formal approach and present a series of mathematical concepts that are needed for a deeper understanding of blockmodeling ideas. Our goal is to lay the foundations for a discussion of cluster analysis (Chapter 5), conventional blockmodeling (Chapter 6), and generalized blockmodeling (Chapters 7–11). The main topics in this chapter are relations (Section 3.2), some basic ideas on functions and homomorphisms (Section 3.3), and basic algebra (Section 3.4).

As the basis for all these topics is set theory, we begin with some basic ideas concerning sets.

3.1 BASIC SET THEORY

In the mathematical expressions presented here, we use the following abbreviations for phrases taken from a natural (verbal) language[1]:

$\vee$	. . . or . . .	$\wedge$	. . . and . . .
$\neg$	not . . .		
$\Rightarrow$	. . . implies . . .	$\Leftrightarrow$	. . . if and only if . . .
$\exists$	there exists	$\forall$	for all
:	. . . such that . . .		
=	value of . . . equal to the value of . . .		
:=	. . . equal by definition to . . .		

We start by introducing the basic predicate, $\in$, of membership:

$$x \in Y := x \text{ belongs to } Y,$$

---

1 It is standard to use "iff" to represent "if and only if" (second item in the second column). The first occurence of this in the following discourse comes with our discussion of groupoids in Section 3.4. We use it in various places in technical discussions.

or x is an element of Y. If Y is a group of people, x represents a person in the group.

In applications of set theory, we often restrict attention to some special set S. This set is called a basic set, or a *universe*. An example is the set of all people in an organization with attention confined to that organization.

We use

$$\mathbb{N}, \mathbb{Z}, \mathbb{Q}, \mathbb{R}, \mathbb{N}^+$$

to denote the sets of natural numbers, integers, rational numbers, real numbers, and positive integers, respectively. Note that $0 \in \mathbb{N}$.

Let $P_A(x)$ be a property of elements of the universe S. The property $P_A(x)$ determines the set

$$A = \{x : P_A(x)\}.$$

If P_A is female employee and S is a social organization, then A is the set of female employees of the organization.

Two sets A and B are equal, $A = B$, if and only if they consist of the same elements:

$$A = B := \forall x : (x \in A \Leftrightarrow x \in B).$$

It follows that a set is uniquely determined by its elements. There is exactly one set without elements – the empty set, denoted by $\emptyset$ or by $\{\ \}$.

We also define the predicates $\notin$ (is not a member of), $\neq$ (is not equal to), $\subseteq$ (is contained in), and $\subset$ (is strictly contained in) by the following:

$$x \notin A := \neg(x \in A),$$
$$A \neq B := \neg(A = B),$$
$$A \subseteq B := \forall x : (x \in A \Rightarrow x \in B),$$
$$A \subset B := (A \subseteq B) \wedge \neg(A = B).$$

These predicates have the following properties:

S1. $A = B \Leftrightarrow (A \subseteq B) \wedge (B \subseteq A)$.
S2. $(A \subseteq B) \wedge (B \subseteq C) \Rightarrow A \subseteq C$.
S3. $(A \subset B) \wedge (B \subseteq C) \Rightarrow A \subset C$.
S4. $A \subset B \Rightarrow \exists x : (x \in B \wedge x \notin A)$.
S5. $\emptyset \subseteq A$.
S6. $A \subseteq A$.

Set operations. We next define some basic operations with sets. One is the *union*, $A \cup B$, of two sets A and B. $A \cup B$ contains elements that belong to A or to B, or to both. As an example, if A is the set of all girls in a school and B is the set of all boys in the school, $A \cup B$ is the set of all children in the school. A second operation is *intersection*, $A \cap B$. It consists of elements belonging to both sets. If

A is the set of all girls in a school and B is the set of left-handed children, $A \cap B$ is the set of left-handed girls. The difference $A \setminus B$ is the set of elements in A but not in B. In the children example, $A \setminus B$ is the set of right-handed girls. More formally, we state the following.

Union:

$$x \in A \cup B := x \in A \vee x \in B \quad \text{or} \quad A \cup B := \{x : x \in A \vee x \in B\}.$$

Intersection:

$$x \in A \cap B := x \in A \wedge x \in B \quad \text{or} \quad A \cap B := \{x : x \in A \wedge x \in B\}.$$

Difference:

$$x \in A \setminus B := x \in A \wedge x \notin B \quad \text{or} \quad A \setminus B := \{x : x \in A \wedge x \notin B\}.$$

With respect to the universe, we can define the *complement*, A^c, as the set of elements not in A. With S the set of children in a school and A the set of girls, the complement is the set of children who are not girls, that is, the boys:

$$A^c := S \setminus A.$$

Some properties of set operations are listed next. We encourage readers not familiar with set theory to construct examples and work through these properties.

Idempotency:

$$A \cup A = A, \qquad\qquad A \cap A = A.$$

Commutativity:

$$A \cup B = B \cup A, \qquad\qquad A \cap B = B \cap A.$$

Associativity:

$$A \cup (B \cup C) = (A \cup B) \cup C, \qquad A \cap (B \cap C) = (A \cap B) \cap C.$$

Distributivity:

$$A \cap (B \cup C) = (A \cap B) \cup (A \cap C), \quad A \cup (B \cap C) = (A \cup B) \cap (A \cup C).$$

Absorption:

$$A \cup (A \cap B) = A, \qquad\qquad A \cap (A \cup B) = A.$$

The basic properties of sets $\emptyset$ and S are as follows:

$$A \cup \emptyset = A, \qquad\qquad A \cap \emptyset = \emptyset,$$
$$A \cup S = S, \qquad\qquad A \cap S = A.$$

For the complement, we have

$$A \cup A^c = \mathcal{S}, \qquad\qquad A \cap A^c = \emptyset,$$
$$(A^c)^c = A.$$

The De Morgan laws are as follows:

$$(A \cup B)^c = A^c \cap B^c, \qquad\qquad (A \cap B)^c = A^c \cup B^c.$$

Relations of set operations with set inclusion $\subseteq$ are

$$A \subseteq B \iff A \cup B = B \iff A \cap B = A.$$

Next, we define another operation with sets, that is, the *symmetric difference*, $\oplus$, as the set of all elements that belong to sets A and B but not to both.

$$A \oplus B := (A \cup B) \setminus (A \cap B).$$

For example, let A be the set of girls in a school and B the set of left-handed children.[2] $A \oplus B$ is the union of the right-handed girls and the left-handed boys. Here are some properties[3]:

D1. $A \oplus B = (A \setminus B) \cup (B \setminus A)$.
D2. $A \oplus \emptyset = A$.
D3. $A \oplus A = \emptyset$.
D4. $A \oplus B = B \oplus A$.
D5. $A \oplus (B \oplus C) = (A \oplus B) \oplus C$.

If we know that $X \oplus A$ exists, know that it equals B, and want to know what is X, then we have to solve the equation $X \oplus A = B$, given B. We need to know that there is at least one solution and whether there is a unique solution or not. Given that $X \oplus A = (X \setminus A) \cup (A \setminus X)$, the only possible solution is $A \oplus B$, and it is unique. That is, $X \oplus A = B$ always has a unique solution $X = A \oplus B$.

The power set. The power set of set A is the set of all its subsets:

$$\mathcal{P}(A) = \{X : X \subseteq A\}.$$

For example, if a, b, and c are members of a triad (as A), the power set is

$$\mathcal{P}(\{a, b, c\}) = \{\emptyset, \{a\}, \{b\}, \{c\}, \{a, b\}, \{a, c\}, \{b, c\}, \{a, b, c\}\}.$$

---

2 We assume there are no ambidextrous children.
3 Again, we encourage readers not familiar with these ideas to work through some constructed examples.

We have

$$\mathcal{P}(A) \cap \mathcal{P}(B) = \mathcal{P}(A \cap B),$$
$$\mathcal{P}(A) \cup \mathcal{P}(B) \subseteq \mathcal{P}(A \cup B),$$
$$A \subseteq B \Rightarrow \mathcal{P}(A) \subseteq \mathcal{P}(B).$$

We denote the cardinality, the number of elements, of set A by $\text{card}(A)$ or by $|A|$. For finite sets A and B, the following hold:

$$\text{card}(A \cup B) + \text{card}(A \cap B) = \text{card}(A) + \text{card}(B),$$
$$\text{card}(A \cup B) - \text{card}(A \cap B) = \text{card}(A \oplus B),$$

and for $B \subseteq A$,

$$\text{card}(A \setminus B) = \text{card}(A) - \text{card}(B).$$

The power set, $\mathcal{P}(A)$, for a finite set A with n elements, $\text{card}(A) = n$, has 2^n elements, that is, $\text{card}(\mathcal{P}(A)) = 2^n$.

The sets used in social network analysis are usually finite.

Families of sets. As a stepping stone toward partitions and clustering, the core of blockmodeling, we consider the idea of families. Let $\mathcal{A} = \{A_1, A_2, A_3, \ldots\}$ be a set of sets, also called a family. As an example, suppose someone from the Smith family marries someone from the Jones family; then the married couple belongs to both families.[4] The key idea is that the families can have nonempty intersections. Consider the people of the world and the sets defined in terms of nationalities. These sets form a family of sets. A person with dual nationality belongs to at least two of the families. The union of all of the families is simply the people of the world.

We extend the notions of union and intersection to families.

For a family $\mathcal{A} = \{A_j\}$, the union of sets in a family consists of all elements that belong to at least one set A_j of the family $\mathcal{A}$. More formally,

$$\bigcup_{X \in \mathcal{A}} X := \{x : \exists X \in \mathcal{A} : x \in X\}.$$

The intersection for families is defined in a similar fashion. It consists of all elements that belong to all sets of the family $\mathcal{A}$:

$$\bigcap_{X \in \mathcal{A}} X := \{x : \forall X \in \mathcal{A} : x \in X\}.$$

---

4   Of course, social conventions may dictate that the two families become one family.

For convenience, we use also the abbreviations

$$\cup \mathcal{A} := \bigcup_{X \in \mathcal{A}} X \quad \text{and} \quad \cap \mathcal{A} := \bigcap_{X \in \mathcal{A}} X.$$

A generalized distributivity holds:

$$B \cap (\bigcup_{X \in \mathcal{A}} X) = \bigcup_{X \in \mathcal{A}} (B \cap X)$$

$$B \cup (\bigcap_{X \in \mathcal{A}} X) = \bigcap_{X \in \mathcal{A}} (B \cup X).$$

Sometimes we index the sets from family $\mathcal{A}$ with indices from the index set, I:

$$\mathcal{A} = \{A_i : i \in I\}.$$

In these cases, we use the notation

$$\bigcup_{i \in I} A_i := \cup \mathcal{A} \quad \text{and} \quad \bigcap_{i \in I} A_i := \cap \mathcal{A}.$$

Clusterings and partitions. Blockmodeling is a collection of techniques for creating clusterings and partitions. A family $\mathcal{A}$ of nonempty subsets of a set A, $A_i \subseteq A$ is called a clustering of A. The sets A_i are also called clusters.

It is a covering of the set A if and only if each element of A belongs to some set of $\mathcal{A}$,

$$\bigcup_{i \in I} A_i = A,$$

and it is a complete clustering or a *partition* if and only if its member sets are pairwise disjoint (have no elements in common):

$$i \neq j \Rightarrow A_i \cap A_j = \emptyset.$$

For a partition, $\mathcal{A}$, of a finite set, A, it holds that

$$\text{card}(A) = \sum_{i \in I} \text{card}(A_i).$$

In a covering, some clusters can overlap.

A clustering $\mathcal{A}$ is hierarchical if and only if

$$\forall A_i, A_j \in \mathcal{A} : A_i \cap A_j \in \{\emptyset, A_i, A_j\},$$

and it is a complete hierarchical clustering if also $\forall x \in A : \{x\} \in \mathcal{A}$ and $A \in \mathcal{A}$.

For example,

$$\mathcal{A} = \{\{a\}, \{b\}, \{c\}, \{d\}, \{e\}, \{f\}, \{a, e\}, \{b, d\}, \{b, d, f\}, \{a, b, c, d, e, f\}\}$$

is a complete hierarchical clustering of the set $A = \{a, b, c, d, e, f\}$. Note that if $A_i = \{a, e\}$ and $A_j = \{b, d\}$, then $A_i \cap A_j = \emptyset$, or, if $A_i = \{b, d\}$ and $A_j = \{b, d, f\}$, then $A_i \cap A_j = \{b, d\} = A_i$. Both illustrate the idea of hierarchy: Two clusters are either disjoint or one is contained in the other.

The Cartesian product. An ordered pair (x, y) is one in which the order of x and y is important and

$$(x, y) = (u, v) \Leftrightarrow (x = u) \wedge (y = v).$$

The Cartesian product is defined as the set of all ordered pairs (dyads) in which the first element comes from one set and the second element comes from another set. More formally,

$$A \times B := \{(x, y) : x \in A \wedge y \in B\}.$$

Some properties of the Cartesian product are as follows:

$$A \times (B \cup C) = A \times B \cup A \times C,$$
$$A \times (B \cap C) = A \times B \cap A \times C,$$
$$A \times (B \setminus C) = (A \times B) \setminus (A \times C),$$
$$A \times B = \emptyset \Leftrightarrow (A = \emptyset) \vee (B = \emptyset).$$

The notion of the Cartesian product can be extended to families of sets. The idea of an ordered dyad extends to an ordered n-tuple (n elements instead of two). We first define an ordered n-tuple $(x_1, x_2, \ldots, x_n)$, $x_i \in A_i$, $i \in 1, \ldots, n$, where

$$(x_1, x_2, \ldots, x_n) = (y_1, y_2, \ldots, y_n) \Leftrightarrow \forall i \in 1, \ldots, n : x_i = y_i.$$

The Cartesian product of the family $\mathcal{A} = \{A_1, A_2, \ldots, A_n\}$ is a set of ordered n-tuples where the ith element comes from the ith set, A_i.

$$\underset{i=1}{\overset{n}{\times}} A_i := \{(x_1, \ldots, x_i, \ldots, x_n) : x_i \in A_i, i \in 1, \ldots, n\}.$$

3.2 RELATIONS

Because a simple social network is defined as a set of social actors and one or more (social) relations defined over them, relation is a fundamental notion for social network analysis. We provide an intuitive treatment of (social) relations together with several examples in Chapter 1. Here, we provide some formal definitions and explore some of the properties of relations.

In set theory, every subset R of the Cartesian product $A \times B$ is called a (binary) relation on $A \times B$. We call the set $A \times B$ a *context* of the relation R. Being clear about the context of a relation is important.

In practice there are many different relations. In addition to those used in Chapter 1, we have the following examples.

- x is a friend of y;
- x is a sister of y;
- x is communicating by e-mail with y;
- y is citing x; and
- y belongs to x.

Although these examples are stated in the form of relational ties (dyadic pairs), this is a kind of shorthand statement. We assume there is a set of actors for which the relational ties are stated. So for the statement "x is a friend of y" we assume, for a set A, that $x, y \in A$. The relation "friendship" is the set of all of the specific friendship relational ties and is a subset of $A \times A$. For the statement "y belongs to x" there are two sets, A and B, with $x \in A$ and $y \in B$. An example used in several places in this book features women, $\{x\}$, attending events, $\{y\}$. The relation is made up of all of the pairs of specific women attending specific events. We denote the set of all binary relations on $A \times B$ by **Rel**(A, B):

$$\mathbf{Rel}(A, B) = \{R : R \subseteq A \times B\}.$$

Therefore,

$$R \in \mathbf{Rel}(A, B) \Leftrightarrow R \subseteq A \times B.$$

Let $R \in \mathbf{Rel}(A, B)$ be a binary relation. If $A \neq B$, we say that R is a relation *from* the set A *to* the set B. An example is the classic Deep South data for 18 women and 14 events shown in Table 1.3. It is a membership relation as described in Section 1.1.1. Often such data are referred to as two-mode (relational) data. If $A = B$, we say that R is a relation *on* the set A. The marriage ties of the Florentine families (described in Table 1.2) provides an example.

For binary relations we usually use the *infix* notation:

$$x R y := (x, y) \in R.$$

For example "3 is less than 7" is written as $3 < 7$ instead of $(3, 7) \in <$.

Some binary relations. Some special binary relations are as follows.
The *total* or *universal* relation is

$$T_{A,B} = A \times B.$$

The *empty* or *void* relation is

$$\emptyset_{A,B} = \emptyset.$$

The *identity* or *diagonal* relation is

$$I_A = \{(x, x) : x \in A\}.$$

We use the symbols I and T when the context $A \times B$ is evident from the discussion.

The domain and range of a binary relation. The domain of a binary relation $R \in \mathbf{Rel}(A, B)$ is the set of elements "related from,"

$$\mathcal{D}R = \{x \in A : \exists y \in B : xRy\},$$

and its range is the set of elements "related to,"

$$\mathcal{R}R = \{y \in B : \exists x \in A : xRy\}.$$

Evidently, $\mathcal{D}R \subseteq A$ and $\mathcal{R}R \subseteq B$.

Example 3.1 We illustrate these ideas with the helping relation for the 14 workers in the BWR presented in Section 2.1.2 in Table 2.10(a) in more detail.

$$A = \{I_1, I_3, W_1, W_2, W_3, W_4, W_5, W_6, W_7, W_8, W_9, S_1, S_2, S_4\},$$

$$\begin{aligned}
\text{helps} = \quad & \{(W_1, W_3), (W_1, W_9), (W_1, S_1), (W_2, W_3), (W_2, W_4), \\
& (W_2, S_1), (W_3, W_2), (W_4, W_1), (W_4, W_3), (W_4, W_6), \\
& (W_5, W_3), (W_6, W_3), (W_6, W_7), (W_6, W_8), (W_6, W_9), \\
& (W_7, S_4), (W_8, W_6), (W_8, W_7), (W_8, W_9), (W_9, S_4), \\
& (S_1, W_7), (S_2, W_6), (S_4, W_4), (S_4, W_8)\},
\end{aligned}$$

$$\mathcal{D} \text{ helps} = \{W_1, W_2, W_3, W_4, W_5, W_6, W_7, W_8, W_9, S_1, S_2, S_4\},$$

$$\mathcal{R} \text{ helps} = \{W_1, W_2, W_3, W_4, W_6, W_7, W_8, W_9, S_1, S_4\}. \quad \square$$

For a single set of actors (one-mode data), the domain and range of R need not be the same. See Example 3.1. This is shown also in Table 3.1 with the row labeled $\mathcal{R}$ and the column labeled $\mathcal{D}$. For two-mode data with $A \cap B = \emptyset$, they are necessarily different.

Some properties of the domain $\mathcal{D}R$ are

$$\begin{aligned}
\mathcal{D}R = \emptyset &\Leftrightarrow R = \emptyset, & B \neq \emptyset &\Rightarrow \mathcal{D}(A \times B) = A, \\
\mathcal{D}(R \cup S) &= \mathcal{D}R \cup \mathcal{D}S, & \mathcal{D}(R \cap S) &\subseteq \mathcal{D}R \cap \mathcal{D}S, \\
R \subseteq S &\Rightarrow \mathcal{D}R \subseteq \mathcal{D}S, & \mathcal{D}I_A &= A.
\end{aligned}$$

In words, for the first row, the domain of R is empty only when R is empty. If B is not empty, then the domain of $A \times B$ is A. For the second row, the domain of the union of R and S is the union of the domain of R and domain of S. The domain of the intersection of R and S is a subset of the intersection of the domains of R and S. For the third row, if R is contained within S, the domain of R is contained within the domain of S. The domain of the identity relation on A is A.

Analogous properties hold also for the range of a binary relation, $\mathcal{R}R$.

The relational matrix. For computational and other purposes, the relation $R \in \mathbf{Rel}(A, B)$ is often represented by its matrix (i.e., the sociomatrix): a binary

Table 3.1. A Matrix Representation of the BWR Helping Relation

Helps		1	2	3	4	5	6	7	8	9	10	11	12	13	14	$\mathcal{D}$
I_1	1	0	0	0	0	0	0	0	0	0	0	0	0	0	0	0
I_3	2	0	0	0	0	0	0	0	0	0	0	0	0	0	0	0
W_1	3	0	0	0	0	1	0	0	0	0	0	1	1	0	0	1
W_2	4	0	0	0	0	1	1	0	0	0	0	0	1	0	0	1
W_3	5	0	0	0	1	0	0	0	0	0	0	0	0	0	0	1
W_4	6	0	0	1	0	1	0	0	1	0	0	0	0	0	0	1
W_5	7	0	0	0	0	1	0	0	0	0	0	0	0	0	0	1
W_6	8	0	0	0	0	1	0	0	0	1	1	1	0	0	0	1
W_7	9	0	0	0	0	0	0	0	0	0	0	0	0	0	1	1
W_8	10	0	0	0	0	0	0	0	1	1	0	1	0	0	0	1
W_9	11	0	0	0	0	0	0	0	0	0	0	0	0	0	1	1
S_1	12	0	0	0	0	0	0	0	0	1	0	0	0	0	0	1
S_2	13	0	0	0	0	0	0	0	1	0	0	0	0	0	0	1
S_4	14	0	0	0	0	0	1	0	0	0	1	0	0	0	0	1
$\mathcal{R}$		0	0	1	1	1	1	0	1	1	1	1	1	0	1	

(Boolean) matrix $\mathbf{B}(R) = [b(R)(x, y)]$ defined by

$$b(R)(x, y) = \begin{cases} 1 & (x, y) \in R \\ 0 & (x, y) \notin R \end{cases}.$$

Example 3.2 Here,

$$R = \{(a, d), (c, a), (c, f), (d, d), (d, f), (f, a), (f, b)\}$$

is a relation on $A = \{a, b, c, d, e, f\}$ and its matrix is

$$\mathbf{B}(R) = \begin{bmatrix} 0 & 0 & 0 & 1 & 0 & 0 \\ 0 & 0 & 0 & 0 & 0 & 0 \\ 1 & 0 & 0 & 0 & 0 & 1 \\ 0 & 0 & 0 & 1 & 0 & 1 \\ 0 & 0 & 0 & 0 & 0 & 0 \\ 1 & 1 & 0 & 0 & 0 & 0 \end{bmatrix},$$

where the rows and columns are indexed or labeled in the order a, b, c, d, e, and f. □

Example 3.3 The matrix representation of the BWR helping relation from Example 3.1 **B**(helps) is given in Table 3.1.[5] We note that the range, $\mathcal{R}$, takes the value 1 whenever there is a 1 in the corresponding column of the matrix and the domain, $\mathcal{D}$, takes the value 1 whenever there is a 1 in the corresponding row of the matrix. □

5 This is also in Table 2.10 in Chapter 2.

3.2.1   Operations with binary relations

Context change. A relation $R \in \mathbf{Rel}(A, B)$, defined for a context $A \times B$, can be transferred to a new context $C \times D$ by the following definition:

$$R|C \times D := R \cap C \times D.$$

Obviously, $R|C \times D \in \mathbf{Rel}(C, D)$.

When $C \times D \subseteq A \times B$, we usually say that $R|C \times D$ is a restriction of relation R to the context $C \times D$; it is an extension when $A \times B \subseteq C \times D$.

Example 3.4   Consider A as a set of boys and B as a set of girls with the relation R as "likes" $R \subseteq A \times B$. Often, a distinction is made between teenagers and younger children. If C is the set of teenage boys ($C \subset A$) and D is the set of teenage girls ($D \subset B$), then the restriction of the relation R to teenagers is $R|C \times D$. Attention is confined to liking ties among teenagers.   □

Set operations. Because relations are sets, in principle, we can use all standard set theoretic operations (see Section 3.1) on them, that is, union ($\cup$), intersection ($\cap$), difference ($\setminus$), symmetric difference ($\oplus$), and complement (superscript c), and compare them in terms of inclusion $\subseteq$. However, because we attached relations to contexts, we also have to specify an appropriate context. If the contexts of relations are the same, there is no problem – this is also the context of the resulting relation. When the contexts are different, we will adapt the most natural approach and embed relations in the smallest common context. For example, the intersection of relations $R \in \mathbf{Rel}(A, B)$ and $Q \in \mathbf{Rel}(C, D)$ is the relation $R \cap Q \in \mathbf{Rel}(A \cup C, B \cup D)$. For operations defined in this way, all of the usual properties hold (see Section 3.1).

Let $R, S \in \mathbf{Rel}(A, B)$. Then we have, for the corresponding matrices,

$$\mathbf{B}(R \cup S) = \mathbf{B}(R) \vee \mathbf{B}(S),$$
$$\mathbf{B}(R \cap S) = \mathbf{B}(R) \wedge \mathbf{B}(S),$$
$$\mathbf{B}(R \setminus S) = \mathbf{B}(R) \setminus \mathbf{B}(S),$$

where

$$\mathbf{C} = \mathbf{B}_1 \vee \mathbf{B}_2, \qquad c(x, y) = b_1(x, y) \vee b_2(x, y),$$
$$\mathbf{C} = \mathbf{B}_1 \wedge \mathbf{B}_2, \qquad c(x, y) = b_1(x, y) \wedge b_2(x, y),$$
$$\mathbf{C} = \mathbf{B}_1 \setminus \mathbf{B}_2, \qquad c(x, y) = b_1(x, y) \wedge \neg b_2(x, y).$$

Example 3.5

$$A = \{a_1, a_2\},$$
$$B = \{b_1, b_2, b_3\},$$
$$R = \{(a_1, b_1), (a_2, b_1), (a_2, b_2)\},$$
$$S = \{(a_1, b_2), (a_2, b_2), (a_2, b_3)\},$$

$$\mathbf{B}(R) = \begin{bmatrix} 0 & 0 & 1 & 0 & 0 \\ 0 & 0 & 1 & 1 & 0 \\ 1 & 1 & 0 & 0 & 0 \\ 0 & 1 & 0 & 0 & 0 \\ 0 & 0 & 0 & 0 & 0 \end{bmatrix},$$

$$\mathbf{B}(S) = \begin{bmatrix} 0 & 0 & 0 & 1 & 0 \\ 0 & 0 & 0 & 1 & 1 \\ 0 & 0 & 0 & 0 & 0 \\ 1 & 1 & 0 & 0 & 0 \\ 0 & 1 & 0 & 0 & 0 \end{bmatrix},$$

$$\mathbf{B}(R) \vee \mathbf{B}(S) = \begin{bmatrix} 0 & 0 & 1 & 1 & 0 \\ 0 & 0 & 1 & 1 & 1 \\ 1 & 1 & 0 & 0 & 0 \\ 1 & 1 & 0 & 0 & 0 \\ 0 & 1 & 0 & 0 & 0 \end{bmatrix},$$

$$\mathbf{B}(R) \wedge \mathbf{B}(S) = \begin{bmatrix} 0 & 0 & 0 & 0 & 0 \\ 0 & 0 & 0 & 1 & 0 \\ 0 & 0 & 0 & 0 & 0 \\ 0 & 1 & 0 & 0 & 0 \\ 0 & 0 & 0 & 0 & 0 \end{bmatrix},$$

$$\mathbf{B}(R) \setminus \mathbf{B}(S) = \begin{bmatrix} 0 & 0 & 1 & 0 & 0 \\ 0 & 0 & 1 & 0 & 0 \\ 1 & 1 & 0 & 0 & 0 \\ 0 & 0 & 0 & 0 & 0 \\ 0 & 0 & 0 & 0 & 0 \end{bmatrix}. \quad \square$$

Example 3.6 By using set operations on relations, we can reveal interesting connections between these relations. In Chapter 2 we described five relations among workers in the BWR: game playing, positive affect, negative affect, helping, and conflict over windows (see Tables 2.8–2.10). Consider the results of the following operations on these relations:

$$\text{negative} \cap \text{positive} = \emptyset,$$
$$\text{negative} \cap \text{helps} = \{(W_6, W_7)\},$$
$$\text{positive} \setminus \text{games} = \{(W_7, S_1), (S_1, W_7)\}.$$

In words, we state the following: (i) there is no actor who both likes and dislikes another actor; (ii) there is only one pair of actors (W_6 and W_7) who dislike each other yet one (W_6) helps the other (W_7); and (iii) among the actors who like each other, only W_7 and S_1 do not play games together. $\square$

Table 3.2. Two Hypothetical Binary Relations

		Friend				Best Friend			
Actor	a	b	c	d	e	a	b	c	d	e
a	0	1	0	1	0	0	1	0	0	0
b	1	0	0	0	1	1	0	0	0	0
c	0	1	0	0	0	0	1	0	0	0
d	0	1	1	0	1	0	0	0	0	1
e	0	1	0	1	0	0	0	0	1	0

3.2.2 Comparing relations

The relation $R \in \mathbf{Rel}(A, B)$ is contained (included) in the relation $Q \in \mathbf{Rel}(C, D)$ if and only if $R \subseteq Q$, $A \subseteq C$, and $B \subseteq D$.

Example 3.7 Consider the two (socio)matrices in Table 3.2. The left matrix (binary relation) illustrates the relation "friend" for a set of five actors $\{a, b, c, d, e\}$. We can imagine these people being asked to name their single "best friend." Actors a and b are mutual best friends as are d and e, but c's choice of b as a best friend is not reciprocated. In this example, $A = B$ and $C = D$. If we denote best friend and friend by R and S, respectively, it is clear that $R \subset S$. □

Example 3.8 Consider the set of three hypothetical matrices in Table 3.3. The center matrix displays a relation for six actors $\{a, b, c, d, e, f\}$ at a particular point in time denoted by T_1. Let R be the relation for T_1. Imagine that f leaves the group but there are no changes beyond the departure of f. The resulting matrix, labeled T_2^a with relation S^a, is on the left. It is clear that $\{a, b, c, d, e\}$ is a subset of $\{a, b, c, d, e, f\}$ (for rows and columns) and $S^a \subset R$. However, if the departure of f prompts c to choose d and to no longer choose b, as shown in the panel labeled T_2^b, the relation S^b is not a subset of R. □

Relations $R \in \mathbf{Rel}(A, B)$ and $Q \in \mathbf{Rel}(C, D)$ are equal if and only if they are mutually contained in each other, that is, if and only if $R = Q$, $A = C$, and $B = D$.

Table 3.3. Three Binary Relations

S^a / T_2^a					R / T_1						S^b / T_2^b				
	a	b	c	d	e		a	b	c	d	e	f		a	b	c	d	e
a	0	1	0	1	0	a	0	1	0	1	0	0	a	0	1	0	1	0
b	1	0	0	0	1	b	1	0	0	0	1	1	b	1	0	0	0	1
c	0	1	0	0	0	c	0	1	0	0	0	0	c	0	0	0	1	0
d	0	1	1	0	1	d	0	1	1	0	1	1	d	0	1	1	0	1
e	0	1	0	1	0	e	0	1	0	1	0	0	e	0	1	0	1	0
						f	1	0	1	0	1	0						

When one relation is nested inside the other, a comparison of the two relations is straightforward, but when two relations are not directly comparable in this sense, we need to define measures that capture the difference between the relations. We do this by using dissimilarity measures in the set **Rel**(A, B).[6] Assume that A and B are finite. One example of a dissimilarity measure is the Hamming distance, which is defined as

$$d_{\mathrm{H}}(R, S) = \text{card}(R \oplus S),$$

where $R, S \in$ **Rel**(A, B) and card denotes the size of a set, in this case of the symmetric difference between R and S. When this is applied to T_2^a and T_2^b in Table 3.3, we see that (c, b) is an element of S^a but not of S^b. Similarly, (c, d) is in S^b but is not in S^a. The Hamming distance is therefore $d_H(S^a, S^b) = 2$ and counts the total number of times there is a 1 in one matrix but not in the other. Intuitively, for Table 3.3, it seems the measure is small: the two matrices have many corresponding elements. In general, however, it is necessary to normalize such scores. One normalization is (using h in place of H)

$$d_h(R, S) = \frac{\text{card}(R \oplus S)}{\text{card}(A \times B)}.$$

For this simple example, card$(A \times B)$ is 25. The normalized measure is $d_h(S^a, S^b) = 2/25$. Other distances can also be introduced in the set **Rel**(A, B). For example,

$$d_u(R, S) = \begin{cases} 0 & R = S = \emptyset \\ \dfrac{\text{card}(R \oplus S)}{\text{card}(R \cup S)} & \text{otherwise} \end{cases} .$$

For this example, $S^a \cup S^b$ has 11 elements and the normalized measure is $d_u(S^a, S^b) = 2/11$.

Another dissimilarity that could be used is

$$d_m(R, S) = \begin{cases} 0 & R = S = \emptyset \\ \dfrac{\max(\text{card}(R \setminus S), \text{card}(S \setminus R))}{\max(\text{card}(R), \text{card}(S))} & \text{otherwise} \end{cases} .$$

In this example, card$(S^a \setminus S^b)$ is 1, as is card$(S^b \setminus S^a)$, making the numerator 1. We see that card$(S^a) = $ card$(S^b) = 10$, and thus $d_m(S^a, S^b) = 1/10$.

This methodology for comparing two relations can be used in at least two ways. In Chapter 1 we introduced the idea of one social relation constraining another – where the relations were "authority" and "friendship" in an organization. The comparison measures introduced here permit the measurement of the correspondence between such relations and facilitate the study of the constraint of one relation on another. In both Chapters 1 and 2 we discussed examples in which a social

---

6 In Chapter 5 (Section 5.3), we define a set of dissimilarity measures and examine some of their properties.

network has multiple relations such as the BWR and the SG networks. If two relations differ little from each other, using both may be a way of dealing with measurement error. However, if two relations differ greatly, we may need to be cautious when analyzing them jointly. Comparing them by using the methods of this section allows an analyst to drop redundant relations and to know when there are major differences between relations. We pursue this further with the BWR data in Section 5.4.1. We note that there is considerable debate over the use of multiple relations, which is a topic we consider further in the final chapter.

Dissimilarity properties. It is possible to examine the properties of dissimilarities; the following three properties are the most common.

1. There is zero distance between identical relations:

$$d(R, S) = 0 \Leftrightarrow R = S.$$

2. There is symmetry:

$$d(R, S) = d(S, R).$$

3. There is triangle inequality:

$$\forall Q \in \mathbf{Rel}(A, B) : d(R, S) \le d(R, Q) + d(Q, S).$$

We say also that $(\mathbf{Rel}(A, B), d)$ is a metric space when these properties hold.

It has to be stressed that $R = S$ means the equality of descriptions (as sets of pairs) of relations. There can exist conceptually different relations with the same description.

For $d \in \{d_H, d_h\}$, we can prove the following property:

$$R \cap S \subseteq Q \subseteq R \cup S \Leftrightarrow d(R, S) = d(R, Q) + d(Q, S).$$

We further consider the properties of dissimilarity measures in Chapter 5.

We can also measure the determinacy of relation S by relation R by introducing the *determinacy* coefficient:

$$K(R \Rightarrow S) = \begin{cases} 1 & S = \emptyset \\ \dfrac{\mathrm{card}(R \cap S)}{\mathrm{card}(S)} & \text{otherwise} \end{cases}.$$

The larger the determinacy coefficient, the more the relation S is determined by R.[7]

For the simple relations described in Table 3.3, it is clear that the relation R, at T_1, determines S^a completely (as constructed, with the only change being f's departure from the network) and thus that the measure of determinacy is $K(R \Rightarrow S^a) = 1$. All of the ties in S are ties in $R \cap S$. However, R does not determine S^b

---

7 We do *not* mean this in causal sense.

Table 3.4. Joint Playing Games and Positive Ties in the BWR

	I_1	I_3	W_1	W_2	W_3	W_4	W_5	W_6	W_7	W_8	W_9	S_1	S_2	S_4
I_1	0	0	0	0	1	0	0	0	0	0	0	0	0	0
I_3	0	0	0	0	0	0	0	0	0	0	0	0	0	0
W_1	0	0	0	0	1	1	0	0	0	0	0	1	0	0
W_2	0	0	0	0	0	0	0	0	0	0	0	0	0	0
W_3	1	0	1	0	0	1	0	0	0	0	0	1	0	0
W_4	0	0	1	0	1	0	0	0	0	0	0	1	0	0
W_5	0	0	0	0	0	0	0	0	0	0	0	0	0	0
W_6	0	0	0	0	0	0	0	0	0	0	0	0	0	0
W_7	0	0	0	0	0	0	0	0	0	1	1	0	0	0
W_8	0	0	0	0	0	0	0	0	1	0	1	0	0	1
W_9	0	0	0	0	0	0	0	0	1	1	0	0	0	1
S_1	0	0	1	0	1	1	0	0	0	0	0	0	0	0
S_2	0	0	0	0	0	0	0	0	0	0	0	0	0	0
S_4	0	0	0	0	0	0	0	0	0	1	1	0	0	0

completely: (c, b) is a member of R but is not a member of S^b whereas (c, d) is in S^b but is not in R. Because $\text{card}(R \cap S) = 9$ and $\text{card}(S) = 10$, $K(R \Rightarrow S^b) = 9/10$. All but one of S's elements are in $R \cap S$. If $A_1 = \{a, b, c, d, e, f\}$, then the context is given by $A_1 \times A_1$. In the computation for this example, the tie that did not persist (c, b) is irrelevant for computing K. Because all of the ties involving f in R are ignored, the context $A_2 \times A_2$ where $A_2 = \{a, b, c, d, e\}$ could be assumed. Note that $S|A_2 \times A_2$ is equal to the restriction $R|A_1 \times A_1$.

We can define also the *mutual determinacy* coefficient:

$$K(R \Leftrightarrow S) = \begin{cases} 1 & R = S = \emptyset \\ \dfrac{\text{card}(R \cap S)}{\text{card}(R \cup S)} & \text{otherwise} \end{cases} = 1 - d_u(R, S).$$

For R in S^a, $\text{card}(R \cup S^a) = 15$ and $\text{card}(R \cap S^a) = 10$, giving $K(R \Leftrightarrow S^a) = 10/15$. Here, the ties involving f are relevant and the context is $A_1 \times A_1$. For R and S^b, $\text{card}(R \cup S^b) = 16$ and $\text{card}(R \cap S^b) = 9$, making $K(R \Leftrightarrow S^b) = 9/16$. Finally, $K(S^a \Leftrightarrow S^b) = 9/11$ because $\text{card}(S^a \cap S^b) = 9$ and $\text{card}(S^a \cup S^b) = 11$.

Example 3.9 Consider again the BWR helping ties together with the positive ties. There are 56 game-playing ties and 26 positive ties. The intersection of the two relations is given in Table 3.4.

There are 24 ties that are both positive and game playing. If R is game playing and S represents the positive ties, then the determinacy coefficient in which game playing determines positive ties is $24/26 = 0.92$. On the other hand, the determinacy coefficient in which positive ties determine game playing is $24/56 = 0.43$. People who play games together in the BWR tend to like each other, but liking is much less likely to generate the playing of games. Table 3.5 shows the union of

Table 3.5. BWR: Playing Games or Positive Ties

	I_1	I_3	W_1	W_2	W_3	W_4	W_5	W_6	W_7	W_8	W_9	S_1	S_2	S_4
I_1	0	0	1	1	2	1	0	0	0	0	0	0	0	0
I_3	0	0	0	0	0	0	0	0	0	0	0	0	0	0
W_1	1	0	0	1	2	2	1	0	0	0	0	2	0	0
W_2	1	0	1	0	1	1	0	0	0	0	0	1	0	0
W_3	2	0	2	1	0	2	1	0	0	0	0	2	0	0
W_4	1	0	2	1	2	0	1	0	0	0	0	2	0	0
W_5	0	0	1	0	1	1	0	0	1	0	0	1	0	0
W_6	0	0	0	0	0	0	0	0	1	1	1	0	0	0
W_7	0	0	0	0	0	0	1	1	0	2	2	1	0	1
W_8	0	0	0	0	0	0	0	1	2	0	2	0	0	2
W_9	0	0	0	0	0	0	0	1	2	2	0	0	0	2
S_1	0	0	2	1	2	2	1	0	1	0	0	0	0	0
S_2	0	0	0	0	0	0	0	0	0	0	0	0	0	0
S_4	0	0	0	0	1	0	0	0	1	2	2	0	0	0

the positive ties and the game-playing ties. A 1 indicates a single relation (either positive or game playing) and a 2 indicates that both ties are present. Note that the 2s in Table 3.5 correspond exactly to the 1s in Table 3.4. The count of the union of ties (with a 2 counted only once) is 58. The coefficient of mutual determinacy is $24/58 = 0.41$.

In contrast, consider negative ties and helping ties. There are 24 helping ties and 38 negative ties. The two relations have only one tie (W_6, W_7) in common. The determinacy coefficient in which helping determines negative ties is $1/38 = 0.026$, and the coefficient in which negative ties determines helping is $1/24 = 0.042$. The coefficient of mutual determinacy is $1/61 = 0.016$. All of this is consistent with the two relations' having a tiny overlap. □

Some additional properties of this coefficient are as follows:

$$0 \le K(R \Leftrightarrow S) \le K(R \Rightarrow S) \le 1,$$
$$K(R \Rightarrow S) = 1 \quad \Leftrightarrow \quad S \subseteq R,$$
$$K(R \Leftrightarrow S) = 1 \quad \Leftrightarrow \quad K(R \Rightarrow S) = K(S \Rightarrow R) = 1 \quad \Leftrightarrow \quad R = S.$$

3.2.3 Special operations

In addition to standard set theoretic operations, there are some special operations. We start with the converse of a relation.

The converse relation. For a relation $R \in \mathbf{Rel}(A, B)$, its converse or transposed relation $R^{-1} \in \mathbf{Rel}(B, A)$ is defined by

$$R^{-1} = \{(x, y) : yRx\},$$

or, in an alternative notation,

$$x R^{-1} y \Leftrightarrow y R x.$$

For the matrix of the converse relation, we have

$$\mathbf{B}(R^{-1}) = \mathbf{B}(R)^{\mathrm{T}},$$

where the superscript T denotes matrix transposition. Using the BWR example, we see that if R is "helping," then R^{-1} is the relation "being helped." We note that the matrix of converse relation is not the inverse of $\mathbf{B}(R)$.

For $R, S \in \mathbf{Rel}(A, B)$ we have the following:

$$(R^{-1})^{-1} = R, \qquad \mathcal{D}R^{-1} = \mathcal{R}R,$$
$$(R \cup S)^{-1} = R^{-1} \cup S^{-1}, \qquad (R \cap S)^{-1} = R^{-1} \cap S^{-1}.$$

Immediate successors, predecessors, and neighbors. The set of immediate successors of the element x is the set

$$R(x) := \{y : x R y\},$$

and the set of its immediate predecessors, $R^{-1}(x)$. The set $R \cup R^{-1}(x) = R(x) \cup R^{-1}(x)$ consists of all its immediate neighbors.

These notions can be extended also to sets of vertices. Let $B \subseteq A$; then

$$R(B) := \bigcup_{x \in B} R(x).$$

It holds that

$$R(B_1 \cup B_2) = R(B_1) \cup R(B_2),$$
$$R(B_1 \cap B_2) \subseteq R(B_1) \cap R(B_2),$$
$$B_1 \subseteq B_2 \Rightarrow R(B_1) \subseteq R(B_2).$$

Product of relations. Thus far, our discussion has been focused on relations and comparisons of relations. Relations can also be coupled. For example, we can consider a "friend of a friend" relation: if a has b as a friend and b has c as a friend, then c is a friend of a friend of a. An anthropological example is "mother's brother" (or maternal uncle), a much studied relation: if b is the mother of a and c is a brother of b, then c is the maternal uncle of a. The intuition is to move from one node to a second node in one relation and then move from the second node to the third node in the second relation.

To formalize these ideas, let $R \in \mathbf{Rel}(A, B)$ and $S \in \mathbf{Rel}(B, C)$; then the "product" of relations R and S is this relation[8] (see Figure 3.1):

$$R * S = \{(x, z) \in A \times C : \exists y \in B : (x R y \wedge y S z)\} \in \mathbf{Rel}(A, C),$$

---

8 In traditional mathematics, there is another product, denoted by $S \circ R$, that is related to our product by the equality $S \circ R = R * S$. In essence, this is a notational difference. We use $R * S$ since it is congruent with the applications of relations for the analysis of graphs and networks.

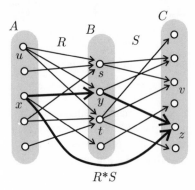

Figure 3.1. Product of relations.

or, in matrix form,

$$\mathbf{B}(R * S) = \mathbf{B}(R) \times \mathbf{B}(S),$$

where

$$\mathbf{C} = \mathbf{B}_1 \times \mathbf{B}_2, \quad c(x, z) = \bigvee_{y \in B} b_1(x, y) \wedge b_2(y, z).$$

In Figure 3.1, the bolded tie of R from $x \in A$ to $y \in B$ and the bolded tie of S from $y \in B$ to $z \in C$ follow each other to create the bolded tie $R * S$ from $x \in A$ to $z \in C$.

Example 3.10 Consider the hypothetical example in Table 3.6, with R being a friendship relation. On the left is the matrix for R and on the right is the matrix for the friend-of-a-friend relation created by $R \times R$. The tie between a and e in this relation comes from d's being a friend of e and a's being a friend of d. All of the remaining ties in the friend-of-a-friend relation can be traced in the same way. □

In general, the product of relations is not a commutative operation, not even on **Rel**(A, A). For example,

$$\text{brother} * \text{father} \subseteq \text{uncle},$$

$$\text{father} * \text{brother} \subseteq \text{father}.$$

Table 3.6. Friend and Friend-of-a-Friend Relations

	B(R)						**B(R) × B(R)**				
	a	b	c	d	e		a	b	c	d	e
a	0	0	0	1	0		0	0	0	0	1
b	0	0	0	0	1		1	0	1	0	0
c	1	1	0	0	0		0	0	0	1	1
d	0	0	0	0	1		1	0	1	0	0
e	1	0	1	0	0		1	1	0	1	0

The product, when defined, is associative:

$$R * (S * T) = (R * S) * T.$$

If R is "mother of," and S is "brother of," and T is "father of," then the product $R * S * T$ defines an identified kinship tie. (As determined by the society, this may or may not be empirically recognized by the members of the society.) If $R = S = T$, for example, in a friendship network, the product is "friend of a friend of a friend." If R is "relative of," S is a "friend of," and T is a "coworker of," then the product relation $R * S * T$ is a "relative of a friend of a coworker" relation.[9]

Some additional properties of the product of relations are included in the following array:

$$R * (S \cup T) = R * S \cup R * T, \qquad (R \cup S) * T = R * T \cup S * T,$$
$$R * (S \cap T) \subseteq R * S \cap R * T, \qquad (R \cap S) * T \subseteq R * T \cap S * T,$$
$$R \subseteq S \Rightarrow R * T \subseteq S * T, \qquad R \subseteq S \Rightarrow T * R \subseteq T * S,$$
$$I_A * R = R * I_B = R, \qquad \emptyset * R = R * \emptyset = \emptyset,$$
$$(R * S)^{-1} = S^{-1} * R^{-1}, \qquad R \subseteq R * R^{-1} * R.$$

The first property states that the product of R and $S \cup T$ is the same as forming the union of the product $R * S$ and the product $R * T$. Similarly, the product of $R \cup S$ and T is the same as the union of the products $R * T$ and $S * T$. The last property states that the product of the three relations – R, R^{-1}, and R – contains R. That is, some ties can be "created" through the product that are not in R. (Whether $R * R^{-1} * R$ properly contains R or equals R depends on R. For example, for R in Table 3.6, $R * R^{-1} * R = R$.) All of the other properties in the array can be expressed in a similar fashion, and we encourage readers to do so.

The first two rows in this array concern distributive properties; in the following paragraphs, in our discussion of the transitive closure of a relation (in Section 4.2.2), we also need the generalized distributivity:

$$R * (\bigcup_{i \in I} S_i) = \bigcup_{i \in I} (R * S_i), \qquad (\bigcup_{i \in I} S_i) * R = \bigcup_{i \in I} (S_i * R),$$
$$R * (\bigcap_{i \in I} S_i) \subseteq \bigcap_{i \in I} (R * S_i), \qquad (\bigcap_{i \in I} S_i) * R \subseteq \bigcap_{i \in I} (S_i * R).$$

We emphasize that $R * R^{-1}$ is not always equal to I_A. For example, let $A = \{a, b, c\}$ and $R = \{(a, c), (b, c)\} \in \mathbf{Rel}(A, A)$. Then $R^{-1} = \{(c, a), (c, b)\}$ and

$$R * R^{-1} = \{(a, a), (a, b), (b, a), (b, b)\}.$$

Since the product of relations is associative, we can define for $R \in \mathbf{Rel}(A, A)$ as its nth power R^n, $n \in \mathbb{N}$:

$$R^n = R * R * \cdots * R.$$

---

9   Although the product can be defined, the meaning of such a constructed relation might not have empirical value.

We can also define this recursively[10]:

$$R^0 = I \qquad \text{and} \qquad R^{n+1} = R * R^n.$$

The following properties hold:

$$R^{m+n} = R^m * R^n, \qquad (R^m)^n = R^{mn},$$
$$R^n \cup S^n \subseteq (R \cup S)^n, \qquad (R^{-1})^n = (R^n)^{-1},$$

and

$$R^{(n)} := \bigcup_{i=0}^{n} R^i = (I \cup R)^n$$

for all $m, n \in \mathbb{N}$. However, we *cannot* define $R^{-n} := (R^{-1})^n$ because, as noted earlier, $R * R^{-1} = I$ does not always hold. It follows that it is not possible to extend the properties to all integers $\mathbb{Z}$.

3.3   FUNCTIONS

In set theory, a function is a special type of relation.

A binary relation $R \in \mathbf{Rel}(A, B)$ is a *partial* or *mapping* if and only if

$$\forall x \in A, \forall y_1, y_2 \in B : (xRy_1 \wedge xRy_2 \Rightarrow y_1 = y_2).$$

An element $x \in A$ can be mapped to at most one element in B. For notational convenience and by convention, we use f instead of R when denoting functions; instead of $f \in \mathbf{Rel}(A, B)$ we write

$$f : A \to B \qquad \text{or} \qquad A \xrightarrow{f} B \qquad \text{or} \qquad f \in B^A$$

and read the following: f is a function from A to B. Instead of $(x, y) \in f$ we write

$$f : x \mapsto y \qquad \text{or} \qquad y = f(x).$$

Here x is the *argument*, and y is the *value* or *image* of the element x. This is illustrated in Figure 3.2.

A function f is completely determined by the set of pairs

$$\{(x, f(x)) : x \in \mathcal{D}f\},$$

which is called also a *graph*[11] of the function f.

A function $f : A \to B$, for which

$$\mathcal{D}R = A$$

holds, is *everywhere defined* (over A).

When a function, f, is defined on a Cartesian product $A = A_1 \times A_2 \cdots A_n$, we usually denote its value for the argument $(x_1, x_2, \ldots, x_n)$ by $f(x_1, x_2, \ldots, x_n)$.

---

10   Note that $0 \in \mathbb{N}$.
11   This use of "graph" is not the same as that in Chapter 4.

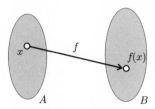

Figure 3.2. A function.

We can extend the notion of an image, as we have done in the general case of relations, to the subsets of the set A. Let $C \subseteq A$; then

$$f(C) = \{y \in B : \exists x \in C : y = f(x)\} = \bigcup_{x \in C} \{f(x)\},$$

and we know also that

$$f(\emptyset) = \emptyset,$$
$$f(C_1 \cup C_2) = f(C_1) \cup f(C_2),$$
$$f(C_1 \cap C_2) \subseteq f(C_1) \cap f(C_2).$$

In general $\mathcal{R}f = f(A) \subseteq B$; in the case when $f(A) = B$, we say that function f is *surjective* and that it maps the set A *onto* the set B.

If a function f assigns different images to different elements,

$$\forall x, y \in \mathcal{D}f : (x \neq y \Rightarrow f(x) \neq f(y)),$$

or, equivalently,

$$\forall x, y \in \mathcal{D}f : (f(x) = f(y) \Rightarrow x = y),$$

we say that the function f is *injective*.

An everywhere defined function f is *bijective* if and only if it is injective and surjective.

These concepts are illustrated in Figure 3.3. On the left, there is an element, b_5 (and b_2), that has no x such that $f(x) = b_5$. In the middle figure, every element of B is the image of an element in A. On the right, every element of A is mapped to a single element in B and each element of B is an image of a single element in A.

A *restriction* of function $f : A \to B$ to the set $C \subseteq A$ is called the function

$$f|C := f \cap C \times B.$$

This is illustrated in Figure 3.4. All that is meant by the idea of a restriction is that the function is defined for a subset of the domain. In Figure 3.4 the function is restricted to the members of C. All of the elements of $A \setminus C$ are ignored when the

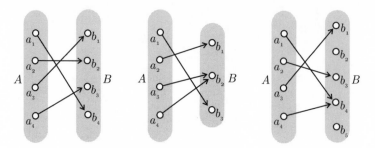

Figure 3.3. An everywhere defined function from A to B, a surjective function, and a bijective function.

function is restricted in this way. Conversely, let $C \subseteq A$ and $f : A \to B$. Function f is an *extension* of function $g : C \to B$ if and only if $f|C = g$.

I_A, a *unit* relation on the set A, is an everywhere defined function. It is often denoted by id_A and called the *identity* function on A:

$$\forall x \in A : \mathrm{id}_A(x) = x.$$

A *constant* function on the set A is called the function $f : A \to B$ for which it holds:

$$\exists b \in B \, \forall x \in A : f(x) = b.$$

A *permutation* is a bijective mapping of a set onto itself.

Let $\mathbb{B} = \{0, 1\}$. A *characteristic* function of the set $C \subseteq A$ is called the function $\chi_C : A \to \mathbb{B}$:

$$\chi_C(x) = \begin{cases} 1 & x \in C \\ 0 & x \notin C \end{cases}.$$

These four functions are illustrated in Figure 3.5. The identity function maps a set, A, to itself by mapping each element of A to itself. The permutation function

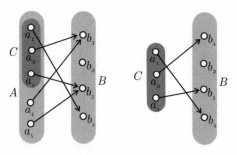

Figure 3.4. Restriction of a function.

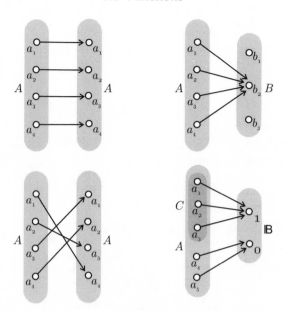

Figure 3.5. Identity, constant, permutation, and characteristic functions.

maps every element of A to another element of A and so creates a permutation of the elements. As shown in Figure 3.5, every element is mapped to a distinct other element. It is not necessary that every element be mapped to another element under a permutation. So, for example, if a_1 is mapped to a_1, a_2 is mapped to a_2, a_3 is mapped to a_4, and a_4 is mapped to a_3, then the function described by this is still a permutation. The identity function is a special case of a permutation and is called the *identity permutation*. The constant function maps every element of A to a single element of B. For a charateristic function, the set B has only two elements. In Figure 3.5 we have labeled them 0 and 1. Under the characteristic function, the elements of A are grouped into two subsets. One subset is mapped to the element 0 and the other subset is mapped to 1.

3.3.1 Products of functions ⊙

We define the product (composition) $*$ of relations in Section 3.2. Because functions are relations, products of functions are thus already defined. In classical mathematics (mathematical analysis), another product $f \circ g$ of functions $g : A \to B$ and $f : B \to C$ is usually used. It is defined by

$$f \circ g(x) := f(g(x))$$

or

$$y = f \circ g(x) := \exists z \in B : (z = g(x) \wedge y = f(z)),$$

or, in relational notation,

$$x(f \circ g)y := \exists z \in B : (xgz \wedge zfy).$$

Therefore, $f \circ g = g * f$.

Theorem 3.1 *The product $f \circ g$ of functions $g : A \to B$ and $f : B \to C$ is also a function from A to C.*

However, the relation f^{-1} is not always a function. The conditions under which f^{-1} is a function are given in the following theorem.

Theorem 3.2 *Let $f \in \mathbf{Rel}(A, B)$ be a function. Then the relation f^{-1} is a function if and only if f is injective. Then f^{-1} is also injective.*

Some additional properties include the following.

Theorem 3.3 *Let $f : A \to B$ be an injective function and $C_1, C_2 \subseteq A$. Then*

$$f(C_1 \cap C_2) = f(C_1) \cap f(C_2),$$
$$f(C_1 \setminus C_2) = f(C_1) \setminus f(C_2).$$

Theorem 3.4 *Let $f : A \to B$ be an injective, everywhere defined function. Then*

$$f^{-1} \circ f = \mathrm{id}_A,$$

and, if it is also surjective,

$$f \circ f^{-1} = \mathrm{id}_B.$$

Theorem 3.5 *Let $f : A \to B$ and $g : B \to C$ be both injective and surjective functions; then the function $g \circ f$ is also injective and surjective.*

Theorem 3.6 *Let $f : A \to B$, $g : B \to C$, and $g \circ f$ be functions. Then*

- *if $g \circ f$ is surjective, then g is surjective;*
- *if $g \circ f$ is injective, then f is injective;*
- *if $g \circ f$ is bijective, then g is surjective and f is injective.*

3.3.2   Relational homomorphisms

Let $R \in \mathbf{Rel}(A, B)$ and $S \in \mathbf{Rel}(C, D)$. A mapping $h : A \cup B \to C \cup D$ is a *homomorphism* of relation R to relation S if and only if

$$\forall x \in A, y \in B : (xRy \Rightarrow h(x)Sh(y)),$$

and it is an *embedding* if and only if

$$\forall x \in A, y \in B : (xRy \Leftrightarrow h(x)Sh(y)).$$

3.4 BASIC ALGEBRA ⊙

Algebraic operations are just special types of functions. We shall restrict our discussion to binary operations of the form

$$* : A \times B \to C,$$

or by elements

$$* : (a, b) \mapsto c$$

for $(a, b) \in \mathcal{D}* \subseteq A \times B$ and $c \in C$. This is usually written, using the *infix* notation, also as $c = a * b$.

In the case when $A = B = C$, the operation $*$ is said to be *internal* in A. For example, addition (+) is an internal operation in the set of real numbers $\mathbb{R}$ (or in the set of natural numbers $\mathbb{N}$) since it assigns to every pair of reals $(a, b) \in \mathbb{R}^2$ another real number $a + b \in \mathbb{R}$, their sum:

$$+ : (7, 4) \mapsto 11 \qquad \text{or} \qquad 7 + 4 = 11.$$

When the sets A and B have a small number of elements, a binary operation $*$ is often represented by its Cayley table:

$*$	b
a	$a * b$

For example, the compositions ∘ of rotations for a multiple of 90 degrees: $r = \text{Rot}\,0$, $s = \text{Rot}\,90$, $t = \text{Rot}\,180$, $u = \text{Rot}\,270$ can be described by the following Cayley table:

∘	r	s	t	u
r	r	s	t	u
s	s	t	u	r
t	t	u	r	s
u	u	r	s	t

An ordered pair $(A, *)$, where A is a set with an internal and everywhere defined binary operation $*$, is called a *groupoid*. For example, the rotations form with a composition, ∘, a groupoid $(\{r, s, t, u\}, \circ)$.

A groupoid is an example of an algebraic structure. There are several algebraic structures based on a groupoid that are obtained by imposing some additional properties on it. We list some of these properties.

Commutativity:

$$\forall a, b \in A : a * b = b * a.$$

Associativity:

$$\forall a, b, c \in A : a * (b * c) = (a * b) * c.$$

Both of these properties hold for the rotations, $\circ$, example.

An *idempotent* element of a groupoid $(A, *)$ is called an element $a \in A$ for which

$$a * a = a.$$

A groupoid $(A, *)$ is *idempotent* iff all its elements are idempotent.

An *identity* or *neutral* element of a groupoid $(A, *)$ is called an element $e \in A$ for which

$$\forall a \in A : a * e = e * a = a.$$

The identity in the rotations example is r. By definition, an identity is always an idempotent element since $e * e = e$.

An *absorption* element of a groupoid $(A, *)$ is called an element $s \in A$ for which

$$\forall a \in A : s * a = a * s = s.$$

A *regular element* in a groupoid $(A, *)$ is called an element $a \in A$ for which

$$\forall b, c \in A : ((a * b = a * c \Rightarrow b = c) \land (b * a = c * a \Rightarrow b = c)).$$

An element $a \in A$ of a groupoid $(A, *, e)$ with identity e is *invertible* if

$$\exists a' \in A : a' * a = a * a' = e.$$

The element $a' \in A$ is then called the *inverse* element of $a \in A$.

A commutative groupoid $(A, *)$ is often also called the *Abelian* groupoid.

An associative groupoid $(A, *)$ is called a *semigroup*. In a semigroup the order of computation is not important – we can omit the brackets. In an Abelian semigroup the order of elements in an expression is also not important. Semigroups have been used to study images of a blockmodel. See Boyd (1969, 1991) and Bonacich (1979) for discussions of using semigroups in this fashion.

An idempotent Abelian semigroup $(A, *)$ is called a *semilattice*. An example is $(\mathbb{R}, \max)$.

As another example, consider the set of all undirected graphs on four vertices $\mathcal{G}_4 = \{G_i : i = 1, \ldots, 11\}$ shown in Figure 3.6. In $\mathcal{G}_4$ we define two binary operations $*$ and $\triangle$, where $G_i * G_j$ is the smallest graph containing (subgraphs isomorphic to) both G_i and G_j and $G_i \triangle G_j$ is the largest graph contained in both G_i and G_j. For example, $G_4 * G_5 = G_8$, $G_6 * G_{10} = G_{10}$, $G_5 \triangle G_4 = G_2$, and so

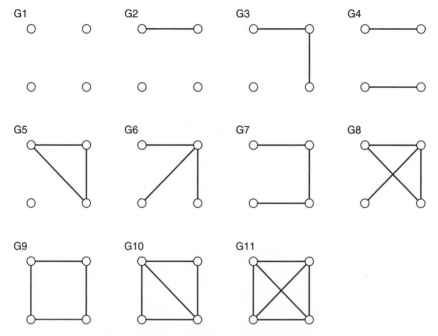

Figure 3.6. The set of edge graphs on four vertices.

on. In determining the results of operations $*$ and $\triangle$, we can use as a help the containment relation displayed on the left side of Figure 3.7. The structures $(\mathcal{G}_4, *)$ and $(\mathcal{G}_4, \triangle)$ are both semilattices.

Now consider the subset of $\mathcal{G}_4$ consisting of all connected graphs $\mathcal{C}_4\{G_i : i = 6, \ldots, 11\}$; see the right side of Figure 3.7. The structure $(\mathcal{C}_4, *)$ is also a semilattice, but the structure $(\mathcal{C}_4, \triangle)$ is not since the result of $G_6 \triangle G_9$ (and some others) is not defined. There is no connected graph on four vertices contained in both G_6 and G_9.

$(\mathcal{P}(A), \cup, \emptyset)$ is a semilattice with identity $\emptyset$ and absorption element A.

In a semigroup $(A, *)$ we can define the nth power a^n of an element $a \in A$ as

$$a^n = \underbrace{a * a * \cdots * a}_{n},$$

or, recursively,

P0. $a^1 \quad = a$
P1. $a^{n+1} = a^n * a, \qquad n \in \mathbb{N}^+.$

It is easy to verify that for all $n, m \in \mathbb{N}^+$, the following hold:

$$a^n * a^m = a^{n+m} \qquad \text{and} \qquad (a^n)^m = a^{nm}.$$

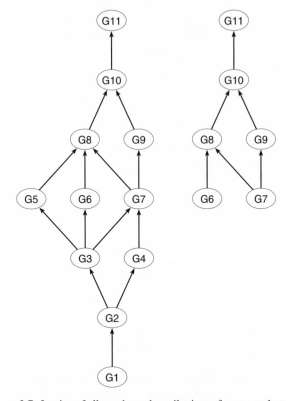

Figure 3.7. Lattice of all graphs and semilattices of connected graphs.

A semigroup $(A, *, e)$ with identity e is termed a *monoid*. In a monoid we can extend the power to the 0 exponent by $a^0 = e$. Some examples of monoids are as follows.

(**Rel**$(A, A), *, I)$ is a monoid with identity I.

$(\mathbb{N}, +, 0)$ is an Abelian monoid with identity 0 in which all elements are regular.

$(\mathbb{R}, \cdot, 1)$ is an Abelian monoid with identity 1 and absorption element 0 in which all elements, except 0, are regular.

A monoid $(A, *, e)$ in which every element is invertible is called a *group*. In a group, we can extend the power of elements to include negative exponents by $a^{-n} = (a^{-1})^n$ for $n \in \mathbb{N}$.

The groupoid of rotations example described above is a group.

$(\mathcal{P}(A), \oplus, \emptyset)$ is an Abelian group with $X' = X$.

$(\mathbb{R} \setminus \{0\}, \cdot, 1)$ is an Abelian group with $a' = a^{-1}$.

Extensive discussions of the uses of algebra for studying social relations can be found in Boyd (1991) and Pattison (1993).

3.5   TRANSITIONS TO CHAPTERS 4 AND 9

In Chapter 4, we build on the foundations described in this chapter and provide an extended treatment of social relations and graphs. Chapter 4 is critical in establishing the foundations for our discussion of conventional blockmodeling and generalized blockmodeling. In Chapter 10 we discuss signed networks, and some additional mathematical foundations for this extension are provided in Chapter 9, where algebraic structures with two operations are discussed.

4

RELATIONS AND GRAPHS FOR
NETWORK ANALYSIS

In this chapter we continue our presentation of a series of mathematical concepts that provide a deeper understanding of blockmodeling ideas. Our goal is to lay the foundations for a discussion of both conventional blockmodeling (in Chapter 6) and our generalized approach to partitioning social networks (in Chapters 6–11).

The main topics in this chapter are a more detailed discussion of graphs (Section 4.1), a presentation of some types of binary relations (Section 4.2), and some basic ideas of partitions and equivalence relations (Section 4.3). The first two sections build toward Section 4.3, which considers ideas at the core of block-modeling. We consider acyclic relations (Section 4.4), a topic used later in this chapter and in Chapter 11. This is followed by materials on orders (Section 4.5) and a short statement about networks (Section 4.6) using materials developed in this chapter. Centrality (Section 4.7) is the last topic considered in this chapter. We do not deal with graph or network centralization, for it is not used in our discussion of blockmodeling.

4.1 GRAPHS

Graphs allow us to describe many social network situations very precisely. We provided a preliminary – and intuitive – discussion of graphs in Chapter 1, where we used a variety of examples. In this section, we take a more formal approach to graphs. Binary relations, as noted in Section 3.2, are closely related to graphs and provide our point of departure.

A *graph* is an ordered triple $\mathbf{G} = (\mathcal{V}, \mathcal{E}, \mathcal{A})$. The set $\mathcal{V}$ is the *vertex set* of the graph $\mathbf{G}$; $\mathcal{E}$ is the set of *edges* (undirected lines), and $\mathcal{A}$ is the set of *arcs* (directed lines) of $\mathbf{G}$: $\mathcal{V}$, $\mathcal{E}$, and $\mathcal{A}$ are pairwise disjoint sets. The sets $\mathcal{E}$ and $\mathcal{A}$ can be empty. If $\mathcal{A} = \emptyset$, the graph $\mathbf{G}$ is *undirected*. The marriage ties of elite families in Florence in the 15th century (see Figure 1.2) provide an example of this kind of graph. A graph is *directed* if $\mathcal{E} = \emptyset$. This is illustrated by an organizational hierarchy (see Figure 1.3). The Little League (LL) baseball team shown in Figure 1.1 is another directed graph.[1] To each line p from $\mathcal{L} = \mathcal{E} \cup \mathcal{A}$ belongs a pair of vertices – its *endpoints*. In the case of an arc, one vertex is its *initial* vertex and the other vertex is its *terminal* vertex. For the line between Tom and Frank in Figure 1.1, Tom is the initial vertex and Frank is the terminal vertex (endpoint). For undirected graphs there are simply end vertices; for example, the Medici family and the Barbadori family are the ends of an edge. Given the definition above of $\mathcal{L}$, we sometimes use $\mathbf{G} = (\mathcal{V}, \mathcal{L})$ as a shorthand statement for a graph.

We use $e(u : v)$ to denote that an edge e has end vertices u and v; or, equivalently, $e(u : v)$. Similarly, $a(u, v)$ says that u is the initial and v is the terminal vertex of arc a. A line $p \in \mathcal{L}$ *joins* its end vertices and an arc $a \in \mathcal{A}$ *joins* its initial vertex *to* its terminal vertex. When both ends of a line are the same, we call it a *loop*. A vertex that is not an end of any line is an *isolate*, and it is said to be *isolated*. Two lines are *parallel* if they have the same endpoints.

Let us denote by $\mathcal{V}^{(2)}$ the set of all one- or two-element subsets[2] of the set of vertices $\mathcal{V}$:

$$\mathcal{V}^{(2)} = \{\{u, v\} : u, v \in \mathcal{V}\}.$$

We can describe the relations between lines and vertices by the following functions:

endpoints of a line:	$\text{ext} : \mathcal{L} \to \mathcal{V}^{(2)}$;
initial vertex of an arc:	$\text{ini} : \mathcal{A} \to \mathcal{V}$;
terminal vertex of an arc:	$\text{ter} : \mathcal{A} \to \mathcal{V}$;
twin vertex (partial function):	$\text{twin} : \mathcal{V} \times \mathcal{L} \to \mathcal{V}$.

They have these properties:

$$
\begin{aligned}
p(u : v) &\Rightarrow \text{ext}(p) = \{u, v\}, & a(u, v) &\Rightarrow \text{ext}(a) = \{u, v\}, \\
a(u, v) &\Rightarrow \text{ini}(a) = u, & a(u, v) &\Rightarrow \text{ter}(a) = v, \\
a(u, v) &\Rightarrow \text{twin}(u, a) = v, & a(u, v) &\Rightarrow \text{twin}(v, a) = u, \\
p(u : v) &\Rightarrow \text{twin}(u, p) = v.
\end{aligned}
$$

Example 4.1 Consider the LL baseball team in Figure 1.1. Also see Table 2.15 (in Section 2.2.1), which gives the binary matrix for the relation "best friend." We consider the arc between Tom and Frank: $a(\text{Tom, Frank})$. Here, $\text{ext}(a) = \{\text{Tom, Frank}\}$, $\text{ini}(a) = \text{Tom}$, $\text{ter}(a) = \text{Frank}$, and $\text{twin}(\text{Frank}, a) = \text{Tom}$. $\square$

We *extend* our notation for edges and arcs to all lines as follows: let $p \in \mathcal{L}$; then

$$p(u, v) := (p \in \mathcal{E} \wedge p(u : v)) \vee (p \in \mathcal{A} \wedge p(u, v)),$$

---

1 The relation is directed because of the way the sociometric question was asked. The ties between, for example, Frank and Ron are two arcs and are *not* a single edge.

2 These include $\{u, u\} = \{u\}$.

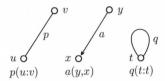

Figure 4.1. Lines.

the line *p joins* vertex u *to* vertex v, and

$$p(u\!:\!v) := p(u, v) \vee p(v, u),$$

the line *p joins* vertex u *with* vertex v.

We use the abbreviation

$$uLv := \exists p \in \mathcal{L} : p(u, v),$$

which essentially defines the *adjacency* relation. Elements u and v are adjacent if $p(u, v)$ belongs to $\mathcal{L}$.

Representations by graphs offer intuitive meanings for relations. This can be done pictorially, as in Figures 1.1 and 1.2 (provided the graph is not large). A continuous curve is used for each of its lines connecting the small circles representing its endpoints (see Figure 4.1). For an arc, we indicate its direction by an arrow on the curve. Often we call this representation of a graph a *picture of a graph*. On the right, q is a loop at t.

A graph **G** is *finite* if and only if the sets $\mathcal{V}$ and $\mathcal{L}$ are finite. All graphs considered in this book are finite unless otherwise noted. We denote the number of vertices by n, and the number of lines by m:

$$n = \mathrm{card}(\mathcal{V}) \qquad \text{and} \qquad m = \mathrm{card}(\mathcal{L}).$$

A graph **G** is *simple* if and only if for each pair of vertices $u, v \in \mathcal{V}$ (see Figure 4.2) the following hold:

- Either they are not endpoints of the same line; or
- $u = v$ and there is exactly one directed loop at u; or
- $u \neq v$ and there is exactly one edge and no arc with u, v as endpoints; or
- $u \neq v$ and there is at most one arc in each direction and no edge with u, v as endpoints.

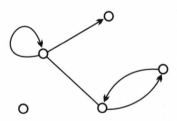

Figure 4.2. A simple graph.

Simple directed graphs are called also *relational* or *Berge* graphs. Overwhelmingly, social network analysts have focused their attention on simple graphs. In simple graphs, every line is uniquely determined by its endpoints and its type (directed or undirected). Therefore we can denote an edge with endpoints u and v by $(u : v)$ and an arc with initial vertex u and terminal vertex v by (u, v). The set of arcs $\mathcal{A}$ of a relational graph $\mathbf{G} = (\mathcal{V}, \emptyset, \mathcal{A})$ is in bijection with its adjacency relation (see Section 2.2):

$$R_A = \{(u, v) : \exists a \in \mathcal{A} : a(u, v)\} \in \mathbf{Rel}(\mathcal{V}, \mathcal{V}).$$

Example 4.2 Consider the relation in the following table:

	a	b	c	d	e	f
a	0	0	0	1	0	0
b	0	0	0	0	0	0
c	1	0	0	0	0	1
d	0	0	0	1	0	1
e	0	0	0	0	0	0
f	1	1	0	0	0	0

We can represent this relation by the graph in Figure 4.3. Note that each line drawn in the figure corresponds to a 1 contained in the relational matrix.

Consider the graph represented in Figure 4.3 and also focus on the matrix for this example. We obtain the list of sets of immediate successors by reading the rows of the table:

$$\begin{aligned} R(a) &= \{d\}, & R(d) &= \{d, f\}, \\ R(b) &= \emptyset, & R(e) &= \emptyset, \\ R(c) &= \{a, f\}, & R(f) &= \{a, b\}. \end{aligned}$$

We obtain the list of predecessors (see Section 3.2.3 for the definition of R^{-1}) by

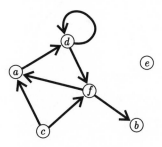

Figure 4.3. Graph of relation R.

reading the columns of the table:

$$R^{-1}(a) = \{c, f\}, \qquad R^{-1}(d) = \{a, d\},$$
$$R^{-1}(b) = \{f\}, \qquad R^{-1}(e) = \emptyset,$$
$$R^{-1}(c) = \emptyset, \qquad R^{-1}(f) = \{c, d\}.$$

Using N to denote $R \cup R^{-1}$, we see that the sets of neighbors are

$$N(a) = \{c, d, f\}, \qquad N(d) = \{a, d, f\},$$
$$N(b) = \{f\}, \qquad N(e) = \emptyset,$$
$$N(c) = \{a, f\}, \qquad N(f) = \{a, b, c, d\}. \quad \square$$

The representation of the binary relation by a graph, as shown in Figure 4.3, provides a visualization of the relation and can be used to support our intuitions about relations. Such pictures can also be misleading (see Chapter 6, Section 6.5.)

Lists of successors or neighbors are often used to represent graphs on files for use with computer programs.

Subgraphs. A graph $\mathbf{H} = (\mathcal{V}', \mathcal{A}', \mathcal{E}')$ is a *subgraph* of a graph $\mathbf{G} = (\mathcal{V}, \mathcal{E}, \mathcal{A})$, denoted by $\mathbf{H} \subseteq \mathbf{G}$, if and only if $\mathcal{V}' \subseteq \mathcal{V}$, $\mathcal{E}' \subseteq \mathcal{E}$, and $\mathcal{A}' \subseteq \mathcal{A}$. Note that since $\mathbf{H}$ is itself a graph, all endpoints of lines from $\mathcal{L}' = \mathcal{E}' \cup \mathcal{A}'$ should be in $\mathcal{V}'$, that is, $\text{ext}(\mathcal{L}') \subseteq \mathcal{V}'$. When $\mathcal{V}' = \mathcal{V}$, $\mathbf{H}$ is a *spanning subgraph* of $\mathbf{G}$.

Figure 4.4 shows a graph $\mathbf{G}$ and various subgraphs. The subgraph $\mathbf{H}$ is a spanning subgraph of $\mathbf{G}$.

Another type of subgraph is one that is *induced by a vertex set* $\mathcal{V}' \subseteq \mathcal{V}$:

$$\mathcal{L}' = \mathcal{L}(\mathcal{V}') = \{p \in \mathcal{L} : \exists u, v \in \mathcal{V}' : p(u : v)\}.$$

Given a set of vertices $\mathcal{V}'$, the subgraph induced by $\mathcal{V}'$ has all of the lines linking the nodes contained in $\mathcal{V}'$ that are in $\mathcal{L}$. In Figure 4.4, the subgraph I is induced by the vertex set $\{a, b, c, e, f\}$. The subgraph N is not induced by this vertex set because the edge $(c : e)$ is not in N.

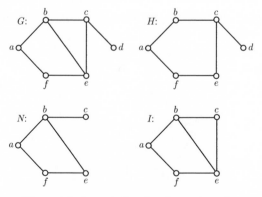

Figure 4.4. A graph $\mathbf{G}$ and various subgraphs.

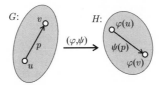

Figure 4.5. Homomorphism.

Subgraphs also can be *induced by a line set* $\mathcal{L}' \subseteq \mathcal{L}$:

$$\mathcal{V}' = \mathcal{V}(\mathcal{L}') = \{v \in \mathcal{V} : \exists p \in \mathcal{L}' \exists u \in \mathcal{V} : p(u\!:\!v)\} = \bigcup_{p \in \mathcal{L}'} \text{ext}(p) = \text{ext}\,\mathcal{L}'.$$

Given a set of lines $\mathcal{L}'$, all of the vertices joined by lines from $\mathcal{L}'$ must be in the vertex set, $\mathcal{V}'$.

Homomorphisms between graphs. In our intuitive discussion of blockmodeling in Chapter 1, we described how one smaller (and simpler) network could represent the essential structure of a larger network. The simpler network is an image of the larger structure. More formally, this kind of representation can be described in terms of *homomorphisms*. Let $\mathbf{G} = (\mathcal{V}, \mathcal{E}, \mathcal{A})$ and $\mathbf{H} = (\mathcal{V}', \mathcal{E}', \mathcal{A}')$ be graphs. A pair of mappings (φ, ψ), $\varphi \colon \mathcal{V} \to \mathcal{V}'$, and $\psi \colon \mathcal{L} \to \mathcal{L}'$ determines a *weak homomorphism* of graph $\mathbf{G}$ in graph $\mathbf{H}$ if and only if the following holds:

$$\forall u, v \in \mathcal{V} \,\forall p \in \mathcal{L} : (p(u\!:\!v) \Rightarrow \psi(p)(\varphi(u)\!:\!\varphi(v))).$$

In words, if u is mapped to $\varphi(u)$ and v is mapped to $\varphi(v)$ under φ and $p(u\!:\!v)$ is a line in $\mathbf{G}$, then the line $\psi(p)(\varphi(u)\!:\!\varphi(v))$ must be the image of $p(u\!:\!v)$ under the mapping ψ.

The pair of mappings (φ, ψ) determines a *strong homomorphism* of graph $\mathbf{G}$ in graph $\mathbf{H}$ if and only if the following holds

$$\forall u, v \in \mathcal{V} \,\forall p \in \mathcal{L} : (p(u, v) \Rightarrow \psi(p)(\varphi(u), \varphi(v))).$$

Under a *strong* homomorphism, direction matters and edges must be mapped to edges. If (some) edges are mapped to arcs – for example if the edge $p(u : v)$ is mapped to the arc $a(x, y)$ under ψ – the mapping is not a strong homomorphism since from $p(v, u)$ it follows $a(y, x)$.

A transformation of a graph $\mathbf{G} = (\mathcal{V}, \mathcal{E}, \mathcal{A})$ into its *undirected skeleton* $S(\mathbf{G}) = (\mathcal{V}, \mathcal{E}')$, where

$$\mathcal{E}' = \{(u\!:\!v) : u, v \in \mathcal{V}, u \neq v, \exists p \in \mathcal{L} : p(u\!:\!v)\},$$

is a weak homomorphism.

A similar transformation of a given graph $\mathbf{G} = (\mathcal{V}, \mathcal{E}, \mathcal{A})$ is to its *directed skeleton* a simple directed graph $DS(\mathbf{G}) = (\mathcal{V}, \mathcal{A}')$, where

$$\mathcal{A}' = \{(u, v) : u, v \in \mathcal{V} \wedge \exists p \in \mathcal{L} : p(u, v)\}$$

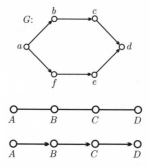

Figure 4.6. A weak and a strong homomorphic image of **G**.

is a homomorphism only for directed graphs since it assigns to each edge of **G** a pair of arcs in $DS(\mathbf{G})$.

As a further example, consider the graph in Figure 4.6. Let the mappings φ and ψ be

v	a	b	c	d	e	f
$\varphi(v)$	A	B	C	D	C	B

and

p	(a,b)	(a,f)	(b,c)	(c,d)	(e,d)	(f,e)
$\psi(p)$	$(A:B)$	$(A:B)$	$(B:C)$	$(C:D)$	$(C:D)$	$(B:C)$

The mapping pair (φ, ψ) is a weak homomorphism, as shown in the graph in Figure 4.6 (middle figure).

Suppose φ is the same but

p	(a,b)	(a,f)	(b,c)	(c,d)	(e,d)	(f,e)
$\psi(p)$	(A,B)	(A,B)	(B,C)	(C,D)	(C,D)	(B,C)

The pair of mappings, (φ, ψ), is a strong homomorphism, as shown in Figure 4.6 (bottom figure).

Isomorphism of two graphs ⊙. If the mappings (φ, ψ) are bijections and the implication $(\Rightarrow)$ in the condition in the definition of a homomorphism is replaced by the equivalence $(\Leftrightarrow)$ – the mappings determine an embedding – the graphs **G** and **H** are weakly (strongly) *isomorphic*. We write: $\mathbf{G} \sim \mathbf{H}$, that is, graphs **G** and **H** are weakly isomorphic, and $\mathbf{G} \approx \mathbf{H}$, that is, graphs **G** and **H** are strongly isomorphic. When an isomorphism (ϕ, ψ) maps a graph **G** to itself, it is called an *automorphism*.

For example,

v	a	b	c	d	e	f
$\varphi(v)$	a	f	e	d	c	b

determines an automorphism of the graph from Figure 4.6.

Let **Gph** be the set of all graphs. An *invariant* of a graph is a mapping $i :$ **Gph** $\to \mathbb{R}$ that is constant over isomorphic graphs. The number of vertices, the number of arcs, and the number of edges are all invariants for isomorphic graphs. Throughout the rest of this chapter, additional graph invariants are defined. We distinguish between a weak invariant,

$$\mathbf{G} \sim \mathbf{H} \Rightarrow i(\mathbf{G}) = i(\mathbf{H}),$$

and a strong invariant,

$$\mathbf{G} \approx \mathbf{H} \Rightarrow i(\mathbf{G}) = i(\mathbf{H}).$$

Equivalently, $i(\mathbf{G}) \neq i(\mathbf{H}) \Rightarrow \neg(\mathbf{G} \sim \mathbf{H})$ for a weak invariant and $i(\mathbf{G}) \neq i(\mathbf{H}) \Rightarrow \neg(\mathbf{G} \approx \mathbf{H})$ for strong invariants.[3] As a result, invariants have an important role in examining the isomorphism of two graphs. In the following paragraphs we define several invariants.

Invariants on families of graphs are called structural properties. Formally, we state the following: Let $\mathcal{F} \subseteq$ **Gph** be a family of graphs. A property $q: \mathcal{F} \to \mathbb{R}$ is *structural* on $\mathcal{F}$ iff

$$\forall \mathbf{G}, \mathbf{H} \in \mathcal{F} : (\mathbf{G} \approx \mathbf{H} \Rightarrow q(\mathbf{G}) = q(\mathbf{H})).$$

Similary, a vertex property $s(\mathbf{G}, v)$, $v \in \mathcal{V}(\mathbf{G})$ is structural on $\mathcal{F}$ iff

$$\forall \mathbf{G}, \mathbf{H} \in \mathcal{F}, v \in \mathcal{V} : (\mathbf{G} \approx \mathbf{H} \Rightarrow s(\mathbf{G}, v) = s(\mathbf{H}, \varphi(v)))$$

for every isomorphism (φ, ψ) between **G** and **H**.

If these conditions are satisfied only for a weak isomorphism ($\sim$), the property is said to be *weakly structural*.

Stars. One early intuition in the application of graph theoretic ideas to social networks was to count the number of lines incident at a particular vertex. These lines can be counted in categories – for example, arcs and edges. We can also distinguish, and count, lines coming into vertices or out from vertices. The numbers of lines of selected types (e.g., arc or edge, incoming or outgoing, or all) with endpoints in a given set of vertices are termed *line-degrees*. Formally, we define these counts by using stars.

A star at a vertex $v \in \mathcal{V}$ is the set of all lines having v as an endpoint:

$$\mathcal{L}(v) = \{p : v \in \text{ext}(p)\}.$$

---

3 A weak invariant does not consider the direction of lines, whereas the strong invariant is based on preserving the directions of lines.

Figure 4.7. Star.

This is illustrated in Figure 4.7, where the solid circle represents v. We can define other types of stars:

$$\mathcal{L}_0(v) = \{p : \text{ext}(p) = \{v\}\},$$

$$\mathcal{E}(v) = \{p : p \in \mathcal{E} \wedge v \in \text{ext}(p)\},$$

$$\mathcal{A}_{\text{ter}}(v) = \{p : p \in \mathcal{A} \wedge \text{ter}(p) = v\},$$

$$\mathcal{A}_{\text{ini}}(v) = \{p : p \in \mathcal{A} \wedge \text{ini}(p) = v\}.$$

Here $\mathcal{L}_0(v)$ is the set of loops at v and $\mathcal{E}(v)$ is the set of edges incident with v. In addition, $\mathcal{A}_{\text{ter}}(v)$ is the set of arcs incident *to* v, and $\mathcal{A}_{\text{ini}}(v)$ is the set of the arcs incident *from* v.

Degrees. In most discussions of degree centrality, degree is implicitly considered as a property of vertices. There is a more general language applicable for all graphs – and not only simple graphs. Using stars, we can, for example, define the degree of all lines at the vertex u:

$$\deg(u) = \text{card}(\mathcal{L}(u)).$$

The degree of all lines between vertices u and v is

$$\deg(u, v) = \text{card}(\mathcal{L}(u) \cap \mathcal{L}(v)).$$

The degree of all lines to vertex u from vertex v is

$$\text{indeg}(u, v) = \text{card}((\mathcal{E}(u) \cap \mathcal{E}(v)) \cup (\mathcal{A}_{\text{ter}}(u) \cap \mathcal{A}_{\text{ini}}(v))).$$

This is a count of both edges between u and v and the arcs from v to u. The degree of all arcs from vertex u to vertex v is

$$\text{outdeg}_A(u, v) = \text{card}(\mathcal{A}_{\text{ini}}(u) \cap \mathcal{A}_{\text{ter}}(v)).$$

The degrees are structural properties.

Several relations hold among degrees. These include

$$\deg(u, v) = \deg(v, u), \qquad \text{indeg}(u, v) = \text{outdeg}(v, u)$$

and

$$\deg(u) = \sum_{v \in \mathcal{V}} \deg(u, v).$$

Also,

$$\sum_{v \in \mathcal{V}} \text{indeg}_A(v) = \sum_{v \in \mathcal{V}} \text{outdeg}_A(v) = \text{card}(\mathcal{A}).$$

When we want to express explicitly that some number refers to a given graph **G**, we append the graph name to it. For example, $\deg(u, v; \mathbf{G})$ denotes the degree of lines between vertices u and v in graph **G**.

We can look at the set of lines with an endpoint in a vertex u in two ways. The first is globally: we see the entire line. The second is locally: we see halflines, that is, we see only a segment of the line – in which case we count loops twice. To express the second way of counting, we introduce the notion of *valency*,

$$\text{val}(u) = \deg(u) + \deg_0(u),$$

where $\deg_0(u) = \text{card}(\mathcal{L}_0(u))$ is the number of loops at vertex u. It is easy to see that

$$\sum_{u \in \mathcal{V}} \text{val}(u) = 2m.$$

Each line (edge or arc) has two vertices and loops are counted twice. This leads immediately to a result that is known as the *handshaking lemma*.

Theorem 4.1 *In a graph there is always an even number of vertices of odd valency.*

Using valencies, we can introduce two graph invariants. They are *minimum degree*,

$$\delta(\mathbf{G}) = \min_{v \in \mathcal{V}} \text{val}(v),$$

and *maximum degree*,

$$\Delta(\mathbf{G}) = \max_{v \in \mathcal{V}} \text{val}(v).$$

Neighbors. Two vertices are neighboring iff they are the endpoints of the same line. As in the case of stars, we can introduce several sets of neighbors of a given vertex.

set of (proper) neighbors of vertex v : $\text{ext}(\mathcal{L}(v)) \setminus \{v\}$;
set of (direct) predecessors of vertex v : $\text{ext}(\mathcal{E}(v) \cup \mathcal{A}_{\text{ter}}(v))$;
set of (direct) successors of vertex v : $\text{ext}(\mathcal{E}(v) \cup \mathcal{A}_{\text{ini}}(v))$.

The cardinalities of these sets are termed *vertex-degrees*. In simple graphs, the line-degrees are equal to the corresponding vertex-degrees.

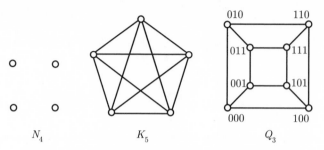

Figure 4.8. A null graph, a complete graph, and a cube.

4.1.1   Examples of graphs

In our discussion of blockmodeling (in Chapters 1, 6, and 7), we use some special types of graphs or subgraphs. They include those defined in this section.

The *null* graph on n vertices is $N_n = (\mathcal{V}, \emptyset)$, card($\mathcal{V}$) = n. These graphs contain no lines; the degree of all vertices is 0. The graph N_4 is shown in Figure 4.8. In Chapter 6, these will be used as *null blocks*. The null graph on a single vertex is called trivial.

The *complete* graph on n vertices is $K_n = (\mathcal{V}, \mathcal{E})$, card($\mathcal{V}$) = n, $\mathcal{E} = \{(u:v) : u, v \in \mathcal{V} \wedge u \neq v\}$. Here card($\mathcal{E}$) = $\frac{1}{2}n(n-1)$. Figure 4.8 also shows K_5. Clearly the cliques discussed in Chapter 1 are complete (sub)graphs, and we will use complete subgraphs as (perfect) one-blocks in Chapter 6. The *directed complete* graph, DK_n, on n vertices is defined as $DK_n = (\mathcal{V}, \mathcal{A})$, card($\mathcal{V}$) = n, $\mathcal{A} = \{(u, v) : u, v \in \mathcal{V}\}$. Here card($\mathcal{A}$) = n^2.

The third graph, Q_3, in Figure 4.8 is a three-dimensional *cube*. (Generally, Q_k denotes the k-dimensional cube graph.) These kinds of graphs are applied in coding theory and the vertices are binary words, for example 010 or 101. Intuitively, an edge between vertices exists where there is a single binary difference in the word. Thus, in Figure 4.8, the vertex 000 has edges with the vertices 001, 010, and 100 only. Similarly, vertex 111 has edges with the vertices 011, 110, and 101 only.

When all vertices of a graph have the same valency r, we say that the graph is r-*regular*. A three-regular graph is usually called a *cubic* graph. See Figure 4.9 for

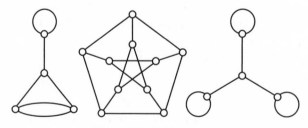

Figure 4.9. Cubic graphs.

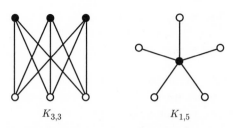

$K_{3,3}$ $K_{1,5}$

Figure 4.10. Complete bipartite graphs.

some examples. The Everett graph (Figure 6.1) is a cubic graph. Note also that N_4 is zero regular, K_5 is four-regular, and Q_3 is cubic.

A graph $\mathbf{G} = (\mathcal{V}, \mathcal{L})$ is *bipartite* if and only if the vertex-set can be partitioned into two sets X and Y such that each line has its endpoints in both sets:

$$\forall p \in \mathcal{L} \, \exists u \in X \, \exists v \in Y : p(u : v).$$

We consider bipartite graphs in Chapter 6 (Section 6.1.5) and extend them to k-partite graphs and in Chapter 8 on two-mode blockmodeling. A simple undirected graph $((X, Y), \mathcal{E})$, $r = \mathrm{card}(X)$, $s = \mathrm{card}(Y)$, with edge-set $\mathcal{E} = \{(u : v) : u \in X, v \in Y\}$, is called a *complete bipartite* graph and denoted by $K_{r,s}$. Figure 4.10 shows two complete bipartite graphs $K_{3,3}$ and $K_{1,5}$. The graph $K_{1,n}$ is called also an $(n + 1)$ *star*.

Cliques. A clique in a graph is a maximal complete subgraph. This means that a subset $W \subseteq V$ determines a clique iff the subgraph $(W, \mathcal{L}(W))$ induced by W is a complete graph and there is no vertex in $V \setminus W$ that is linked by edges to all vertices of W.

We see that $\omega(\mathbf{G})$, the *clique number* of a graph $\mathbf{G}$, equals the size of the largest clique in graph $\mathbf{G}$. This is another graph invariant.

In empirical applications, the notion of clique is usually too stringent. There were several attempts to "soften" it. For example, a k clique of graph $\mathbf{G} = (V, \mathcal{L})$ is a clique in the graph $(V, R_{\mathcal{L}}^{(k)})$. All vertices in a k clique can reach others on W in at most k steps. Using the idea of restricting a relation (introduced in Section 3.2.1), we find that a *k-plex* is a maximal subgraph $\mathbf{H} = (W, R_{\mathcal{L}}|W)$ on $n_{\mathbf{H}} = \mathrm{card}(W)$ vertices such that, for every $v \in W$, it holds $n_{\mathbf{H}} - \mathrm{deg}_{\mathbf{H}}(v) \leq k$. In other words, at each vertex at most k lines are missing. A one-plex is a clique.

Another algorithmic objection for the use of cliques is the result of work by Moon and Moser (1965), who showed that the maximum possible number of cliques in a graph grows exponentially with the number of vertices.

k cores and p cores. A k core, or a core of order k, in a graph $\mathbf{G} = (V, \mathcal{L})$ is a maximal subgraph $\mathbf{H}_k = (W_k, \mathcal{L}(W_k))$ such that for each $v \in W$ it holds $\mathrm{deg}_{\mathbf{H}}(v) \geq k$. The core of maximum order is also called a *main* core: Its order is called a *core number* of $\mathbf{G}$ and is denoted by $\mathrm{core}(\mathbf{G})$. This is another graph invariant.

A core $\mathbf{H}_k$ need not be connected. In a graph, k-cores are nested: $i < j \Rightarrow W_j \subseteq W_i$. There exists a simple and efficient algorithm to determine the hierarchy of cores. It is based on recursive deletion of all vertices of degree less than k, $k = 1, 2, \ldots$.

Replacing deg in the definition by indeg or outdeg, we obtain k-incores and k-outcores. We can obtain several other types of cores by first transforming graph $\mathbf{G}$ and applying the notion to the transformed graph.

A p-core, $p \in [0, 1]$, in a graph $\mathbf{G} = (V, \mathcal{L})$ is a maximal subgraph $\mathbf{H}_p = (W_p, \mathcal{L}(W_p))$ such that for each $v \in W$ it holds $\deg_{\mathrm{H}}(v) \geq p \cdot \deg_{\mathrm{G}}(v)$ and that each of its connected components is two-connected.

Again we can replace deg in the definition by indeg or outdeg. There also exists a simple and efficient algorithm to determine p-cores.

Triads. For three different vertices $u, v, w \in \mathcal{V}$ of the graph $\mathbf{G} = (\mathcal{V}, \mathcal{L})$, the subgraph $\mathbf{T}(u, v, w)$ induced by them is called a triad.

In social network analysis we usually deal with relational graphs without loops. For such graphs, there are 16 isomorphism classes of triads presented in Figure 4.11,

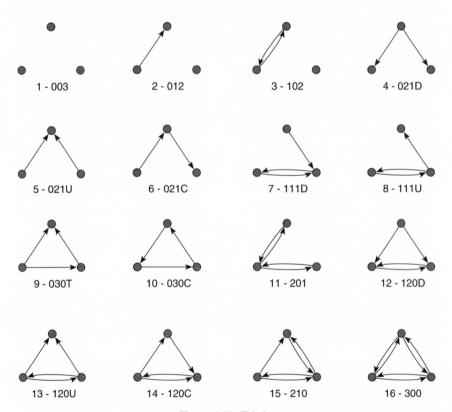

Figure 4.11. Triads.

where they are labeled 1 through 16. The additional labeling comes from the practice of counting the number of mutual (M) ties, the number of asymmetric (A) ties, and the number of null (N) ties. These labels are called MAN labels. In the first isomorphism class, 003 denotes the presence of only three null ties. For the second isomorphism class, 012 denotes the presence of zero M ties, one A tie, and two N ties. All the remaining labels can be read in the same fashion. There are some distinct isomorphism classes whose MAN counts are identical (e.g., 021). When this happens, a fourth character is used to distinguish the isomorphism classes. They are U (used for up), D (used for down), C (used for the presence of a cycle), and T (used for the presence of a transitive triple). The vector of their cardinalities is called the *triad census*. There exist $\binom{n}{3}$ triads in a given graph with n vertices.

4.1.2   *Traveling on a graph*

Here we define the ideas of walk, path, and length of a walk or path; on the basis of these concepts, we define several types of connectedness. These notions were mentioned briefly in Section 1.2.1 and are used frequently in the chapters following this one.

A finite sequence of vertices and lines of graph $\mathbf{G} = (\mathcal{V}, \mathcal{L})$,

$$S = v_0, s_1, v_1, s_2, v_2, \ldots, s_k, v_k,$$

is a walk from v_0 to v_k on $\mathbf{G}$ iff

$$\bigwedge_{i=1}^{k} s_i(v_{i-1}, v_i).$$

The number k is the *length* of the walk S, and we write $|S| = k$. Vertex v_0 is the *initial* and vertex v_k the *terminal* vertex of the walk S. When needed, we denote this walk by $S(v_0, v_k)$. When $v_0 = v_k$, the walk is *closed* and is called a *circuit*. The walk is *simple* and called a *trail* iff all its lines are different; and it is an *elementary* walk if and only if all its vertices (except the initial and terminal vertices) are different. A nonelementary walk is shown in Figure 4.12, where $v_i = v_j$ is on the walk twice. Each elementary walk is also simple.

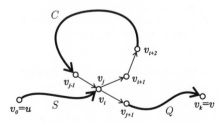

Figure 4.12. Nonelementary walk.

The length of a (proper) elementary walk cannot exceed $|\mathcal{V}| - 1$ nor $|\mathcal{V}|$ in the case of a closed walk. The length of a simple walk cannot exceed $|\mathcal{L}|$.

A simple walk on $\mathbf{G} = (\mathcal{V}, \mathcal{L})$ that contains all of the lines from $\mathcal{L}$ is called a *Eulerian* walk, and an elementary walk that contains all of the vertices from $\mathcal{V}$ is called a *Hamiltonian* walk.

When the sequence S satisfies a weaker condition,

$$\bigwedge_{i=1}^{n} s_i(v_{i-1} : v_i),$$

it is called a *semiwalk* or *chain*. The line between v_{i-1} and v_i need not be oriented from v_{i-1} to v_i. All the concepts introduced for walks can be defined also for semiwalks. If $S(u, v)$ is a semiwalk from u to v, then the reversed sequence $\tilde{S}(u, v)$ is a semiwalk from v to u.

In the set $\mathcal{S}^*(\mathbf{G})$ of all walks for a graph $\mathbf{G}$, we can define the operation of *concatenation*, $\circ$, of walks as follows. If $v_k = u_0$, then we call the *concatenation* of walks $S = v_0, s_1, v_1, s_2, \ldots, s_k, v_k$ and $Q = u_0, q_1, u_1, q_2, \ldots, q_l, u_l$ the walk

$$S \circ Q = v_0, s_1, v_1, s_2, \ldots, s_k, v_k (= u_0), q_1, u_1, q_2, \ldots, q_l, u_l.$$

The idea is that the terminal vertex of one walk is the intitial vertex for the next walk. Some properties of concatenation $\circ$ as an operator follow. It is associative:

$$S \circ (Q \circ T) = (S \circ Q) \circ T.$$

For two walks, S and Q,

$$|S \circ Q| = |S| + |Q|.$$

If C is a closed walk and $S \circ C \circ Q$ is a walk, then $S \circ Q$ is also a walk (see Figure 4.12). From this property, we see that that if there exists a walk from u to v, then there also exists an elementary walk from u to v.

Sometimes it is useful to introduce a null walk in the vertex $v : Z_v = v$. We have

$$|Z_v| = 0 \quad \text{and} \quad Z_v \circ S(v, u) = S(v, u) \circ Z_u = S(v, u).$$

Walks and semiwalks connect nonneighboring vertices of a graph. In doing so, they determine several types of *connectedness*. The vertex v is *reachable* from the vertex u if there exists a walk from u to v. Vertices u and v are

- strongly connected if u and v are mutually reachable;
- unilaterally connected if u is reachable from v *or* v is reachable from u;
- weakly connected if there exists a semiwalk from u to v; and
- disconnected if they are not weakly connected.

These ideas can also be extended to graphs. A graph $\mathbf{G}$ is (weakly) strongly connected if and only if each pair of its vertices is (weakly) strongly connected.

A connected two-regular undirected graph is called a *cycle*. A cycle on n vertices is denoted by C_n. Figure 4.13 shows C_5. If we delete any edge from the cycle we obtain a *path*. A path on n vertices is denoted by P_n. Figure 4.13 also shows P_4.

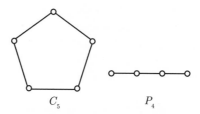

Figure 4.13. A cycle and a path.

Note that if the first and last vertices are joined by an edge, a cycle C_4 would result. If we add a new vertex to a cycle C_n and connect it by an edge with each of the vertices on the cycle, we get a *wheel*: W_{n+1}. See W_6 in Figure 4.14. If we orient (assign directions to some edges) a cycle C_n, we obtain a *semicycle*. A strongly connected directed semicycle is called a *directed cycle* (where all arcs point in the same direction) and is denoted by DC_n. In a similar way, we can also introduce *semipaths* and *directed paths*.

The subgraph induced by an elementary walk is (weakly) isomorphic to a path or a cycle. We often use terms such as Hamiltonian path or cycle for it.

A graph containing no semicycle as a subgraph is called a *semiforest*. If it is also connected, it is called a *semitree*. An undirected semitree is a *tree*. An example of a tree is the graph T shown in Figure 4.14.

Theorem 4.2 *A graph* **G** *is weakly connected if and only if it contains a spanning semitree.*

A variety of graph properties can be defined through the idea of deleting vertices or deleting lines (edges and arcs).

The *vertex connectivity* κ of graph **G** is the minimum number of vertices that have to be deleted, together with the incident lines, from a graph to obtain a disconnected graph or a trivial graph N_1. For the star shown in Figure 4.7, the value of κ is 1.

The *line connectivity* λ of graph **G** is the minimum number of lines that have to be deleted from a graph to obtain either a disconnected graph or a trivial graph N_1.

Whitney (1932) proved this inequality: $\kappa(\mathbf{G}) \le \lambda(\mathbf{G}) \le \delta(\mathbf{G})$.

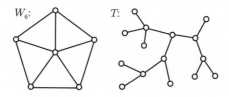

Figure 4.14. A wheel and a tree.

A k-vertex-cutset is called the set C of k vertices of the graph $\mathbf{G}$ for which the graph induced by the set $\mathcal{V} \setminus C$ is disconnected or is trivial.

A k-line-cutset is called the set C of k lines of the graph $\mathbf{G}$ for which the graph induced by the set $\mathcal{L} \setminus C$ is disconnected or is trivial.

A graph $\mathbf{G}$ is k-connected if and only if $\kappa(\mathbf{G}) \geq k$ and is k-line-connected if and only if $\lambda(\mathbf{G}) \geq k$.

The connection between connectivity and semiwalks in a graph is given by the following variant of Menger's theorem.

Theorem 4.3 (Whitney) *A graph* $\mathbf{G}$ *is k-vertex/edge connected if and only if each pair of its vertices is connected by at least k-vertex/line disjoint semiwalks.*

Geodesics. For a given pair of vertices $u, v \in \mathcal{V}$, a shortest path from u to v is called a *geodesic* from u to v and its length the *geodesic distance* from u to v and denoted $d(u, v)$. If v is not reachable from u, then we set $d(u, v) = \infty$.

The subgraph $\mathbf{Geo}(u, v)$ induced by all geodesics from u to v is called a *geodesic subgraph* from u to v. Let w, t lie in the same order on a geodesic from u to v; then $w, t \in \mathcal{V}(\mathbf{Geo}(u, v))$ and $\mathbf{Geo}(w, t) \subseteq \mathbf{Geo}(u, v)$.

For the geodesic distance, it holds $d(u, w) + d(w, v) \geq d(u, v)$, $d(u, v) \geq 0$ and $d(u, v) = 0 \Leftrightarrow u = v$. Also note that, in general, $d(u, v)$ can be different from $d(v, u)$. In undirected or symmetric directed graphs, $d(u, v) = d(v, u)$ for all $u, v \in \mathcal{V}$ (d is a distance) and also $\mathbf{Geo}(u, v) = \mathbf{Geo}(v, u)$.

The *eccentricity* of a vertex v is

$$e(v) = \max_{u \in \mathcal{V}} d(v, u),$$

the *radius* of a graph $\mathbf{G}$ is

$$r(\mathbf{G}) = \min_{v \in \mathcal{V}} e(v),$$

and the *diameter* of a graph $\mathbf{G}$ is

$$D(\mathbf{G}) = \max_{v \in \mathcal{V}} e(v).$$

For a strongly connected graph $\mathbf{G}$, we have $r(\mathbf{G}) \leq D(\mathbf{G}) \leq 2r(\mathbf{G})$ and $D(\mathbf{G}) \leq n - 1$.

A vertex v is a *central vertex* if $e(v) = r(\mathbf{G})$. The set of all central vertices $C(\mathbf{G}) = \{v : e(v) = r(\mathbf{G})\}$ is the (geodesic) *center* of graph $\mathbf{G}$.

Let $v \in \mathcal{V}$ be a vertex such that every other vertex of $\mathbf{G}$ is reachable from it. Then the sets

$$\mathcal{V}_k = \{u \in \mathcal{V} : d(v, u) = k\}, \ k \leq e(v)$$

form a partition of $\mathcal{V}$ with the property that, if $\mathbf{G}$ is undirected, all links of $\mathbf{G}$ are only inside sets $\mathcal{V}_k$ and between the consecutive sets,

$$p(u, w) \wedge u \in \mathcal{V}_k \Rightarrow w \in \mathcal{V}_k \cup \mathcal{V}_{k+1},$$

or, in the case of a general graph,

$$p(u, w) \wedge w \in \mathcal{V}_k \Rightarrow u \in \mathcal{V}_i, i \geq k - 1;$$

that is, only backward arcs can jump across levels.

4.1.3 Graph coloring

The graph coloring problem can be stated as follows. If the vertices $\mathcal{V}$ of a given undirected graph $\mathbf{G} = (\mathcal{V}, \mathcal{E})$ have to be colored such that no edge has both ends colored with the same color, what is the smallest number of different colors needed to color the graph?

This is one of the basic graph theory problems, and several other problems can be reduced to it.

Let $\mathbf{G} = (\mathcal{V}, \mathcal{E})$ be a simple undirected graph and C a set of colors. A *coloring* of $\mathbf{G}$ is a mapping $c : \mathcal{V} \to C$ that satisfies the condition

$$\forall u, v \in \mathcal{V} : ((u : v) \in \mathcal{E} \Rightarrow c(u) \neq c(v)).$$

The *spectrum* of a coloring, c, is the set of used colors $c(\mathcal{V})$. Its cardinality – the number of used colors – is denoted by

$$\chi(c; \mathbf{G}) = \mathrm{card}(c(\mathcal{V})).$$

A graph $\mathbf{G}$ is r-colorable iff there exists a coloring c such that $\chi(c; \mathbf{G}) \leq r$. Of special interest is a graph invariant

$$\chi(\mathbf{G}) = \min_{c \text{ is a coloring}} \chi(c; \mathbf{G})$$

called the *chromatic number* of the graph $\mathbf{G}$. We also say that the graph $\mathbf{G}$ is χ-chromatic.

Because the labels of colors are not important, we can select some standard set of colors, for example $C_n = 1, \ldots, n$.

Chromatic number. Directly from the definition of $\chi(\mathbf{G})$, we have the following.

1. $\chi(\mathbf{G}) \leq \chi(c; \mathbf{G}) \leq \mathrm{card}(\mathcal{V})$.
2. $\mathbf{H} \subseteq \mathbf{G} \Rightarrow \chi(c; \mathbf{H}) \leq \chi(c; \mathbf{G})$.
3. Let $\mathbf{G}_i$ be the connected components of the graph $\mathbf{G}$; then $\chi(c; \mathbf{G}) = \max_i \chi(c; \mathbf{G}_i)$.
4. $\chi(\mathbf{G}) \leq \Delta(\mathbf{G}) + 1$.
5. $\chi(\mathbf{G}) \leq \mathrm{core}(G) + 1$.

If we apply Steps 2 and 3 on an optimal coloring c^*, $\chi(c^*; \mathbf{G}) = \chi(\mathbf{G})$, we get

2′. $\mathbf{H} \subseteq \mathbf{G} \Rightarrow \chi(\mathbf{H}) \leq \chi(\mathbf{G})$.
3′. $\chi(\mathbf{G}) = \max_i \chi(\mathbf{G}_i)$.

From Step 2′ it follows that

$$\chi(\mathbf{G}) \geq \omega(\mathbf{G}),$$

where $\omega(\mathbf{G})$ is the clique number of the graph $\mathbf{G}$ – the size of the largest clique in $\mathbf{G}$. The following equality holds for a complete graph: $\chi(K_n) = \omega(K_n) = n$.

Theorem 4.4 (König) $\chi(G) \leq 2$ *iff the graph $\mathbf{G}$ contains no odd cycle.*

Theorem 4.5 (Brooks)   *In a connected graph $\mathbf{G}$ different from the complete graph or the odd cycle, with $\Delta(\mathbf{G}) \geq 3$,*

$$\chi(\mathbf{G}) \leq \Delta(\mathbf{G}).$$

Tutte showed that graphs exist with $\omega(\mathbf{G}) = 2$ and $\chi(\mathbf{G})$ arbitrarily large (see Chartrand and Oellerman 1992:309). Erdös (1959, 1961) and Lovász (1968) proved that, for any pair of natural numbers r and s, there exists an r-chromatic graph in which the girth, that is, the length of the shortest cycle, is greater than s.

An interesting view on $\chi(\mathbf{G})$ also provides the following theorem.

Theorem 4.6 (Roy, Gallai)   *Let $\mathbf{G}' = (\mathcal{V}, \mathcal{A}(\mathcal{E}))$ be a directed graph obtained from the graph $\mathbf{G} = (\mathcal{V}, \mathcal{E})$ by arbitrarily directing its edges. Let k be the length of the longest simple walk on $\mathbf{G}'$; then*

$$\chi(\mathbf{G}) \leq k + 1.$$

A *planar* graph is one that can be represented by a picture in a plane without any crossing of the curves representing the lines. In 1976, Appel and Haken, using a computer, gave a positive answer to a more than 100-year-old four-color problem: Every planar graph can be properly colored with at most four colors (Appel and Haken 1977a, 1977b). The four-color theorem was the first theorem with a proof so large that a human mathematician was not able to check it in a standard way.

Coloring algorithms ▷. Theoretical results about the complexity of the algorithms (Karp 1972; Aho, Hopcroft, and Ullman 1976) showed that the coloring problem is an NP-complete problem (no convenient method is known).

Algorithms exist that can produce in a reasonable amount of time (some days) minimal colorings for graphs with up to 100 vertices. What about the larger graphs? In general we have to be satisfied with some good, but not necessarily minimal, coloring.

Most of the coloring procedures for large graphs are an elaboration of the idea of sequential coloring: In the order determined by a permutation of vertices, color the vertices with the (lowest) for a current vertex free color – color not yet used for its neighbors. For every graph there exists a permutation that yields, by using sequential coloring, a minimal coloring.

4.2   TYPES OF BINARY RELATIONS

In this section, we return to our discussion of binary relations and present some of their properties formally. We then provide an interesting and useful extension of a relation in which the extended relation (a closure) has some required property not present in the original relation.

4.2.1 Properties of relations

There are many properties of binary relations. For each of the following properties, the standard definition is also expressed with the use of operations on relations and followed by the interpretation in graph-theoretic terms.

Let $R \in \mathbf{Rel}(A, A)$. This can also be viewed as the relational graph $\mathbf{G} = (A, R)$. The relation R is said to be *reflexive* if and only if

$$\forall x \in A : xRx, \qquad\qquad I \subseteq R.$$

The relational graph has a loop at every vertex.

It is said to be *irreflexive* if and only if

$$\forall x \in A : \neg xRx, \qquad\qquad R \cap I = \emptyset.$$

Every vertex of the relational graph has no loop.

It is *symmetric* if and only if

$$\forall x, y \in A : (xRy \Rightarrow yRx), \qquad\qquad R = R^{-1}.$$

All arcs in the relational graph are in reciprocating pairs.

It is *asymmetric* if and only if

$$\forall x, y \in A : \neg(xRy \wedge yRx), \qquad\qquad R \cap R^{-1} = \emptyset.$$

The relational graph has no loops, and no arc is in a reciprocating pair.

It is *antisymmetric* if and only if

$$\forall x, y \in A : (xRy \wedge yRx \Rightarrow x = y), \qquad\qquad R \cap R^{-1} \subseteq I.$$

No arc in the relational graph is in a pair. Loops are permitted.

It is *transitive* if and only if

$$\forall x, y, z \in A : (xRy \wedge yRz \Rightarrow xRz), \qquad\qquad R^2 \subseteq R.$$

If in the relational graph we can reach a vertex from another vertex in two steps, we can reach it also in one step.

It is *intransitive* if and only if

$$\forall x, y, z \in A : (xRy \wedge yRz \Rightarrow \neg xRz), \qquad\qquad R^2 \cap R = \emptyset.$$

If in the relational graph we can reach a vertex from another vertex in two steps, we *cannot* reach it also in one step.

It is *comparable* if and only if[4]

$$\forall x, y \in A : (x \neq y \Rightarrow xRy \vee yRx), \qquad\qquad T \setminus I \subseteq R \cup R^{-1}.$$

Each pair of different vertices is an endpoint-set of an arc: if xRy is not in the graph, yRx must be present.

---

4   $T = A \times A$; see Section 3.2.

It is strictly comparable if and only if

$$\forall x, y \in A : (xRy \vee yRx), \qquad\qquad R \cup R^{-1} = T.$$

The relational graph has a loop in every vertex and each pair of different vertices is an endpoint-set of an arc.

4.2.2   Closures

In general, relations need not have any of the properties listed in Section 4.2.1. For example, a binary relation need not have a specific property, say, transitivity. We can try to extend a given relation R so that the new (extended) relation does have the specific property. If the smallest such relation exists, and is uniquely defined, we call it a closure of R with respect to the property. For example, if the extended relation is transitive, we will call it the transitive closure of R.

Let $P(R)$ be a property of relations and $R \in \mathbf{Rel}(A, A)$. The relation $S \in \mathbf{Rel}(A, A)$ is a P closure of R if and only if it satisfies these conditions:

$$R \subseteq S,$$

$$P(S),$$

$$\forall Q \in \mathbf{Rel}(A, A) : ((R \subseteq Q) \wedge P(Q) \Rightarrow S \subseteq Q).$$

In words, R is contained within S; S has the property P; and, if Q is another relation containing R with this property, S is contained in Q. But because the P closure of a relation R is unique, and if S is the P closure of R, S is the smallest relation containing R with the property P. Evidently, a relation R has the property P if and only if it is its own P closure.

The following is clear.

Theorem 4.7   *The relation* $\hat{R} := R \cup R^{-1}$ *is a symmetric closure of the relation R.*

One of the most studied properties of binary relations is transitivity, for social networks (both human and nonhuman) are said to exhibit transitivity. For example, let R be the relation "friend of." If xRy and yRz, then there is an increased likelihood (beyond chance) that xRz. Methods for determining if a relation is transitive (and measuring the transitivity of a binary relation) are useful. The rest of this section focuses on this issue.

We start by observing that if the relation R is transitive, we have for every $k \in \mathbb{N}^+$, $R^k \subseteq R$. We next introduce two new relations, $R^\star$ and $\overline{R}$, that are based on the relation R:

$$xR^\star y := \exists k \in \mathbb{N} : xR^k y,$$

$$x\overline{R}y := \exists k \in \mathbb{N}^+ : xR^k y,$$

or, equivalently,

$$R^\star = \bigcup_{k\in\mathbb{N}} R^k \quad \text{and} \quad \overline{R} = \bigcup_{k\in\mathbb{N}^+} R^k.$$

The only difference between these relations is that k is restricted to the positive integers for $\overline{R}$. Several interesting properties hold for these two relations.

$$
\begin{array}{ll}
R^k \cup R^\star = R^\star, k \geq 0, & R^k \cup \overline{R} = \overline{R}, k > 0, \\
R^\star \quad\;\; = I \cup \overline{R}, & \overline{R} \quad\;\; = R * R^\star = R^\star * R, \\
R^\star * R^\star = R^\star, & R^k * R^\star = R^\star * R^k, k \geq 0, \\
(R^\star)^\star \;\; = R^\star, & (R^\star)^{-1} = (R^{-1})^\star, \\
R^\star \cup S^\star \subseteq (R \cup S)^\star, & \overline{R} \cup \overline{S} \subseteq \overline{(R \cup S)}.
\end{array}
$$

If the relation R is transitive, we have also

$$\overline{R} = R, \qquad R^\star = I \cup R,$$

and, for R, S reflexive,

$$(R \cup S)^\star = (R * S)^\star.$$

The relations R^k, $R^\star$, and $\overline{R}$ are important tools for the analysis of the connectivity structure of the relation R. Their meaning stems from the following theorems.

Theorem 4.8 *The relation $\overline{R}$ is a transitive closure of R and $R^\star$ is a transitive and reflexive closure of relation R.*

Theorem 4.9

a. $x R^k y$ if and only if, in the graph $\mathbf{G} = (A, R)$, there exists a walk of length k from x to y.
b. $x R^\star y$ if and only if, in the graph $\mathbf{G} = (A, R)$, there exists a walk from x to y.
c. $x \overline{R} y$ if and only if, in the graph $\mathbf{G} = (A, R)$, there exists a nonnull walk from x to y.

4.2.3 Computing the transitive closure ▷

For programmers, we need to be able to compute the closures $R^\star$ and $\overline{R}$ efficiently. Since $R^\star = I \cup \overline{R}$, we can restrict our attention to computing the reflexive closure $\overline{R}$.

One possibility for computing $R^\star$ is given by the following property.

Proposition 4.10 *Let $R \in \mathbf{Rel}(A, A)$, where A is a finite set. Then*

$$R^\star = \bigcup_{i=0}^{s} R^i = R^{(s)} = (I \cup R)^s, \qquad s \geq |A| - 1.$$

We can obtain $R^\star$ by computing the sequence $(I \cup R)^{2^k}$, $k = 1, 2, \ldots$.

This algorithm is not the best possible one. A much more efficient algorithm (with many fathers, such as Kleene, Warshall, Floyd and Roy) is as follows.

If we represent the relation R with its matrix $\mathbf{B}(R)$,

var b : **array** $[1..n, 1..n]$ **of** *boolean*;

then the following program segment (in PASCAL)

for $j := 1$ **to** n **do for** $i := 1$ **to** n **do if** $b[i, j]$ **then**
    for $k := 1$ **to** n **do** $b[i, k] := b[i, k]$ **or** $b[j, k]$;

transforms the matrix into the matrix $\mathbf{B}(\overline{R})$ of transitive closure $\overline{R}$.

This procedure has a variant that can be implemented by using bitwise operations. Suppose that the relation is represented (by rows) by the table of sets of direct successors of vertices:

var r : **array** $[1..n]$ **of set of** $1, \ldots, n$;

then the procedure can be written in this form:

for $j := 1$ **to** n **do for** $i := 1$ **to** n **do**
    if j **in** $r[i]$ **then** $r[i] := r[i] + r[j]$.

4.2.4 Special elements

In analyses of a relation, special elements of a set A with respect to the relation $R \in \mathbf{Rel}(A, A)$ can play an important role.

An element $x \in A$ is an *initial* element or a *source* if and only if

$$\forall y \in A : (y \neq x \Rightarrow \neg yRx) \qquad \text{or} \qquad R^{-1}(x) \subseteq \{x\}.$$

An initial element x has no predecessors.

An element $x \in A$ is a *terminal* element or a *sink* if and only if

$$\forall y \in A : (y \neq x \Rightarrow \neg xRy) \qquad \text{or} \qquad R(x) \subseteq \{x\}.$$

A terminal element x has no successors.

An element $x \in A$ is the *first* element if and only if

$$\forall y \in A : (y \neq x \Rightarrow x\overline{R}y) \qquad \text{or} \qquad \overline{R}(x) \cup \{x\} = A,$$

and an element $x \in A$ is the *last* element if and only if

$$\forall y \in A : (y \neq x \Rightarrow y\overline{R}x) \qquad \text{or} \qquad \overline{R}^{-1}(x) \cup \{x\} = A.$$

A first element can reach every other vertex, and a last element can be reached from all the other vertices.

Example 4.3 The left-hand-side relation in Figure 4.15 has two initial elements x and u. There is no terminal element in this graph, but v, y, and z are last elements. Also, x and u are not first elements as neither can reach the other. Note that if the arc from z to v is reversed, z becomes a terminal element.

For the relation on the right-hand side of Figure 4.15, all three elements a, b, and c are simultaneously the first and the last elements. $\square$

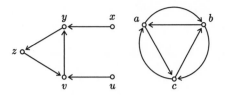

Figure 4.15. Special elements in graphs.

Theorem 4.11 *x is an R-first or initial element if and only if it is an R^{-1}-last (terminal) element.*

Theorem 4.12 *If the relation R is antisymmetric and x a first element, x is also initial. If the relation R is comparable and x an initial element, x is also first.*

4.2.5 Tournaments ▷

A relation $R \in \mathbf{Rel}(A, A)$ is a tournament if and only if it is asymmetric and comparable. These are relations that result from round-robin tournaments in which players engage in a game that cannot end in a tie and in which every player plays with each other exactly once.

In tournaments we have, for every vertex $x \in A$,

$$\text{indeg } x + \text{outdeg } x = n - 1.$$

A tournament is acyclic if and only if it is transitive. A Hamiltonian path exists in every tournament. If a tournament is strongly connected, then it has also a Hamiltonian cycle.

4.3 PARTITIONS AND EQUIVALENCE RELATIONS

As outlined in Chapter 1 (Sections 1.4.2 and 1.4.3), equivalence and partitions are the most central ideas in blockmodeling. In all of our subsequent chapters, it is difficult to find a page where one or the other concept is not mentioned. Here, we provide the definitions and some properties of these two ideas.

A relation $R \in \mathbf{Rel}(A, A)$ is an *equivalence* (relation) if and only if it is reflexive, symmetric, and transitive. We denote the set of all equivalence relations over the set A by $\mathbf{Eqv}(A)$.

Example 4.4 Consider the following example as a relation, denoted by R, for a network of eight vertices $\{a, b, c, d, e, f, g, h\}$. Imagine the relation as "friend-ship" and as allowing actors to be their own friends.

The relation is clearly reflexive. If x is a member of this network, then xRx holds for each vertex: There are 1s on the main diagonal. The relation R is also symmetric: If x and y are two vertices, then xRy occurs only when yRx; for example aRb with bRa and the matrix is symmetric about the main diagonal.

Finally, R is transitive: If x, y, z denote vertices, then whenever xRy and yRz are present, so too is xRz. See the triples $\{c, d, e\}$ and $\{f, g, h\}$. $\square$

Theorem 4.13   *A relation $R \in \mathbf{Rel}(A, A)$ is an equivalence if and only if*

$$\mathcal{D}R = A \qquad \text{and} \qquad R^{-1} * R = R.$$

Partitions and equivalences are essentially the two sides of the same coin. This is demonstrated with the example. The obvious partition of the vertices into the sets $\{a, b\}, \{c, d, e\}$, and $\{f, g, h\}$ is fully consistent with the relation R. An equivalence relation partitions the vertices into subsets of equivalent vertices. More formally, we state the following.

Theorem 4.14   *Let $\mathcal{A} = \{A_i\}_{i \in I}$ be a partition of the set A; then the relation*

$$\mathrm{eqv}\,(\mathcal{A}) := \{(x, y) : \exists X \in \mathcal{A} : (x \in X \wedge y \in X)\} = \bigcup_{i \in I} A_i \times A_i$$

is an equivalence on A.

It follows that every partition determines some equivalence. This is an important idea, for the primary goal of blockmodeling is to partition the vertices into clusters (subsets). In thinking about this, we need to be careful. *Every* partition defines an equivalence relation *regardless* of the relation R describing a network. For example, we could partition the eight vertices into the clusters $\{a, f, g\}, \{b, h\}$, and $\{c, d, e\}$. This defines an equivalence relation as a member of $\mathbf{Eqv}(A)$. Whereas this partition belongs to $\mathbf{Eqv}(A)$, it seems far removed from R. So, R is special because a (social) relation as its partition also has meaning in terms of the relation itself. In constructing a blockmodel, more is sought than *a* partition. Partitions are sought that do have meaning with regard to the relation. For example, we seek a structural equivalence or a regular equivalence as partitions with specific properties. We pursue these ideas further in Chapter 6. Before we discuss clustering – establishing partitions – in Chapter 5, we present some additional ideas concerning equivalence relations.

These results are illustrated by the simple example with eight vertices (see Table 4.1).

Table 4.1. A Hypothetical Friendship Relation

	a	b	c	d	e	f	g	h
a	1	1	0	0	0	0	0	0
b	1	1	0	0	0	0	0	0
c	0	0	1	1	1	0	0	0
d	0	0	1	1	1	0	0	0
e	0	0	1	1	1	0	0	0
f	0	0	0	0	0	1	1	1
g	0	0	0	0	0	1	1	1
h	0	0	0	0	0	1	1	1

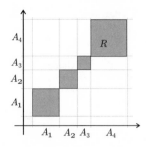

Figure 4.16. Squares – the Cartesian product of the partition.

We can also think in terms of the Cartesian product of the partition, as shown in Figure 4.16. The graph of an equivalence relation is a set of disjoint cliques. The representation is shown in terms of a clustering imposed on the elements of the Cartesian product of the vertices. This creates a set of so-called blocks defined by the Cartesian product of the clusters. The shaded blocks will be uniformly 1 whereas the other blocks will be uniformly 0. In terms of how blockmodels get represented, imagine the ordinand axis flipped so that it point downward. In a matrix form we get one-blocks along the main diagonal. Note also that when a blockmodel is established, the nonclique rectangles are constructed.

Let $R \in \mathbf{Eqv}(A)$. The *equivalence class* of the element $x \in A$ is called the set of its neighbors $[x] := R(x) = \{y : xRy\}$.

Theorem 4.15 *Let $R \in \mathbf{Eqv}(A)$. Then the family of equivalence classes $A/R :=$ $\{[x] : x \in A\}$ is a partition of the set A and*

$$xRy \Leftrightarrow [x] = [y] \qquad \text{and} \qquad \neg xRy \Leftrightarrow [x] \cap [y] = \emptyset.$$

Theorem 4.16

a. If $R \in \mathbf{Eqv}(A)$, then eqv $(A/R) = R$.
b. If $\mathcal{A}$ is a partition of A, then $A/\text{eqv}(\mathcal{A}) = \mathcal{A}$.

Example 4.5 We consider again the BWR game-playing relation. This relation is shown in the first panel of Table 4.2. As described in Section 2.1.2, Roethlisberger and Dickson (1939) obtained the following partition into cliques (classes or clusters):

$$\mathcal{C} = \{ \{I_1, W_1, W_2, W_3, W_4, S_1\}, \{I_3\}, \{W_5\}, \{W_6, W_7, W_8, W_9, S_4\}, \{S_2\} \}.$$

This partition determines the equivalence relation eqv($\mathcal{C}$), which is shown in the middle panel of the table.

If we compute the relation

$$\text{games} \setminus \text{eqv}(\mathbf{C}),$$

we get the matrix in the bottom panel. The only element that is in relation with others is W_5. It is adjacent to $\{W_1, W_3, W_4, W_7, S_2\}$. All these elements except W_7 are in the first class of the partition $\mathbf{C}$. If we construct another partition by including

Table 4.2. BWR Games and an Equivalence Relation

	I_1	I_3	W_1	W_2	W_3	W_4	W_5	W_6	W_7	W_8	W_9	S_1	S_2	S_4
						Playing Games								
I_1	0	0	1	1	1	1	0	0	0	0	0	0	0	0
I_3	0	0	0	0	0	0	0	0	0	0	0	0	0	0
W_1	1	0	0	1	1	1	1	0	0	0	0	1	0	0
W_2	1	0	1	0	1	1	0	0	0	0	0	1	0	0
W_3	1	0	1	1	0	1	1	0	0	0	0	1	0	0
W_4	1	0	1	1	1	0	1	0	0	0	0	1	0	0
W_5	0	0	1	0	1	1	0	0	1	0	0	1	0	0
W_6	0	0	0	0	0	0	0	0	1	1	1	0	0	0
W_7	0	0	0	0	0	0	1	1	0	1	1	0	0	1
W_8	0	0	0	0	0	0	0	1	1	0	1	0	0	1
W_9	0	0	0	0	0	0	0	1	1	1	0	0	0	1
S_1	0	0	1	1	1	1	1	0	0	0	0	0	0	0
S_2	0	0	0	0	0	0	0	0	0	0	0	0	0	0
S_4	0	0	0	0	0	0	0	0	1	1	1	0	0	0
						eqv (**C**)								
I_1	1	0	1	1	1	1	0	0	0	0	0	1	0	0
I_3	0	1	0	0	0	0	0	0	0	0	0	0	0	0
W_1	1	0	1	1	1	1	0	0	0	0	0	1	0	0
W_2	1	0	1	1	1	1	0	0	0	0	0	1	0	0
W_3	1	0	1	1	1	1	0	0	0	0	0	1	0	0
W_4	1	0	1	1	1	1	0	0	0	0	0	1	0	0
W_5	0	0	0	0	0	0	1	0	0	0	0	0	0	0
W_6	0	0	0	0	0	0	0	1	1	1	1	0	0	1
W_7	0	0	0	0	0	0	0	1	1	1	1	0	0	1
W_8	0	0	0	0	0	0	0	1	1	1	1	0	0	1
W_9	0	0	0	0	0	0	0	1	1	1	1	0	0	1
S_1	1	0	1	1	1	1	0	0	0	0	0	1	0	0
S_2	0	0	0	0	0	0	0	0	0	0	0	0	1	0
S_4	0	0	0	0	0	0	0	1	1	1	1	0	0	1
						Games \ Equivalence								
I_1	0	0	0	0	0	0	0	0	0	0	0	0	0	0
I_3	0	0	0	0	0	0	0	0	0	0	0	0	0	0
W_1	0	0	0	0	0	0	1	0	0	0	0	0	0	0
W_2	0	0	0	0	0	0	0	0	0	0	0	0	0	0
W_3	0	0	0	0	0	0	1	0	0	0	0	0	0	0
W_4	0	0	0	0	0	0	1	0	0	0	0	0	0	0
W_5	0	0	1	0	1	1	0	0	1	0	0	1	0	0
W_6	0	0	0	0	0	0	0	0	0	0	0	0	0	0
W_7	0	0	0	0	0	0	1	0	0	0	0	0	0	0
W_8	0	0	0	0	0	0	0	0	0	0	0	0	0	0
W_9	0	0	0	0	0	0	0	0	0	0	0	0	0	0
S_1	0	0	0	0	0	0	1	0	0	0	0	0	0	0
S_2	0	0	0	0	0	0	0	0	0	0	0	0	0	0
S_3	0	0	0	0	0	0	0	0	0	0	0	0	0	0

W_5 in the first cluster, we get a new partition,

$$\mathbf{C}' = \{ \{I_1, W_1, W_2, W_3, W_4, W_5, S_1\}, \{I_3\}, \{W_6, W_7, W_8, W_9, S_4\}, \{S_2\} \},$$

for which

$$\text{games} \setminus \text{eqv}(\mathbf{C}') = \{(W_5, W_7), (W_7, W_5)\}.$$

We can compute the determinacy coefficient (see Section 3.2.2): $K(\text{games} \Rightarrow \text{eqv}(\mathbf{C}')) \approx 1$ and $K(\text{eqv}(\mathbf{C}') \Rightarrow \text{games}) \approx 1$. The games relation can be almost completely explained by belonging to the same clique. $\square$

In applications of equivalences, we often select in each class a uniquely defined element c, called a *representative* of the class. The set $C \subseteq A$ is a *set of representatives* for a partition $\mathcal{A} = \{A_i\}_{i \in I}$ if and only if

$$\forall i \in I : \text{card}(A_i \cap C) = 1,$$

or, in other words,

$$\forall i \in I \, \exists c \in C : A_i \cap C = \{c\}.$$

Most of the equivalences used in applications are defined as follows. Let $f : A \to B$ be a function. Then the relation $R \in \mathbf{Rel}(A, A)$ defined by

$$x R y := f(x) = f(y)$$

is an equivalence.

In fact, every equivalence $R \in \mathbf{Eqv}(A)$ can be expressed in this way since for the function $f : A \to A/R$, $f : x \mapsto [x]$ it holds that

$$x R y \Leftrightarrow f(x) = f(y).$$

The relation of weak connectedness R^W and the relation of strong connectedness R^S in a relational graph (A, R), see Section 4.1.2, are equivalences; we have

$$R^W = (\hat{R})^\star \quad \text{and} \quad R^S = R^\star \cap (R^\star)^{-1}.$$

Relation $(\hat{R})^\star$ is also the *equivalence closure* of relation R.

The elements $x, y \in A$ are structurally equivalent, $x \equiv y$, for $R \in \mathbf{Rel}(A, A)$ if and only if $R(x) = R(y)$ and $R^{-1}(x) = R^{-1}(y)$. The structural equivalence $\equiv$ is an equivalence relation.

For the relation represented by the graph in Figure 4.17, we get

$$A/R^W = \{A\},$$
$$A/R^S = \{\{a, d, e\}, \{b\}, \{c, i\}, \{f, g, h\}\}.$$

We also note that both types of isomorphism described in Section 4.1 are equivalence relations on the set of all graphs **Gph** and $\approx \subset \sim$ holds.

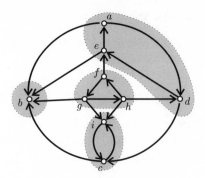

Figure 4.17. A relational graph and its strong components.

4.4   ACYCLIC RELATIONS

In Chapter 11, we focus on acyclic structures as a form of blockmodel. In this section, some basic notions and theorems about acyclic relations are given.

A relation $R \in \textbf{Rel}(A, A)$ is *acyclic* if and only if

$$\forall x \in A \; \forall k > 0 : \neg x(R \setminus I)^k x,$$

that is, if its graph, except for loops, contains no cycles. This condition can also be written in the form $\overline{(R \setminus I)} \cap I = \emptyset$. We denote by $\textbf{Acy}(A)$ the set of all acyclic relations on A.

A relation $R \in \textbf{Rel}(A, A)$ is *strictly acyclic* if and only if

$$\forall x \in A \; \forall k > 0 : \neg x R^k x,$$

that is, if its graph contains no cycles and also loops are not allowed. This condition can also be written in form $\overline{R} \cap I = \emptyset$. Each strictly acyclic relation is also acyclic.

When dealing with acyclic relations, instead of using the general symbol R, we denote the relation with a more suggestive symbol $\sqsubseteq$. We also define relations $\sqsubset := \sqsubseteq \setminus I, \underline{\sqsubseteq} := \sqsubseteq \cup I, \sqsupseteq := \sqsubseteq^{-1}, \sqsupset := \sqsubset^{-1}$ and sets

$$\uparrow (x) = \{y : x \sqsubseteq y\},$$
$$\downarrow (x) = \{y : y \sqsubseteq x\},$$
$$[x, y] = \uparrow (x) \cap \downarrow (y).$$

Here $\sqsubset$ is a $\sqsubseteq$ with loops deleted and $\underline{\sqsubseteq}$ is a $\sqsubseteq$ with loops added.

Theorem 4.17   *If the relation $\sqsubseteq \in \textbf{Acy}(A)$ is an acyclic relation, then $\sqsubset$ is a strictly acyclic relation.*

Theorem 4.18   *If the relation $\sqsubseteq$ is (strictly) acyclic, then its inverse relation $\sqsupseteq$ and its restriction $\sqsubseteq |_B = \sqsubseteq \cap B \times B$, $B \subseteq A$ are also both (strictly) acyclic.*

For an acyclic relation $\sqsubseteq \in \textbf{Acy}(A)$, the initial and terminal elements are called *minimal* and *maximal* elements, respectively.

The set of all minimal elements in A is denoted by Min A; Max A is the set of its maximal elements.

Theorem 4.19 *Let the relation $\sqsubseteq \in$ **Acy**(A); then in the set A there exists at most one first and at most one last element.*

Because for an acyclic relation $\sqsubseteq \in$ **Acy**(A) the first or last element, when it exists, is uniquely determined, it deserves a special name. It is called the *least–greatest* (also *minimum–maximum*) element.

Theorem 4.20 *For an acyclic relation $\sqsubseteq \in$ **Acy**(A) over a finite, nonempty set A, there is at least one minimal and at least one maximal element.*

Adding a single source s connected to all minimal elements and a single sink t connected from all maximal elements creates a *standardized acyclic network*.

4.4.1 Levels

A function $h: A \to 1, \ldots,$ card $h(A)$ satisfying the condition, $x \neq y \wedge x \sqsubseteq y \Rightarrow i(x) < i(y)$, is called a level function. This notion is useful in studying ranked-clusters systems and hierarchies.

A minimal (using the smallest number of levels) level function can be produced by use of the following procedure:

$S := A; j := 1;$
while $S \neq \emptyset$ **do**
  $B := $ Min S;
  for $x \in B$ **do** $h(x) := j$;
  $j := j + 1$;
  $S := S \setminus B$
end;

There can exist different minimal level functions.

Most social systems – ranging from tiny domestic groups to the entire world system of societies – are stratified in some fashion. In the context of small groups and social networks, our major focus in this book, there seems to be a universal tendency toward ranking and hierarchy in some form. However, *stratification, ranking*, and *hierarchy* are notoriously ambiguous terms in their usage. In an attempt to provide some rigor to thinking about ranked social systems, we make use of certain terms in a precise fashion. We use *stratified sociometric system* as a loose term to label the notion of a stratified social structural (network) system. This is no more than a label, and these systems can vary in distinctive ways. We need a way of characterizing these differences. In Chapter 7, within the rubric of a generalized treatment of blockmodeling, we discuss the ranked-clusters model as a way of representing stratified sociometric systems. Intuitively, actors form subgroups and are distributed across levels. Our point of departure is the concept of a level, and we introduce it here. We also note that implicit in most discussions of ranking is the idea that social actors are ordered in some fashion given the sets of social relations over them. We provide definitions of orders in Section 4.5.

4.5   ORDERS

Among transitive relations, we often encounter, besides equivalences, different types of orders:

- *preorder*: transitive, reflexive;
- *weak order*: transitive, reflexive, comparable;
- *order*: transitive, antisymmetric;
- *partial order*: transitive, reflexive, antisymmetric;
- *linear order*: transitive, antisymmetric, reflexive, comparable;
- *strict partial order*: transitive, irreflexive; and
- *strict linear order*: transitive, irreflexive. comparable.

A linearly ordered subset of A is called a *chain*.

We denote with $\mathbf{Ord}(A)$ the set of all orders (transitive and antisymmetric relations) on A.

Example 4.6   Let $C = \{C_1, \ldots, C_k\}$ and $\mathcal{D} = \{D_1, \ldots, D_m\}$ be partitions of the set A. We say that $\mathcal{D}$ is a refinement of C, denoted $\mathcal{D} \preceq C$, if and only if

$$\forall D \in \mathcal{D} \exists C \in C : D \subseteq C.$$

The refinement relation $\preceq$ is a partial order.   □

Often in the definition of strict orders, asymmetry is required instead of irreflexivity. However, these definitions are equivalent as follows.

Theorem 4.21   *A transitive relation is irreflexive if and only if it is asymmetric.*

Theorem 4.22   *If the relation $R \in \mathbf{Rel}(A, A)$ is transitive, then the relation $R \setminus I$ is transitive also. If the relation $R \in \mathbf{Rel}(A, A)$ is antisymmetric, then the relation $R \setminus I$ is asymmetric.*

If a relation R has a property (transitive, reflexive, irreflexive, symmetric, asymmetric, antisymmetric, or comparable), then the relation R^{-1} has the same property. Therefore, for the previously defined types, the following theorems are given.

Theorem 4.23   *Let $R \in \mathbf{Rel}(A, A)$ be a relation of any of the listed types. A relation R and relation R^{-1} are of the same type.*

Because all properties in the definitions of types of transitive relations are universally quantified (start with $\forall$), their validity is preserved when the relation is restricted to some subset. Therefore, we have the following theorems.

Theorem 4.24   *Let $R \in \mathbf{Rel}(A, A)$ be a relation of any of the listed types. Then the relation $R|_B = R \cap B \times B$, $B \subseteq A$ is of the same type.*

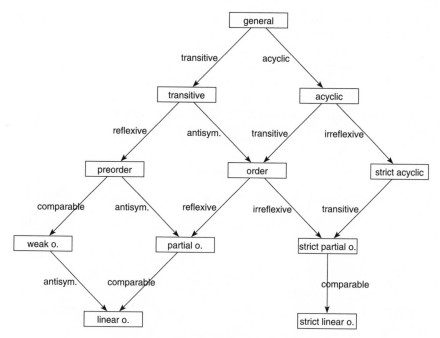

Figure 4.18. Types of transitive relations.

Theorem 4.25 *Every order is an acyclic relation, and every strict order is a strictly acyclic relation.*

Theorem 4.26 *If the relation $\sqsubseteq \in \mathbf{Ord}(A)$, then $\sqsubseteq$ is a partial order and $\sqsubset$ is a strict partial order.*

4.5.1 Factorization

Suppose that on the set A we have a relation $R \in \mathbf{Rel}(A, A)$ and an equivalence $\sim \in \mathbf{Eqv}(A)$. The equivalence $\sim$ partitions the set A into equivalence classes that form the family $A/\sim$. In $A/\sim$ we can define the *factor* relation $\mathbf{r} = R/\sim \in \mathbf{Rel}(A/\sim, A/\sim)$:

$$\mathbf{r} = R/\sim := \{\exists x \in X \exists y \in Y : xRy\}.$$

Later we will see that all blockmodels can be described in these terms. The factor relation is the image of a blockmodel.

Theorem 4.27 *Let $R \in \mathbf{Rel}(A, A)$. The relation $\sqsubseteq := R/R^S$ is acyclic on A/R^S. If R is a preorder then $\sqsubseteq$ is a partial order on A/R^S. If R is a tournament then $\sqsubseteq$ is a linear order on A/R^S.*

For a relation $R \in \mathbf{Rel}(A, A)$, we know that the strong connectivity relation R^S is an equivalence. It partitions the set A into equivalence classes (strong components) that form a family A/R^S. In it, we can define the factor relation $\sqsubseteq = R/R^S$. This is shown in Figure 4.19, which displays the factorization of the graph in Figure 4.17. The elements of the factor relation are simply the clusters $\{a, d, e\}$, $\{b\}$, $\{c, i\}$, and $\{f, g, h\}$ that form the strong components of the graph in Figure 4.17.

We note that each relation $R \in \mathbf{Rel}(A, A)$ can be extended to a preorder by determining its reflexive and transitive closure $R^\star$, which is also a *preorder closure* of R.

4.5.2   Hasse diagram

What can be said about the graph of an order? It has no cycle of length greater than 1.

For an order $\sqsubseteq \in \mathbf{Ord}(A)$ over a finite set A, the relation *covers* are defined by

$$\sqsubset\!\!\cdot := \sqsubset \setminus \sqsubset^2.$$

The relation $\sqsubset\!\!\cdot$ is strictly acyclic, and $\overline{\sqsubset\!\!\cdot} = \sqsubset$. The graph $H = (A, \sqsubset\!\!\cdot)$ is also called the *Hasse graph* of the order $\sqsubseteq$.

In Figure 4.18 the Hasse graph of inclusions among different types of orders is presented.

The notion of a Hasse relation or graph can be introduced for any acyclic relation $\sqsubseteq \in \mathbf{Acy}(A)$ over a finite set A by

$$\sqsubset\!\!\cdot := \sqsubset \setminus \sqsubset * \overline{\sqsubset\!\!\cdot}.$$

The relation $\sqsubset\!\!\cdot$ is the minimal relation contained in $\sqsubseteq$ that preserves the reachability in the original relation, that is, $\overline{\sqsubset\!\!\cdot} = \overline{\sqsubset}$.

Since in the Hasse graph of an acyclic relation $\sqsubseteq$ there are no cycles, we can draw it in such a way that the arcs are going only from lower to higher vertices; therefore, the arrows are superfluous. The picture obtained after removing arrows is called the *Hasse diagram* of $\sqsubseteq$. See Figure 6.8 in Chapter 6 and Figure 11.1 in Chapter 11.

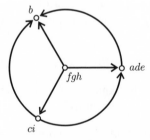

Figure 4.19. The graph of a factor relation $\sqsubseteq$.

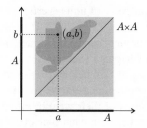

Figure 4.20. Topological reorder matrix.

4.5.3 Numberings

In applications of acyclic relations over finite sets, it is often useful to extend the relation to a linear order that is described by an injective function (see Section 3.3),

$$i : A \to 1, \dots, |A|,$$

called a *compatible numbering* of A (for the relation $\sqsubseteq$) if and only if

$$x \neq y \Rightarrow i(x) \neq i(y) \qquad \text{and} \qquad x \neq y \wedge x \sqsubseteq y \Rightarrow i(x) < i(y).$$

The following can be shown.

Theorem 4.28 *For every acyclic relation $\sqsubseteq \in \mathbf{Acy}(A)$ over a finite set A, a compatible numbering exists.*

A compatible numbering can be produced by the following procedure, also called a *topological sort*:

$B := A; j := 0;$
while $B \neq \emptyset$ **do**
    select $x : x$ is a minimal element of B;
    $j := j + 1;$
    $i(x) := j;$
    $B := B \setminus \{x\}$
end;

If we reorder the elements of the set A in the order defined by the numbering i, then in the corresponding matrix all 1s are on or above the diagonal (See Figure 4.20). Topological orderings are usually not unique.

4.6 NETWORKS

The structure of a network $\mathbf{N}$ is determined by its graph $\mathbf{G} = (\mathcal{U}, \mathcal{L})$. The properties of units and lines can be described by additional functions. We get a network,

$$\mathbf{N} = (\mathcal{U}, \mathcal{L}, \mathcal{F}_{\mathcal{U}}, \mathcal{F}_{\mathcal{L}});$$

$f : \mathcal{U} \to X$ from $\mathcal{F}_{\mathcal{U}}$ is a property of units (vertices), and $g : \mathcal{L} \to Y$ from $\mathcal{F}_{\mathcal{L}}$ is a property of lines.

This rather forbidding statement can be illustrated by the example of the Florentine network introduced in Chapter 1 (Section 1.1.1) and especially in Figure 1.2. In this example, $\mathcal{U}$ is the set of families and $\mathcal{L}$ is the set of marriage ties. Also, letting $X = \mathbb{R}$, an example of the function, we see that $f : \mathcal{U} \to X$ is the mapping of the families to the measures of their wealth. Finally, suppose we had a count of the number of marriages between each pair of families. Then $Y = \mathbb{N}$ and an example of $g : \mathcal{L} \to Y$ would be the mapping of the (qualitative) marriage relation to $\mathbb{N}$, the count of marriages between families.

4.7   CENTRALITY IN NETWORKS

Centrality measures are examples of structural properties used in the indirect blockmodeling approach (see Section 6.3). They also provide us with basic insight about some of the most interesting units in a network. We consider only vertex measures to describe the vertices in the network and ignore measures of network centralization because we do not use them for blockmodeling.

It seems that the most important distinction between centrality measures for vertices is based on the decision of whether the relation $R \in \mathbf{Rel}(\mathcal{U}, \mathcal{U})$ describing a network $\mathbf{N} = (\mathcal{U}, R)$ is considered as directed or undirected (symmetric). This gives us two main types of centrality measures.

- There is the directed case with measures of importance; there are two subgroups: measures of influence, based on relation R, and measures of support, based on relation R^{-1}.
- There is the undirected case, with measures of centrality, based on relation $\hat{R}$.

For symmetric relations $R = R^{-1} = \hat{R}$, and therefore all types of measures coincide.

Another important division of centrality measures is between

- local measures, which consider only immediate neighbors of a given vertex; and
- global measures, which consider all vertices connected by paths with a given vertex.

Other general discussions of centrality measures can be found in Hoivik and Gleditsch (1975), Freeman (1977, 1979), Hummon, Doreian, and Freeman (1990), and Wasserman and Faust (1994).

Degree measures. Let us consider some ways of constructing vertex measures. Let $S \in \mathbf{Rel}(\mathcal{U}, \mathcal{U})$ be a relation. We can base a measure on the cardinality of the set $S(x)$. To ensure comparability of measures for relations on different sets, we normalize it by dividing it with the maximal possible value $d_{\max}$. This gives us a measure

$$c(x; S) = \frac{\operatorname{card}(S(x))}{d_{\max}}.$$

It holds that $0 \le c(x; S) \le 1$.

As special cases of this measure we get the following:

measure	definition
local influence	$c(x; R)$
local support	$c(x; R^{-1})$
local centrality	$c(x; \hat{R})$
global influence	$c(x; \overline{R})$
global support	$c(x; \overline{R^{-1}})$
global centrality	$c(x; \overline{\hat{R}})$

These measures are examples of structural vertex properties.

Let $\mathcal{F} \subseteq \mathbf{Rel}(\mathcal{U}, \mathcal{U})$ be a family of relations and $n = \text{card}(\mathcal{U})$. We can define

$$d_{\max} = \max\{\text{card}(S(x)) : x \in \mathcal{U} \wedge S \in \mathcal{F}\}.$$

We have: $d_{\max} = n$ if $\mathcal{F} = \mathbf{Rel}(\mathcal{U}, \mathcal{U})$; $d_{\max} = n - 1$, for all irreflexive relations over $\mathcal{U}$; and $d_{\max} = \Delta(S)$ for $\mathcal{F} = \{S\}$. The relation $S \setminus I$ is always irreflexive. Note also that for an irreflexive relation R, its transitive closure $\overline{R}$ need not be irreflexive.

If the graph of relation R is not connected, other normalizations can be considered – for example, based on the maximal cardinality of activity regions $a(x; R) = \text{card}(\overline{R}^{-1} \cup \overline{R}(x))$ or on the cardinality of the (strongly) connected component to which a given vertex belongs.

Measures of closeness. For a strongly connected network $(\mathcal{U}, S)$, Sabidussi (1966) introduced the following measure of *closeness* (in normalized form, see Freeman 1977 – in the original definition, the denominator was 1):

$$cl(x; S) = \frac{n - 1}{\sum_{y \in \mathcal{U}} d(x, y)},$$

where $d(x, y)$ is the geodesic distance from x to y. It holds that $0 \leq cl(x; S) \leq 1$.

To extend the definition to general networks, we can set

$$cl(x; S) = \begin{cases} \dfrac{\text{card}(\overline{S}(x) \setminus \{x\})}{\sum_{y \in \overline{S}(x)} d(x, y)} \cdot \dfrac{\text{card}(\overline{S}(x))}{n} & \overline{S}(x) \neq \emptyset \\ 0 & \overline{S}(x) = \emptyset \end{cases}.$$

For strongly connected networks, $\overline{S}(x) = \mathcal{U}$ and we get the original definition.

We distinguish

measure	definition
outcloseness	$cl(x; R)$
incloseness	$cl(x; R^{-1})$
(total) closeness	$cl(x; \hat{R})$

Measures of betweenness. Freeman (1977, 1979) and Gould (1987) defined *betweenness* of a vertex x by

$$b(x; S) = \frac{1}{(n-1)(n-2)} \sum_{\substack{y,z \in \mathcal{U}:n(y,z) \neq 0 \\ y \neq z, x \neq y, x \neq z}} \frac{n(y, z; x)}{n(y, z)},$$

where $n(y, z)$ is the number of geodesics from y to z and $n(y, z; x)$ is the number of geodesics from y to z passing through x. It holds that $0 \leq b(x; S) \leq 1$ and $b(x; S) = b(x; S^{-1})$.

We distinguish

measure	definition
betweenness	$b(x; R)$
weak betweenness	$b(x; \hat{R})$

Flow measures. Degree, closeness, and betweenness measures are based on the economy assumption; communications use the geodesics. Bonacich (1971), Bolland (1988), and Stephenson and Zelen (1989) proposed two indices that consider all possible communication paths.

Let $a(x, y; k)$ denote the number of all walks from vertex x to vertex y of length not exceeding k, and let $A(k)$ be a matrix of all these numbers $A(k) = [a(x, y; k)]$. Evidently $A(1) = R$. Then the number of all walks from vertex x of length not exceeding k equals

$$v(x; k) = \sum_{y \in \mathcal{U}} a(x, y; k).$$

Let $v^*(k) = \max\{v(x; k) : x \in \mathcal{U}\}$; then the Bonacich index for vertex x is defined by

$$B(x) = \lim_{k \to \infty} \frac{v(x; k)}{v^*(k)}.$$

It can be shown that $B(x)$ equals the xth component of normalized eigenvector ($\max_x B(x) = 1$) of the relational matrix R corresponding to the largest eigenvalue $\lambda_{\max}$.

The Stephenson and Zelen index is defined only for symmetric and connected networks. It is also based on the total flow in a network, weighting each walk by the reciprocal of its length.

Here is its definition in the general case. Let $A = [a(x, y)]$ be a symmetric network matrix. We compute from it a new matrix $B = [b(x, y)]$ determined by

$$b(x, y) = \begin{cases} 1 + \sum_{z \in \mathcal{U}} a(x, z) & x = y \\ 1 - a(x, y) & x \neq y \end{cases}.$$

Let $C = [c(x, y)] = B^{-1}$ and define

$$k = \frac{1}{n} \sum_{y \in \mathcal{U}} (c(y, y) - 2c(x, y)).$$

The value of k is identical for all $x \in \mathcal{U}$. Then the *Stephenson and Zelen* index for vertex x is determined by

$$I(x) = \frac{1}{k + c(x, x)}.$$

4.7.1 *Algorithmic aspects*

It can be shown (Batagelj 1994) that the transitive closure matrix and matrices of number and length of geodesics can be computed by Fletcher's algorithm (Fletcher 1980) as closure matrices over a corresponding semiring. Semirings are discussed in Chapter 9.

In computing of flow indices we need an algorithm for determining the largest eigenvalue and the corresponding eigenvector and an algorithm for inverting a matrix. These algorithms can be found in any book on numerical analysis (e.g., Conte and de Boor 1981; Press et al. 1986).

4.8 SUMMARY AND TRANSITION

We have presented a formal statement of relations and graphs as a foundation for blockmodeling. Using some basic ideas of set theory, we described relations in Section 3.2 and graphs in Section 4.1. Blockmodeling is a set of techniques for partitioning graphs and constructing mappings from graphs to their images. The key ideas for doing this concern subgraphs, homomorphisms between graphs, binary relations, and equivalence relations. We included material on operations with binary relations together with a set of tools for comparing relations – topics not usually considered in applications of blockmodeling. Our reason for doing this is that establishing blockmodels is not the end of a complete blockmodeling analysis. We need a framework for comparing graphs and for comparing blockmodels as graphs.

The topics considered in this chapter are some of the foundations for block-modeling. Our discussion of equivalence relations included material on clusters and partitions of vertices into clusters. We did not discuss how these partitions can be established. Before taking a detailed look at blockmodeling, we use Chapter 5 to consider techniques from cluster analysis. This makes the clustering aspect of blockmodeling explicit. It also emphasizes the need to select partitioning techniques carefully from a very large set of options for establishing clusters.

Blockmodeling is best viewed as a set of general tools for clustering social actors and social relations in meaningful ways. Our primary goal in Chapters 3–5 is to provide a formal foundation for a general treatment of blockmodeling. In

Chapter 3, we introduced some set theoretic ideas and formally defined relations as mathematical objects because we will represent social relations in these terms. In this chapter, our attention has been focused on developing relational concepts and graph theoretic ideas as tools that will be useful for network analysis. The third part of our presentation of the formal foundations for blockmodeling comes in Chapter 5, where we discuss cluster analytic techniques. Starting in Chapter 6, we draw on these foundations for an integrated treatment of blockmodeling. Before moving to Chapter 5, we briefly reconsider some of the materials in this chapter as they relate to clustering.

Looking at a graph in terms of its subgraphs (Section 4.1) can be viewed as a clustering of the graph. In Section 4.1.2, we provided definitions of weakly connected and strongly connected graphs. If a graph is not weakly connected, it is possible to analyze the weak components separately (subgraphs of **G** that are weakly connected). If a graph is not strongly connected, it can be analyzed in terms if its strong components (subgraphs of **G** that are strongly connected). The vertices in each strong component $\mathbf{H}_i$ can be shrunk (condensed) to a single point, H_i^* (Harary, Norman, and Cartwright 1965), and the resulting graph with vertices $\{H_i^*\}$ is an acyclic graph (Section 4.4). In essence, the **G** has been clustered (factored) and the resulting graph can be analyzed.

The idea of a k-core was introduced in Section 4.1.1, and this idea can be mobilized to cluster a graph in terms of nested subgraphs (depending on the sequenced values of k). This provides a powerful tool for locating boundaries of subgraphs within graphs. See Doreian and Woodard (1992) for an application of k-cores to locate the boundary of a network of social service organizations when the empirical boundary was unknown.

The idea of graph homomorphism was defined in Section 4.1 and provides a coherent framework for comparing graphs in systematic ways. Blockmodeling creates a (new) clustered network (graph) from an (original) network with a structure determined by the nature of the clustering and the distribution of the ties in the social network. Using homomorphisms provides a way of analyzing the structure of the clustered network in relation to the original network. We turn now to an explicit discussion of clustering methods in Chapter 5.

5

CLUSTERING APPROACHES

Regardless of whether old methods are used or new methods are created, all efforts to blockmodel social networks involve clustering. It is useful, then, to consider some the many tools and *ideas* that have been created by cluster analysts. We describe the essential ideas and discuss a variety of methods that have value for clustering social networks. With regard to conventional blockmodeling concerns, the materials in Sections 5.1–5.4 are essential. Readers can move directly to Chapter 6 from the end of Section 5.4. In Section 5.5 a nonstandard approach of simultaneously clustering attribute and relational (network) data is discussed.

5.1 AN INTRODUCTION TO CLUSTER ANALYTIC IDEAS

Grouping units into clusters so that those within a cluster are as similar to each other as possible, whereas units in different clusters are as dissimilar as possible, is a very old problem. Many different (partial) solutions have been proposed. Although the clustering problem is intuitively simple and understandable, providing general solution(s) is difficult and remains a very current activity. New data sets and new problems provide the impetus for finding more solutions. The increasing number of recent papers on this topic, in both theoretical and applied statistical journals, is notable.[1]

There are two main reasons for this lively interest and the creation of many new procedures in this area. First, prior to 1960, clustering problems were solved separately in different scientific fields with little concern for integration across specific solutions – a characteristic of the early stages in the development of any discipline. Attempts to unify different problems and solutions first appeared in the 1960s, with Sokal and Sneath (1963) providing the first extensive statement. With this as a point of departure, cluster analysis developed as a specific data

---

1 Further, the *Journal of Classification* was established in 1984, and the International Federation of Classification Societies was formed in 1985.

analytic field. Second, the development of cluster analysis was greatly influenced by developments in computing technology. These allowed the application of more demanding computational procedures and the processing of large data sets. Theoretical results in computer science were also important, especially the theoretical work on computational complexity. The result that most of the clustering problems are NP hard was proven early on by Brucker (1978). NP hard means, in this case, that it is believed that there are no efficient, exact algorithms for solving most of the clustering problems. Therefore, it is not surprising that many problems were, and still are, being solved with heuristic approaches more or less adapted to the specifics of particular problems.

Of course, these reasons interact with each other. Developments in computing technology and the creation of new theoretical results are applied in different scientific fields. These applications have features specific to the different fields with the risk that clustering procedures will proliferate with much redundancy across fields of application. In turn, this motivates further unifying work to integrate many clustering developments. Such cycles of activity produce great benefits for both the fields of application and cluster analysis. We believe that the topics we consider under blockmodeling also have this feature. *With the use of known clustering procedures, network partitioning will benefit, whereas the use of criterion functions based on network concepts of equivalence may prove useful for cluster analysis.*

5.2   USUAL CLUSTERING PROBLEMS

Cluster analysis (known also as classification and taxonomy) mainly deals with the following general problem: Given a set of units $\mathcal{U}$, determine subsets, called clusters, C, that are homogeneous or well separated according to the measured variables. The set of clusters forms a clustering. This problem can be formulated as an optimization problem.

Determine the clustering $\mathbf{C}^*$ for which

$$P(\mathbf{C}^*) = \min_{\mathbf{C} \in \Phi} P(\mathbf{C}),$$

where $\mathbf{C}$ is a clustering of a given set of units or actors $\mathcal{U}$, Φ is the set of all feasible clusterings, and $P : \Phi \rightarrow \mathbb{R}$ is a *criterion function*.

Because the set of feasible clusterings is finite, a solution of the clustering problem always exists. However, since this set is usually very large, it is not easy to find an optimal solution.

There are several types of clusterings, such as partition, hierarchy, pyramid, fuzzy clustering, and clustering with overlapping clusters. The most frequently used clusterings are partition and hierarchy – a feature shared by this book. A clustering $\mathbf{C} = \{C_1, C_2, \ldots, C_k\}$ is a partition of the set of units $\mathcal{U}$ if

$$\bigcup_i C_i = \mathcal{U}, \qquad i \neq j \Rightarrow C_i \cap C_j = \emptyset.$$

A clustering $\mathbf{H} = \{C_1, C_2, \ldots, C_k\}$ is a hierarchy if, for each pair of clusters C_i and C_j from $\mathbf{H}$,

$$C_i \cap C_j \in \{C_i, C_j, \emptyset\},$$

and it is a complete hierarchy if, for each unit x, $\{x\} \in \mathbf{H}$ and $\mathcal{U} \in \mathbf{H}$ (also see Section 3.1).

Clustering criterion functions can be constructed *indirectly* as a function of a suitable (dis)similarity measure between pairs of units (e.g., Euclidean distance) or *directly* (see below). In most cases, the criterion function is defined indirectly. For partitions into k clusters, the Ward criterion function

$$P(\mathbf{C}) = \sum_{C \in \mathbf{C}} \sum_{x \in C} d(x, t_C)$$

is usually used, where t_C is the center of the cluster C and is defined as

$$t_C = (\bar{u}_{1C}, \bar{u}_{2C}, \ldots, \bar{u}_{mC}),$$

where $\bar{u}_{iC}$ is the average of the variable U_i, $i = 1, \ldots, m$, for the units from the cluster C and d is the squared Euclidean distance.

5.2.1 An example

Consider the set of five units $\mathcal{U} = \{a, b, c, d, e\}$ for which there are measurements in terms of two variables (U and V):

	a	b	c	d	e
U	1	2	3	5	5
V	1	3	2	3	5

The units are presented graphically in Figure 5.1.

We group the units into two clusters (a partition) by using the following criterion function:

$$P(\mathbf{C}) = \sum_{C \in \mathbf{C}} \sum_{x \in C} d(x, t_C),$$

where $t_C = (\bar{u}_C, \bar{v}_C)$ is the center of the cluster C and the dissimilarity d is the Euclidean distance.

All possible partitions into two clusters, together with the calculated values of the criterion function, are shown in Table 5.1. The lowest value of the criterion function is (for the last partition)

$$P(\mathbf{C}_{15}) = 5.41.$$

The best clustering (partition) for this criterion function is therefore

$$\mathbf{C}^* = \{\{a, b, c\}, \{d, e\}\}.$$

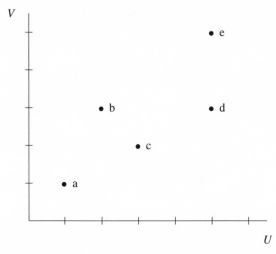

Figure 5.1. Graphical presentation of five units and the optimal clustering into two clusters.

From the graphical display, this is the obvious solution. For this simple example, we can search the set of all 15 possible clusterings. In general, however, if there are n units, there are

$$2^{n-1} - 1$$

different partitions with two clusters. The number of partitions exponentially increases with the number of units. In the case of clustering n units into k clusters,

Table 5.1. All Partitions and Values of the Criterion
Function

C	C_1	C_2	t_1	t_2	$P(\mathbf{C})$
1	a	$bcde$	(1.0, 1.0)	(3.75, 3.25)	6.65
2	b	$acde$	(2.0, 3.0)	(3.50, 2.75)	8.18
3	c	$abde$	(3.0, 2.0)	(3.25, 3.00)	8.67
4	d	$abce$	(5.0, 3.0)	(2.75, 2.75)	7.24
5	e	$abcd$	(5.0, 5.0)	(2.75, 2.25)	5.94
6	ab	cde	(1.5, 2.0)	(4.33, 3.33)	6.66
7	ac	bde	(2.0, 1.5)	(4.00, 3.67)	7.21
8	ad	bce	(3.0, 2.0)	(3.33, 3.33)	9.58
9	ae	bcd	(3.0, 3.0)	(3.33, 2.67)	9.48
10	bc	ade	(2.5, 2.5)	(3.67, 3.00)	8.48
11	bd	ace	(3.5, 3.0)	(3.00, 2.67)	9.34
12	be	acd	(3.5, 4.0)	(3.00, 2.00)	8.08
13	cd	abe	(4.0, 2.5)	(2.67, 3.00)	8.58
14	ce	abd	(4.0, 3.5)	(2.67, 2.33)	9.11
15	de	abc	(5.0, 4.0)	(2.00, 2.00)	5.41

the number of all possible partitions is equal to the second-order Stirling number:

$$\mathcal{S}(n, k) = \frac{1}{k!} \sum_{i=0}^{k} (-1)^{k-i} \binom{k}{i} i^n.$$

If we wanted to cluster the preceding five units into three clusters, we could search for the best clustering over the set of 25 partitions. In contrast, the number of all possible partitions of 30 units into 10 clusters is

$$\mathcal{S}(30, 10) = 173, 373, 343, 599, 189, 364, 594, 756.$$

This large number is daunting because a set of size 30 is quite small. Often, clustering involves several hundreds or thousands of units! Clearly, searching across all partitions to locate those partitions with the smallest value of a criterion function is impractical. This is the case for many of the social networks we consider in this book.

5.2.2 The usual steps of solving clustering problems

We list the usual steps of solving a clustering problem (Hansen, Jaumard, and Sanlaville 1993) and use the following sections to describe them. The steps are as follows.

1. Select the set of units $\mathcal{U}$.
2. Measure the appropriate variables for the given problem. Variables can be measured with different scale types. If numerical variables with different scales are used, in most cases they should be standardized.
3. Choose an appropriate dissimilarity between units d for the given problem and the types of variables used.
4. Choose an appropriate type of clustering.
5. Select or create an appropriate criterion function to evaluate the selected type of clustering.
6. Choose or devise an algorithm for the given clustering problem.
7. Determine the clustering(s) that optimize(s) the chosen criterion function with the selected algorithm. An approximate solution may be necessary if there is no exact algorithm or if an excessive amount of computing time is needed to obtain an exact solution.
8. Assess the solutions obtained to see if they have some underlying structure. Descriptive statistics can be used to summarize the characteristics of each cluster.

Prior to an analysis, both the units and the appropriate variables will have been selected by the analyst. For our purposes, the first two steps do not require further discussion.

5.3 (DIS)SIMILARITIES

For solving a clustering problem, the choice of an appropriate (dis)similarity measure between two units is crucial. The issues for us to consider when selecting a (dis)similarity measure include its mathematical properties, its behavior when confronted with data, the nature of the data, and the use made of the (dis)similarity matrix. Several authors (e.g., Gower and Legendre 1986) discuss the properties of dissimilarities and ways the information concerning them guides the choice of a dissimilarity in applications.

A dissimilarity can be described by a mapping, a *measure of dissimilarity*, where a real number is assigned to each pair of units (x, y):

$$d : (x, y) \mapsto R.$$

We usually assume that the following conditions hold:

1. $d(x, y) \geq 0$,   nonnegativity;
2. $d(x, x) = 0$,
3. $d(x, y) = d(y, x)$,   symmetry.

If, for a dissimilarity measure, the following two conditions also hold,

4. $d(x, y) = 0 \Longrightarrow x = y$;
5. $\forall z : d(x, y) \leq d(x, z) + d(z, y)$,   triangle inequality;

then the dissimilarity is called a *distance*.

There is a large literature dealing with a wide range of (dis)similarities. Some elaborated overviews of these measures can be found in, for example, Sokal and Sneath (1963), Clifford and Stephenson (1975:49–82), Everitt (1974:49–59), Gordon (1981:13–32), Lorr (1983:22–44), and Hubálek (1982).

Most often, the dissimilarity is based on the descriptions of units by selected variables. In the case in which units have more complicated structures (e.g., networks), some invariants (e.g., triadic counts in a network) are used as variables (see Section 5.3.1.). The other possibility is to define a dissimilarity of structures in a direct way (e.g., the smallest number of steps to transform one structure to the other).

In most cases, the types of variables describing the units limit the choice of an appropriate (dis)similarity measure. We briefly discuss two of the most used types of measures: measures for numerical data and measures for binary data.

5.3.1   (Dis)similarity measures for numerical data

When the clustered units are described with numerical variables, Euclidean distance is used frequently. For the units x and y decribed by m numerical variables,

$$x = (x_1, x_2, \ldots, x_m),$$
$$y = (y_1, y_2, \ldots, y_m),$$

the Euclidean distance is defined in the following way:

$$d(x, y) = \sqrt{\sum_{i=1}^{m} (x_i - y_i)^2}.$$

The Manhattan distance is used often:

$$d(x, y) = \sum_{i=1}^{m} |x_i - y_i|.$$

Both distances are special cases of the Minkowsky distance:

$$d(x, y) = \left(\sum_{i=1}^{m} |x_i - y_i|^r \right)^{\frac{1}{r}}, \qquad r > 0$$

If $r = 1$, then we have the Manhattan distance, and for $r = 2$ we have the Euclidean distance. When deciding on the most appropriate distance measure for solving a given clustering problem, we find it useful to consider the following property of the Minkowsky distance: the larger the value r, the stronger the influence of larger differences $|x_i - y_i|$ on the distance between units. In the limited case ($r = \infty$), the Minkowsky distance becomes

$$d(x, y) = \max_i |x_i - y_i|.$$

It is also called the Chebyshev distance.

The attribute data in Table 5.2 present the Florentine families (see also Section 1.1.1) and two variables: family wealth (measured in the year 1427) and number of council seats held by family members in the years 1282–1344.

Table 5.2. Attribute Data for Florentine
Families

		Family Wealth	Council Seats
Acciaiuoli	1	10.448	53
Albizzi	2	35.730	65
Barbadori	3	55.351	N/A
Bischeri	4	44.378	12
Castellani	5	19.691	22
Ginori	6	32.013	N/A
Guadagni	7	8.127	21
Lamberteschi	8	41.727	0
Medici	9	103.140	53
Pazzi	10	48.233	a
Peruzzi	11	49.313	42
Pucci	12	2.970	0
Ridolfi	13	26.806	38
Salviati	14	9.899	35
Strozzi	15	145.896	74
Tornabuoni	16	48.258	N/A

Note: N/A indicates that data are not available. The letter "a" indicates a special case of the Pazzi family.

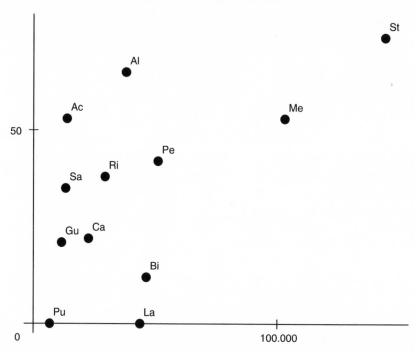

Figure 5.2. Florentine families according to wealth and number of council seats.

The places of the families are graphicaly presented in two-dimensional space, where the dimensions are family wealth and the number of council seats of families (see Figure 5.2). Two clusters of similar families are seen nicely from this figure: the Strozzi and Medici families with very high values on both variables and all others

Table 5.3. Standardized Data on Wealth and
Number of Council Seats

		Family Wealth	Council Seats
Acciaiuoli	1	−0.76	0.79
Albizzi	2	−0.14	1.31
Bischeri	3	0.07	−0.97
Castellani	4	−0.53	−0.54
Guadagni	5	−0.82	−0.59
Lamberteschi	6	0.01	−1.49
Medici	7	1.51	0.79
Peruzzi	8	0.19	0.32
Pucci	9	−0.94	−1.49
Ridolfi	10	−0.36	0.15
Salviati	11	−0.77	0.02
Strozzi	12	2.55	1.70

Table 5.4. Euclidean Distances among Florentine Families

		1	2	3	4	5	6	7	8	9	10	11	12
Acciaiuoli	1	0.0											
Albizzi	2	0.6	0.0										
Bischeri	3	3.8	5.3	0.0									
Castellani	4	1.8	3.6	0.6	0.0								
Guadagni	5	1.9	4.0	0.9	0.1	0.0							
Lamberteschi	6	5.8	7.9	0.3	1.2	1.5	0.0						
Medici	7	5.1	3.0	5.2	5.9	7.3	7.5	0.0					
Peruzzi	8	1.1	1.1	1.7	1.3	1.8	3.3	2.0	0.0				
Pucci	9	5.2	8.5	1.3	1.1	0.8	0.9	11.2	4.6	0.0			
Ridolfi	10	0.6	1.4	1.4	0.5	0.7	2.8	3.9	0.3	3.0	0.0		
Salviati	11	0.6	2.1	1.7	0.4	0.4	2.8	5.8	1.0	2.3	0.2	0.0	
Strozzi	12	11.8	7.4	13.3	14.5	16.6	16.7	1.9	7.5	22.4	10.9	13.9	0.0

with much lower values. The second cluster can be divided in two subclusters: a group of families with low values in both variables, and a group with low values on wealth but higher values on the number of council seats.

Because the variables are measured on different scales, we standardize both variables before calculating the distances between families (see Step 2 in Section 5.2.2). The most usual standardization is

$$z_{ij} = \frac{x_{ij} - \mu_j}{\sigma_j},$$

where x_{ij} is the value of the variable X_j for the unit i, μ_j is the arithmetic mean, and σ_j is the standard deviation of the variable X_j. The standardized data for wealth and number of council seats of the 12 Florentine families are given in Table 5.3. We consider only the 12 families with all available data. The Euclidean distances between the families are given in Table 5.4. We return to this example in Section 5.4.1.

It is also possible to use the Pearsonian (1926) correlation coefficient[2] as a similarity measure:

$$r(x, y) = \frac{\sum_{i=1}^{m}(x_i - \mu_x)(y_i - \mu_y)}{\sqrt{\sum_{i=1}^{m}(x_i - \mu_x)^2 \sum_{i=1}^{m}(y_i - \mu_y)^2}},$$

where

$$\mu_x = \frac{1}{m}\sum_{i=1}^{m} x_i$$

and

$$\mu_y = \frac{1}{m}\sum_{i=1}^{m} y_i.$$

---

2   We note that this correlation coefficient is not affected by linear transformations of either variable.

There are many other distance measures on $\mathbb{R}^m$. For example, the Mahalanobis generalized distance (1936) is defined as

$$d(x, y) = (x - y)'\Sigma^{-1}(x - y),$$

where Σ is a variance–covariance matrix of variables within clusters. This measure considers (which most of other measures do not) the relationship between variables. If the Pearsonian correlation between variables is 0 and the variables are standardized, then the Mahalanobis distance is the square of the Euclidean distance.

There are two interesting dissimilarity measures defined for units having only positive values of the variables. One is the Lance–Williams (1966) dissimilarity measure:

$$d(x, y) = \frac{\sum_{i=1}^{m} |x_i - y_i|}{\sum_{i=1}^{m} (x_i + y_i)}.$$

The Canberra distance is the other (Lance and Williams 1967):

$$d(x, y) = \sum_{i=1}^{m} \frac{|x_i - y_i|}{|x_i + y_i|}.$$

They are both very sensitive for very small values (around zero).

5.3.2   (Dis)similarity measures for binary data

Many similarity measures have been defined for units described by binary variables. They are determined mostly by the frequencies of the contingency table for a pair of units for which the similarity is measured. The contingency table for the units x and y where the values of all m variables are $+$ and $-$ is

		Unit y	
		$+$	$-$
Unit x	$+$	a	b
	$-$	c	d

The sum of all four frequencies is equal to the number of variables ($a + b + c + d = m$). The frequency a counts how many variables the units x and y both have as a positive response, and d counts the joint occurrence of negative responses. The frequencies b and c count the number of variables for which the units have different responses.

Many matching similarity measures are known in the literature (e.g., Hubálek 1982; Batagelj and Bren 1995) and include the following.

1. There is the Sokal–Michener similarity (1958):

$$\frac{a+d}{a+b+c+d}.$$

2. There is the first Sokal–Sneath similarity (1963):

$$\frac{2(a+d)}{2(a+d)+b+c}.$$

3. There is the Rogers–Tanimoto similarity (1960):

$$\frac{a+d}{a+d+2(b+c)}.$$

4. There is the Russell–Rao similarity (1940):

$$\frac{a}{a+b+c+d}.$$

5. There is the Jaccard similarity (1908):

$$\frac{a}{a+b+c}.$$

6. There is the Czekanowski similarity (1913):

$$\frac{2a}{2a+b+c}.$$

7. There is the second Sokal–Sneath similarity (1963):

$$\frac{a}{a+2(b+c)}.$$

8. There is the Kulczynski similarity (1927):

$$\frac{a}{b+c}.$$

All of these similarity measures, except the last, are defined in the interval from 0 to 1. The first three measures would give us the same order of pairs of units. We say that these measures are order equivalent (Batagelj and Bren 1995). The fifth, sixth, and seventh similarity measures are also order equivalent. The notion of equivalency of similarity measures is an important one in cluster analysis. Some of the clustering methods give exactly the same solutions when different but equivalent similarity measures are used between units (e.g., the minimum and maximum hierarchical methods described in Section 5.4.1).

It is possible to measure the dissimilarities between relations. In Section 3.2.2, four such dissimilarities were defined: d_H (Hamming distance), d_h (normalized Hamming distance), d_u, and d_m.

5.4 CLUSTERING ALGORITHMS

In general, most of the clustering problems are NP hard. For this reason, different efficient heuristic algorithms for producing good clustering solutions have been created (see Step 7 in Section 5.2.2). Most of the statistical systems such as SAS and SPSS have implemented the hierarchical and leader algorithms discussed in the next two sections. We note that there are many other algorithms and approaches. Of these, the relocation algorithm described in Section 5.4.3 is particularly useful.

5.4.1   The hierarchical approach

Agglomerative hierarchical clustering algorithms usually assume that all relevant information on the relationships between the n units from the set $\mathcal{U}$ is summarized by a symmetric pairwise dissimilarity matrix $D = [d_{ij}]$. The scheme of the agglomerative hierarchical algorithm is as follows.

Each unit is a cluster: $C_i = \{x_i\}$, $x_i \in \mathcal{U}$, $i = 1, 2, \ldots, n$;
repeat while there exist at least two clusters:
   determine the nearest pair of clusters C_p and C_q:
      $d(C_p, C_q) = \min_{u,v} d(C_u, C_v)$;
   fuse the clusters C_p and C_q to form a new cluster
      $C_r = C_p \cup C_q$;
   replace C_p and C_q by the cluster C_r;
   determine the dissimilarities between the cluster C_r
      and other clusters.

According to the last step of this algorithm, we have to determine the dissimilarity d between the newly formed cluster C_r and all other previously established clusters. This can be done in many different ways, each of which determines a different hierarchical clustering method. Suppose that we have three clusters C_i, C_j, and C_k in a certain iteration of the hierarchical procedure with the dissimilarities between them as shown in Figure 5.3.

Suppose further that the clusters C_i and C_j are the closest. They are fused to form a new cluster $C_i \cup C_j$. The methods of creating the dissimilarity between the new cluster and an extant cluster C_k include the following.

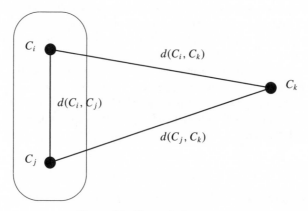

Figure 5.3. Three clusters.

- There is the *minimum method*, or single linkage (Florek et al. 1951; Sneath 1957):

$$d(C_i \cup C_j, C_k) = \min(d(C_i, C_k), d(C_j, C_k)).$$

- There is the *Maximum method*, or complete linkage (McQuitty 1960):

$$d(C_i \cup C_j, C_k) = \max(d(C_i, C_k), d(C_j, C_k)).$$

- There is the *McQuitty method* (McQuitty 1966, 1967):

$$d(C_i \cup C_j, C_k) = \frac{d(C_i, C_k) + d(C_j, C_k)}{2}.$$

The dissimilarities between the new cluster and the other clusters can be determined according to the structure of each cluster. Three ways of obtaining these dissimilarities are as follows.

- There is the *average method* (Sokal and Michener 1958),

$$d(C_i \cup C_j, C_k) = \frac{1}{(n_i + n_j)n_k} \sum_{u \in C_i \cup C_j} \sum_{v \in C_k} d(u, v),$$

where n_i denotes the number of units in the cluster C_i.
- There is the *Gower method* (Gower 1967),

$$d(C_i \cup C_j, C_k) = d^2(t_{ij}, t_k),$$

where t_{ij} denotes the centroid of the fused cluster $C_i \cup C_j$ and t_k the center of the cluster C_k.
- There is the *Ward method* (Ward 1963):

$$d(C_i \cup C_j, C_k) = \frac{(n_i + n_j)n_k}{(n_i + n_j + n_k)} d^2(t_{ij}, t_k).$$

The resulting clustering (hierarchy) can be represented graphically by means of the clustering tree (dendrogram).

In cases with well-separated clusters, all hierarchical methods give the same solution.

Clustering of Florentine families. At this point, we return to the Florentine families. The dendrograms based on the dissimilarities between the Florentine families presented in Table 5.4 were obtained by using the minimum, maximum, and Ward methods, respectively, and are presented in Figure 5.4. All three hierarchical methods gave the same two-cluster solution: the Strozzi and Medici families in one cluster and all others in the second, which is consistent with the graphical representation of the families in two-dimensional space in Figure 5.2. The dendrograms differ in detail but the three-cluster solution is

$$C_1 = \{\text{Bischeri, Castellani, Guadagni, Lamberteschi, Pucci}\},$$
$$C_2 = \{\text{Acciaiuoli, Albizzi, Peruzzi, Ridolfi, Salviati}\},$$
$$C_3 = \{\text{Medici, Strozzi}\},$$

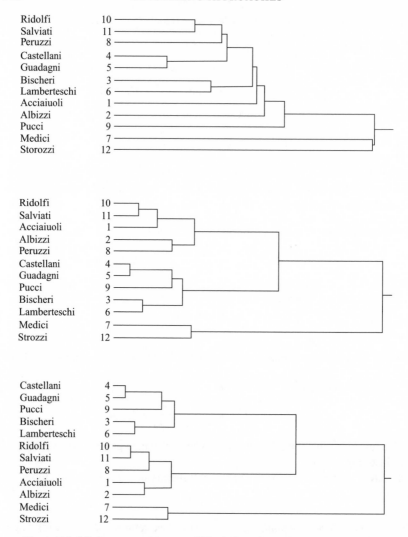

Figure 5.4. Minimum, maximum, and Ward clusterings of Florentine families.

and it is the same for the maximum and Ward methods. However, it is not obtained when the minimum method is used. The second cluster from the two-cluster solution does not consist of two well-separated subclusters (see Figure 5.2). In such cases, different methods can provide different clustering solutions.

Clustering relations. In Section 3.2.2, four dissimilarity measures between relations are defined. We computed three of them $(d_h, d_u, \text{and } d_m)$ for five of the BWR relations described in detail in Section 2.1.2: playing games, positive affect, negative affect, helping, and conflict over windows. These are shown in Table 5.5. Note

Table 5.5. *Dissimilarity Matrices d_h, d_u, and d_m of Five BWR Relations*

d_h	Help	Games	Positive	Negative	Conflict
Help	0.00000	0.22449	0.16327	0.30612	0.22449
Games		0.00000	0.17347	0.37755	0.27551
Positive			0.00000	0.32653	0.24490
Negative				0.00000	0.30612
Conflict					0.00000
d_u					
Help	0.00000	0.70968	0.78049	0.98361	0.83019
Games		0.00000	0.58621	0.88095	0.72973
Positive			0.00000	1.00000	0.85714
Negative				0.00000	0.88235
Conflict					0.00000
d_m					
Help	0.00000	0.67857	0.65385	0.97368	0.76316
Games		0.00000	0.57143	0.82143	0.64286
Positive			0.00000	1.00000	0.78947
Negative				0.00000	0.78947
Conflict					0.00000

that only the upper triangle is shown because these measures are symmetric – the distance of R from S is the same as the distance of S from R.

The five relations were clustered for each of the dissimilarity measures by using the Ward hierarchical method. The resulting clusterings (hierarchies) are represented graphically by dendrograms in Figure 5.5. The range of values of the dissimilarity measures are given with the dendrograms.

Clearly, the partitions differ, showing that both the measures and the relations differ. For d_h, the helping and positive ties are the least dissimilar, yet for d_u and d_m, the game-playing and positive ties are the least dissimilar. This implies that, on the technical side, we need to select dissimilarity measures with care, and, on the substantive side, we can explore the nature of the relations among the relations.

Some properties of hierarchical procedures. Agglomerative hierarchical procedures are very popular because they are very simple and their solutions can be presented nicely by dendrograms. In general, they are also very quick, for some hundreds of units and users do not need to have an explicit idea about the number of clusters hidden within the data. The most frequently used methods are the minimum, maximum, and Ward methods, but here also the user can have difficulties in choosing the right method. The minimum method is very effective for finding long, nonelliptic clusters (with a sausage shape). If there are overlapping clusters,

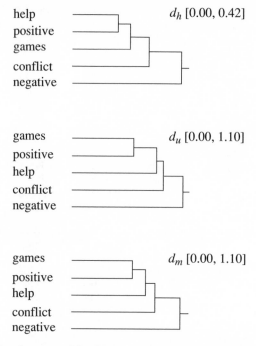

Figure 5.5. Dendrograms of five BWR relations for three dissimilarity measures.

the effect of using the minimum method is chaining, where, in each iteration, only one unit is added to a cluster. For example, there is some chaining effect in the hierarchical clustering of Florentine families obtained by the minimum method. From Figure 5.4 we can see that the larger cluster consists of two overlapping clusters. The maximum method searches for very cohesive clusters. The minimum and maximum methods are invariant under all transformations of the (dis)similarity measure that do not change the ordering of pairs of units.

The agglomerative clustering procedures can be connected with the optimizational clustering approach by means of a (clustering) criterion function. Using this, we can see the "greediness" of the agglomerative algorithm. The early fusion of clusters can preclude the later formation of more optimal clusters: Clusters fused early cannot be separated later even if the early fusion is incorrect. The negative effects of greediness are usually noticed at the higher levels of agglomeration (with smaller numbers of clusters). This also means that the clusterings into lower numbers of clusters are less reliable. This suggests that some other clustering algorithm (e.g., local optimization procedures such as the leader – see Section 5.4.2 – or relocation algorithms – see Section 5.4.3) should also be used to check solutions from the agglomorative procedures.

Several authors (e.g., Everitt 1974; Mojena 1977) have studied, comparatively, the performance of agglomerative methods by using artificially generated data. These studies show that the Ward method is the most suitable for finding ellipsoidal clusters, that the minimum method is preferable for longer chaining clusters, and that the maximum method is best for spherical clusters.

5.4.2 The leader algorithm

Among the nonhierarchical procedures, the most popular is the leader algorithm (Hartigan 1975), or K-MEANS (e.g., MacQueen 1967), or the dynamic clusters algorithm (Diday 1974). It assumes that users can determine the number of clusters of the partition they want to obtain.

The basic scheme of the leader algorithm is as follows.

Determine the initial set of leaders $\mathcal{L} = \{l_i\}$;
repeat
> determine the clustering $\mathbf{C}$ in a way that classifies
> > each unit with the nearest leader;
> for each cluster $C_i \in \mathbf{C}$ compute its centroid $\overline{C_i}$.
> > The centroid $\overline{C_i}$ determines the new leader l_i
> > of the cluster C_i;

until the leaders do not change.

Very large sets of units can be efficiently clustered by using the leader algorithm, whereas the standard agglomerative hierarchical procedures have some limits on the number of units. The leader algorithm is a *local* optimization procedure. Different initial sets of leaders can provide different local optima and corresponding partitions. Consequently, several initial sets of leaders should be used to assess the set of obtained solutions[3] to the clustering problem.

Clustering of Florentine families. For example, the problem of clustering of Florentine families into three clusters based on the standardized data (see Table 5.3) was analyzed also by use of the leader algorithm. The resulting clusters are exactly the same as the ones obtained by maximum or Ward hierarchical methods:

$C_1 = \{$Bischeri, Castellani, Guadagni, Lamberteschi, Pucci$\}$,

$C_2 = \{$Acciaiuoli, Albizzi, Peruzzi, Ridolfi, Salviati$\}$,

$C_3 = \{$Medici, Strozzi$\}$.

The leaders (also centroids) of each cluster are shown in the following table,

	l_1	l_2	l_3
wealth	−0.44	−0.37	2.03
priors	−1.02	0.52	1.25
n_i	5	5	2
d_{max}	0.69	0.82	0.69

---

3 Users usually forget that the leader algorithm is a local optimization procedure and are satisfied with the solutions obtained from only one set of inital leaders.

where n_i denotes the number of units in the cluster C_i and d_{max} denotes the maximal distance between the leader l_i and the units in the cluster C_i. The latter measures the homogeneity of the cluster. The results show that the first cluster consists of families with the lowest economic and political power. The second cluster is low on wealth and high on number of council seats, and the third has very high values on both variables.

5.4.3   The relocation algorithms

These algorithms assume that the user can specify the number of clusters of the partition.

The scheme of the relocation algorithm is as follows.

Determine the initial clustering $\mathbf{C}$;
while
> there exist $\mathbf{C}$ and $\mathbf{C}'$
> such that $P(\mathbf{C}') \leq P(\mathbf{C})$, where $\mathbf{C}'$ is obtained
> by moving a unit x_i from cluster C_p
> to cluster C_q in the clustering $\mathbf{C}$ or by interchanging
> units x_i and x_j between two clusters;

repeat:
> substitute $\mathbf{C}'$ for $\mathbf{C}$.

Although different criterion functions can be used in this approach, the Ward criterion function is used most often.

The relocation algorithm is very efficient for solving specific clustering problems. Because it is a local optimization procedure, different initial clusterings must be used. We discuss this method in the following sections and use it extensively in Chapters 6–11.

Clustering of Florentine families. For example, the clustering of Florentine families into three clusters according to their wealth and number of council seats can also be obtained by use of a relocation method. The obtained clustering (based on Euclidean distances and Ward criterion function) is exactly the same as the one obtained by the maximum or Ward hierarchical approaches and the leader algorithm.[4]

5.5   CONSTRAINED CLUSTERING

For constrained clustering, grouping similar units into clusters has to satisfy some additional conditions. This class of problems is also relatively old. One of the most

---

4   The value of the Ward criterion function for the best obtained clustering into three clusters is the same as the one obtained by the leader algorithm ($P(\mathbf{C}) = 4.49$).

frequently treated problems in this field is regionalization: Clusters of similar geographical regions have to be found, according to some chosen characteristics, where the regions included in a cluster also have to be geographically connected. A number of analytical approaches to this problem have been taken. The majority of authors (e.g., Gordon 1973, 1980, 1987; Lebart 1978; Lefkovitch 1980; Ferligoj and Batagelj 1982; Perruchet 1983; Legendre 1987) solve this problem by adapting standard clustering procedures, especially agglomerative hierarchical algorithms and local optimization clustering procedures. While determining the clusters, they use a test to ensure that the units placed in the same clusters also satisfy the additional condition of, for example, geographical contiguity. The geographic contiguity can be presented by the following relation:

$$x_i \ R \ x_j \equiv \text{the unit } x_i \text{ is geographically contiguous with the unit } x_j.$$

Such a constraint is generally called a relational constraint. Ferligoj and Batagelj (1982, 1983) first treated this clustering problem for general symmetric relations and then for nonsymmetric relations.[5] Murtagh (1985) provided a review of clustering with symmetric relational constraints. It is also possible to work with other nonrelational conditions, as discussed in the next section. A more recent survey of constrained clustering was given by Gordon (1996), and a discussion of some constrained clustering problems was given by Batagelj and Ferligoj (1998, 2000).

5.5.1 The constrained clustering problem

The constrained clustering problem can be expressed as follows. Determine the clustering $\mathbf{C}^*$ for which the criterion function P has the minimal value among all clusterings from the set of feasible (permissible) clusterings $\mathbf{C} \in \Phi$, where Φ is determined by the constraints. In short, we seek $\mathbf{C}^*$ such that

$$P(\mathbf{C}^*) = \min_{\mathbf{C} \in \Phi} P(\mathbf{C}).$$

Various types of the constraints are discussed below.

Relational constraints. Generally, the set of feasible clusterings for this type of constraint can be defined as

$$\Phi(R) = \{\mathbf{C} : \mathbf{C} \text{ is a partition of } \mathcal{U} \text{ and each cluster } C \in \mathbf{C} \text{ is a subgraph}$$
$$(C, R \cap C \times C) \text{ in the graph } (\mathcal{U}, R) \text{ with the required type of}$$
$$\text{connectedness}\}.$$

---

5   Friendship among human actors, as a social network, provides an example of this.

We can define different types of sets of feasible clusterings for the same relation R (Ferligoj and Batagelj 1983). Some examples of clusterings with relational constraint $\Phi^i(R)$ are given in the table here[6]:

Type of Clusterings	Type of Connectedness
$\Phi^1(R)$	weakly connected units
$\Phi^2(R)$	weakly connected units that contain at most one center
$\Phi^3(R)$	strongly connected units
$\Phi^4(R)$	clique
$\Phi^5(R)$	the existence of a trail containing all the units of the cluster

In the clustering type $\Phi^2(R)$, a center of a cluster C is the set of units $L \subseteq C$ iff the subgraph induced by L is strongly connected and

$$R(L) \cap (C - L) = 0,$$

where $R(L) = \{y : \exists x \in L : xRy\}$.

The first four types of connectedness are presented in Figure 5.6.

When R is symmetric, $\Phi^1(R) = \Phi^3(R)$.

The set of feasible clusterings $\Phi^i(R)$ are linked in terms of the nature of the relations specified in the constraints. For example,

- $\Phi^4(R) \subseteq \Phi^3(R) \subseteq \Phi^2(R) \subseteq \Phi^1(R)$;
- $\Phi^4(R) \subseteq \Phi^5(R) \subseteq \Phi^2(R)$;
- If the relation R is symmetric, then $\Phi^3(R) = \Phi^1(R)$;
- If the relation R is an equivalence relation, then $\Phi^4(R) = \Phi^1(R)$.

From the relation R, we can also determine, for each clustering type $\Phi^i(R)$ the minimum number of clusters in the clusterings belonging to $\Phi^i(R)$:

$$\omega^i(R) = \min_{\mathbf{C} \in \Phi^i(R)} \operatorname{card}(\mathbf{C}).$$

For some clustering types the minimum number of clusters is as follows.

$\omega^1(R) =$ the number of weakly connected components;

$\omega^2(R) =$ the number of strongly connected subsets in the set $\mathcal{U}$;

$\omega^3(R) =$ the number of strongly connected components;

$\omega^4(R) =$ the cardinality of a minimal cover of the graph $(\mathcal{U}, R)$ with cliques.

---

6   For the definitions of types of connectedness, see Section 4.1.2.

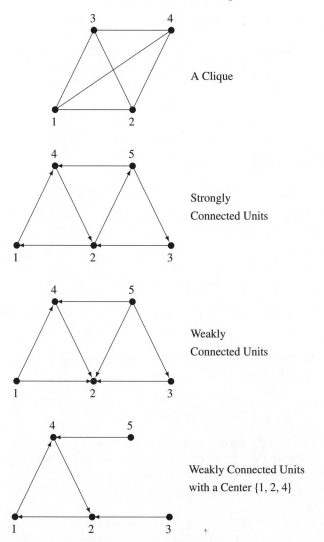

Figure 5.6. Types of connectedness.

Constraining variables. The set of feasible clusterings for this partiticular type of constraint is defined as follows (Ferligoj 1986):

$$\Phi[a, b] = \{\mathbf{C} : \mathbf{C} \text{ is a partition of } \mathcal{U} \text{ and for each cluster}$$
$$C \in \mathbf{C} \text{ holds} : v_C \in [a, b]\},$$

where v_C is a value determined by values of the constraining variable, V, for the units in the cluster C.

Consider a geographical region where areas have to be clustered. Areas in a specific cluster must be geographical neighbors (satisfying a relational constraint) and be as similar as possible with regard to some characteristics (consistent with the usual clustering problem). Additionally, there is a constraining variable V that must be considered. As an example, the number of inhabitants V in the region (cluster C) has to be greater than a given value a:

$$v_C = \sum_{x \in C} v_x > a.$$

The following property always holds:

$$[a, b] \subseteq [c, d] \Rightarrow \Phi_k[a, b] \subseteq \Phi_k[c, d].$$

Before solving a constrained clustering problem, we must analyze the constraints. In doing so, the following questions should be considered:

- Is the constraining interval $[a, b]$ selected in accordance with v_U and the number of clusters k?
- Do the constraints ensure a nonempty set of feasible clusterings $\Phi_k[a, b]$?

Of course, this kind of analysis depends on the type of the function v_C that is chosen.

An optimizational constraint. The set of feasible clusterings for an optimizational constraint is defined as

$$\Phi(F) = \{ \mathbf{C} : \mathbf{C} \text{ is a partition of } U \text{ and for a second criterion } F \text{ the condition}$$
$$F(\mathbf{C}) < f \text{ has to be satisfied} \}.$$

The value f of the second criterion is a threshold value that determines the number of clusterings in the set of feasible clusterings. Actually, this is a two-criteria clustering problem: the first criterion is the clustering criterion P and the second is the constrained criterion F. This type of clustering problem is treated in Section 5.6.

We note that a combination of the mentioned three types of constraints (relational, constraining variable, and optimizational) can be considered simultaneously.

5.5.2 Solving constrained clustering problems

Standard clustering algorithms can be adapted for solving constrained clustering problems. We consider the agglomerative hierarchical and the relocation type of algorithms.

A modified hierarchical algorithm. One straightforward modification of a standard agglomerative hierarchical algorithm is described by this scheme.

Each unit is a cluster: $C_i = \{x_i\}$, $x_i \in \mathcal{U}$, $i = 1, 2, \ldots, n$;
repeat while there exist at least two clusters, which
by fusion, give a feasible clustering:

determine the nearest pair of clusters C_p and C_q:
$$d(C_p, C_q) = \min\{d(C_u, C_v) : C_u \text{ and } C_v, u \neq v, \text{ and}$$
$$\text{fuse to form a feasible clustering}\};$$
fuse clusters C_p and C_q into a new cluster $C_r = C_p \cup C_q$;
replace the clusters C_p and C_q by the cluster C_r;
determine the dissimilarities d between the cluster C_r
and other clusters.

Ferligoj and Batagelj (1983) have shown that it is possible to apply such a modified agglomerative algorithm only for cases in which the constraint has a divisibility property. The constraint $T(C)$ is divisible if, for each cluster consisting at least of two units, the following holds:

$$\exists C_1, C_2 \neq \emptyset :$$
$$(C_1 \cup C_2 = C \;\wedge\; C_1 \cap C_2 = \emptyset \;\wedge\; T(C_1) \;\wedge\; T(C_2)).$$

Unfortunately, the constraint on a variable is usually not divisible.

For relational constraints, it is also necessary to determine the relation between the newly formed cluster $C_r = C_p \cup C_q$ and other clusters in a way that the feasibility of the clusterings is preserved in each step of the clustering procedure. Ferligoj and Batagelj (1983) found strategies of adjusting relations for the following clustering types from Section 5.5.1: $\Phi^1(R)$ (a tolerant strategy), $\Phi^2(R)$ (a leader strategy), and $\Phi^5(R)$ (a strict strategy).

A modified relocation algorithm. The main idea of a scheme for an adapted relocation algorithm can be presented as follows.

Determine the initial feasible clustering **C**;
while

there exist **C** and **C**′
such that $P(\mathbf{C}') \leq P(\mathbf{C})$, where **C**′ is obtained by
moving of a unit x_i from cluster C_p to cluster C_q
in the clustering **C** or by interchanging units x_i and x_j
between two clusters, and the units in each new cluster
satisfy the constraints;
repeat

substitute **C**′ for **C**.

The following two features must be part of any algorithm of this type:

- an efficient testing procedure to assess whether each cluster obtained by transitions, or by interchanges, does satisfy the constraints and
- a method for generating initial clusterings that are feasible.

However, for some constraints, the second problem may be NP hard. In addition, the first feature can lead to very complicated graph theoretical problems. For these reasons, clustering problems with relational constraints may be better solved by adapting agglomerative algorithms or by appropriately constructed new algorithms. A modified relocation algorithm can be used for solving clustering problems with optimizational constraints. These problems can also be solved efficiently by multicriteria clustering algorithms in which the first criterion is the clustering criterion and the second is the constraint criterion (see Section 5.6).

5.5.3 The structure enforcement coefficient

To study the influence of constraints on the clustering solutions, we can use the structure enforcement coefficient (Ferligoj 1986) if $P(\mathbf{C} \geq 0)$,

$$K = \frac{P(\mathbf{C}_c^*) - P(\mathbf{C}^*)}{P(\mathbf{C}_c^*)},$$

where $\mathbf{C}^*$ is the best obtained clustering without constraints and $\mathbf{C}_c^*$ is the best obtained clustering with constraints $(P(\mathbf{C}_c^*) \geq P(\mathbf{C}^*))$. The coefficient K is not defined if $P(\mathbf{C}_c^*) = 0$. In this case let $K = 0$. The coefficient K is defined for the interval $[0, 1]$ and measures the relative growth of the criterion function that is due to the influence of constraints imposed on the clustering.

5.5.4 An empirical example

This example is drawn from a study of the educational career plans for all Slovene students who made the transition to high school in 1981 (Ferligoj and Lapajne 1986). Each student has a set of preferences as to which high school he or she wants to attend. Because it is not possible to honor all of these preferences, some students have to choose another school. It is assumed that there is some structure to these preferences: If students cannot go to their most preferred school, then they choose another school that is close to their first choice.

For a particular cohort, data were collected at three time points.

1. One point was a time prior to the student's actually making his or her choices (using a questionnaire concerning preferences on vocational choices).
2. Another point was at the time when the student made his or her applications.
3. Another point was at the time of the student's enrollment in the first class of the high school (which may or may not be the preferred choice).

For this example, we consider the movements between the first time point preference (vocational choice) and the third time point (actual enrollment).

The data come from the follow-up study of the first generation of Grade 8 students (aged 15–16 years) who enrolled in the first class of the reformed career-oriented educational programs in Slovenia in 1981–1982. The whole generation (about 28,500 students) was followed on the basis of data collected by an employment service (Lapajne 1984). From this study, we selected the 17 programs of secondary career-oriented education with the greatest number of students – about 19,000 students remained in the database. The programs considered are these[7]:

AG	Agriculture	FT	Food Technology
CH	Chemistry	BU	Business
MT	Metallurgy	AD	Administration
EE	Electrical Energy	CS	Computer Science
EL	Electronics	PE	Pedagogical
CN	Civil Engineering	MD	Medical
CA	Carpentry	NS	Natural Sciences and Mathematics
TE	Textiles	SS	Social Sciences and Linguistics
CM	Commercial		

The movements between these programs can be represented by a valued network $(\mathcal{U}, R, w)$. The set $\mathcal{U}$ are units (in our case programs), and the elements of the set R are arcs (movements between programs). The value w on an individual arc is the percentage of students that have moved from one program to another.

There are data available on the students that came from the employment service. We focus on the following variables that were aggregated over the 17 selected programs:

- the average school grades over the four last years of primary school and the first year of high school (eight variables),
- the average of the Slovene version of the General Aptitude Tests Battery (GATB), taken in the seventh class of the primary school (seven variables),
- sociodemographic variables (including percent of girls and percent of different types of the father's education), (five variables).

We focus on these characteristics of students in career-oriented educational programs and the movements between the desired vocational choices and actual enrollments. We use clustering tools to examine the extent to which the movements are due to the similarity of the programs (which is defined by the student preference structures over them).

To study this problem empirically, we simultaneously used methods for analyzing characteristics of the students (in programs) and the network movement of students between programs. We used the clustering with relational constraints approach as follows. The clustering criterion function was constructed in terms of the program similarities according to the characteristics of the students in them. The movements between the programs were treated as constraints. In general, the clustering with constraints problem, stated in this way, is a two-criteria optimization problem. One is the optimization according to the student characteristics (the clusters consist of the most similar programs), and other is the optimization over

7   The program on Administration means simple clerical secretarial work (lowest level white-collar work).

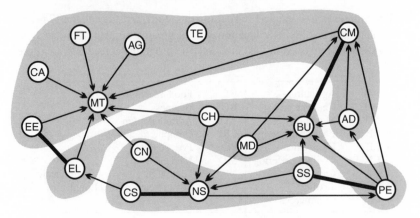

Figure 5.7. Clustering *without* constraints into three clusters.

the valued network (the clusters consist of programs with the highest movements between them). A two-criteria optimization problem can be reduced to a single optimization problem in at least two ways (see the next section on multicriteria clustering):

- combine both criteria into a single criterion function, and
- have one criterion determine the criterion function, with the other setting the feasible (permissible) clusterings: clusterings are feasible if the value of the second criterion function is smaller or greater (as determined by the nature of the criterion function) than a specified threshold.

We used the second approach where a threshold p was used to reduce the valued movement matrix to a binary relation R in the following way.

$x \ R \ y \equiv$ if the movement w from the program x to the program
y is greater than p.

For each threshold value of p we obtained a binary relation, and we solved the clustering problem by using algorithms that implement clustering by relational constraints.

To determine an appropriate threshold, we analyzed the network of movements first. When the threshold level is decreased, the constraining relation is enriched (by having more arcs).[8] It seems that important changes in solutions appear when there is a change in the connectivity structure of the constraining relation, that is, when two components are joined by an arc that is newly created with a change in the threshold.

---

8 It is possible to solve the problem sequentially for all possible distinct relations. This would be
   extraordinarily time consuming and unnecessary.

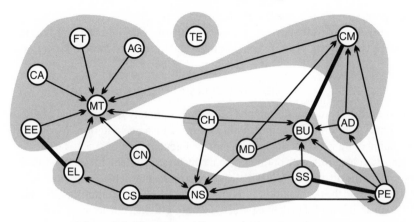

Figure 5.8. Clustering *with* constraint into four clusters.

Before clustering, we standardized all variables. We measured the dissimilarity between programs by using Euclidean distance. We then used the maximum agglomerative clustering method. Figure 5.7 presents the three-cluster solution in which the thick lines represent symmetric ties (i.e., flows in both directions). The cluster at the bottom of the figure consists of CS, NS, SS, and CN programs. The students in these programs have the best school grades, the best GATB results, and, mostly, fathers with at least a high school education. The programs in the cluster at the top of Figure 5.7 comprise MT, CA, EE, CM, AD, TE, FT, and AG. Compared with the first group, this group is at the opposite extreme on the set of student attributes. The third group, consisting of EL, CH, MD, BU, and PE programs, is located between the other two groups in Figure 5.7.

We considered three threshold levels for p, each defining a set of elements to be taken from the relational matrix: those with at least 1% of the volume of movements, those having at least 3%, and those with at least of 5% of movements. In the case of $p = 1\%$, the relation is so rich that it does not constrain, in any way, the clustering solution. When $p = 3\%$ is used, the differences between obtained clustering without constraints and with relational constraints are also minimal. In the case of $p = 5\%$, there are fewer represented movements between programs (see Figure 5.7). In clustering with this relational constraint, we considered both the tolerant and the leader strategies. Although the considered relation ($p = 5\%$) has fewer arcs, the same clustering (into four clusters[9]) is found by use of both strategies. Comparing the clustering without constraints with constrained clustering, we can see some differences. In the constrained clustering, TE becomes a singleton in a cluster and the EL program moves from the middle cluster to the bottom cluster of the diagram (see Figure 5.8). This suggests that the vocational movements are strongly (but not completely) related to the student characteristics

---

9 Note that the network data are not used to obtain the clustering shown in Figure 5.7.

of the programs. This is true if we considered a very stringent relational constraint ($p = 5\%$). For p less than 5%, this is even more true. For p greater than 5%, there would be very few moves between programs and the analysis would be irrelevant.

5.6   MULTICRITERIA CLUSTERING

Some clustering problems cannot be solved appropriately with classical clustering algorithms if they require optimization over more than one criterion. We discussed an example of a two-criteria optimization problem in Section 5.5.1. There, it was treated as a clustering with optimizational constraint problem. In general, solutions optimal for the distinct criteria will differ from each other. This creates the problem of trying to find the best solution so as to satisfy as many of the criteria as possible. In this context, it is useful to define the set of Pareto-efficient clusterings: A clustering is Pareto efficient if it cannot be improved on any criterion without sacrificing on some other criterion.

A multicriteria clustering problem can be approached in different ways:

- by reducing it to a clustering problem with a single criterion, one that is obtained as a combination of the given criteria;
- by using consensus clustering techniques (e.g., Day 1986) applied to clusterings obtained by single-criterion clustering algorithms for each criterion;
- by using constrained clustering algorithms where a selected criterion is considered as the clustering criterion and all others determine the constraints (see Section 5.5); or
- by using (or creating) direct algorithms. Hanani (1979) proposed an algorithm based on the dynamic clusters algorithm (see Section 5.4.2). Ferligoj and Batagelj (1992) proposed modified relocation algorithms and modified agglomerative hierarchical algorithms.

5.6.1   A multicriteria clustering problem

In a multicriteria clustering problem (Φ, P_1, P_2, ..., P_k), we have several criterion functions P_t, $t = 1, \ldots, k$ over the same set of feasible clusterings Φ, and our aim is to determine the clustering $\mathbf{C} \in \Phi$ in such a way that

$$P_t(\mathbf{C}) \to \min, \qquad t = 1, \ldots, k.$$

In the ideal case, we are searching for the dominant set of clusterings. The solution $\mathbf{C}_0$ is the dominant solution if for each solution $\mathbf{C} \in \Phi$ and, for each criterion P_t, it holds that

$$P_t(\mathbf{C}_0) \le P_t(\mathbf{C}), \qquad t = 1, \ldots, k.$$

Usually the set of dominant solutions is empty. Therefore, the problem arises of finding a solution to the problem that is as good as possible according to each of the given criteria. Formally, the Pareto-efficient solution is defined as follows.

For $\mathbf{C}_1, \mathbf{C}_2 \in \Phi$, solution $\mathbf{C}_1$ *dominates* solution $\mathbf{C}_2$ if and only if

$$P_t(\mathbf{C}_1) \le P_t(\mathbf{C}_2), \qquad t = 1, \ldots, k,$$

and for at least one $i \in 1, \ldots, k$ the strict inequality $P_i(\mathbf{C}_1) < P_i(\mathbf{C}_2)$ holds. We denote the dominance relation by $\prec$, where $\prec$ is a strict partial order. The set of Pareto-efficient solutions, Π, is the set of minimal elements for the dominance relation:

$$\Pi = \{\mathbf{C} \in \Phi : \neg \exists \mathbf{C}' \in \Phi : \mathbf{C}' \prec \mathbf{C}\}.$$

In other words, the solution $\mathbf{C}^* \in \Phi$ is Pareto efficient if there exists no other solution $\mathbf{C} \in \Phi$ such that

$$P_t(\mathbf{C}) \le P_t(\mathbf{C}^*), \qquad t = 1, \ldots, k$$

with strict inequality for at least one criterion. A Pareto clustering is a Pareto-efficient solution of the multicriteria clustering problem.

Since the optimal clusterings for each criterion are Pareto-efficient solutions, the set Π is not empty. If the set of dominant solutions is not empty then it is equal to the set of Pareto-efficient solutions.

5.6.2 Solving discrete multicriteria optimization problems

Multicriteria clustering problems are approached here as a multicriteria optimization problem, which is one that has been treated by several authors (e.g., MacCrimmon 1973; Zeleny 1974; Podinovskij and Nogin 1982; Homenjuk 1983; Chankong and Haimes 1983). In the clustering case, we are dealing with discrete multicriteria optimization (the set of feasible solutions is finite), which means that many very useful theorems in the field of multicriteria optimization do not hold, especially those that require convexity (Ferligoj and Batagelj 1992).

It was proven that, if for each of the given criteria, there is a unique solution, then the minimal number of Pareto-efficient solutions to the given multicriteria optimization problem equals the number of different minimal solutions of the single-criterion problems (Ferligoj and Batagelj 1992).

Although several strategies haven been proposed for solving multicriteria optimization problems explicitly (e.g., Chankong and Haimes 1983), the most common is the conversion of the multicriteria optimization problem to a single-criterion problem.

5.6.3 Direct multicriteria clustering algorithms

We can approach the multicriteria clustering problem efficiently by using direct algorithms. Here, we discuss two types of direct algorithms: a version of the relocation algorithm, and the modified agglomerative (hierarchical) algorithms.

A modified relocation algorithm. The idea of the modified relocation algorithm for solving the multicriteria clustering problem follows from the definition of a Pareto-efficient clustering. The scheme of the algorithm is as follows.

Determine the initial clustering $\mathbf{C}$;
while
> in the neighborhood of the current clustering $\mathbf{C}$
> there exists a clustering $\mathbf{C}'$ which dominates the clustering $\mathbf{C}$

repeat move to clustering $\mathbf{C}'$.

In a relocation algorithm, the *neighborhood* of a given clustering is usually defined by moving a unit from one cluster to another cluster or by interchanging two units from different clusters. This neighborhood structure does not always lead to a Pareto-efficient solution. The richer the neighborhood clustering structure, and the simpler the structure of the data, the larger the probability that the procedure attains Pareto-efficient clustering. Because the solutions obtained by the proposed procedure cannot be improved by local transformations, we call them *local Pareto clusterings*.

The basic procedure should be repeated many times (at least hundreds of times), and the obtained solutions should be reviewed. An efficient review of the obtained solutions can be done systematically with the following metaprocedure.

Determine the optimal clusterings according to each criterion
function $P_t, t = 1, \dots, k$, and put them into the set of local
Pareto clusterings Π;
repeat
> determine with the basic procedure the current
> local Pareto clustering $\mathbf{C}$;
> **if** there does not exist a clustering $\mathbf{C}_p \in \Pi : \mathbf{C}_p \prec \mathbf{C}$
> **then** include $\mathbf{C}$ in the set of local Pareto clusterings:
> $$\Pi := \Pi \cup \{\mathbf{C}\}$$
> and exclude from the set Π clusterings dominated by $\mathbf{C}$:
> $$\Pi := \Pi \setminus \{\mathbf{C}' \in \Pi : \mathbf{C} \prec \mathbf{C}'\}.$$

With this metaprocedure, the clusterings obtained through the modified relocation algorithm are put in the criterion space inside the region initially determined by optimal clusterings according to each single criterion (see Figure 5.10 in the following example); at the same time it is tested to see if it (the currently obtained clustering) should be included in the set of local Pareto clusterings Π. With the inclusions and exclusions of clusterings through the iterations, the set Π approaches the true set of Pareto clusterings.

An agglomerative hierarchical approach. Agglomerative hierarchical clustering algorithms usually assume that all relevant information on the relationships between the n units from the set $\mathcal{U}$ is summarized by a symmetric pairwise dissimilarity matrix $D = [d_{ij}]$. In the case of multicriteria clustering, we assume we have k dissimilarity matrices $D^t, t = 1, \dots, k$, each summarizing all relevant information obtained, for example, in the k different situations. The problem is to find the best hierarchical solution that satisfies all k dissimilarity matrices as much as possible.

One approach to solving the multicriteria clustering problem combines the given dissimilarity matrices (at each step) into a composed matrix. The modified agglomerative hierarchical algorithm is as follows.

Each unit is a cluster: $C_i = \{x_i\}$, $x_i \in \mathcal{U}, i = 1, 2, \ldots, n$;
repeat while there exist at least two clusters:
    construct matrix $D = f(D^t; t = 1, \ldots, k)$;
    find in D the nearest pair of clusters C_p and C_q:
        $d(C_p, C_q) = \min_{u,v} d(C_u, C_v)$;
    fuse clusters C_p and C_q into a new cluster $C_r = C_p \cup C_q$;
    replace the clusters C_p and C_q by the cluster C_r;
    for each dissimilarity matrix $D^t, t = 1, \ldots, k$:
        determine the dissimilarities d^t between the cluster C_r
        and other clusters.

The derived matrix $D = [d_{ij}]$ can, for example, be defined as follows:

$$d_{ij} = \max(d_{ij}^t; t = 1, \ldots, k),$$
$$d_{ij} = \min(d_{ij}^t; t = 1, \ldots, k),$$
$$d_{ij} = \sum_{t=1}^{k} \alpha_t d_{ij}^t, \quad \sum_{t=1}^{k} \alpha_t = 1.$$

Following this approach, one of several *decision rules* (see, e.g., pessimistic, optimistic, Hurwicz, and Laplace below) for making decisions under uncertainty (Chankong and Haimes 1983; French 1986) can be used at the composition and selection step of the procedure. Then the scheme of the modified agglomerative algorithm is as follows.

Each unit is a cluster: $C_i = \{x_i\}$, $x_i \in \mathcal{U}, i = 1, 2, \ldots, n$;
normalize each dissimilarity matrix $D^t, t = 1, \ldots, k$;
repeat while there exist at least two clusters:
    determine the nearest pair of clusters C_p and C_q, $d_{pq} = d(C_p, C_q)$
        according to a given decision rule;
    fuse clusters C_p and C_q into a new cluster $C_r = C_p \cup C_q$;
    replace the clusters C_p and C_q by the cluster C_r;
    for each dissimilarity matrix $D^t, t = 1, \ldots, k$:
        determine the dissimilarities d^t between the cluster C_r
        and the other clusters.

The normalization step is not always necessary, especially when dissimilarities are obtained with the same variables and the same dissimilarity measure on different occasions.

In the pair selection step of the algorithm, the decision rules can have different forms (Batagelj and Ferligoj 1990).

- There is Wald's (pessimistic) rule:

$$d_{pq} = \min_{i,j} \max_t d_{ij}^t.$$

- There is the optimistic rule:

$$d_{pq} = \min_{i,j} \min_t d_{ij}^t.$$

- There is Hurwicz's rule with a pessimism index α, $0 \le \alpha \le 1$:

$$d_{pq} = \min_{i,j} \left(\alpha \max_t d_{ij}^t + (1 - \alpha) \min_t d_{ij}^t \right).$$

- There is Laplace's principle of insufficient reason:

$$d_{pq} = \frac{1}{k} \min_{i,j} \sum_{t=1}^{k} d_{ij}^t.$$

The obtained hierarchical solution can be represented graphically by the dendrogram whose levels are the dissimilarities $d(C_p, C_q)$ from the selection step.

Another approach is to perform the selection step by searching for the Pareto-nearest pair of clusters: The pair of clusters (C_i, C_j) is Pareto nearest if there exists no other pair of clusters (C_p, C_q) such that

$$d_{pq}^t \le d_{ij}^t \qquad t = 1, \ldots, k,$$

and, for at least one dissimilarity matrix, strict inequality holds.

In this case, at each selection step there can exist more than one Pareto-nearest pair of clusters. This means that the proposed procedure gives several (Pareto) hierarchical solutions. If a smaller set of solutions is desired, additional decision rules have to be built into the procedure. If, at each selection step, the pair of clusters that has minimal value according to a particular criterion is chosen, the resulting hierarchical solution is the same as the hierarchical clustering obtained according to the dissimilarity matrix on which this criterion is based. One possible decision rule is this: At each step, select that pair of clusters (from the set of Pareto-nearest pairs of clusters) for which the sum or product of all values of criterion functions is minimal.[10] Because there is no single fusion level at each step, there is no simple graphical presentation of a solution by a dendrogram.

5.6.4   An example

To illustrate the proposed algorithms for multicriteria clustering, we need raw data (or similarity matrices) obtained under different conditions or in different ways. Our simple example has six units:

$$\mathcal{U} = \{x_1, x_2, x_3, x_4, x_5, x_6\}.$$

---

10   In the case of a multiplicative rule, the normalization of the dissimilarity matrices is not necessary.

Table 5.6. *Six Units at Two Time Points and Their Squared*
Euclidean Distances

Units	Y_1^1	Y_2^1	Y_1^2	Y_2^2		1	2	3	4	5	6
1	0	0	1	0	1	0	2	4	10	20	18
2	1	1	2	1	2	2	0	2	4	10	8
3	0	2	0	3	3	10	8	0	10	16	10
4	3	1	3	0	4	4	2	18	0	2	4
5	4	2	4	3	5	18	8	16	10	0	2
6	3	3	2	4	6	17	9	5	17	5	0

Two variables (Y_1 and Y_2) are measured for these units at two time points. The data are given on the left side of Table 5.6 and displayed in two-dimensional space (Figure 5.9).

The squared Euclidean distance matrices for both time points are presented on the right side of Table 5.6. (The distances for the first time point are in the upper triangle, whereas the lower triangle has the distances for the second time point.)

All feasible clusterings into two clusters with the corresponding value of the Ward criterion function at each time point are listed in Table 5.7. From this table, it is clear that the best clustering for the first time point is

$$\mathbf{C}_7 = \{\{x_1, x_2, x_3\}, \{x_4, x_5, x_6\}\}$$

with $P_1(\mathbf{C}_7) = 5.33$. For the second time point, the best solution is

$$\mathbf{C}_{11} = \{\{x_1, x_2, x_4\}, \{x_3, x_5, x_6\}\}$$

with $P_2(\mathbf{C}_{11}) = 11.33$. Because these two solutions are not identical, a dominant solution does not exist.

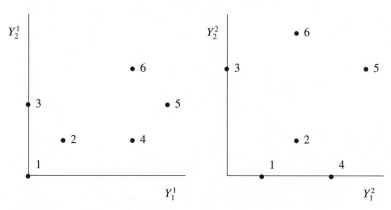

Figure 5.9. Six units in two-dimensional space for both time points.

Table 5.7. The Set of All Feasible Clusterings into Two Clusters

	C	$P_1(C)$	$P_2(C)$			C	$P_1(C)$	$P_2(C)$
1	{12345}{6}	16.00	19.20		17	{1345}{26}	19.50	23.50
2	{12346}{5}	14.40	18.40		18	{1346}{25}	19.00	21.75
3	{1234}{56}	9.00	13.50		19	{134}{256}	14.67	18.00
4	{12356}{4}	18.40	19.60		20	{1356}{24}	19.50	18.75
5	{1235}{46}	15.50	24.00		21	{135}{246}	18.67	24.00
6	{1236}{45}	12.00	17.75		22	{136}{245}	16.00	17.33
7	{123}{456}	5.33	17.33		23	{13}{2456}	9.50	17.75
8	{12456}{3}	16.00	18.40		24	{1456}{23}	15.00	21.75
9	{1245}{36}	17.00	13.50		25	{145}{236}	17.33	18.00
10	{1246}{35}	19.50	20.75		26	{146}{235}	20.00	23.33
11	{124}{356}	14.67	11.33		27	{14}{2356}	17.00	14.75
12	{1256}{34}	20.00	23.75		28	{156}{234}	18.67	22.67
13	{125}{346}	18.67	22.67		29	{15}{2346}	19.50	23.75
14	{126}{345}	18.67	24.00		30	{16}{2345}	20.00	24.00
15	{12}{3456}	12.00	18.75		31	{1}{23456}	13.60	19.60
16	{13456}{2}	19.20	24.00					

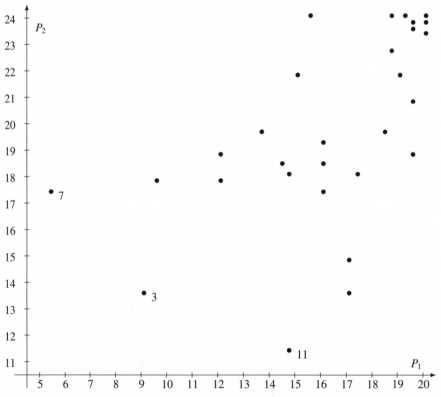

Figure 5.10. All feasible clusterings presented in two-dimensional criterion Space (P_1, P_2).

Feasible clusterings can be presented graphically in two-dimensional criterion space (P_1, P_2) as is shown in Figure 5.10. Three Pareto clusterings can be seen in this figure: $\mathbf{C}_3$, $\mathbf{C}_7$, and $\mathbf{C}_{11}$. Thus, in the Pareto set, we have both of the optimal solutions, each according to a single criterion, and a new clustering, $\mathcal{C}_3$:

$$\mathbf{C}_3 = \{\{x_1, x_2, x_3, x_4\}, \{x_5, x_6\}\}.$$

We now consider the clusterings obtained by the last variant of the modified agglomerative hierarchical algorithm, where in each iteration of the algorithm the Pareto-nearest pair of clusters is obtained. The maximum method was used. We obtained three hierarchical solutions:

$$(((x_1, x_2), x_3), (x_4, (x_5, x_6))),$$
$$((((x_1, x_2), x_4), x_3), (x_5, x_6)),$$
$$(((x_1, x_2), x_4), (x_3, (x_5, x_6))).$$

Although we used a different criterion function, the three hierarchical solutions obtained give the same three Pareto results into two clusters as were obtained by complete search.

5.7 TRANSITION TO BLOCKMODELING

Clearly, there are many ways in which clustering problems can be solved. There are a large number of (dis)similarity measures and many clustering procedures. This variety gives us some pause for thought: We need to be clear about the clustering methods used, or adapted, for partitioning social networks. The methods we propose in Chapter 6 all use criterion functions that are constructed explicitly in terms of network equivalence ideas. They can be constructed indirectly by means of appropriately defined (dis)similarity measures (compatible with considered equivalence) or directly by use of network data, which accounts for the use of the terms *indirect* and *direct*. In the direct approach, we primarily use the relocation algorithm described in Section 5.4.3.

The clustering with relational constraint approach gives a tool to analyze the mixed data: attribute and relational (network) data. The multicriteria clustering approach can be used for the analysis of multiple networks.

6

AN OPTIMIZATIONAL APPROACH TO CONVENTIONAL BLOCKMODELING

Our explicit treatment of blockmodeling starts here and continues to the end of the book. We remind readers that blockmodeling provides a way of discerning fundamental structures in networks and permits the delineation of role systems. As a practical matter, most of the prior empirical work on blockmodeling was done within an approach that we have characterized as conventional blockmodeling (Section 1.5), and it is our point of departure here. Given our broader objective of replacing all of the features of conventional blockmodeling with the features of what we have called generalized blockmodeling, this chapter breaks naturally into two parts. One contains the foundational ideas of blockmodeling and the other develops the essential foundations of generalized blockmodeling. An indirect method proceeds by analyzing some transformation of the network data, whereas a direct method works with the network data themselves. *By the end of this chapter, we develop a direct method to replace the indirect method and an optimization approach for delineating and fitting blockmodels.* In this chapter, we stay within the framework of using structural and regular equivalence. The development of new block types, together with new types of blockmodels, starts in Chapter 7.

6.1 CONVENTIONAL BLOCKMODELING

The procedural goal of blockmodeling is to identify, in a given network, clusters (classes) of units (actors) that share structural characteristics defined in terms of some relation R. Each cluster forms a *position*. The units within a cluster have the same or similar connection patterns. Clusters form a partition $\mathbf{C} = \{C_1, C_2, \ldots, C_k\}$, which is a special type of clustering of the set of units $\mathcal{U}$ (see Section 5.2). As mentioned in Chapter 4, each partition determines an equivalence relation (and vice versa). We use $\sim$ to denote the equivalence relation determined by a partition $\mathbf{C}$.

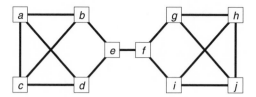

Figure 6.1. The Everett network.

A clustering C also partitions the relation R into *blocks:*

$$R(C_i, C_j) = R \cap C_i \times C_j.$$

Each block is defined in terms of units belonging to clusters C_i and C_j and consists of all arcs from units in cluster C_i to units in cluster C_j. If $i = j$, the block $R(C_i, C_i)$ is called a diagonal block.

Unfortunately, the term *block* is ambiguous because it has two meanings in the blockmodeling literature. In one usage, the block is the set of units grouped together in the blockmodel. See, for example, Schwartz and Sprinzen (1984:109). In this sense, the block is a cluster of units. We do not like this usage of the term and much prefer a second usage: *a block is a relation between two clusters of units.* A blockmodel with k positions (clusters) has k^2 blocks. Of these, there are k diagonal blocks and $k(k-1)$ nondiagonal blocks.

A *blockmodel* consists of structures obtained by identifying all units from the same cluster of the clustering C. A blockmodel can be presented by a reduced graph or by a relational matrix called an *image matrix*. The vertices in the reduced graph represent the positions, each of them defined by a cluster of units, and arcs represent relations between positions defined by the structure of relations between the clusters of units, that is, blocks. Therefore, for an exact definition of a blockmodel, we must be precise about which blocks produce an arc in the reduced graph and which do not.

The partition is constructed by using structural information contained in R *only*, and units in the same cluster are equivalent to each other in terms of R *alone*. These units share a common structural position within the network.[1]

As an example, we consider a network with 10 units, also known as the Everett network[2] (Borgatti and Everett 1989). The graph of this network is presented in Figure 6.1 together with a relation matrix in Table 6.1.

For example, consider the clustering into $k = 3$ clusters:

$$C = \{\{a, c, h, j\}, \{b, d, g, i\}, \{e, f\}\}.$$

1   In general, the statement can be extended to include several relations $\{R_t\}$.
2   It is used as the International Association of Social Network Analysts (INSNA) logo.

Table 6.1. The Everett Network

	a	b	c	d	e	f	g	h	i	j
a	0	1	1	1	0	0	0	0	0	0
b	1	0	1	0	1	0	0	0	0	0
c	1	1	0	1	0	0	0	0	0	0
d	1	0	1	0	1	0	0	0	0	0
e	0	1	0	1	0	1	0	0	0	0
f	0	0	0	0	1	0	1	0	1	0
g	0	0	0	0	0	1	0	1	0	1
h	0	0	0	0	0	0	1	0	1	1
i	0	0	0	0	0	1	0	1	0	1
j	0	0	0	0	0	0	1	1	1	0

The intuition here is based on regular equivalence.[3] The clustering partitions the relational matrix into nine blocks as shown in Table 6.2, where the blocks are constructed by permuting the rows and columns of the relational matrix. The array of positions defined by the clusters, together with the induced relations for them, is the blockmodel. Establishing blockmodels from empirical relational data is the so-called blockmodeling problem. We note that this is a rather limited statement of the problem. As outlined in Chapter 1, the idea of the blockmodeling problem can be extended to prespecifying blockmodels (in whole or in part) and testing them. Ways for doing this are discussed in detail in Section 7.4.

This blockmodel can be presented as the three-node graph with its image matrix in Table 6.2. The blocks are represented by the elements of the image matrix. The first cluster $\{a, c, h, j\}$ is represented by the position (vertex) C_1, the second cluster $\{b, d, g, i\}$ by the position C_2, and the third cluster $\{e, f\}$ by the position C_3. The elements of the image matrix are either 0s or 1s. For this blockmodel, each 0 represents a block composed entirely of 0s, such as the tie from C_1 to C_3. Blocks having at least one 1 in each row and column in the top panel of Table 6.1 are represented by 1 in the image matrix shown in the second panel of Table 6.2. Both C_1 and C_3 have self-loops representing the idea that, for both, there are ties among the units defining these diagonal blocks. This simple graph shows a very comprehensible (simplified) structure of the network. Each unit from the cluster C_3 is connected to at least one unit of the same cluster and to at least one unit of cluster C_2.

6.1.1   Definitions of equivalences

Blockmodeling, as a set of empirical procedures, is based on the idea that units in a network can be grouped according to the extent to which they are equivalent in terms of some meaningful definition of equivalence. In general, and without

---

3   An intuitive statement of regular equivalence was given in Section 1.3, and a formal definition is provided in the next section.

Table 6.2. Partition of the Everett Network
into Three Clusters and its Image

	a	c	h	j	b	d	g	i	e	f
a	0	1	0	0	1	1	0	0	0	0
c	1	0	0	0	1	1	0	0	0	0
h	0	0	0	1	0	0	1	1	0	0
j	0	0	1	0	0	0	1	1	0	0
b	1	1	0	0	0	0	0	0	1	0
d	1	1	0	0	0	0	0	0	1	0
g	0	0	1	1	0	0	0	0	0	1
i	0	0	1	1	0	0	0	0	0	1
e	0	0	0	0	1	1	0	0	0	1
f	0	0	0	0	0	0	1	1	1	0

	C_1	C_2	C_3
C_1	1	1	0
C_2	1	0	1
C_3	0	1	1

surprise, different definitions of equivalence usually lead to distinct partitions. Regardless of the definition, there are two basic approaches to the equivalence of units in a given network (compare Faust 1988):

- The equivalent units have the same connection pattern to the *same* neighbors.
- The equivalent units have the same or similar connection pattern to (possibly) *different* neighbors.

The first type of equivalence is formalized by the notion of structural equivalence and the second by the notion of regular equivalence. The latter is a generalization of the former.

Structural equivalence. Lorrain and White (1971) provided one definition of an equivalence: Units are equivalent if they are connected to the rest of the network in identical ways. Such units are said to be structurally equivalent. A permutation $\varphi : \mathcal{U} \to \mathcal{U}$ is an automorphism of the relation R if and only if

$$\forall x, y \in \mathcal{U} : (x R y \Rightarrow \varphi(x) R \varphi(y)).$$

The units x and y are structurally equivalent (we write $x \equiv y$) if and only if the permutation (transposition) $\pi = (xy)$ is an automorphism of the relation R (Borgatti and Everett 1989).

In other words, x and y are structurally equivalent if and only if

s1. $xRy \Leftrightarrow yRx$
s2. $xRx \Leftrightarrow yRy$
s3. $\forall z \in \mathcal{U} \setminus \{x, y\} : (xRz \Leftrightarrow yRz)$
s4. $\forall z \in \mathcal{U} \setminus \{x, y\} : (zRx \Leftrightarrow zRy)$

This can be expressed also in matrix form: $x_i \equiv x_j$ if and only if

s1'. $r_{ij} = r_{ji}$
s2'. $r_{ii} = r_{jj}$
s3'. $\forall k \neq i, j : r_{ik} = r_{jk}$
s4'. $\forall k \neq i, j : r_{ki} = r_{kj}$

The matrix form of the definition of structural equivalence can also be extended to the case in which r_{ij} are real numbers.

We can illustrate these ideas by using Figure 6.1. Both b and d are connected to exactly the same other units $\{a, c, e\}$ and are structurally equivalent. In the same fashion, units g and i are structurally equivalent because they are each directly linked to h, j, and f. Additionally, a and c are structurally equivalent as are h and j. There are no other sets of structurally equivalent units in Figure 6.1.

Although the definition is unequivocal, its empirical implementation has varied. Most empirical analyses using this approach force us to recognize that there are few *exact* structural equivalences in network data. For the network of the Little League (LL) baseball team shown in Figure 1.1, only Jeff, Jay, and Sandy are structurally equivalent. In order to establish an empirically based blockmodel, it is necessary to use the idea of approximate structural equivalence. Actors are clustered together if they are almost structurally equivalent. In many applications, this notion was weakened to something like sufficiently structurally equivalent without much concern for how large a departure from exact structural equivalence is acceptable. For the indirect approach mentioned in Section 1.6 and described in Section 6.1.4, this takes the form of using some (dis)similarity measure – for example, one selected from those described in Section 5.3. This creates the situation in which the definition of approximate structural equivalence can be operationalized differently, as is the case for Breiger et al. (1975), who used correlations, and for Burt (1976), who used Euclidean distances for measures of structural equivalence among two units.

In broad terms, blockmodeling tools are empirical partitioning (clustering) procedures. Usually, there are few formal assessments of how well the blockmodels fit the data. In the approach taken here, we present ways of blockmodeling that incorporate measures of adequacy. The adequacy of these procedures can be pursued and is discussed in the following sections of this chapter.

```
0 0 0 0 0        1 0 0 0
0 0 0 0 0        0 1 0 0
0 0 0 0 0        0 0 1 0
0 0 0 0 0        0 0 0 1

1 1 1 1 1        0 1 1 1
1 1 1 1 1        1 0 1 1
1 1 1 1 1        1 1 0 1
1 1 1 1 1        1 1 1 0
```

Figure 6.2. Ideal blocks for structural equivalence.

From the definition of structural equivalence, it follows that only four possible ideal diagonal blocks can appear (Batagelj, Ferligoj, and Doreian 1992):

$$\text{null, } b_{ij} = 0; \qquad \text{diag null, } b_{ij} = 1 - \delta_{ij};$$
$$\text{complete, } b_{ij} = 1; \qquad \text{diag complete, } b_{ij} = \delta_{ij}.$$

Here δ_{ij} is the Kronecker delta function[4] and $i, j \in C$. The blocks that are all 0 are called null, and the blocks with only 1s are complete blocks.[5] Examples of these structural blocks are presented in Figure 6.2.

For the nondiagonal blocks, $R(C_u, C_v)$, $u \neq v$, only null blocks and complete blocks are admissible.

Regular equivalence. Attempts to generalize structural equivalence date back at least to Sailer (1978) and have taken various forms. Integral to all formulations is the idea that units are equivalent if they link in equivalent ways to other units that are also equivalent. Regular equivalence, as defined by White and Reitz (1983), is one such generalization.

The equivalence relation $\approx$ on $\mathcal{U}$ is a regular equivalence on network $\mathbf{N} = (\mathcal{U}, R)$ if and only if for all $x, y, z \in \mathcal{U}$, $x \approx y$ implies both

R1. $xRz \Rightarrow \exists w \in \mathcal{U} : (yRw \wedge w \approx z)$.
R2. $zRx \Rightarrow \exists w \in \mathcal{U} : (wRy \wedge w \approx z)$.

In Figure 6.1, the pair of vertices, a and c, is connected to the rest of the structure in the same way as the h and j pair. The four vertices are regularly equivalent. In a similar way, b, d, g, and i are regularly equivalent. Finally, e and f are regularly equivalent. This is the partition described earlier in this section. Table 6.2 displays the relation matrix whose rows and columns have been permuted into a form compatible with the blockmodel according to the partition $\mathbf{C}$. As was the case with structural equivalence, regular equivalence implies the existence of ideal blocks. The nature of these ideal blocks follows from the following theorem (Batagelj, Doreian, and Ferligoj 1992).

---

4 This is defined as $\delta_{ij} = 0$ if $i \neq j$ and $\delta_{ij} = 1$ if $i = j$.
5 The labels for the diagonal blocks are a little awkward, but their meaning is clear. The null diagonal block with 1s in its diagonal is empirically rare.

```
0 0 0 0 0       1 0 1 0 0
0 0 0 0 0       0 0 1 0 1
0 0 0 0 0       0 1 0 0 0
0 0 0 0 0       1 0 1 1 0
```

Figure 6.3. Ideal blocks for regular equivalence.

Theorem 6.1   *Let* $\mathbf{C} = \{C_i\}$ *be a partition corresponding to a regular equivalence* $\approx$ *on the network* $\mathbf{N} = (\mathcal{U}, R)$. *Then each block* $R(C_u, C_v)$ *is either null or has the property that there is at least one 1 in each of its rows and in each of its columns. Conversely, if for a given clustering* $\mathbf{C}$, *each block has this property, then the corresponding equivalence relation is a regular equivalence.*

Proof: We first prove that in each row of a nonnull block there is at least one 1. Suppose that the block $R(C_u, C_v)$ is not null. Then there exist $x \in C_u$ and $z \in C_v$ such that $r_{xz} = 1$ (i.e., $x R z$). If $C_u = \{x\}$ the proposition follows; otherwise, take $y \in C_u$, $y \neq x$. From the definition of $\mathbf{C}$ it follows that $x \approx y$, and further, by R1, there exists $w \in \mathcal{U}$ such that $y R w$ and $w \approx z$ or equivalently $r_{yw} = 1$ and $w \in C_v$. Therefore we have at least one 1 also in the row corresponding to y in the block $R(C_u, C_v)$. A similar argument, using R2, establishes the property for columns.

To prove the converse, we first prove that the condition R1 holds. Let $x, y \in C_u$. If the block $R(C_u, C_v)$ is null, then the condition R1 holds vacuously; otherwise, there exist $z, w \in C_v$ (therefore $z \approx w$) such that $r_{xz} = 1$ and $r_{yw} = 1$ (i.e., $x R z$ and $y R w$). The condition R1 holds. By a similar argument, the condition R2 holds. $\square$

From this theorem it follows that regular equivalence produces two types of blocks:

- null blocks, which have all entries as 0; and
- one-covered blocks, which have at least one 1 in each row and column.

We use the term regular for these one-covered blocks.

Examples of the ideal blocks for regular equivalence are presented in Figure 6.3. We can see nicely that the regular blocks shown in Table 6.2 form a partition of the Everett 10-node network that is regular.

Automorphic equivalence.   The idea of automorphic equivalence was proposed by Winship (1974, 1988), Mandel (1983), Winship and Mandel (1983), and Borgatti and Everett (1992a). Automorphic equivalence is based on the idea that equivalent units occupy indistinguishable structural locations in the graph. In Chapter 4, we described two networks (graphs) as isomorphic if there is a one-to-one mapping φ of the units $\mathcal{U}$ of $\mathbf{N} = (\mathcal{U}, R)$ to the units $\mathcal{U}'$ of $\mathbf{N}' = (\mathcal{U}', R')$, where $\varphi(x) R' \varphi(y)$ in $\mathbf{N}'$ if and only if $x R y$ in $\mathbf{N}$. The structural properties of $\mathbf{N}$ are preserved exactly in $\mathbf{N}'$. This idea is used here with φ as a one-to-one mapping of $\mathbf{N}$ to itself with the same preserving features of an isomorphism. The units x and y are automorphically equivalent, $x \cong y$, if and only if there exists an automorphism $\varphi : \mathcal{U} \to \mathcal{U}$ of the

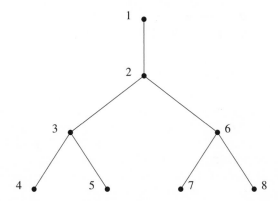

Figure 6.4. A simple graph for illustrating types of equivalences.

relation R such that

$$\varphi(x) = y$$

holds. In Figure 6.1, e and f are automorphically equivalent; the set (b, d, g, h) forms an automorphically equivalent cluster and (a, c, h, j) forms the other automorphically equivalent cluster.[6]

A comparison of some equivalences. The following relation can be proven for these three types of equivalences, where, for a relation R, **Str**(R) is the set of structural equivalences of R, **Aut**(R) is the set of automorphic equivalences of R, and **Reg**(R) is the set of regular equivalences of R:

$$\textbf{Str}(R) \subseteq \textbf{Aut}(R) \subseteq \textbf{Reg}(R).$$

In words, a structural equivalence is also an automorphic equivalence and an automorphic equivalence is also a regular equivalence. This is illustrated by the relation R shown in Figure 6.4. The three exact equivalences are, respectively, structural, automorphic, and regular:

$$\equiv \; = \{\{4, 5\}, \{7, 8\}, \{1\}, \{2\}, \{3\}, \{6\}\},$$
$$\cong \; = \{\{4, 5, 7, 8\}, \{3, 6\}, \{1\}, \{2\}\},$$
$$\approx \; = \{\{1, 4, 5, 7, 8\}, \{2, 3, 6\}\}.$$

Structural equivalence is a very stringent requirement for a network – at least for nontrivial partitions that do not have most vertices as singletons in clusters. Automorphic and regular equivalences have weaker requirements and are more often found in a given network. We also know that, for a network there is, in general, a nonempty set of regular partitions that form a lattice (Borgatti and Everett 1989). In the graphs, especially symmetric graphs, that are constructed

---

6 In this example, both automorphic equivalence and regular equivalence generate the same partition.
   In general, they generate different partitions – as is shown in the next section.

to illustrate equivalence concepts, there tend to be many regular partitions. For example, the graph in Figure 6.1 has 134 regular partitions.

6.1.2   Equivalence and k-partite graphs

A special class of graphs is made up of k-partite graphs (which are defined in Section 4.1.1). It is clear that these graphs have a blocked form in which there are null blocks on the diagonal. The blocks off the diagonal, in general, are not null (although this need not be the case). The complete k-partite graph is one in which all pairs of vertices from different clusters are linked by edges.

Let $\mathbf{G} = (\mathcal{U}, \mathcal{E})$, where $\mathcal{U}$ is the set of vertices of the graph and $\mathcal{E}$ is the set of edges of the graph. Let R be the relation given by $\mathcal{E}$.

Theorem 6.2   *The partition of a complete k-partite graph, **G**, determines an exact structural equivalence.*

Proof: Consider two clusters C_i and C_j with $i \neq j$. Let a_p and a_q be any two vertices in C_i. By definition $a_p R a_q$ does not hold, and the first two conditions for structural equivalence hold trivially. From the complete block structure of R, both a_p and a_q have edges with all elements in C_j. Further, this is true for all clusters C_j. Thus, a_p and a_q are structurally equivalent. This holds for all vertices in C_i, making them all structurally equivalent. This holds for all clusters C_i, where $1 \leq i \leq k$.   □

Theorem 6.3   *The partition of a k-partite graph, **G**, where each vertex $a_p \in C_i$ has an edge with at least one member of each of the other clusters C_j, determines an exact regular equivalence.*

Proof: Let C_i and C_j be any two clusters of the partition of the k-partite graph, and let a_p and a_q be any vertices in C_i. There are no vertices in any cluster without edges involving vertices of each of the other clusters. For a_p there is some vertex, for instance $c_p \in C_j$, such that $a_p R c_p$. Similarly, for a_q there is some vertex, for instance $c_q \in C_j$, such that $a_q R c_q$. This holds for all p and q, and all C_j. Thus, if c_p and c_q are equivalent, then a_p and a_q are also equivalent. However, the same argument holds for c_p and c_q, which implies that all elements in C_i are regularly equivalent. The argument holds for all i, j. Hence, the partition determines an exact regular equivalence.   □

6.1.3   Establishing conventional blockmodels

On the basis of an analyst's substantive concerns, some form of equivalence is selected. The problem of establishing a partition of units in a network, in terms of a considered equivalence, is a special case of the clustering problem that was formulated in Chapter 5. This requires selecting a (dis)similarity measure, computing the (dis)similarities, and applying some clustering algorithm in which a

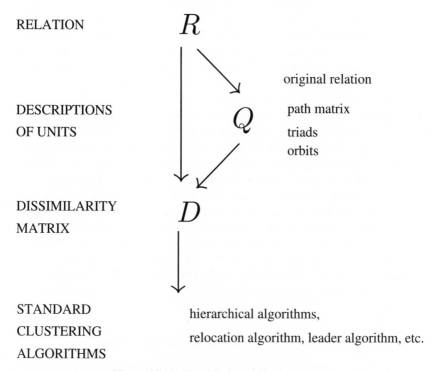

Figure 6.5. Indirect blockmodeling approach.

criterion function is used to ensure that units within a cluster are maximally similar (or minimally dissimilar) to each other and are minimally similar (or maximally dissimilar) to units in other clusters. This task is made more coherent if the equivalence can be expressed in terms of a compatible (dis)similarity measure between pairs of units that reflects the considered equivalence. As an integral part of conventional blockmodeling, an indirect approach is used.

6.1.4 *The indirect blockmodeling approach*

The indirect blockmodeling approach solves the blockmodeling problem by defining a (dis)similarity measure between pairs of units first and then, on this basis, an appropriate clustering criterion function; for example, Ward's (1963) criterion function (see Section 5.4), is selected. For this indirect approach, some typical steps, as shown in Figure 6.5, have to be considered. This indirect approach is implemented in both STRUCTURE and CONCOR,[7] two widely used partitioning algorithms for structural equivalence. They are included in UCINET VI (Borgatti

---

7 Actually, CONCOR has elements of both approaches. See our discussion in Batagelj, Doreian, and Ferligoj (1992b).

et al. 2004).[8] In CONCOR, iterated correlations are used to generate a sequence of binary splits of the set of units,[9] whereas in STRUCTURE, dissimilarity measures are created first and then clustering procedures are used. Once the partitions are created, they can be evaluated.[10] Additionally, attempts are made to interpret the composition of clustered units in terms of R and in terms of attributes of the units in the cluster (see also Wasserman and Faust 1994).

In this process, we first select a description of the units. For example, a description can consist of the row and column of the original relational matrix for the selected unit. Another example is the distribution of triads for each unit (its triadic spectrum; see Hummell and Sodeur 1987). Batagelj, Doreian, and Ferligoj (1992b) discussed some of these descriptions. The next step of the indirect approach is the definition of a dissimilarity measure. This is a crucial step for the indirect approach, for not all dissimilarities are consistent with the selected equivalence. Here, the most important requirement is that the selected dissimilarity measure be compatible[11] with the considered equivalence (Batagelj, Doreian, and Ferligoj 1992b). On the basis of the selected dissimilarity measure, different efficient clustering algorithms can be used such as the hierarchical algorithms, the relocation algorithm, or the leader algorithm presented in Chapter 5.

6.1.5   Measuring the equivalence of pairs of units

In this section we discuss the first step of the indirect approach – obtaining a dissimilarity matrix for structural equivalence. Although the definition of structural equivalence is local (in the sense of being connected to *some* other units), it has global implications because both location and position in networks are defined in terms of *all* other units in a network. We start by considering properties of units and then move to properties of pairs of units. With this done, we consider some dissimilarity measures. This is more than a technical exercise because, if the indirect approach is used, we must know that a selected measure is compatible (defined in this section) with either structural or regular equivalence depending on which is used. This point is emphasized in Section 6.1.6.

Properties of units. The property $t : \mathcal{U} \rightarrow \mathbb{R}$ is *structural* if, for every automorphism φ of the relation R, and every unit $x \in \mathcal{U}$, it holds that

$$t(x) = t(\varphi(x)).$$

---

8   At this time, STRUCTURE is no longer maintained as a generally available program. However, some of its procedures can be found in UCINET.

9   This feature makes it a divisive procedure in which coarse clusters are established and the clusters are partitioned further.

10   For example, in STRUCTURE, a confirmatory factor analysis was used to evaluate the adequacy of a partition.

11   We define this concept in Section 6.1.5.

Let u be an instance of an x, and let $t(u)$ be a structural property of the unit u. Then we have

$$x \equiv y \Rightarrow t(x) = t(y).$$

Some examples of a structural property include

$$t(u) = \text{the degree of unit } u \text{ (the number of neighbors of } u),$$

or (see Batagelj 1990)

$$t(u) = \text{number of units at distance } d \text{ from the unit } u,$$

or (see Burt 1990)

$$t(u) = \text{number of triads of type } x \text{ at the unit } u.$$

Centrality measures (Freeman 1979) are further examples of structural properties.

The collection of structural properties $t_1, t_2, \ldots, t_m$ is *complete* (for structural equivalence) if, and only if, for each pair of units x and y,

$$(\forall i, 1 \le i \le m : t_i(x) = t_i(y)) \Rightarrow x \equiv y$$

is satisfied. The number and distribution of triads involving a unit (its triadic spectrum) are not complete. The path of length 3 provides a simple counterexample. The extreme units have the same triadic spectrum, but they are not structurally equivalent.

We can define the description of the unit u as

$$[u] = [t_1(u), t_2(u), \ldots, t_m(u)].$$

As a simple example, t_1 could be degree centrality, t_2 could be closeness centrality, and t_3 could be betweenness centrality. The dissimilarity between units u and v could be defined as

$$d(u, v) = D([u], [v]),$$

where D is some (standard) dissimilarity between real vectors. In the simple example, D could be the Euclidean distance between the centrality profiles.

In the case in which the dissimilarity D has the property

$$D([u], [v]) = 0 \Rightarrow [u] = [v]$$

and the properties $t_1, t_2, \ldots, t_m$ are complete, then

$$d(u, v) = 0 = D([u], [v]) \Leftrightarrow [u] = [v] \Leftrightarrow \forall i : t_i(u) = t_i(v) \Leftrightarrow u \equiv v.$$

Therefore, we finally have

$$d(u, v) = 0 \Leftrightarrow u \equiv v.$$

Properties of pairs of units. A property $q : \mathcal{U} \times \mathcal{U} \to \mathbb{R}$ is *structural* if, for every automorphism φ of the relation R, and for every pair of units $x, y \in \mathcal{U}$, the following holds:

$$q(x, y) = q(\varphi(x), \varphi(y)).$$

For example, q can be the original relation R:

$$q(u, v) = r(u, v).$$

Fiksel (1980) provided another example:

$$q(u, v) = \text{number of common neighbors of units } u \text{ and } v.$$

As a final example,

$$q(u, v) = \text{length of the shortest path from } u \text{ to } v.$$

We note that if the union of the neighborhoods of u and v is identical to the intersection of their neighborhoods, then u and v are structurally equivalent (Fiksel 1980).

Let $q(u, v)$ be a structural property of units u and v. Then, if $x \equiv y$, we have

q1.　$q(x, y) = q(y, x)$.
q2.　$q(x, x) = q(y, y)$.
q3.　$\forall z \in \mathcal{U} \setminus \{x, y\} : q(x, z) = q(y, z)$.
q4.　$\forall z \in \mathcal{U} \setminus \{x, y\} : q(z, x) = q(z, y)$.

The property q is *sensitive* if properties q1–q4 imply also that $x \equiv y$. An example of a nonsensitive property is

$$q(u, v) = \begin{cases} 1 & u R^\star v \\ 0 & \text{otherwise,} \end{cases}$$

where $R^\star$ is the transitive and reflexive closure of R. For a sensitive property q, we can describe each unit u by a vector

$$[u] = [q(u, x_1), q(u, x_2), \ldots, q(u, x_n), q(x_1, u), \ldots, q(x_n, u)]$$

and define the dissimilarity between units $u, v \in \mathcal{U}$ as

$$d(u, v) = D([u], [v]),$$

where D is a dissimilarity between the corresponding descriptions. Some examples of relevant dissimilarities, together with a discussion of their appropriateness, follow.

Dissimilarities. We consider the following list of dissimilarities[12] between units x_i and x_j, where the description of the unit consists of the row and column of the property matrix.

12　The first two were introduced in Section 5.3.1.

The Manhattan distance is

$$d_m(x_i, x_j) = \sum_{s=1}^{n} (|q_{is} - q_{js}| + |q_{si} - q_{sj}|).$$

The Euclidean distance is

$$d_E(x_i, x_j) = \sqrt{\sum_{s=1}^{n} ((q_{is} - q_{js})^2 + (q_{si} - q_{sj})^2)}.$$

The truncated Manhattan distance is

$$d_s(x_i, x_j) = \sum_{\substack{s=1 \\ s \neq i,j}}^{n} (|q_{is} - q_{js}| + |q_{si} - q_{sj}|).$$

The truncated Euclidean distance (Faust 1988) is

$$d_S(x_i, x_j) = \sqrt{\sum_{\substack{s=1 \\ s \neq i,j}}^{n} ((q_{is} - q_{js})^2 + (q_{si} - q_{sj})^2)}.$$

The corrected Manhattan-like dissimilarity ($p > 0$)[13] is

$$d_c(p)(x_i, x_j) = d_s(x_i, x_j) + p \cdot (|q_{ii} - q_{jj}| + |q_{ij} - q_{ji}|).$$

The corrected Euclidean-like dissimilarity (Burt and Minor 1983) is

$$d_e(p)(x_i, x_j) = \sqrt{d_S(x_i, x_j)^2 + p \cdot ((q_{ii} - q_{jj})^2 + (q_{ij} - q_{ji})^2)}.$$

The corrected dissimilarity is

$$d_C(p)(x_i, x_j) = \sqrt{d_c(p)(x_i, x_j)}.$$

It is easy to verify that all expressions from the list define a dissimilarity, that is, that $d(x, y) \geq 0$, $d(x, x) = 0$, and $d(x, y) = d(y, x)$. Each of the dissimilarities from the list can be assessed to see whether or not it is also a distance.[14]

Compatibility. For procedures based on structural equivalence, we expect the best results if we use a dissimilarity *d compatible* with structural equivalence. That is, we expect the best results if

$$x_i \equiv x_j \Leftrightarrow d(x_i, x_j) = 0.$$

Not all the dissimilarities from the preceding list are compatible with structural equivalence.

---

13   The parameter p can take any positive value. Typically, $p = 1$ or $p = 2$, where these values count the number of times the corresponding diagonal pairs are counted.

14   A dissimilarity d is a distance if $d(x, y) = 0 \Rightarrow x = y$ and $d(x, y) + d(y, z) \geq d(x, z)$.

If q is sensitive, for dissimilarities d_m and d_E we have only

$$d(x_i, x_j) = 0 \Rightarrow x_i \equiv x_j.$$

The converse does not hold. For the matrix

$$\mathbf{R} = \begin{bmatrix} 0 & 1 \\ 1 & 0 \end{bmatrix}$$

the units x_1 and x_2 are structurally equivalent, but (for $q = r$) $d_m(x_1, x_2) = 2$ and $d_E(x_1, x_2) = \sqrt{2}$.

If q is a structural property, for dissimilarities d_S and d_s we have only

$$x_i \equiv x_j \Rightarrow d(x_i, x_j) = 0.$$

Again, the converse does not hold. For the matrix

$$\mathbf{R} = \begin{bmatrix} 1 & 1 \\ 0 & 0 \end{bmatrix}$$

for $q = r$, $d_S(x_1, x_2) = d_s(x_1, x_2) = 0$, but the units x_1 and x_2 are not structurally equivalent.

If a structural property q is sensitive, the dissimilarities d_c, d_C, and d_e are compatible with structural equivalence.

To see this, suppose that $x_i \equiv x_j$. Then, from the properties q1–q4 this follows:

q1'. $q_{ij} - q_{ji} = 0$.
q2'. $q_{ii} - q_{jj} = 0$.
q3'. $\forall k \neq i, j : q_{ik} - q_{jk} = 0$.
q4'. $\forall k \neq i, j : q_{ki} - q_{kj} = 0$.

Therefore all the terms that occur on the right-hand-side expressions in the definitions of dissimilarities d_c, d_C, and d_e are zero. Hence also $d_c(x_i, x_j) = d_C(x_i, x_j) = d_e(x_i, x_j) = 0$. We have proved

$$x_i \equiv x_j \Rightarrow d(x_i, x_j) = 0.$$

To prove also that

$$d(x_i, x_j) = 0 \Rightarrow x_i \equiv x_j,$$

we prove the equivalent statement

$$x_i \not\equiv x_j \Rightarrow d(x_i, x_j) \neq 0.$$

By assumption, q is sensitive. If $x_i \not\equiv x_j$, it follows that for at least one pair of units x_u, x_v, $\{u, v\} \cap \{i, j\} \neq \emptyset$, at least one of the properties q1–q4 does not hold. This means that $q_{uv} \neq q_{vu}$ or equivalently $q_{uv} - q_{vu} \neq 0$. The dissimilarities d_c, d_C, and d_e have value zero exactly when all the terms are zero. Therefore, in this case they are different from zero.

We emphasize that if a property is sensitive, then the corrected Manhattan d_c, corrected Euclidean d_e, and corrected dissimilarity d_C are all compatible with

Table 6.3. Everett Network – Corrected Euclidean Dissimilarities

a	b	c	d	e	f	g	h	i	j	
0.00	2.00	0.00	2.00	2.00	3.46	3.46	3.46	3.46	3.46	a
–	0.00	2.00	0.00	2.83	2.83	3.46	3.46	3.46	3.46	b
–	–	0.00	2.00	2.00	3.46	3.46	3.46	3.46	3.46	c
–	–	–	0.00	2.83	2.83	3.46	3.46	3.46	3.46	d
–	–	–	–	0.00	2.83	2.83	3.46	2.83	3.46	e
–	–	–	–	–	0.00	2.83	2.00	2.83	2.00	f
–	–	–	–	–	–	0.00	2.00	0.00	2.00	g
–	–	–	–	–	–	–	0.00	2.00	0.00	h
–	–	–	–	–	–	–	–	0.00	2.00	i
–	–	–	–	–	–	–	–	–	0.00	j

structural equivalence. For each, two units are structurally equivalent exactly when their dissimilarities are zero.

An example. We return to the Everett network in Figure 6.1 to consider it in terms of structural equivalence. We have already shown that the following are pairs of structurally equivalent units: $\{a, c\}$, $\{b, d\}$, $\{g, i\}$, and $\{h, j\}$. These are the only clusters containing more than one structurally equivalent unit. To illustrate the issue of compatibility for the indirect approach, we used the corrected Euclidean-like dissimilarity measure on the original relation ($p = 2$) to obtain the measures shown in Table 6.3 (in upper triangular form).

Using the Ward method with the agglomerative algorithm (described in Chapter 5), we clustered the units of the network. The resulting dendrogram in Figure 6.6 shows nicely the four pairs of structurally equivalent units. Suppose, however, that we used the uncorrected Euclidean distance as a measure of the extent to which pairs of actors are dissimilar (not structurally equivalent). The measures shown in Table 6.4 differ from those shown in Table 6.3. Notice that, in Table 6.3, $d_e(a, c) = 0$ as it should because a and c are structurally equivalent. However,

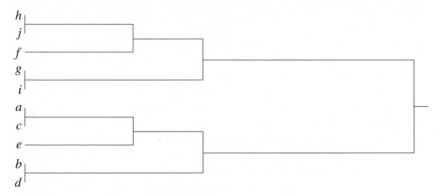

Figure 6.6. Everett network – indirect approach (Ward).

Table 6.4. Everett Network – Uncorrected Euclidean Distances

a	b	c	d	e	f	g	h	i	j	
0.00	2.83	2.00	2.83	2.00	3.46	3.46	3.46	3.46	3.46	a
–	0.00	2.83	0.00	3.64	2.83	3.46	3.46	3.46	3.46	b
–	–	0.00	2.83	2.00	3.46	3.46	3.46	3.46	3.46	c
–	–	–	0.00	3.46	2.83	3.46	3.46	3.46	3.46	d
–	–	–	–	0.00	3.46	2.83	3.46	2.83	3.46	e
–	–	–	–	–	0.00	3.46	2.00	3.46	2.00	f
–	–	–	–	–	–	0.00	2.83	0.00	2.83	g
–	–	–	–	–	–	–	0.00	2.83	2.00	h
–	–	–	–	–	–	–	–	0.00	2.83	i
–	–	–	–	–	–	–	–	–	0.00	j

in Table 6.4, $d_E(a, c) = 2$. The same problem occurs for j and h. In addition, other dissimilarity measures change in magnitude when an uncorrected Euclidean distance is used. Although it is clear that sensitive and compatible measures can be defined for structural equivalence, defining such measures seems far more difficult for regular equivalence.

6.2   OPTIMIZATION AND BLOCKMODELING

There are at least three serious problems in the indirect approach found within conventional blockmodeling. One is that compatible (dis)similarity measures have to be used. Although this can be done for structural equivalence, it seems unlikely that such a measure can be specified for regular equivalence. Furthermore, if other equivalence types are specified, it will be necessary to construct compatible (dis)similarity measures for them also. We propose a more general approach that does not require the use of (dis)similarity measures for all pairs of units. A second problem is more fundamental. Although criterion functions are central in cluster analysis, their use within indirect blockmodeling has remained implicit and not tightly coupled to the specific equivalence concept informing a blockmodeling effort. We propose bringing criterion functions to center stage so that they reflect exactly the equivalence concept mobilized for a blockmodeling analysis. A third problem with using indirect methods for conventional blockmodeling is that there are no explicit measures of fit that are integral to the process of fitting blockmodels. We propose optimizing well-defined criterion functions to identify blockmodels so that the minimized criterion function becomes a direct measure of how well a blockmodel fits the network data.

The construction of these criterion functions stems from the observation that a specified equivalence type implies a set of permitted (ideal) blocks. For structural equivalence, these blocks are the null and complete blocks; for regular equivalence, the ideal blocks are the null and regular blocks. Given an empirical block and a

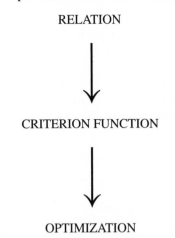

Figure 6.7. Direct blockmodeling approach.

corresponding ideal block, it is a straightforward matter to construct a measure of the extent to which the empirical block departs from the ideal block. Of course, there will be alternative ways of constructing such measures, and we do need to be careful about which measure is chosen.[15] This measure can be constructed for each block, and these discrepancies can be combined (usually by addition) to create a measure of the overall difference between an empirical blockmodel and a corresponding ideal blockmodel. This measure forms the criterion function, and we seek partitions of a network (into clusters of units and blocks as clusters of ties) that minimize this criterion function. For obvious reasons, we call this the direct blockmodeling approach for establishing blockmodels. The typical steps for the direct blockmodeling approach are shown in Figure 6.7.

6.2.1 The direct blockmodeling approach

Assume that we have a single relation network $\mathbf{N} = (\mathcal{U}, R)$. Let Θ denote the set of all equivalence relations of a selected type (e.g., regular or structural equivalence) over $\mathbf{N}$. Every equivalence relation $\sim$ on $\mathcal{U}$ determines a partition $\mathbf{C}$ of $\mathcal{U}$, and vice versa. Let Φ denote the set of all partitions corresponding to the relations from Θ.

If we are able to construct a criterion function $P(\mathbf{C})$ with the properties

P1. $P(\mathbf{C}) \geq 0$,
P2. $P(\mathbf{C}) = 0 \Leftrightarrow \sim \in \Theta$,

then we can express the problem of establishing a partition of a network, in terms of a specific type of equivalence, as a clustering problem. If there are exact

---

15 Even so, each such measure will be a direct reflection of the discrepancy between an empirical block and an ideal block.

equivalences, then (by P2) the minimal value of $P(\mathbf{C})$ is 0. In the case in which Θ is empty, the optimization approach gives the solution(s) that differ(s) least from some ideal case.

Given a clustering $\mathbf{C} = \{C_1, C_2, \ldots, C_k\}$, let $\mathcal{B}(C_u, C_v)$ denote the set of all ideal blocks corresponding to block $R(C_u, C_v)$. Then the total inconsistency of clustering $\mathbf{C}$ (with an ideal clustering) can be expressed as the sum of inconsistencies within blocks (block inconsistencies) across all blocks:

$$P(\mathbf{C}) = \sum_{C_u, C_v \in \mathbf{C}} p(C_u, C_v).$$

The block inconsistency is

$$p(C_u, C_v) = \min_{B \in \mathcal{B}(C_u, C_v)} \delta(R(C_u, C_v), B),$$

where the term $\delta(R(C_u, C_v), B)$ measures the deviation (number of inconsistencies) of the block $R(C_u, C_v)$ from the ideal block B. Of course, the function δ has to be compatible with the selected type of equivalence.

6.2.2 A criterion for structural equivalence

The ideal blocks for structural equivalence are discussed in Section 6.1.1. The term $\delta(R(C_u, C_v), B)$ can be expressed, for nondiagonal blocks, as

$$\delta(R(C_u, C_v), B) = \sum_{x \in C_u, y \in C_v} |r_{xy} - b_{xy}|.$$

In this expression, r_{xy} is the observed tie and b_{xy} is the corresponding value in an ideal block. It is easy to verify that a criterion function $P(\mathbf{C})$ defined in this fashion is sensitive to structural equivalence:

$$P(\mathbf{C}) = 0 \Leftrightarrow \mathbf{C} \text{ defines structural equivalence.}$$

As defined, the deviation between blocks is based on the assumption that the inconsistency $0 \to 1$ is equiprobable[16] with the inconsistency $1 \to 0$. To deal with instances in which the assumption is not be valid, we introduce two parameters, α and β, to weight the two types of inconsistencies. Let B^* be a solution of an optimization problem from the expression for $p(C_u, C_v)$. Then we can redefine p, for example, as follows:

$$p(C_u, C_v) = \alpha \, \text{card}\{(x, y) \in C_u \times C_v : r_{xy} > b^*_{xy}\}$$
$$+ \beta \, \text{card}\{(x, y) \in C_u \times C_v : r_{xy} < b^*_{xy}\}.$$

Selecting large α ($\alpha = 100$) and small β ($\beta = 1$), optimizing $P(\mathbf{C})$, we are primarily seeking solutions with the least number of inconsistencies of the type $0 \to 1$ and, as a secondary criterion, among them solutions with the least number

---

16 In addition, it is invariant to the transformation of complementing the relation $R \to \mathcal{U} \times \mathcal{U} \setminus R$. Empirically this case is not infrequent.

of inconsistencies of the type $1 \rightarrow 0$. If we reverse the magnitudes of the weights, greater emphasis is placed on the $1 \rightarrow 0$ inconsistencies. The option chosen rests on substantive concerns. When a block has very few departures from an ideal block, then the terms *null block* and *complete block* in a description of an empirical blockmodel are unambiguous. There is a special – but not infrequent – case in which the number of 0s is the same as the number of 1s in a block $R(C_u, C_v)$. For this we select 1s in a block for B^* if $\alpha \geq \beta$ and 0s in a block otherwise.

The values of the criterion function decrease as the number of clusters specified for structural equivalence increases. This illustrates a general result.

Theorem 6.4 *For establishing optimal partitions of units in a network, based on the concept of structural equivalence, the optimized values of the criterion function decrease monotonically*[17] *with the number of clusters.*

Proof: Consider an optimal partition with k clusters and let the value of the criterion function be f. Next consider an optimal partition with $k + 1$ clusters that has been obtained from the k-cluster partition by splitting a cluster of that partition. This split induces splits in the blocks for the split cluster. Consider an off-diagonal block split into two subblocks. If this were a null block split into two null subblocks, the same 1s would remain inconsistencies and the criterion function would remain at f. However, if a subblock is now a one block, then there must be more 1s than 0s and the criterion function will drop below f to some value denoted by f_p. A similar argument holds for a one block split into two subblocks with the role of 0s and 1s reversed. For the diagonal blocks there will be a split into four subblocks, and an argument similar to the one used for off-diagonal blocks holds for them. There may be a partition into $k + 1$ clusters that is not nested inside an optimal partition into k clusters. Let the criterion function be f_q. By the above argument, an optimal partition into k clusters can have a cluster split to create a partition with a criterion function of f_p or f. If the criterion function f_q is above f or f_p, it is not optimal. The criterion function of the optimal partition will be bounded above by f or by $f_p < f_q$.   □

6.2.3 A criterion for regular equivalence

The construction of the criterion function for regular equivalence is based on ideal blocks discussed in Section 6.1.2.

As a measure of regularity of a block, the quantity

$$\delta(R(C_u, C_v), B) = \begin{cases} \text{number of 1-covered rows or columns} & B \text{ is null block} \\ \text{number of 0 rows or columns} & B \text{ is regular block} \end{cases}$$

can be used. From Theorem 6.3, it follows that the criterion function $P(\mathbf{C})$, so defined, is sensitive to regular equivalence:

$$P(\mathbf{C}) = 0 \Leftrightarrow \mathbf{C} \text{ defines a regular equivalence.}$$

17   In general, this is not a strictly monotonic decrease.

In Chapter 7 another measure of regularity of a block is defined that also gives a sensitive criterion function to regular equivalence.

6.2.4   A clustering algorithm

In the case of the direct blockmodeling approach, where an appropriate criterion function to capture the selected equivalence is constructed, one of the local optimization clustering procedures can be used to solve the given blockmodeling problem (Batagelj et al., 1992).

We propose using the relocation algorithm introduced in Section 5.4.3.

Determine the initial clustering $\mathbf{C}$;
repeat:
> **if** in the neighborhood of the current clustering $\mathbf{C}$
> there exists a clustering $\mathbf{C}'$ such that $P(\mathbf{C}') < P(\mathbf{C})$
> **then** move to clustering $\mathbf{C}'$.

Usually, the neighborhood is determined by two transformations: moving a unit from one cluster to another cluster, and interchanging two units from different clusters.

To obtain a so-called good solution and an impression of its quality, we repeat the procedure with different (random) initial partitions $\mathbf{C}$. If the procedure is repeated many times (i.e., some hundreds or thousands of times), all or most[18] of the partitions of the selected type of equivalence (structural or regular) in a given network can be found.

6.2.5   Two artificial examples

We use two of the networks that we considered earlier to illustrate the direct approach for constructing blockmodels. We use the first to examine both structural and regular equivalences, and we use the second for regular equivalence only.

We first note that both networks are small enough for us to search through all possible partitions. In general, of course, we cannot do this for large networks. We do so here only as a demonstration that the direct clustering methods we are considering do locate the exact structural equivalence partitions.

The Everett network. The Everett 10-node network (see Figure 6.1 and Table 6.1) was searched for all structural equivalence partitions into 1–10 clusters. The results are presented in Table 6.5. The relocation procedure was then repeated

---

18 Because this is a local optimization procedure, there is no guarantee that we will identify all partitions with a minimized criterion function. This is a price we are prepared to pay. For small networks, with roughly 12 or fewer units, an exhaustive search can be done (see the next section) and all optimal blockmodels can be identified. As the size of the network grows, the risk of missing some optimal partitions increases (which accounts for the need for multiple repetitions).

Table 6.5. Number of Clusters and Structural
Equivalence: Direct Approach

Number of Clusters	Minimum Value Criterion Function	Number of Different Obtained Partitions
1	30	1
2	14	1
3	10	2
4	6	1
5	4	2
6	0	1
7	0	4
8	0	6
9	0	4
10	0	1

300 times for each number of clusters. Because the analyzed network is rather simple, these were enough to obtain all of the exact solutions. These are all congruent with the indirect solution presented in the Ward dendrogram in Figure 6.6. Note the monotone decline in the size of the minimum value of the criterion function.

We also searched the Everett network for regular equivalence partitions. By means of an exhaustive search, all exact regular equivalences in the network were found. Table 6.6 shows the distribution of the number of clusters in a partition and the number of different obtained regular partitions. In addition, we used the relocation procedure with our proposed criterion function. All of the exact regular

Table 6.6. All Regular Partitions of the
Everett Network

Number of Clusters	Number of All Partitions	Number of Regular Partitions
1	1	1
2	511	94
3	9,330	7
4	34,105	12
5	42,525	4
6	22,827	1
7	5,880	4
8	750	6
9	45	4
10	1	1
Total	106,975	134

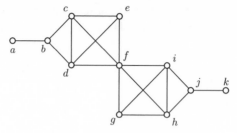

Figure 6.8. Second artificial example.

partitions were obtained with 300 repetitions of the local optimization (relocation) algorithm.[19]

The table shows that, for each number of clusters, there exists at least one regular partition. There are 94 different regular partitions into two clusters, and larger numbers of clusters have considerably fewer partitions. The unique regular partitions into six clusters is exactly the coarsest structural equivalence partition with six clusters.[20]

A second artificial network. The second network we use to illustrate the direct approach is shown in Figure 6.8. It is also small enough for an exhaustive search. Table 6.7 displays the results of that search.

There are the following 21 regular partitions of this network.

There is the 11-cluster partition:

$$P_1 = \{\{a\}, \{b\}, \{c\}, \{d\}, \{e\}, \{f\}, \{g\}, \{h\}, \{i\}, \{j\}, \{k\}\}.$$

There are the 10-cluster partitions:

$$P_2 = \{\{c, d\}, \{a\}, \{b\}, \{e\}, \{f\}, \{g\}, \{h\}, \{i\}, \{j\}, \{k\}\},$$
$$P_3 = \{\{h, i\}, \{a\}, \{b\}, \{c\}, \{d\}, \{e\}, \{f\}, \{g\}, \{j\}, \{k\}\}.$$

There are the nine-cluster partitions:

$$P_4 = \{\{c, d\}, \{h, i\}, \{a\}, \{b\}, \{e\}, \{f\}, \{g\}, \{j\}, \{k\}\}.$$

There are the six-cluster partitions:

$$P_5 = \{\{a, k\}, \{b, j\}, \{c, h\}, \{d, i\}, \{e, g\}, \{f\}\},$$
$$P_6 = \{\{a, k\}, \{b, j\}, \{c, i\}, \{d, h\}, \{e, g\}, \{f\}\}.$$

There are the five-cluster partitions:

$$P_7 = \{\{a, k\}, \{b, j\}, \{c, d, h, i\}, \{e, g\}, \{f\}\},$$

---

19 As a practical matter, it is good to increase the number of repetitions when the size (*n*) of the network increases or the number of positions (*k*) specified is increased. Adopting this strategy lowers the risk of missing optimal partitions.

20 All of the regular partitions into higher numbers of clusters yield all the corresponding structural equivalence partitions.

Table 6.7. All Regular Partitions of the
Second Network

Number of Clusters	Number of All Partitions	Number of Regular Partitions
1	1	1
2	1,023	10
3	28,501	0
4	145,750	1
5	246,730	3
6	179,487	2
7	63,987	0
8	11,880	0
9	1,155	1
10	55	2
11	1	1
Total	678,570	21

$$P_8 = \{\{a, k\}, \{b, j\}, \{c, h\}, \{d, i\}, \{e, f, g\}\},$$
$$P_9 = \{\{a, k\}, \{b, j\}, \{c, i\}, \{d, h\}, \{e, f, g\}\}.$$

There is the four-cluster partition:

$$P_{10} = \{\{a, k\}, \{b, j\}, \{c, d, h, i\}, \{e, f, g\}\}.$$

There are the two-cluster partitions:

$$P_{11} = \{\{a, c, g, k\}, \{b, d, e, f, h, i, j\}\},$$
$$P_{12} = \{\{a, c, h, k\}, \{b, d, e, f, g, i, j\}\},$$
$$P_{13} = \{\{a, c, i, k\}, \{b, d, e, f, g, h, j\}\},$$
$$P_{14} = \{\{a, d, g, k\}, \{b, c, e, f, h, i, j\}\},$$
$$P_{15} = \{\{a, d, h, k\}, \{b, c, e, f, g, i, j\}\},$$
$$P_{16} = \{\{a, d, i, k\}, \{b, c, e, f, g, h, j\}\},$$
$$P_{17} = \{\{a, e, g, k\}, \{b, c, d, f, h, i, j\}\},$$
$$P_{18} = \{\{a, e, h, k\}, \{b, c, d, f, g, i, j\}\},$$
$$P_{19} = \{\{a, e, i, k\}, \{b, c, d, f, g, h, j\}\},$$
$$P_{20} = \{\{a, f, k\}, \{b, c, d, e, g, h, i, j\}\}.$$

There is the one-cluster partition:

$$P_{21} = \{\{a, b, c, d, e, f, g, h, i, j, k\}\}.$$

These partitions form the lattice displayed in Figure 6.9.

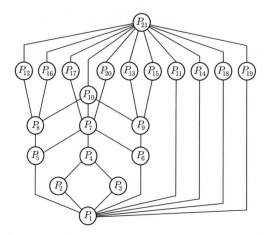

Figure 6.9. The lattice of regular partitions of Figure 6.8.

6.3   REPRESENTING PARTITIONS

Faust and Wasserman (1992:13) described three ways in which a partition can be represented: as a density table, as an image matrix (e.g., Table 6.2), and as a reduced (image) graph (e.g., Figure 6.2). All of these forms are useful for role analyses. However, the decision to proceed with a particular partition in terms of any of the representations considered by Faust and Wasserman rests on a prior representation – a representation that is more intuitive and visual. This is the conjunction of the partition established in some fashion and a particular diagram of the network. To illustrate this we consider the 12-node network on the left in Figure 6.10. Table 6.8 gives the count of all regular partitions. There are three regular partitions with five clusters. One of these is the partition shown on the

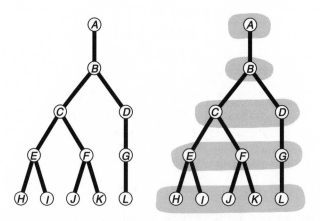

Figure 6.10. An obvious five-cluster regular partition of the 12-node network.

Table 6.8. 12-Node Network – All Regular
Partitions

Number of Clusters	Total Number of Partitions	Number of Regular Partitions
1	1	1
2	2,047	1
3	86,526	27
4	611,501	0
5	1,379,400	3
6	1,323,652	0
7	627,396	0
8	159,027	1
9	22,275	2
10	1,705	1
11	66	2
12	1	1
Total	4,213,597	39

right side in Figure 6.10, which has the obvious partition imposed on it, which is consistent with the way the network is drawn on the left side.

However, from Table 6.8 there are two other exact regular partitions with five clusters. One of these is shown on the left side of Figure 6.11, where the partition is imposed on the network as drawn in Figure 6.10. At face value, the partition and the network are not consistent. However, if the network is redrawn as shown on the right side of Figure 6.11, this partition appears consistent with the network. The third exact, regular partition is shown in Figure 6.12, where it is imposed on the network as it was originally drawn. Here the partition seems even less consistent with the network. Yet the network can be redrawn in another way that makes this

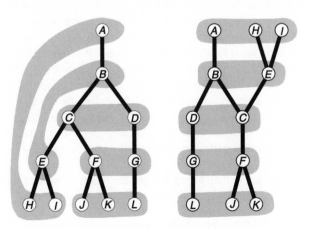

Figure 6.11. A second five-cluster regular partition of the 12-node network.

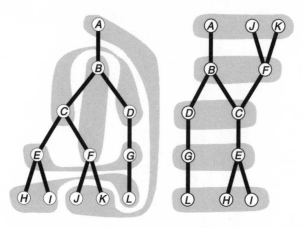

Figure 6.12. A third five-cluster regular partition of the 12-node network.

partition also appear consistent with the structure of the network. Of course, all of the exact, regular partitions of the units of the network are consistent with the structure. It is only the appearance of the network that differs. The importance of this example is that the appearance of a network, in a particular diagram, may cloud our judgment of whether a partition that has been established is consistent with the network structure. Both of the partitions on the left side of Figure 6.11 or Figure 6.12, if imposed on the network as drawn in Figure 6.10, could lead the analyst to conclude that the partition is not consistent with the network structure. In this case, none of the representational forms (i.e., density table, image matrix, and image graph) would be invoked and the informal visual examination of the network would have eliminated a potential role analysis.

Serious implications are suggested by this example. All that the blockmodeling procedures do is find partitions consistent with a particular type of equivalence: They solve the blockmodeling problem. The direct approach makes this very explicit. In general, it returns multiple partitions with some optimal value of the criterion function. There is no way in which such a technical procedure can choose among equally well-fitting partitions. It seems that additional substantive or ethnographic information is needed for making that selection. For an ongoing study, or one with rich documentation,[21] this is unproblematic. For relational data, with little description beyond those data, there will be real difficulties in selecting an appropriate representation. Another implication is that regular equivalence is a subtle and general equivalence. By using it, we face getting many seemingly strange partitions that are fully consistent with this equivalence type.

Consider again the graph in Figure 6.8 and the image shown in Figure 6.13. One of the 21 exact, regular partitions of this network is P_7, and Table 6.9 displays the

21   The BWR data (see Chapter 2) provide an example.

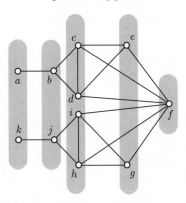

Figure 6.13. A redrawn version of Figure 6.8.

adjacency matrix in a blocked and permuted form consistent with P_7. By inspection, it is clearly a regular partition because the blocks are either null or one covered. In Figure 6.8, it is clear that f is the most central unit in the network. Cluster P_5 has only f as a member and does not appear as central in Figure 6.13. The issue is not whether Figure 6.13 is a distorted version of Figure 6.8. Rather, with multiple, equally well-fitting partitions, we have to examine alternative potential interpretations. This is another reminder that the initial picture we draw of a network – if we draw one at all – may mislead us. A seemingly strange regular partition can force us to reconsider the shape of the network(s) we study. This seems a beneficial outcome. We can push this further. When the indirect approach – especially with the use of hierarchical clustering methods – to blockmodeling is used, there seems to be

Table 6.9. A Regular Equivalence Partition of
Figure 1.8

·	a	k	b	j	c	d	h	i	e	g	f
a	0	0	1	0	0	0	0	0	0	0	0
k	0	0	0	1	0	0	0	0	0	0	0
b	1	0	0	0	1	1	0	0	0	0	0
j	0	1	0	0	0	0	1	1	0	0	0
c	0	0	1	0	0	1	0	0	1	0	1
d	0	0	1	0	1	0	0	0	1	0	1
h	0	0	0	1	0	0	0	1	0	1	1
i	0	0	0	1	0	0	1	0	0	1	1
e	0	0	0	0	1	1	0	0	0	0	1
g	0	0	0	0	0	0	1	1	0	0	1
f	0	0	0	0	1	1	1	1	1	1	0

Table 6.10. *Transatlantic Industries – Structural Equivalences and Direct Solutions*

Number of Clusters	1	2	3	4	5	6	7	8	9	10	11	12	13
Cluster Function	37	29	23	20	17	13	10	8	5	3	0	0	0
Number of Partitions	1	1	2	1	3	3	1	3	2	3	1	3	1

a tendency to select and interpret *the* blockmodel.[22] The direct approach permits the identification of multiple, equally well-fitting blockmodels. At a minimum, this forces us to think further about the blockmodels that have been established, which is another beneficial outcome.

6.4 SOME EMPIRICAL EXAMPLES

We now consider some empirical examples that include networks described in Chapters 1 and 2. Each direct partitioning effort starts with a specification of the number, k, of clusters of units. The first step of the relocation method we use – as proposed in Section 6.2.4 – is a random split of the units into k clusters. Given the equivalence selected and the implied ideal block types, the criterion function is calculated. Denote its value by P_1. Randomly selected units in two clusters can be interchanged between the clusters or one unit can be moved from one cluster to another. This gives a new partition and with it a new blockmodel. The criterion function can be calculated for it. Denote this value by P_2. If $P_2 \geq P_1$, the new partition (blockmodel) is discarded. However, if $P_2 < P_1$, we move to the new blockmodel and repeat either the interchange of units between clusters or the movement of one unit from one cluster to another to get a new blockmodel. If there is a drop in the value of the criterion function, we move to new blockmodel. This continues until no further improvement is possible. This so-called best blockmodel is retained and the relocation method is used again. This leads to another best blockmodel (in the next sequence of examined blockmodels), which is also stored. After many repetitions, we select the blockmodel(s) with the smallest identified value of the criterion function. In this sense, the optimization is built into the fitting procedure.

6.4.1 *Two little league baseball teams*

Consider the network of friendship ties that was displayed in Figure 1.1. The social actors are members of an LL baseball team, as reported by Fine (1987). Table 6.10 displays a summary of the partitions established by using the direct approach for structural equivalence. For a given number of clusters in a partition, we provide the optimal value of the criterion function and the number of partitions having that value.[23]

---

[22] There are a variety of ad hoc proposals for selecting some point on the cluster diagram for identifying the blockmodel for an interpretation. At best, this seems fraught with hazard.

[23] There are two partitions into three clusters with the minimum value of 23 for the criterion function and not one as reported by Doreian, Batagelj, and Ferligoj (1994). Finding additional optimal partitions is a strong reminder that this is a local optimization procedure!

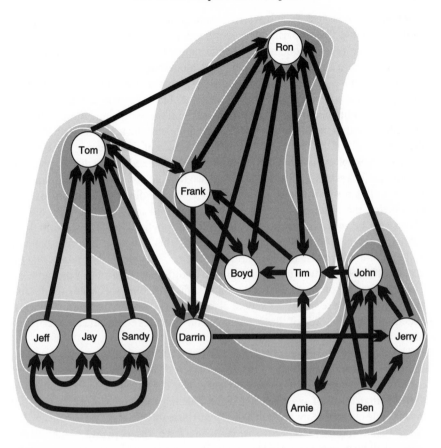

Figure 6.14. Transatlantic industries friendship – partitions with one, two, three, and four clusters.

We note several items that are evident from this table. First, the values of the criterion function decrease as the number of clusters specified for structural equivalence increases (see Theorem 6.4). The second item to note in Table 6.10 is that for $k = 1, 2, 4, 7, 11$, and 13, the partitions are unique. Of course, for $k = 1$ and $k = 13$ this is not news. The unique partitions for $k = 2$ and $k = 4$ are displayed in Figure 6.14 (with one of the two partitions into three clusters) and are nested within each other. For five clusters, there are three distinct partitions, each with a criterion function value of 17. None of these five cluster partitions are nested inside the partitions shown in Figure 6.14. The direct approach using the relocation local optimization procedure is *not* a hierarchical procedure.[24]

The third item to note is that if analysts seek a partition into five clusters, any choice between these three partitions cannot be made on the basis of the criterion

---

24 In contrast, indirect approach procedures such as CONCOR and STRUCTURE all return nested partitions.

function and must rest on substantive considerations. That there can be equally well fitting but different partitions is worth emphasizing again.

As we have noted frequently, when the indirect approach is used, there is no explicit measure of fit for the established blockmodel. However, the criterion function we have defined can be used to evaluate any established blockmodel for a particular equivalence type. Doreian et al. (1994) reported comparisons of the solutions obtained by the direct approach with those obtained through the use of methods within the indirect approach. Regardless of the measure of profile similarity used, all of the indirect solutions have values of the criterion function that are at or, most often, above the minimum values obtained by the direct approach. In general, the results reported therein suggest that the direct approach is superior. However, this observation is rather trivial because the direct approach focuses on minimizing the criterion function we have specified for structural equivalence. There may be other more appropriate criterion functions, and there is no guarantee that the partitions obtained by minimizing this particular criterion function will also minimize those other criterion functions.[25] In general, we expect that the use of different criterion functions will lead to different partitions of the network. Even so, the use of an explicit criterion function of some sort seems preferable to using no measure of fit.[26] We note also that each "impure" empirical block is coded as the nearest "ideal" block and the inconsistencies contribute to the criterion function.

The other LL baseball team discussed by Fine (1987) was Sharpstone Auto. This data set is described in Chapter 2 (Section 2.2.1). The structure of the two teams can be compared in a variety of ways in terms of structural equivalence. Doing so is useful both in terms of substance and technique. In general, placing all of the units into a single cluster means that all of the 1s will be counted as inconsistencies.[27] The Transatlantic Industries and Sharpstone teams have, respectively, 37 and 39 ties that will all be counted as inconsistencies. When partitioned, in terms of structural equivalence, into two clusters, each team is depicted in terms of its leaders and followers. Each team has a unique partition with the minimum inconsistency count. The leading group for Transatlantic Industries is {Ron, Frank, Boyd, and Tim}, with {Justin, Harry, and Whit} as the corresponding group for Sharpstone. The number of inconsistencies in each partition, respectively, is 29 and 17. Clearly,

---

25   For an exact equivalence, they will all return an optimal value of 0 for the criterion function (if they are compatible with the type of equivalence).

26   However, we do caution against the blind use of accepting a partition solely on the basis of a criterion function. Other things being equal, for a given number of clusters, the value of the criterion function provides useful information about the partition. In addition, if an analyst adopts a partition that fits less well than another partition, it seems reasonable to ask for good reasons for that choice. We discuss this further in the context of considering constraints on blockmodels.

27   There are many more 0s than 1s, usually, in the entire network when it is viewed as a single block; the null block is the ideal block. The inconsistency count will be the number of 1s in the network.

Table 6.11. LL Structural Equivalence Partitions

			1	3	4	5	2	6	10	11	12	13	7	8	9
			\multicolumn{15}{c}{Transatlantic Industries}
C_1	Ron	1	0	1	1	1	0	0	0	0	0	0	0	0	0
	Frank	3	1	0	1	0	0	0	0	1	0	0	0	0	0
	Boyd	4	1	1	0	0	1	0	0	0	0	0	0	0	0
	Tim	5	1	1	1	0	0	0	0	0	0	0	0	0	0
C_2	Tom	2	1	1	0	0	0	0	0	1	0	0	0	0	0
C_3	John	6	0	0	0	1	0	0	0	0	1	1	0	0	0
	Jerry	10	1	0	0	0	0	1	0	0	0	0	0	0	0
	Darrin	11	1	0	0	0	1	0	1	0	0	0	0	0	0
	Ben	12	1	0	0	0	0	1	1	0	0	0	0	0	0
	Arnie	13	0	0	0	1	0	1	0	0	0	0	0	0	0
C_4	Jeff	7	0	0	0	0	1	0	0	0	0	0	0	1	1
	Jay	8	0	0	0	0	1	0	0	0	0	0	1	0	1
	Sandy	9	0	0	0	0	1	0	0	0	0	0	1	1	0

			1	2	3	4	6	7	9	10	11	12	5	8	13
			\multicolumn{15}{c}{Sharpstone}
C_1	Justin	1	0	1	1	0	0	1	0	0	0	0	0	0	0
	Harry	2	1	0	1	0	0	1	0	0	0	0	0	0	0
	Whit	3	1	1	0	1	0	0	0	0	0	0	0	0	0
C_2	Brian	4	1	1	0	0	0	0	0	0	0	0	1	0	0
	Ian	6	1	1	1	0	0	0	0	0	0	0	0	0	0
	Mike	7	1	1	0	0	1	0	0	0	0	0	0	0	0
	Dan	9	1	1	1	0	0	0	0	0	0	0	0	0	0
	Ray	10	1	1	1	0	0	0	0	0	0	0	0	0	0
	Cliff	11	1	1	1	0	0	0	0	0	0	0	0	0	0
	Mason	12	1	1	0	1	0	0	0	0	0	0	0	0	0
C_3	Paul	5	1	0	1	0	1	0	0	0	0	0	0	0	0
	Jim	8	1	0	1	1	0	0	0	0	0	0	0	0	0
C_4	Roy	13	0	0	1	0	0	0	0	0	0	0	1	1	0

the drop in inconsistencies for Sharpstone is dramatic. The two image structures differ, as this table shows:

Subgroup	Transatlantic	Sharpstone
Leaders	1 0	1 0
Followers	0 0	1 0

Table 6.12. Image Matrices for
the Two Teams

Transatlantic			
	C_1	C_2	C_3	C_4
C_1	1	0	0	0
C_2	0	0	0	0
C_3	0	0	0	0
C_4	0	1	0	1

Sharpstone			
	C_1	C_2	C_3	C_4
C_1	1	0	0	0
C_2	1	0	0	0
C_3	1	0	0	0
C_4	0	0	1	0

For Transatlantic Industries, there are many ties within the leading subgroup with the followers having ties distributed in a way that is consistent with null blocks, albeit with many inconsistencies. For Sharpstone, there are also many ties within the leading subgroup, but the followers concentrate their friendship choices on the members of the leading subgroup. Truly, they are followers.

There is a unique four-cluster partition for each team. The inconsistency count for Transatlantic Industries has dropped to 20 for $k = 4$. The corresponding number for Sharpstone is 14. The relation matrices, in partitioned form, are given in Table 6.11, and the corresponding image matrix is given in Table 6.12.

Consider the partitioned matrix shown in Table 6.11 (top). There are four clusters that define the 16 blocks in the blockmodel. One product of the direct partitioning approach is a count of the inconsistencies, by block, of the partition. Corresponding to Table 6.11 (top), the distribution of inconsistencies is

$$
\begin{array}{cccc}
2 & 1 & 1 & 0 \\
2 & 0 & 1 & 0 \\
5 & 1 & 7 & 0 \\
0 & 0 & 0 & 0
\end{array}
$$

For cluster C_1, there are two inconsistencies in its block. There is no tie from Frank to Tim, nor is there one from Boyd to Tim in what should be a complete block. For the link from cluster C_1 to cluster C_2, there is one inconsistency. Boyd sends a tie to Tom in what otherwise would be a null block. Similarly, the lone link from Frank in cluster C_1 to Darrin in cluster C_3 is an inconsistency. For the ties from boys in cluster C_2 to boys in cluster C_1, either the two 0s or the two 1s can be viewed as contributing two inconsistencies to the total inconsistency count.

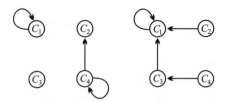

Figure 6.15. The image graphs for the two teams.

We treat the corresponding ideal block as null, and so the ties from Tom to Ron and Frank are the inconsistencies. The tie from Tom to Darrin (in cluster C_3) is another inconsistency. There are five ties from boys in cluster C_3 to boys in cluster C_1, and they are all inconsistent with a null block. In a similar fashion, the seven ties among the boys in cluster C_3 are all inconsistencies. There are no inconsistencies among the ties from boys in cluster C_4. We return to this partition in Chapter 7. For now, we note that 12 of inconsistencies are concentrated in two of the cells. It seems reasonable that, for the model as a whole, the inconsistencies be distributed across all of the cells in roughly the same fashion (controlling for block size). Having the inconsistencies piling up in a small number of cells suggests that we take a closer look at the partition and the distribution of inconsistencies.

Figure 6.15 shows the image graphs for the two teams. Again, it is clear that the Sharpstone team is far more centralized than the Transatlantic Industries team, which is consistent with Fine's (1987) account. Treated separately, the Transatlantic Industries' team seems best represented with the partition into four clusters, and for Sharpstone the partition into two clusters seems best.[28] The image structures make it clear that these groups have very distinct structures. It may be of some interest to note that they were both very successful teams. In one year, Sharpstone was the league champion, and in the next year, Transatlantic Industries finished at the top. For these networks, at least as described here, there is no simple prediction of success from the network structure. Groups with very distinct structures were equally successful. From Fine's (1987) account, Sharpstone had a much more elaborate idioculture than Transatlantic Industries and this stemmed, at least in part, from differences in structure: The followers of the Sharpstone team followed the leaders when the leaders created unique elements that became part of the idioculture.

6.4.2 *The political actor example*

We turn next to another real example, one taken from Doreian and Albert (1989).[29] The actors are prominent political actors in a local community and the social relation is "strong political ally." Figure 6.16 shows the partition established in

---

28 These two partitions have about the same number of inconsistencies, which seems reasonable for a comparison.
29 The political actor network is presented in Section 2.2.2.

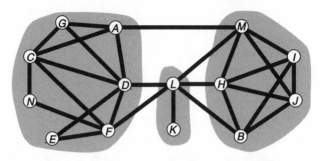

Figure 6.16. Political actor network: structural equivalence (32 inconsistencies).

the original analysis, where there are two political alliances (A, D, F, E, N, C, G) and (B, H, M, I, J) together with a pair of neutral actors (L, K). This partition was established with CONCOR (Breiger et al. 1975) and also with STRUCTURE (Burt 1976). Through the use of UCINET VI (Borgatti et al. 2004), this partition can be replicated under profile similarity by using the product moment correlation as a measure of similarity. (These are all based on structural equivalence.) The partition has immense appeal, particularly with the way in which the network is drawn in Figure 6.16. However, when examined in terms of the criterion function discussed in the previous section, this partition has 32 inconsistencies. Using a direct approach with the same criterion function, we get the different partition shown in Figure 6.17. With only 26 inconsistencies, it is a better fitting partition. The most notable difference between the two partitions is the location of actor L. In Figure 6.16 he is neutral, whereas he is located in one of the two opposed political alliances in Figure 6.17. The location of actors N, E, and K in a separate subset is another difference and may better reflect the peripheral location of these actors.

The major point here is the same as made in Section 6.3: The picture of the network can be drawn in different ways, each consistent with a particular partition. These partitions can also remind us to look more closely at the network and the kinds of equivalence we use.

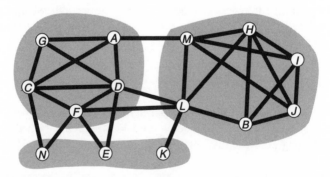

Figure 6.17. Political actor network: structural equivalence (26 inconsistencies).

At a minimum, all of these examples suggest that the visual representation of a network is a very unreliable criterion for assessing empirical partitions. If we seek such an assessment, our attention must be directed elsewhere. We propose using a formally based measure of the goodness of fit. Using such a measure suggests that the partition shown in Figure 6.17 is preferable to the partition shown in Figure 6.16 – provided that the partition makes substantive sense. The partitions shown in Figure 6.16 and Figure 6.17 are rival hypotheses and, in this case, we can distinguish them and choose one as the better representation of the network. However, we again note that the reported partitions of the network in Figure 6.10 into five clusters could not be distinguished by the criterion function because they were all exact, regular partitions. These examples suggest that the acceptance of one partition through the use of a particular diagram may deflect our attention away from other equally legitimate or better partitions.

Of course, using diagrams remains a useful way of presenting results. Indeed, we use many throughout this book. We do not deny that "a picture is worth a thousand words," but we do think that the picture has to be selected carefully. Moreover, if pictures are used as a part of the data analysis, data analysts need a wide range of options: One picture should not preclude the examination of alternative pictures.

6.5 AN ANALYSIS OF A SEARCH AND RESCUE OPERATION

We turn to examine the Kansas SAR network described in Chapter 2 (Section 2.2.4). For this analysis, we use all communication links.[30] Drabek et al. (1981) used CONCOR to partition the (binarized) communication matrix. Their partition is shown in Table 6.13. The labels and names of the organizations are given in Table 2.19.

Drabek et al. (1981) labeled these positions, respectively, as (1) the Authority Position[31]; (2) the Primary Support Position; (3) the Critical Resources Position; (4) the Secondary Support Position, Number 2; and (5) the Secondary Support Position, Number 1. The image matrix for this blockmodel can be represented in two ways:

Position	1	2	3	4	5
1	complete	complete	null	null	complete
2	complete	complete	null	null	null
3	complete	complete	null	null	null
4	complete	null	null	null	null
5	complete	null	null	null	null

---

30 Table A of Appendix III in the Drabek et al. publication makes it clear that this is the relation they used for constructing their blockmodel.
31 They used the term block for position in identifying these positions. Consistent with our use of the terms *block* and *blockmodel*, we relabel them as positions.

Table 6.13. Indirect (CONCOR) Partition for the Kansas SAR Network

	A	E	C	F	G	I	K	D	L	N	B	H	J	S	M	O	P	Q	R	T
A	0	1	1	1	1	1	1	0	0	0	1	0	0	0	0	1	1	1	0	1
E	1	0	1	1	1	0	1	1	1	1	0	0	0	0	1	0	1	1	0	1
C	1	1	0	1	0	1	1	1	0	0	0	0	0	0	0	0	0	1	0	0
F	1	1	1	0	1	1	1	1	1	1	0	0	0	0	0	0	0	0	0	0
G	1	1	1	1	0	1	0	1	0	0	0	0	1	0	0	0	1	0	0	0
I	1	1	1	1	1	0	1	0	0	0	0	0	0	0	0	0	0	1	0	0
K	1	1	1	1	1	1	0	0	1	0	0	0	0	0	0	0	0	0	0	0
D	1	1	1	1	1	1	0	0	0	1	1	0	0	0	0	0	0	0	0	0
L	1	1	0	0	1	0	0	0	0	0	0	0	0	0	0	0	0	1	0	0
N	1	1	1	1	1	1	0	0	1	0	0	0	0	0	1	0	0	1	1	1
B	1	1	1	1	1	1	0	0	0	1	0	0	0	0	0	0	1	1	0	0
H	1	1	0	0	0	0	0	0	0	0	1	0	1	0	0	0	0	0	0	0
J	1	1	0	0	0	0	0	0	0	0	0	0	0	0	0	0	0	0	0	0
S	1	1	0	1	1	1	0	0	0	0	1	0	0	0	0	0	0	1	0	0
M	1	1	0	0	0	0	0	0	0	0	0	0	0	0	0	0	0	0	0	0
O	1	1	1	1	1	1	1	1	1	1	0	0	1	0	1	0	1	1	1	1
P	1	1	0	1	1	0	1	0	0	0	1	0	0	0	0	0	0	0	0	0
Q	1	1	1	1	1	1	0	0	0	1	1	0	1	0	0	0	0	0	0	0
R	1	1	0	0	0	0	0	0	0	1	0	0	0	0	1	0	0	0	0	0
T	1	1	0	0	0	0	0	0	0	0	0	0	0	0	0	1	1	1	0	0

The more conventional representation of the image matrix is

Position	1	2	3	4	5
1	1	1	0	0	1
2	1	1	0	0	0
3	1	1	0	0	0
4	1	0	0	0	0
5	1	0	0	0	0

Fitting a structural equivalence model entails looking for a partition in which the ideal blocks are either complete or null. The first version of the image matrix indicates the closest ideal block types that the established blocks resemble – either complete or null blocks. The second version of the image matrix has the more conventional form. The graph representing this image matrix is in Figure 6.18.

This is a reasonable partition of the network and the graph. However, when the criterion function for structural equivalence is examined, this partition has 79 inconsistencies. Using our direct approach with this criterion function, we

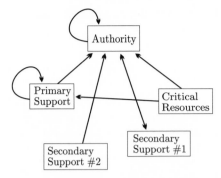

Figure 6.18. A direct (CONCOR) five-cluster partition of the Kansas SAR.

obtained four partitions with only 57 inconsistencies.[32] One of these is shown in Table 6.14. The image graph corresponding to this partition is in Figure 6.19. The image matrix for this partition can be represented as

Position	1	2	3	4	5
1	complete	complete	complete	null	null
2	complete	complete	null	null	null
3	complete	complete	null	null	null
4	complete	null	null	null	null
5	complete	complete	complete	complete	null

or as an image matrix:

Position	1	2	3	4	5
1	1	1	1	0	0
2	1	1	0	0	0
3	1	1	0	0	0
4	1	0	0	0	0
5	1	1	1	1	0

Comparisons between the two images can be made in terms of several features. First, as already mentioned, the second blockmodel has far fewer inconsistencies. Second, it is clear that the composition of the clusters differs. Third, the structures of the two image matrices (and hence the blockmodels) differ. With regard to the composition of the clusters, both have the Sheriff (A) and the Highway Patrol (E) together as the core actors of the network. According to Drabek et al. the Sheriff

---

32   As noted, the relocation algorithm can yield more than one partition with the same optimal criterion function.

Table 6.14. A Direct Partition for the Kansas SAR Network

	A	E	C	F	G	I	B	D	K	N	P	Q	H	J	L	M	R	S	T	O
A	0	1	1	1	1	1	1	0	1	0	1	1	0	0	0	0	0	0	1	1
E	1	0	1	1	1	0	0	1	1	1	1	1	0	0	1	1	0	0	1	0
C	1	1	0	1	0	1	0	1	1	0	0	1	0	0	0	0	0	0	0	0
F	1	1	1	0	1	1	0	1	1	1	0	0	0	0	1	0	0	0	0	0
G	1	1	1	1	0	1	0	1	0	0	1	0	0	1	0	0	0	0	0	0
I	1	1	1	1	1	0	0	0	1	0	0	1	0	0	0	0	0	0	0	0
B	1	1	1	1	1	1	0	0	0	1	1	1	0	0	0	0	0	0	0	0
D	1	1	1	1	1	1	1	0	0	1	0	0	0	0	0	0	0	0	0	0
K	1	1	1	1	1	1	0	0	0	0	0	0	0	0	1	0	0	0	0	0
N	1	1	1	1	1	1	0	0	0	0	0	1	0	0	1	1	1	0	1	0
P	1	1	0	1	1	0	1	0	1	0	0	0	0	0	0	0	0	0	0	0
Q	1	1	1	1	1	1	1	0	0	1	0	0	0	1	0	0	0	0	0	0
H	1	1	0	0	0	0	1	0	0	0	0	0	0	1	0	0	0	0	0	0
J	1	1	0	0	0	0	0	0	0	0	0	0	0	0	0	0	0	0	0	0
L	1	1	0	0	1	0	0	0	0	0	0	1	0	0	0	0	0	0	0	0
M	1	1	0	0	0	0	0	0	0	0	0	0	0	0	0	0	0	0	0	0
R	1	1	0	0	0	0	0	0	0	1	0	0	0	0	0	1	0	0	0	0
S	1	1	0	1	1	1	1	0	0	0	0	1	0	0	0	0	0	0	0	0
T	1	1	0	0	0	0	0	0	0	0	1	1	0	0	0	0	0	0	0	1
O	1	1	1	1	1	1	0	1	1	1	1	1	0	1	1	1	1	0	1	0

took control of the SAR effort after "the County Attorney reassured him that his authority was legitimate" (Drabek et al. 1981:35). His command post was located in a state Highway Patrol van. Although these two actors form the core position, the Sheriff is the dominant actor (and the Highway Patrol is part of the Authority Position by virtue of providing the physical location of the command center).

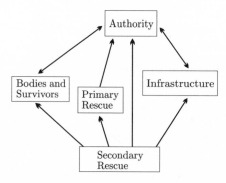

Figure 6.19. A direct five-cluster partition of the Kansas SAR.

We have labeled the second position as "Bodies and Survivors." A temporary morgue was set up by the County Coroner (*C*) at an office of the U.S. Army Corps of Engineers (*I*). The Corps operates the dam that created Lake Pomona, and the lake is within the jurisdiction of the Kansas State Game and Fish Commission (*G*). The uninjured survivors were taken to the State Park Office (*F*). These four actors form a well-defined cluster.

The third position is labeled the "Infrastructure and Lyndon (based) operators." The Civil Defense Office (*B*) has general authority for emergencies of this sort and is based in Lyndon. The County Attorney (*D*) is based there also and, as noted above, assured the Sheriff of his legal authority to take charge of the SAR effort. Both Crable Ambulance (*K*) and the Lyndon Police (*P*) are based in Lyndon and have general resources that are useful in an emergency of the sort that occurred on Lake Pomona. The Shawney County Underwater Rescue Team (*N*) had hardware and expertise that are clearly relevant for this SAR, although they are not based in Lyndon. The American Red Cross (*Q*) has relevant expertise and equipment for the rescue effort. The fourth position can be viewed as the "Primary Rescue Operators" and is made up of organizations directly involved in the physical aspect of rescues (in addition to those located in the third cluster). The "Secondary Rescue Operators" position has only one occupant, the Burlingame Police (*O*), with a strange connection to the rest of the network: They claimed to be in communication with most of the organizations in the SAR network, but few of these organizations made the reciprocal claim. It can best be thought of as a residual position.

If we look more closely at the image matrix, it is clear that the Sheriff and the Highway Patrol communicate with each other (as well as with the organizations in the rest of the network). Organizations in the Bodies and Survivors cluster also communicate with each other. (This block contributes only one inconsistency to the total count.) The block containing the ties from the Infrastructure cluster to the bodies and survivors cluster is almost complete. Its contribution to the inconsistency total is only four. Actors in all the clusters claim to communicate with the two organizations in the Authority cluster. The organizations in the Primary Rescue Operators cluster do not communicate much with each other. That block is close to being null and contributes only two inconsistencies to the inconsistency total. Nor is there any reason to expect that they would communicate with each other. In the main, each has a different expertise set, and these were organized by the actors in the Authority cluster.

Although the two image matrices (and graphs) differ, the differences all involve the Burlingame Police. Instead of a reciprocal link between the authority position and the Secondary Support (Number 1) position in the CONCOR blockmodel, there is an unreciprocated tie from the Secondary Rescue Position to the Authority Position. All of the other links from the residual core to other positions are not reciprocated.

We recognize that we are on dangerous ground with this alternative characterization of the SAR network, for we have far less interpretable material at our disposal and we rely on only one source. Even so, we think that the positions we have identified have more coherence than those identified by Drabek et al. (1981). As supporting evidence, we note that the blockmodel delineated by Drabek and his colleagues has many more inconsistencies than the one we have established by means of local optimization and the use of a criterion function that exactly captures the formal meaning of structural equivalence.

Suppose, for the moment, that on substantive grounds the other blockmodel is the more veridical. At a minimum, the blockmodel established here is a plausible rival hypothesis deserving further attention. We noted in Chapter 5 that any partition defines an equivalence relation. Starting with the blockmodel of Drabek et al., we find it would be necessary to establish the kind of equivalence represented by its partition.

In the idealized examples that we considered earlier, we noted that there can be more than one partition of the network, in terms of a specific type of equivalence, that fit equally well. There are four partitions of the SAR network, each with 57 inconsistencies. These are as follows.

$$\{A, E\}, \{B, D, K, N, P, Q\}, \{C, F, G, I\}, \{H, J, L, M, R, S, T\}, \{O\},$$
$$\{A, E\}, \{B, D, K, N, P, S\}, \{C, F, G, I, Q\}, \{H, J, L, M, R, T\}, \{O\},$$
$$\{A, E\}, \{B, D, K, N, P, Q, S\}, \{C, F, G, I\}, \{H, J, L, M, R, T\}, \{O\},$$
$$\{A, E\}, \{B, D, K, P, S\}, \{C, F, G, I, Q\}, \{H, J, L, M, R, T\}, \{N, O\}.$$

In general, they each require some consideration. The image graph for the partition in which the Shawney County Underwater Rescue Team (N) joins the Burlingame Police (O) is the same as that for the partition explored above with the exception that there is no tie from the Secondary Rescue cluster to the Infrastructure cluster.

The presence of multiple partitions, each indistinguishable from the others in terms of the criterion function, does lead to some interpretational problems. For structural equivalence, it seems reasonable to examine a set of such partitions to see if there are stable subsets of units that always appear together in a cluster. If the set of partitions differs greatly, there is little more to be said with respect to interpretation of the partitions. For this example, there is considerable consistency between the partitions. This consistency can be described in terms of the clusters having stable "cores," and for the partitions of the SAR network they are shown by the following table:

Cluster	Core
Authority	A, E
Bodies and Survivors	C, F, G, I
Infrastructure	B, D, K, P
Primary Rescue Operators	H, J, L, M, R
Secondary Rescue Operators	O

The first two are exactly identified clusters. The core of the Infrastructure cluster is made up of those organizations that really belong: Those not in this core are the Shawney County Rescue Team (N) and the Red Cross (Q). (They are not based in Lyndon although they do have relevant expertise.) The Primary Rescue cluster has five organizations in its core. Trivially, the residual cluster is also a whole cluster. It seems reasonable that, when there is such stability across equally well-fitting partitions, there is a core structure meriting further attention.

6.6   GENERALIZED BLOCKMODELING

This chapter has focused on partitions of networks described in terms of equivalences defined within conventional blockmodeling. The discussion contained throughout Section 6.1 laid the foundation for our subsequent discussion of optimization and blockmodeling in Section 6.2. Once the permitted (ideal) blocks have been identified for a definition of an equivalence type, a criterion function can be defined and used in some optimization procedure. For this purpose, we selected the relocation algorithm described in Sections 5.4.3 and 6.2.4 and used it to identify blockmodels by optimizing the criterion function. With these procedures we have replaced the indirect approach with a direct approach and have incorporated a measure of fit that, in the role of the criterion function, is integral to the procedure for fitting blockmodels.

Chapter 7 extends this line of thought further by expanding the types of blocks that can be used in constructing a blockmodel. In the following chapter we consider partitions of networks in which each block in a blockmodel has its own pattern and the permitted patterns are much more numerous than those for the equivalences discussed in this chapter.

7

FOUNDATIONS FOR GENERALIZED
BLOCKMODELING

In Section 6.1 we stayed within the framework of conventional blockmodeling and showed that structural and regular equivalences induce three special types of blocks: null blocks, complete blocks, and regular (one covered for both rows and columns) blocks. We also noted that different definitions of equivalence can lead to different identified blockmodels. In Section 6.2 we turned our attention toward generalizing blockmodeling by replacing indirect methods with direct methods and using optimization methods to delineate blockmodels and fit them to data. The next step, taken here, in our generalizing process is to expand the permitted types of ideal blocks. In doing this, we note, as we did in Section 4.3, that a partition determines an equivalence relation and vice versa. So, rather than specify new types of equivalences and derive their permitted block types, we simply expand the block types, knowing that partitions in terms of these new block types will determine new equivalences.

By proceeding in this fashion, we are making a subtle change in thinking about equivalences that signals, and emphasizes, a complete break with the indirect approach to establishing blockmodels. By focusing on the block types alone, we dispense with the need to measure the extent to which pairs of units are equivalent. Such measures become irrelevant: We focus instead on identifying and fitting block types. This is done empirically within the direct approach outlined in the previous chapter.

Network analysts often have some theoretical knowledge concerning the structure of the clusterings of units and of the structure of ties between positions (e.g., core periphery, hierarchy). This kind of information can be used to constrain clusterings and to specify blockmodels in advance. In this chapter we discuss how such constrained and prespecified models can be formulated, fitted, and interpreted.

The rest of the chapter is structured as follows. In Section 7.1 we propose the generalization of equivalences by defining new block types. Because of the novelty of doing this, we explore different ways of looking at blocks and keeping track of the inconsistencies between empirical blocks and these (new) block types.

Section 7.2 presents a formal statement of generalized blockmodeling in terms of specifying generalized blockmodels and describing ways of fitting them within the direct (optimization) methods we propose. Some concrete examples are presented in Section 7.3, together with some new ways of diagramming the images of generalized blockmodels. In Section 7.4 we return to the idea, introduced informally in Chapter 1, of prespecifying blockmodels in the sense of identifying clusters or the locations of blocks types in a (generalized) blockmodel. This leads naturally to the idea of defining types of blockmodels, which we discuss in Section 7.5. In Section 7.6 we present some applications of prespecified blockmodels, and we discuss the benefits of using optimization methods in Section 7.7. The concluding section points to futher extensions of block types.

7.1 GENERALIZATION OF EQUIVALENCES

Some examples of block types that can be used to describe ties between the clusters (positions) of a blockmodel (and relations of clusters to themselves) are displayed in Figure 7.1. They are listed also in Table 7.1. For this table and this section, we change our notation for clusters. Rather than denote clusters with symbols like C_i and C_j (in the notation of Chapter 6), we use symbols like X and Y. Our focus here is on types of connections between clusters that are described by the predicates that have to be satisfied by blocks $R(X, Y)$. In essence, our attention is focused on the kinds of graphs we have described as image graphs. However, we have many more options beyond using 0 and 1 for the ties in these graphs. The graph theoretic aspect of this is emphasized by our use of X, Y, Z, and so on, for the clusters.[1]

A clustering $\mathbf{C}$ is consistent with structural equivalence if and only if each of its blocks is either null or complete, and it is consistent with regular equivalence if and only if each of its blocks is either null or regular. Here we relax the requirements for the types of connections and allow a broader class of types. The new types of connections also induce special types of blocks. Consider Table 7.1. The first block shown in Table 7.1 is a complete block with 1s everywhere consistent with structural equivalence. If the block diagonal, then the main diagonal can be 0s, which is the classical conception of the clique. Beneath the complete block in Table 7.1 is a regular block in which rows and columns are one covered. Below the regular block is a null block consistent with both structural (lean fit) and regular equivalence. All of this is familiar from Chapter 6.

The remaining blocks in Table 7.1 are new. The generalizations proposed here start with a weakening of the regular equivalence property. A block is *row-regular* if all of its rows are one covered, and a block is *column-regular* if all of its columns are one covered. These types of connections are displayed also in the middle row of Figure 7.1. Obviously, a regular block is both row-regular and column-regular.

---

1 The tables of this section are also more compact by use of the X, Y, Z labeling. Readers can read this section by using X for C_i, Y for C_j, and Z for C_k in the notation of Chapter 6. When we return to interpreting blockmodels, we revert to the C labeling for clusters.

Table 7.1. Examples of Blocks with Types of Connections

		Y							Y							Y			
X	1	1	1	1	1	X	0	1	0	0	0	X	0	0	1	0	0
	1	1	1	1	1		1	1	1	1	1		0	0	1	1	0
	1	1	1	1	1		0	0	0	0	0		1	1	1	0	0
	1	1	1	1	1		0	0	0	1	0		0	0	1	0	1

      complete   row-dominant   col-dominant

		Y							Y							Y			
X	0	1	0	0	0	X	0	1	0	0	0	X	0	1	0	1	0
	1	0	1	1	0		0	1	1	0	0		1	0	1	0	0
	0	0	1	0	1		1	0	1	0	0		1	1	0	1	1
	1	1	0	0	0		0	1	0	0	1		0	0	0	0	0

      regular   row-regular   col-regular

		Y							Y						Y			
X	0	0	0	0	0	X	0	0	0	1	0		1	0	0	0
	0	0	0	0	0		0	0	1	0	0		0	1	0	0
	0	0	0	0	0		1	0	0	0	0	X	0	0	1	0
	0	0	0	0	0		0	0	0	1	0		0	0	0	0
													0	0	0	1

      null   row-functional   col-functional

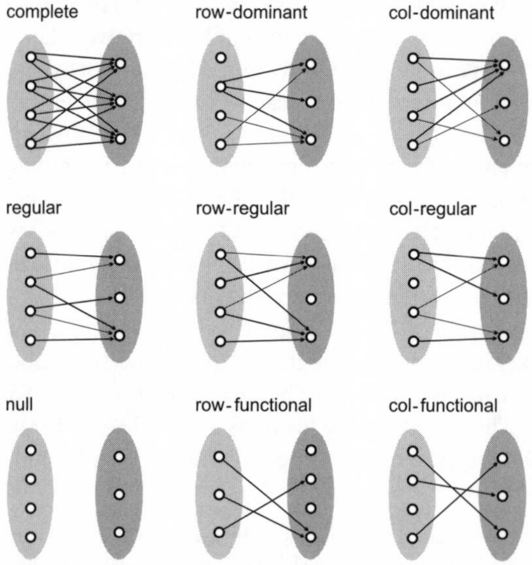

Figure 7.1. Nine types of connection between clusters.

Table 7.2. Types of Connections

Null	$\mathrm{nul}(X, Y; R)$	$\equiv$	$R(X, Y) = \emptyset$
Complete	$\mathrm{com}(X, Y; R)$	$\equiv$	$\forall x \in X \forall y \in Y : (x \neq y \Rightarrow xRy)$
Row dominant	$\mathrm{rdo}(X, Y; R)$	$\equiv$	$\exists x \in X \forall y \in Y : (x \neq y \Rightarrow xRy)$
Col dominant	$\mathrm{cdo}(X, Y; R)$	$\equiv$	$\mathrm{rdo}(Y, X; R^{-1})$
Row regular	$\mathrm{rre}(X, Y; R)$	$\equiv$	$\forall x \in X \exists y \in Y : xRy$
Col regular	$\mathrm{cre}(X, Y; R)$	$\equiv$	$\mathrm{rre}(Y, X; R^{-1})$
Regular	$\mathrm{reg}(X, Y; R)$	$\equiv$	$\mathrm{cre}(X, Y; R) \wedge \mathrm{rre}(X, Y; R)$
Row functional	$\mathrm{rfn}(X, Y; R)$	$\equiv$	$\forall x \in X \exists! y \in Y : xRy$
Col functional	$\mathrm{cfn}(X, Y; R)$	$\equiv$	$\forall y \in Y \exists! x \in X : xRy$

The *row-dominant block* has at least one unit in (cluster) X with ties to all of the units in Y, and the *column-dominant* block has at least one unit in Y receiving ties from all X units. The row-functional block is one in which each unit in X has a tie to exactly one unit in Y – it defines a function $f : X \to Y$. Note that if the block is square the row-functional block is the sparsest possible regular block. Finally, a column-functional block is one in which each unit in Y has exactly one unit in X linked to it. In later chapters some other ideal blocks with their types of connections are introduced.

7.1.1 Some properties of the predicates

Although the examples in Figure 7.1 and Table 7.1 have intuitive appeal, it is useful to examine the connection types in more formal detail. Table 7.2 provides a small step in this direction, where R is the social relation, by introducing a compact notation for the types of connections in Table 7.1. The null block is represented by $\mathrm{nul}(X, Y; R)$ whereas $\mathrm{com}(X, Y; R)$ represents the complete block. A row-dominant block is represented by $\mathrm{rdo}(X, Y; R)$ and a column-dominant block by $\mathrm{cdo}(X, Y; R)$. Note that if R^{-1} is the converse relation of R, a column-dominant block of R is a row-dominant block of R^{-1}. The row-regular and column-regular blocks are represented by $\mathrm{rre}(X, Y; R)$ and $\mathrm{cre}(X, Y; R)$, respectively. Equivalently, a column-regular block of R is a row-regular block of R^{-1}. A regular block is both row-regular and column-regular. Finally, a row-functional block is represented by $\mathrm{rfn}(X, Y; R)$ and a column-dominant block by $\mathrm{cfn}(X, Y; R)$.

The predicates given in Table 7.2 have several characteristic properties. Let X_1, X_2, Y_1, and Y_2 denote clusters and let T denote a generic property (a type of connection or a type of a block). The left column of Table 7.3 lists properties for clusters, and the right column lists those predicates from Table 7.2 possessing those properties. Consider regular blocks and the first row of Table 7.3. If $R(X_1, Y_1)$ and $R(X_2, Y_2)$ are regular blocks of R (i.e., T is reg), then $R(X_1 \cup X_2, Y_1 \cup Y_2)$ is also a regular block of R. Clearly, the same property holds for row-regular and column-regular, blocks. In the second row of Table 7.3, if $R(X_1, Y)$ and $R(X_2, Y)$ are complete blocks for R, then $R(X_1 \cup X_2, Y)$ is also a complete block of R. If a

Table 7.3. Properties of Predicates

Property	T
$T(X_1, Y_1) \wedge T(X_2, Y_2) \Rightarrow T(X_1 \cup X_2, Y_1 \cup Y_2)$	reg, rre, cre
$T(X_1, Y) \wedge T(X_2, Y) \Rightarrow T(X_1 \cup X_2, Y)$	com, rfn, nul, (reg, rre, cre)
$T(X, Y_1) \wedge T(X, Y_2) \Rightarrow T(X, Y_1 \cup Y_2)$	com, cfn, nul, (reg, rre, cre)
$\emptyset \subset Z \subseteq X \wedge T(X, Y) \Rightarrow T(Z, Y)$	com, nul, cdo, rfn, rre
$\emptyset \subset Z \subseteq Y \wedge T(X, Y) \Rightarrow T(X, Z)$	com, nul, rdo, cfn, cre
$T(X, Y) \Rightarrow T(X \cup Z, Y)$	rdo, cre
$T(X, Y) \Rightarrow T(X, Y \cup Z)$	cdo, rre

block is complete it is regular, and regular blocks will also have the property given in the second row of Table 7.3. Both complete and regular blocks are also row-regular and column-regular, and so these two block-type connections also have this property.[2] It is straightforward to show that both row-functional and null blocks also have this property. Similar arguments hold for the third row of this table.

For the fourth row of Table 7.3, the focus of attention is on subclusters. In essence, if Z is a subcluster of X and $R(X, Y)$ is a block of a given type of R, then a property of that block type holds also for the block $R(Z, Y)$. Clearly, if we are considering complete blocks and $R(X, Y)$ is complete, then $R(Z, Y)$ is complete also. If $R(X, Y)$ is null or column dominant or row functional or row regular, then $R(Z, Y)$ will be null or column dominant or row functional or row regular, respectively. Similar arguments hold for the fifth row of this table. For the next row, if $R(X, Y)$ is row-dominant then $R(X \cup Z, Y)$ will be row-dominant for any Z because the row of 1s in the block $R(X, Y)$ will be present in the block $R(X \cup Z, Y)$. The only other connection type with the property in this row is column-regular. The final row is interpreted in the same fashion. Now we examine some relations between the connection types.

Many relations hold among the predicates, some of which are listed below. As noted above, a regular block is both row-regular and column-regular. Complete blocks are both row-dominant and column-dominant. A row-functional block is row-regular and a column-functional block is column-regular. If $X \cap Y = \emptyset$, we are dealing with nondiagonal blocks. If such a block is row-dominant, it is column-regular and such a column-dominant block is row-regular.

$$\text{reg}(X, Y) \Rightarrow \text{cre}(X, Y), \qquad \text{reg}(X, Y) \Rightarrow \text{rre}(X, Y),$$
$$\text{com}(X, Y) \Rightarrow \text{rdo}(X, Y), \qquad \text{rfn}(X, Y) \Rightarrow \text{rre}(X, Y),$$
$$\text{com}(X, Y) \Rightarrow \text{cdo}(X, Y), \qquad \text{cfn}(X, Y) \Rightarrow \text{cre}(X, Y),$$

$$X \cap Y = \emptyset \wedge \text{rdo}(X, Y) \Rightarrow \text{cre}(X, Y),$$
$$X \cap Y = \emptyset \wedge \text{cdo}(X, Y) \Rightarrow \text{rre}(X, Y)$$

---

2   This accounts for the use of parentheses in the second and third rows of Table 7.3.

Another group of predicates is based on size ideas. Two examples of such predicates are

degree density γ	$\text{den}(\gamma)(X, Y; R) \equiv \text{card } R(X, Y) \geq \gamma \text{ card}(X \times Y)$
degree bound n	$\text{deg}(n)(X, Y; R) \equiv \forall x \in X : \text{card}(R(x) \cap Y) \geq n$

The first predicate concerns density with γ defining a density threshold for a block.[3] The second sets a minimum threshold for the number of units needed for the definition of a block. For example, a block could be specified, in part, as having at least two units.

More complicated predicates expressing partial ordering or different types of connectivity can be used. These ideas can be extended to a simultaneous consideration of $X \times Y$ and $Y \times X$. Even n-ary ($n > 2$) predicates could also be considered.[4] Here, we limit our discussion to binary predicates.

7.1.2 Examples

The examples we consider in this section are used to illustrate the process of thinking about blocks in terms of their types and counting inconsistencies for the block types. They are not illustrative of searching for blocks with smaller counts of inconsistencies. We emphasize that measures of inconsistencies in blocks are specific to block types, and a direct comparison of inconsistencies across different types blocks is not in order. A so-called smaller measure need not mean a better fit in a block.

Consider the following permuted and partitioned relation matrix:

$$
\begin{array}{cccc|cccc}
0 & 1 & 1 & 1 & 1 & 1 & 0 & 0 \\
1 & 0 & 1 & 1 & 0 & 1 & 0 & 1 \\
1 & 1 & 0 & 1 & 0 & 0 & 1 & 0 \\
1 & 1 & 1 & 0 & 1 & 0 & 0 & 0 \\
\hline
0 & 0 & 0 & 0 & 0 & 1 & 1 & 1 \\
0 & 0 & 0 & 0 & 1 & 0 & 1 & 1 \\
0 & 0 & 0 & 0 & 1 & 1 & 0 & 1 \\
0 & 0 & 0 & 0 & 1 & 1 & 1 & 0 \\
\end{array}
$$

Viewed from the perspective of structural equivalence, three of the blocks in this blockmodel are fully consistent with this equivalence. In the fourth (upper right)

---

3   In the traditional discussions of blockmodels, a threshold (conventionally denoted by α) is set for a block to be coded as one block. See, for example, Breiger et al. (1975).

4   In some applications, a "do not care" predicate, which is always satisfied (or is always true), can be a useful specification for some blocks. When this is done, the particular block is not considered in assessing the fit of a blockmodel containing it.

the closest ideal block is a null block. This implies that there are six inconsistencies (1s). An alternative way of looking at the set of the blocks is

complete	regular
null	complete

This blockmodel now has zero inconsistencies once the mixed block pattern is permitted. Of course, this pattern is consistent with regular equivalence, and thus a search with regular equivalence types (null and regular) would yield this partition and pattern.[5] However, by including the complete block, the network structure is more precisely described. The key idea here is changing the set of block types. With this in mind, consider the following blockmodel.

0	1	1	1	1	1	0	0
1	0	1	1	0	1	0	**0**
1	1	0	1	0	0	1	0
1	1	1	0	1	0	0	0
0	0	0	0	0	1	1	1
0	0	0	0	1	0	1	1
0	0	0	0	1	1	0	1
0	0	0	0	1	1	1	0

The only change in this blockmodel, compared with the last one above, is that a single 1 in the upper right block is now a 0. The nearest ideal block with structural equivalence is unchanged (null block), and the inconsistency count is now five. The altered block, however, is no longer regular because the fourth column is not one covered. If we look at the additional types of connection, it is clear that this block is row-regular. So the partition pattern for this structure, with zero inconsistencies, is

complete	row-regular
null	complete

.

We return to the Transatlantic Industries (TI) network shown in Figure 1.1. First we reconsider the structural equivalence partition. The permuted and blocked relational matrix is shown as repeated here in Table 7.4. Note, however, that we have changed the order of clusters and blocks. This is the best unique partition,

5   As stated earlier, a complete block is also regular.

Table 7.4. Transatlantic Industries – Structural Equivalence Partition

		2	1	3	4	5	7	8	9	6	10	11	12	13
Tom	2	0	1	1	0	0	0	0	0	0	0	1	0	0
Ron	1	0	0	1	1	1	0	0	0	0	0	0	0	0
Frank	3	0	1	0	1	0	0	0	0	0	0	1	0	0
Boyd	4	1	1	1	0	0	0	0	0	0	0	0	0	0
Tim	5	0	1	1	1	0	0	0	0	0	0	0	0	0
Jeff	7	1	0	0	0	0	0	1	1	0	0	0	0	0
Jay	8	1	0	0	0	0	1	0	1	0	0	0	0	0
Sandy	9	1	0	0	0	0	1	1	0	0	0	0	0	0
John	6	0	0	0	0	1	0	0	0	0	0	0	1	1
Jerry	10	0	1	0	0	0	0	0	0	1	0	0	0	0
Darrin	11	1	1	0	0	0	0	0	0	0	1	0	0	0
Ben	12	0	1	0	0	0	0	0	0	1	1	0	0	0
Arnie	13	0	0	0	0	1	0	0	0	1	0	0	0	0

and the closest ideal blockmodel pattern is

null	null	null	null
null	complete	null	null
complete	null	complete	null
null	null	null	null

The distribution of inconsistencies across the blocks is

0	2	0	1
1	2	0	1
0	0	0	0
1	5	0	7

There are 20 inconsistencies associated with the partition. If we restrict our attention to the connection types consistent with structural equivalence, and if we assume there are four clusters, no improvement is possible. If we want to obtain a "better fitting" blockmodel, it is necessary to expand the connection types we are willing to consider. Ideally, there is a model with zero inconsistencies.[6] Although no improvements can be made when the count of inconsistencies is zero, there may be other partitions fitting equally well. With this in mind, we reconsider the blocks that were located under structural equivalence and use additional connection types. The second block in the first row of the image can be viewed as row-regular, instead

6 Of course, such a partition has to make substantive sense.

of null, as can the fourth block in that row. In the second row of the image matrix the first block is column-regular. The second block in that row is regular. There are no inconsistencies (consistent with structural equivalence) in the blocks in the third row, and those connection types are unchanged. In the bottom row of the image matrix, the first block is column-regular. The second and fourth blocks of this row are row-regular. This pattern of connections can be summarized as

null	row-reg	null	row-reg
col-reg	regular	null	null
complete	null	complete	null
col-reg	row-reg	null	row-reg

with an inconsistency count distribution of

0	0	0	0
0	0	0	1
0	0	0	0
0	0	0	0

.

With a single inconsistency (a 1 in an otherwise null block), this blockmodel appears to be a clear improvement. However, it will not be the best partition if it makes no substantive sense. Again, the objective here is to think about different blocks types rather than just to obtain a low value for some measure. Of course, settling for a partition based on structural equivalence and simply reinterpreting the blocks is rather limited and *cannot* be viewed as a generalized procedure. The initial structural equivalence partition considered in this section has served its purpose of suggesting more general ways of characterizing an image matrix, and we abandon it here.

Within the direct approach we seek partitions when a (different) set of block types is permitted. We keep the null, complete, and regular blocks, add to them the row-dominant and column-dominant connection types, and seek a partition into four clusters of the TI network. The resulting partition is shown in Table 7.5 with the block pattern below it.

There are no inconsistencies: The partition is exact, given the permitted block types. The network with this partition is shown in Figure 7.2 and has a very appealing interpretation.[7] We label the positions as follows: position C_1 corresponds to the cluster (Ron, Tom, Tim, John, Jerry, and Darrin); C_2 to cluster (Ben and Arnie); C_3 to cluster (Jeff, Jay, and Sandy); and C_4 corresponds to cluster (Frank and Boyd). Position C_3 is made up of actors that are between themselves structurally equivalent: internally they are a maximal complete subgraph. Externally

---

7   The change in representing the arrows in this figure reflects the need for representing the expanded set of connection types. See Table 7.6 for a set of such representations.

Table 7.5. A Generalized Partition of the LL Network

			1	2	5	6	10	11	12	13	7	8	9	3	4
C_1	Ron	1	0	0	1	0	0	0	0	0	0	0	0	1	1
	Tom	2	1	0	0	0	0	1	0	0	0	0	0	1	0
	Tim	5	1	0	0	0	0	0	0	0	0	0	0	1	1
	John	6	0	0	1	0	0	0	1	1	0	0	0	0	0
	Jerry	10	1	0	0	1	0	0	0	0	0	0	0	0	0
	Darrin	11	1	1	0	0	1	0	0	0	0	0	0	0	0
C_2	Ben	12	1	0	0	1	1	0	0	0	0	0	0	0	0
	Arnie	13	0	0	1	1	0	0	0	0	0	0	0	0	0
C_3	Jeff	7	0	1	0	0	0	0	0	0	0	1	1	0	0
	Jay	8	0	1	0	0	0	0	0	0	1	0	1	0	0
	Sandy	9	0	1	0	0	0	0	0	0	1	1	0	0	0
C_4	Frank	3	1	0	0	0	0	1	0	0	0	0	0	0	1
	Boyd	4	1	1	0	0	0	0	0	0	0	0	0	1	0

regular	row-dominant	null	row-dominant
col-dominant	null	null	null
col-dominant	null	complete	null
col-dominant	null	null	complete

they all send a tie to Tom, who is a member of position C_1. This means that the tie from C_3 to C_1 is a column-dominant tie. The actors in C_3 send no other ties, making the ties between positions C_3 and C_2 and between positions C_3 and C_4 all null. The internal structure of position C_1 conforms to the regular block type. As John sends ties to Ben and Arnie, the tie from C_1 to C_2 is row-dominant. Similarly, Tim sends ties to both Boyd and Frank, making the tie from C_1 to C_4 also row-dominant. The tie from position C_2 to C_1 is column-dominant, with Ben and Arnie sending ties to John. The ties from C_2 to positions C_3 and C_4 are null. With Frank and Boyd both citing Ron, the tie from C_4 to C_1 is column-dominant. As these two actors also have a reciprocal tie, the internal structure of the position is complete. Finally, no ties go from C_4 to either C_2 or C_3. In the image graph (bottom panel of Figure 7.2), position C_1 is a sociometric star since all other positions have a column-dominant tie to C_1.

This is an appropriate generalization of the equivalence idea. Each block has a particular pattern from those given in Table 7.1. (The structural and regular equivalence block types are part of this set.) Undoubtedly, there are other types of blocks. With such a generalization, it is clear that this is a completely general methodology, one that is applicable to directed or undirected graphs. Blocks are sculpted singly, but always in a context in which other blocks are being sculpted. A procedure for doing this is described in the following section.

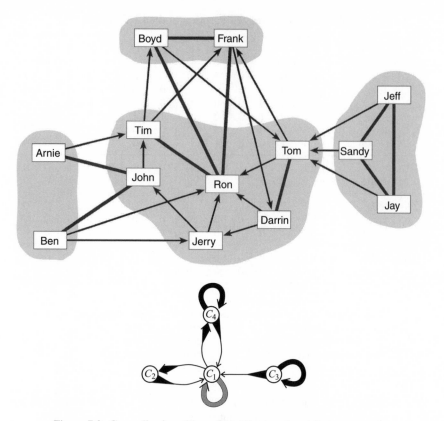

Figure 7.2. Generalized partition of the TI network and its image graph.

7.2   GENERALIZED BLOCKMODELING

Given the argument in the previous section, we propose a generalization of block-modeling that, we believe, will enable analysts to better capture the structure of a network.

7.2.1   Blockmodels

The point of departure is, as before, a network with a set of units $\mathcal{U}$ and a relation $R \subseteq \mathcal{U} \times \mathcal{U}$. Let $\mathcal{Z}$ be a set of positions or images of clusters of units (Batagelj 1997 also used the term *types of units*). In the previous example, 13 boys (the set $\mathcal{U}$) in the TI network were partitioned into four clusters (see Figure 7.2). The set of positions $\mathcal{Z}$ of four clusters consists of C_1, C_2, C_3, and C_4 (see Table 7.5 and Figure 7.2). Let $\mu : \mathcal{U} \to \mathcal{Z}$ denote a mapping that maps each unit to its position. The cluster of units $C(t)$ with the same position $t \in \mathcal{Z}$ is

$$C(t) = \mu^{-1}(t) = \{x \in \mathcal{U} : \mu(x) = t\}.$$

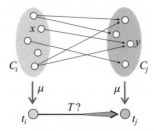

Figure 7.3. Generalized blockmodeling.

Therefore

$$\mathbf{C}(\mu) = \{C(t) : t \in \mathcal{Z}\}$$

is a partition (clustering) of the set of units $\mathcal{U}$.

A *blockmodel* (image or reduced graph) is an ordered quadruple $\mathbf{M} = (\mathcal{Z}, K, \mathcal{T}, \pi)$, where

- $\mathcal{Z}$ is a set of positions;
- $K \subseteq \mathcal{Z} \times \mathcal{Z}$ is a set of connections between positions;
- $\mathcal{T}$ is a set of predicates used to describe the types of connections between clusters in a network (we assume that nul $\in \mathcal{T}$); and
- a mapping $\pi : K \to \mathcal{T} \setminus \{\text{nul}\}$ assigns predicates to connections.

The blockmodel definition is represented in Figure 7.3. A clustering into two clusters $\{C_i, C_j\}$ is shown with arcs from the units of the cluster C_i to the units of the cluster C_j. They form the block $R(C_i, C_j)$. The mapping μ maps each unit to its position (t_i or t_j): all units from C_i are assigned to the position t_i and all units from C_j to t_j. Since the block $R(C_i, C_j)$ is not a null block, there exists a connection from position t_i to position t_j. The mapping π assigns a predicate T to the connection between the two positions. In this case it is a column-regular type of connection.

Let us consider again the TI network and the partition into four clusters (Table 7.5). The set of connections K between the positions is presented by the image graph in Figure 7.2. The set of predicates $\mathcal{T}$ consists of five types of connections: null (nul), regular (reg), complete (com), column-dominant (cdo), and row-dominant (rdo). To each ordered pair of positions was assigned one of the permitted predicates (block types) by the mapping π, for example, reg(A, A), rdo(C_1, C_2), nul(C_1, C_3), rdo(C_1, C_4), and cdo(C_2, C_1); see the block pattern in Section 7.1.

A (surjective) mapping $\mu : \mathcal{U} \to \mathcal{Z}$ determines a blockmodel $\mathbf{M}$ of network $\mathbf{N}$ if and only if it satisfies these conditions:

$$\forall (t, w) \in K : \pi(t, w)(C(t), C(w))$$

and

$$\forall (t, w) \in \mathcal{Z} \times \mathcal{Z} \setminus K : \text{nul}(C(t), C(w)).$$

Note that if $\mathcal{T} = \{\text{nul, com}\}$, we are considering a structural equivalence block-model; if $\mathcal{T} = \{\text{nul, reg}\}$, we are considering a regular equivalence blockmodel.

7.2.2 $\mathcal{T}$-equivalence

Let $\sim$ be an equivalence relation over $\mathcal{U}$. It partitions the set of units $\mathcal{U}$ into clusters

$$[x] = \{y \in \mathcal{U} : x \sim y\}.$$

We say that $\sim$ is *compatible* with $\mathcal{T}$ or $\mathcal{T}$-equivalence over a network **N** if and only if

$$\forall x, y \in \mathcal{U}, \exists T \in \mathcal{T} : T([x], [y]).$$

It is easy to verify that the notion of compatibility for $\mathcal{T} = \{\text{nul, reg}\}$ reduces to the usual definition of regular equivalence (see Chapter 6). Similarly, compatibility for $\mathcal{T} = \{\text{nul, com}\}$ reduces to structural equivalence.

For a compatible equivalence $\sim$, the mapping $\mu \colon x \mapsto [x]$ determines a block-model with $\mathcal{Z} = \mathcal{U}/\sim$.

Having moved to the consideration of more general block types, we need to clarify an implicit change in the term *equivalence*. For structural equivalence, positions are formed and the units in a position are equivalent: They are connected to the same other units. Even when partitions are obtained with inconsistencies, the idea of units in a position being equivalent to each other remains. With the move to regular equivalence, this meaning of equivalence is maintained. Units sufficiently similar are contained in a position – regardless of whether the partition is exact or approximate.

With the generalized block types, partitions are still obtained and the clusters, by definition, are equivalence classes: Units in the same cluster are equivalent given the $\mathcal{T}$-equivalence underlying the partition. For row-regular and column-regular blocks, the idea of units of a cluster being equivalent to each other can be maintained. However, we need to be careful with the row-dominant and column-dominant blocks and the use of the term *equivalent*. From the formulation of these block types, at least one unit will be different from some of the other units in a cluster. Consider this block:

$$\begin{array}{ccccc}
0 & 0 & 0 & 1 & 0 \\
1 & 1 & 1 & 1 & 1 \\
1 & 0 & 0 & 0 & 0 \\
0 & 1 & 1 & 0 & 0
\end{array}$$

The second unit, of a hypothetical position, is connected to all units of the other position. This makes it clearly different to all of the other units in its position in terms of the pattern of ties in the block. As a result, it is *not* equivalent to the other three units of the position in the sense of being structurally identical. We repeat, units within positions (where the positions from a partition of a set of actors and

Table 7.6. *Block Types*

Null	nul	all 0 *	
Complete	com	all 1 *	
Regular	reg	one covered rows and columns	
Row regular	rre	each row is one covered	
Col regular	cre	each column is one covered	
Row dominant	rdo	∃ all 1 row *	
Col dominant	cdo	∃ all 1 column *	
Row functional	rfn	∃! one 1 in each row	
Col functional	cfn	∃! one 1 in each column	
Nonnull	one	∃ at least one 1	

Note: The asterisk indicates this is the case, except for a diagonal block, that differs slightly.

the corresponding blocks partition the relation) are always equivalent in terms of the equivalence relation, and its equivalence classes, that underlies the partition.

Table 7.6 provides a set of visual devices for displaying block types (as types of connections) in generalized blockmodels. As additional block types are defined, additional display devices will be required.

7.2.3 Optimization

Given the approach for blockmodeling presented in Chapter 6 and our discussion of generalized blocks in this chapter, we express the blockmodeling problem (for generalized blocks) as an optimization problem. We use the ideas presented in Chapters 5 and 6.

Given a set of types of connection T and a block $R(X, Y)$, we can determine the strongest (according to the ordering of the set T) type T that is satisfied the most by $R(X, Y)$. In this case we set

$$\pi(\mu(X), \mu(Y)) = T.$$

Our treatment of blockmodeling in Chapter 6 recognized that few empirical blocks were exactly the pure types permitted under the equivalences we considered. Although the examples we used to motivate the reader to consider generalized blocks were such that many blocks were one of the types shown in Figure 7.1, it is clear that the same general empirical problem exists for generalized blocks: It is possible that no type from T is satisfied or that only some are satisfied. We adopt

Table 7.7. Deviations Measures for Types of Blocks

Connection	$\delta(X, Y; T)$	
Null	$\begin{cases} s_t \\ s_t + d - s_d \end{cases}$	nondiagonal diagonal
Complete	$\begin{cases} n_r n_c - s_t \\ n_r n_c - s_t + d + s_d - n_r \end{cases}$	nondiagonal diagonal
Row-dominant	$\begin{cases} (n_c - m_r - 1)n_r \\ (n_c - m_r)n_r \end{cases}$	diagonal, $s_d = 0$ otherwise
Col-dominant	$\begin{cases} (n_r - m_c - 1)n_c \\ (n_r - m_c)n_c \end{cases}$	diagonal, $s_d = 0$ otherwise
Row-regular	$(n_r - p_r)n_c$	
Col-regular	$(n_c - p_c)n_r$	
Regular	$(n_c - p_c)n_r + (n_r - p_r)p_c$	
Row-functional	$s_t - p_r + (n_r - p_r)n_c$	
Col-functional	$s_t - p_c + (n_c - p_c)n_r$	
Density γ	$\max(0, \gamma n_r n_c - s_t)$	

the same strategy as before by introducing the set of *ideal blocks* for a given type $T \in \mathcal{T}$,

$$\mathcal{B}(X, Y; T) = \{B \subseteq K(X, Y) : T(B)\},$$

and we define the *deviation* $\delta(X, Y; T)$ of a block $R(X, Y)$ from the nearest ideal block. We can efficiently test whether a block $R(X, Y)$ is of the type T (from among the types from Table 7.1) by making use of the characterizations of block types in Table 7.6. On the basis of these characterizations, we can construct the corresponding deviation measures (see Table 7.7). We assume that the graphs are binary. The quantities used in the expressions for deviations have the following meaning.

s_t — total block sum = number of 1s in a block,

$n_r = \text{card } X$ — number of rows in a block,

$n_c = \text{card } Y$ — number of columns in a block,

p_r — number of nonnull rows in a block,

p_c — number of nonnull columns in a block,

m_r — maximal row sum,

m_c — maximal column sum,

s_d — diagonal block sum = number of 1s on a diagonal,

d — diagonal error = $\min(s_d, n_r - s_d)$.

Throughout the number of elements in a block is $n_r n_c$.

For the null, complete, row-dominant, and column-dominant blocks, it is necessary to distinguish diagonal blocks and nondiagonal blocks. Consider first the nondiagonal blocks. If the closest ideal block is null, all (s_t) 1s in the block contribute to a deviation measure. For a complete ideal block all $(n_r n_c - s_t)$ 0s in a block contribute to the deviation measure. If the ideal block is row-dominant and there are n_c columns, there would have to be n_c 1s in a row for there to be zero deviation. If there is a row with m_r 1s (where $m_r < n_c$), the contribution to the deviation from that block is $(n_c - m_r)n_r$, where the $(n_c - m_r)$ is multiplied by the number of rows in the block (as the absence of a row of 1s means each row contributes to the deviation). For an ideal column-dominant block the corresponding value is $(n_r - m_c)n_c$. On the diagonal, an ideal null block can have a diagonal with 1s (recall Figure 6.2), and if they are all present there is no contribution to the deviation. If there are fewer 1s there will be a contribution. The diagonal error is $d = \min(s_d, n_r - s_d)$ and the actual contribution to the deviation is $(s_t + d - s_d)$. For a complete ideal diagonal block, the contribution to the deviation is $(n_r n_c - s_t)$ plus $(d + s_d - n_r)$. For both of the diagonal row-dominant (column-dominant) blocks, the deviation is adjusted to allow for having a 0 on a row (column) in a row that otherwise has 1s or a majority of 1s.

For the other ideal block types listed in Table 7.7, there is no need to distinguish diagonal and nondiagonal blocks. For a row-regular ideal block, every row with only 0s in a block will contribute to the deviation. In such a block $(n_r - p_r)$ counts the rows that are not one covered and each such row has n_c columns that all contribute, giving a deviation of $(n_r - p_r)n_c$. For column-regular blocks the contribution is $(n_c - p_c)n_r$. For regular ideal blocks the contribution to the deviation is the sum of the row-regular and column-regular contributions. Note that the deviation for the regular block was defined differently in Chapter 6. Here, having very different types of permitted blocks, the deviations for different types of blocks should be comparable. This is the reason why we define the deviations for regular blocks in this general case in a different way. For a row-functional ideal block, the contributions to the deviation have two sources. Every null row and every row with more than one 1 is inconsistent with this ideal type. There are $(n_r - p_r)$ null rows each with n_c columns, leading to a contribution of $(n_r - p_r)n_c$. If there are p_r rows that are nonnull they can have only a single 1 for consistency with an ideal block. If there is more than one 1 in a row, the contribution that forms the nonnull rows is $(s_t - p_r)$. A similar argument holds for the column-dominant ideal block – the two contributions are $(n_c - p_c)n_r$ and $(s_t - p_c)$. Finally, for a block there are $n_r n_c$ cells and with a density threshold γ there will be $\gamma n_r n_c$ 1s. The number of 1s is s_t, and if $s_t < \gamma n_r n_c$, then the block will have too few 1s and the density threshold will not be reached.

Note that all deviations from Table 7.7 are sensitive:

$$\delta(X, Y; T) = 0 \Leftrightarrow T(R(X, Y)).$$

In δ we can incorporate values v of lines straightforwardly.

On the basis of deviation $\delta(X, Y; T)$, we can define the *block inconsistency* $\varepsilon(X, Y; T)$ of $R(X, Y)$ for type T. Two examples of block inconsistencies are

$$\varepsilon_1(X, Y; T) = w(T)\delta(X, Y; T)$$

and

$$\varepsilon_2(X, Y; T) = \frac{w(T)}{n_r n_c}(1 + \delta(X, Y; T)),$$

where $w(T) > 0$ is a weight of type T. One definition (default) would be to have the types in $\mathcal{T}$ contribute equally. Alternatively, the types in $\mathcal{T}$ can be ordered in importance – in which case, departures from some block types are seen as more important than departures from other block types.

We extend the block inconsistency to the set of feasible types $\mathcal{T}$ by defining

$$\varepsilon(X, Y; \mathcal{T}) = \min_{T \in \mathcal{T}} \varepsilon(X, Y; T)$$

and

$$\pi(\mu(X), \mu(Y)) = \operatorname{argmin}_{T \in \mathcal{T}} \varepsilon(X, Y; T).$$

To make π well defined, we order (the priorities on) the set $\mathcal{T}$ and select the first type from $\mathcal{T}$ that minimizes ε.

We combine block inconsistencies into a *total inconsistency* – the blockmodeling criterion function – where the block inconsistencies are summed across all blocks:

$$P(\mu; \mathcal{T}) = \sum_{(t,w) \in \mathcal{Z} \times \mathcal{Z}} \varepsilon(\mu^{-1}(t), \mu^{-1}(w); \mathcal{T}).$$

Since $\mu^{-1}(t) = C(t)$, $\mu^{-1}(w) = C(w)$, and μ determines a clustering $\mathbf{C}(\mu) = \{C(t) : t \in \mathcal{Z}\}$ (and vice versa), this criterion function can be re-expressed in the clustering terms

$$P(\mathbf{C}; \mathcal{T}) = \sum_{(t,w) \in \mathcal{Z} \times \mathcal{Z}} \varepsilon(C(t), C(w); \mathcal{T}).$$

For a criterion function $P_1(\mu)$, corresponding to the definition of $\varepsilon_1(X, Y; T)$, we have

$$P_1(\mu) = 0 \quad \Leftrightarrow \quad \mu \text{ is an exact blockmodeling.}$$

Also for P_2, corresponding to $\varepsilon_2(X, Y; T)$, we obtain an exact blockmodeling μ if and only if the deviations (inconsistencies) of all blocks are 0.

The foregoing argument leads directly to an optimization problem that can be solved by local optimization procedures – exactly as was done for the conventional blockmodeling problem (see Chapter 6).

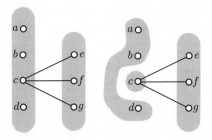

Figure 7.4. Two partitions of a network with zero inconsistencies.

7.3 TWO EXAMPLES OF GENERALIZED BLOCKMODELING

We use two examples to illustrate the application of the procedures described in the previous section. One is artificial (with constructed data) whereas the other uses a data set introduced in Chapter 2.

7.3.1 An artificial network

Consider the network shown in Figure 7.4. This network has two subgroups: $\{a, b, c, d\}$ and $\{e, f, g\}$. These subgroups do communicate with each other but do so in different ways. The members of the first subgroup use c as their representative whereas all members of the second group are involved in the between-subgroup interactions.

Given the narrative for this group, the natural image representation is given by the partition on the left of Figure 7.4. Using only three permitted block types – null, row-dominant and column-dominant – we can specify the blockmodel at the bottom of Table 7.8. This is exactly the structure found at the top of Table 7.8

Table 7.8. A Row-Dominant and
Col-Dominant Partition of Figure 7.4

	e	f	g	a	b	c	d
e	0	0	0	0	0	1	0
f	0	0	0	0	0	1	0
g	0	0	0	0	0	1	0
a	0	0	0	0	0	0	0
b	0	0	0	0	0	0	0
c	1	1	1	0	0	0	0
d	0	0	0	0	0	0	0

null	col-dominant
row-dominant	null

Table 7.9. Structural Equivalence
Partition of Figure 7.4

	c	e	f	g	a	b	d
c	0	1	1	1	0	0	0
e	1	0	0	0	0	0	0
f	1	0	0	0	0	0	0
g	1	0	0	0	0	0	0
a	0	0	0	0	0	0	0
b	0	0	0	0	0	0	0
d	0	0	0	0	0	0	0

(with no inconsistencies). The partition details are shown in Table 7.8 and exactly describe the actual structure with two clusters and four well-defined blocks.

At various places in our treatment of blockmodeling, both traditional and generalized, we have stressed that multiple, equally well-fitting partitions can be fitted to a network. There is another partition that is free of inconsistencies of the network in Figure 7.4. Suppose that a traditional blockmodeling is used within a structural equivalence perspective. There are no such blockmodels with two clusters and zero inconsistencies. However, if a blockmodel is sought with three clusters, there is one without inconsistencies. The clusters are $\{a, b, d\}$, $\{c\}$, and $\{e, f, g\}$. Table 7.9 displays this partition as does the graph on the right side of Figure 7.4. It is clear that the structural equivalence blockmodel is not inconsistent with that in Table 7.8, and a natural interpretation can be provided. Even so, it is a different structural representation.

Of course, the example is an artificial construction. Even if it were empirical, the narrative is incomplete. At a minimum, it would be reasonable to seek data on the interactions within each of the subgroups. It could be that, internally, each member interacts with every other subgroup member. This would be viewed as a clique structure and an exact structural equivalence partition. From the perpective of structural equivalence this may seem odd: One relation can be modeled with three clusters whereas the other requires two clusters. A natural procedure triggered by this example is to seek a partition into two clusters where the first relation is partitioned with null, row-dominant, and column-dominant, blocks but for the second relation only the null and complete blocks are permitted.

7.3.2 A student government network

Consider one of the relations (recall) from the Student Government (SG) discussion network data described in Section 2.2.3. For this example, we restrict the block

Table 7.10. *Optimal Partitions,* $\mathcal{T} = \{$ nul, com, rdo, cdo, reg $\}$

	Partition	P
$\mathbf{C}_1^2$	$\{m_1, pm, m_2, m_3, m_5, m_6, m_7, a_1, a_3\}\{m_4, a_2\}$	1
$\mathbf{C}_2^2$	$\{m_1, a_2\}\{pm, m_2, m_3, m_4, m_5, m_6, m_7, a_1, a_3\}$	1
$\mathbf{C}_1^3$	$\{m_1, pm, m_2, m_3, m_4, m_5, m_7\}\{m_6, a_3\}\{a_1, a_2\}$	0
$\mathbf{C}_2^3$	$\{m_1, m_2, a_2\}\{pm, m_3, m_4, m_5, m_6, m_7\}\{a_1, a_3\}$	0
$\mathbf{C}_3^3$	$\{m_1, m_2\}\{pm, a_3\}\{m_3, m_4, m_5, m_6, m_7, a_1, a_2\}$	0
$\mathbf{C}_4^3$	$\{m_1, m_4\}\{pm, a_3\}\{m_2, m_3, m_5, m_6, m_7, a_1, a_2\}$	0
$\mathbf{C}_1^4$	$\{m_1, m_2\}\{pm, m_4\}\{m_3, m_5, m_6, m_7, a_2\}\{a_1, a_3\}$	0
$\mathbf{C}_2^4$	$\{m_1, m_2, a_2\}\{pm, m_4\}\{m_3, m_5, m_6, m_7\}\{a_1, a_3\}$	0
$\mathbf{C}_3^4$	$\{m_1, m_2, a_2\}\{pm, m_4, m_6, m_7\}\{m_3, m_5\}\{a_1, a_3\}$	0
$\mathbf{C}_1^5$	$\{m_1, m_2\}\{pm, m_3\}\{m_4, a_3\}\{m_5, a_1, a_2\}\{m_6, m_7\}$	1
$\mathbf{C}_2^5$	$\{m_1, m_2, a_2\}\{pm, m_4\}\{m_3, m_5\}\{m_6, m_7\}\{a_1, a_3\}$	1
$\mathbf{C}_3^5$	$\{m_1, m_2, a_2\}\{pm, m_4\}\{m_3, m_6\}\{m_5, m_7\}\{a_1, a_3\}$	1
$\mathbf{C}_4^5$	$\{m_1, a_2\}\{pm, m_3\}\{m_2, a_3\}\{m_4, m_5\}\{m_6, m_7, a_1\}$	1
$\mathbf{C}_5^5$	$\{m_1, a_3\}\{pm, m_5\}\{m_2, m_7, a_1\{m_3, m_4\}\{m_6, a_2\}$	1

types to null, complete, regular, row-dominant, and column-dominant. We selected $P \equiv P_1$ with all weights equal to 1.

The generalized blockmodeling procedure defined by these options was applied for partitions into two to five clusters. Table 7.10 displays the results of these

Table 7.11. *SG Discussion Network Matrix, Rearranged According to* $\mathbf{C}_2^4$

		m_1	m_2	a_2	pm	m_4	m_3	m_5	m_6	m_7	a_1	a_3
C_1	m_1	0	1	0	1	0	0	1	0	0	0	0
	m_2	1	0	0	1	0	1	1	1	1	0	0
	a_2	1	1	0	0	1	1	0	0	0	0	0
C_2	pm	0	0	0	0	0	0	0	0	1	0	0
	m_4	0	0	0	1	0	1	1	1	1	0	0
C_3	m_3	0	0	0	0	0	0	0	1	1	0	0
	m_5	0	0	0	1	1	1	0	1	1	0	0
	m_6	0	0	0	0	0	1	0	0	1	1	1
	m_7	0	0	0	1	0	1	0	1	0	0	1
C_4	a_1	0	0	0	0	0	1	0	1	1	0	1
	a_3	0	0	0	0	0	0	1	0	1	1	0

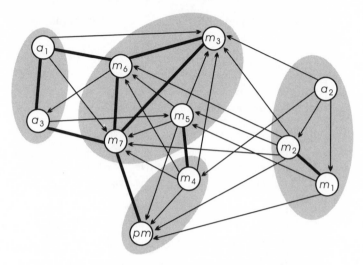

Figure 7.5. A generalized partition of the SG discussion matrix.

analyses. In Table 7.10, $\mathbf{C}_r^s$ labels partitions where s denotes the number of clusters and r is a counting index for partitions into s clusters.

For two-cluster partitions there are two solutions with a minimum inconsistency count of one. If three-cluster partitions are sought, there are four partitions without inconsistency. There are three partitions when attention is focused on four-cluster partitions, all with zero inconsistencies. There are no partitions into five clusters with zero inconsistencies, but there are five partitions with just one inconsistency. For purposes of illustration, we look more closely at the partition labeled $\mathbf{C}_2^4$, where the superscript labels the number of clusters and the suffix identifies a specific partition with this set of block types in $\mathcal{T}$. This is listed in Table 7.11 and is shown in Figure 7.5.

We label the positions of these clusters as $C_1 = \{m_1, m_2, a_2\}$, $C_2 = \{pm, m_4\}$, $C = \{m_3, m_5, m_6, m_7\}$, and $C_4 = \{a_1, a_3\}$. Reading across the first row, we see that the self-loop for C_1 is row regular, the $C_1 \rightarrow C_2$ tie is regular, the $C_1 \rightarrow C_3$ is row dominant, and the tie $C_1 \rightarrow C_4$ is null. Each row can be read the same way, and the summary of the image matrix is shown in Table 7.12 and pictured in Figure 7.6.

Table 7.12. Model Matrix

	C_1	C_2	C_3	C_4
$C_1 = \{m_1, m_1, a_2\}$	rdo	reg	rdo	null
$C_2 = \{pm, m_4\}$	null	rdo	rdo	null
$C_3 = \{m_3, m_5, m_6, m_7\}$	null	rdo	rdo	rdo
$C_4 = \{a_1, a_3\}$	null	null	cdo	com

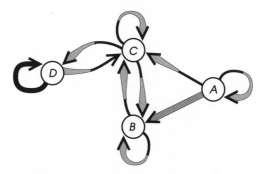

Figure 7.6. Model of the image in Table 7.14.

We compute the numerical values for the entries in this table by using the formulas in Table 7.7.

7.3.3 *Exploring multiple partitions*

In principle, each partition shown in Table 7.10 can be explored in the same fashion. Of course, the choice between the partitions with zero inconsistency cannot be made on technical grounds only; all of these partitions fit equally well. The so-called problem of multiple, equally acceptable partitions is understated in the foregoing narrative. Each plausible set of block types T can contribute a set of well-fitting partitions. Suppose, for the SG data, we select $T = \{\text{nul, rdo, cdo}\}$ and use the generalized blockmodeling procedure. A summary of the relevant partitions is shown in Table 7.13 with the same notational system as before.

As another illustration, the use of $T = \{\text{nul, cdo}\}$ yields the partitions shown in Table 7.14.

In addition, both structural and regular equivalence can be selected. Table 7.15 provides a partial summary of the possible partitions of the SG network. On the left, k denotes the number of clusters in a partition. The remaining columns are for different selections of T, all of which include the null type. Each number gives the value of the optimized criterion functions. For $k = 2$, under structural equivalence the inconsistency score is 29 whereas four is the inconsistency score

Table 7.13. Optimal Partitions with $T = \{$ nul, rdo, cdo $\}$

	Partition	P
$\mathbf{C}_1^2$	$\{m_1, a_2\}\{pm, m_2, m_3, m_4, m_5, m_6, m_7, a_1, a_3\}$	1
$\mathbf{C}_1^3$	$\{m_1, m_4\}\{pm, a_3\}\{m_2, m_3, m_5, m_6, m_7, a_1, a_2\}$	0
$\mathbf{C}_2^3$	$\{m_1, m_2\}\{pm, a_3\}\{m_3, m_4, m_5, m_6, m_7, a_1, a_2\}$	0
$\mathbf{C}_1^4$	$\{m_1, m_2\}\{pm, m_4\}\{m_3, m_5, m_6, m_7, a_2\}\{a_1, a_3\}$	0

Table 7.14. Optimal Partitions with $\mathcal{T} = \{$ nul, cdo $\}$

	Partition	P
$\mathbf{C}_1^2$	$\{m_1, a_2\}\{pm, m_2, m_3, m_4, m_5, m_6, m_7, a_1, a_3\}$	1
$\mathbf{C}_1^3$	$\{m_1, m_4, m_5\}\{pm, m_3, m_6, m_7, a_1, a_3\}\{m_2, a_2\}$	2
$\mathbf{C}_2^3$	$\{m_1, m_4\}\{pm, m_3, m_5, m_6, m_7, a_1, a_3\}\{m_2, a_2\}$	2
$\mathbf{C}_1^4$	$\{m_1, m_2\}\{pm, m_3, a_3\}\{m_4, m_5, m_6, m_7, a_1\}\{a_2\}$	4
$\mathbf{C}_2^4$	$\{m_1, a_2\}\{pm, m_3, a_3\}\{m_2, m_4, m_5\}\{m_6, m_7, a_1\}$	4
$\mathbf{C}_3^4$	$\{m_1, a_2\}\{pm\}\{m_2, m_3, m_4, m_5, m_7\}\{m_6, a_1, a_3\}$	4
$\mathbf{C}_4^5$	$\{m_1, a_2\}\{pm\}\{m_2, m_4, m_5, m_7\}\{m_3, a_1\}\{m_6, a_3\}$	4

under regular equivalence. Corresponding to Table 7.10, the entry in the first row and fourth column (1/2) provides the inconsistency score (1) and the number of optimal partitions (2). The only partitions with an inconsistency score of 0 are those in Table 7.10 and Table 7.6. Attention would most likely be focused on these 10 partitions. In general, a large number of well-fitting partitions will be found, and the choice between them will be substantive and contextual.

For the direct approach, given a set of well-defined block types, there is a set of well-defined measures of fit. In general, the use of different sets of types will yield different partitions of a network. The generality of the method, with the full set of types of connections, will permit, in most cases, the establishment of blockmodels that will fit very well. We suspect that it is possible to fit blockmodels with zero error in most empirical situations. This may be seen as problematic, and one objection to the approach and its methods, as proposed here, could run as follows. All that we have done is look at blocks of a blockmodel, and where a block has errors (within a structural equivalence or a regular equivalence perspective), we have redefined the block type and so eliminated errors by this sleight of hand. We agree! However, we would change the tone and argue that this approach is appropriate and fruitful. The closer examination of the blocks, in terms of block types, leads to a much richer characterization of the fundamental structure(s) of the network. Note also that the partitioning with a general set of types of connections will not, in general, lead to the same partition as those obtained by

Table 7.15. Values of Some Optimal Partitions

k	com	reg	com, reg rdo, cdo	rdo, cdo	cdo	rdo
2	29	4	1/2	1/1	1/1	11
3	23	7	0/4	0/2	2/2	5
4	21	7	0/3	0/1	4/3	3
5	15	6	1/5	2/14	4/1	3

Note: There are no fractions in this table.

use of the regular equivalence types or the structural equivalence types. Not only can the interpretations of the partition change, but the actual clusters located can differ. However, this generality, flexibility, and the ability to establish well-fitting blockmodels come with a price and a caution.

The caution is that the goal is not to minimize a criterion function as such. We know we can always do this. Rather, and here is the price, the set of types must be specified in advance and on substantive grounds. Then, with these theoretically relevant types, the blockmodeling can proceed. With this restatement of the approach, minimizing the criterion function seems appropriate and desirable.

The prime reason for our confidence that exact or near exact partitions will be found is that the row-regular and the column-regular types are extremely weak. This is likely to lead to interpretive problems. It seems fruitful to strive for as strong a set of types of connections as possible. For example, column-dominant implies row regular and is stronger than row-regular and more easily interpreted. We suspect that row-regular and column-regular types (and both the row- and column-functional types) may be needed for very sparse networks and sparse parts of networks.

We emphasize that *substance comes first*. Of course, there is nothing new in stressing this. It already applies to the use of both regular equivalence and structural equivalence. The use of generalized blockmodeling forces the analyst to use theory if well-fitting models can always be found. In general, the practice of mobilizing a partitioning algorithm and interpreting the resulting partition is problematic. Cluster analysts have long known that any partition can be interpreted. We have argued that the use of a network diagram as a validating device is unreliable, yet such diagrams are frequently used this way in the interpretation of partitions. Substance first and the use of an explicit measure of fit seems much preferable. Additionally, there is an element of testing if the analyst specifies the relevant types of connections and then partitions the network in terms of them.

7.4   PRESPECIFIED BLOCKMODELS

Blockmodeling can be used to establish partitions of actors based on their ties with each other (in one or more social relations). In performing such analyses, only the relational data are used. However, network analysts usually know more than this. They have additional information concerning the actors (e.g., demographic attributes and roles), and they may have theoretical hypotheses concerning the structure of the ties between positions (e.g., hierarchy, core periphery,[8] and social

---

8   In an older terminological style, *center periphery* was the preferred terminology. More recently, and especially with the world-system approach of Wallerstein (1974), *core periphery* has become the preferred term. We are indifferent to the use of core and center in this debate. However, we do differentiate the terms in the following way. A core implies some density in a (central) block, and we note that it is possible for a center to be empty as in the case of the baboon network described in Section 7.6.2. In these terms, *center* is a more general term. Whenever we anticipate nonempty centers, we use the term *core*.

Table 7.16. Inductive and Deductive Approaches to Blockmodeling

		Clustering	Blockmodel
Inductive		?	?
Deductive	Prespecification Constraints Constrained Prespecification	? given given	given ? given

circles). This kind of information can be used to specify blockmodels in advance of analyses.

The formal definition of a blockmodel is given in Section 7.2.1. A blockmodel consists of the set of positions (obtained by shrinking clusters into nodes) and connections between positions described by their block types (the mapping π assigns types to connections). A basic prespecified blockmodel is a fixed blockmodel, which means that the set of positions is fixed and each connection between positions has a fixed, prespecified block type. In this case we search for the best-fitted clustering (the mapping μ assigns each unit to its position) in terms of a selected compatible criterion function. It is possible to relax the prespecification by allowing several blockmodels; in other words, a connection between positions could be one of several permitted block types (e.g., regular or complete). It is important to note that in the fitting process under this type of specification, a connection can be of several types. However, in the fitted blockmodel, each connection between positions has a single block type. Here, we discuss how these models can be formulated, fitted, and interpreted.

There are many *exploratory* (inductive) approaches for establishing blockmodels for a set of relations defined over a set of units. Some form of equivalence (a set of block types) is specified, and clusterings and blockmodels are sought that are consistent with the specified equivalence. In all cases, the analyses respond to empirical information (relational data) in order to establish the blockmodel. This is represented in the first row of Table 7.16, where the question marks indicate that something (concerning a blockmodel, a clustering, or both) is not specified before the analysis and has to be established according to the given structural information. In the exploratory mode, only a set of block types defining an equivalence is declared in advance of using blockmodeling.[9] We consider exploratory blockmodeling and inductive blockmodeling to be the same thing.

We argue that blockmodeling can also be used in a *confirmatory* (deductive) mode. Indeed, this is the point of using prespecified blockmodels. Consider the lower panel in Table 7.16. An analyst can start with a specific blockmodel specified, in part or in total, in terms of substance prior to an analysis or on the basis of specific

---

9 Usually, this is done implicitly when structural or regular equivalences are used.

empirical knowledge. This is presented in the first row in the table: The set of clusters is not specified, but the blockmodel (location of at least one block type) has been specified. We call this *prespecification*. The second row of the second panel in Table 7.16 shows the situation in which the analyst has specified one or more of the clusters but has not specified the blockmodel beyond stating the permitted (ideal) block types. This is a case of constraining the structure of the clustering. The constraints can take various forms. Units can be assigned to specific clusters. Units can be specified as belonging together in clusters (regardless of the nature of the clusters). In addition, pairs of units can be specified as never belonging to the same cluster, or the number of units in each cluster can be constrained. Finally, as shown in the last row of Table 7.16, the clustering structure can be constrained and the blockmodel is prespecified and the criterion function evaluated. This is the most stringent type of specification. This is a case of constrained prespecified blockmodeling. A *constrained completely prespecified* blockmodel is one in which the clustering is fixed and all of the locations of block types have been prespecified prior to fitting the blockmodel. When the clustering has been fixed but not *all* of the locations of block types, we have a *constrained blockmodel*; when all of the locations by block types have been prespecified but not the clustering, we have a *completely prespecified* blockmodel. Regardless of the form of the constraints and prespecification, the generalized blockmodeling analysis establishes those solutions that either fit the data perfectly or provide those that are closest to the specified blockmodel and constraints. The value of an appropriate criterion function is used to decide whether or not the specified blockmodel fits to the empirical relational data.[10]

In all of the deductive applications of blockmodeling, the empirical blockmodeling part is done subject to the specifications found in the prespecified blockmodel or the constraints in clusterings. Batagelj, Ferligoj, and Doreian (1998) present methods for doing this.

7.5 BLOCKMODEL TYPES

There are several known and well-studied blockmodels such as a hierarchical model or a core–periphery model. White et al. (1976) and Wasserman and Faust (1994:417–423) describe configurations of ties between positions (blockmodels) and expressed in the image matrices. Their classifications are for k-position blockmodels for $k = 2$ and $k = 4$. For two-position blockmodels there are $2^{2 \times 2} = 16$ possible models, or, generally, for k-position blockmodels $2^{k \times k}$ possible models. They especially considered some types of these models "that display theoretically important structural properties," as shown here.

---

10 Some blocks can be prespecified as "do not care" blocks and ignored in fitting a blockmodel. The residual part of the blockmodel structure can be examined given the fitted partial model.

1. There are cohesive subgroups with intraposition ties and no ties between positions:

$$
\begin{array}{ccc}
1 & 0 & 0 \\
0 & 1 & 0 \\
0 & 0 & 1
\end{array}
$$

2. There is a core–periphery model with one core position (center) that is internally cohesive and connected with all other positions. The other positions (periphery) are all connected to the core position, not connected to each other, and not internally cohesive:

$$
\begin{array}{ccc}
1 & 1 & 1 \\
1 & 0 & 0 \\
1 & 0 & 0
\end{array}
$$

3. There is a centralized model, which is a special case of the core–periphery model, in which all ties are from the core position or toward it:

$$
\begin{array}{ccc}
1 & 1 & 1 \\
0 & 0 & 0 \\
0 & 0 & 0
\end{array}
\quad \text{or} \quad
\begin{array}{ccc}
1 & 0 & 0 \\
1 & 0 & 0 \\
1 & 0 & 0
\end{array}
$$

4. There is a hierarchical model with the positions on a single path:

$$
\begin{array}{ccc}
0 & 1 & 0 \\
0 & 0 & 1 \\
0 & 0 & 0
\end{array}
\quad \text{or} \quad
\begin{array}{ccc}
0 & 0 & 0 \\
1 & 0 & 0 \\
0 & 1 & 0
\end{array}
$$

5. There is a transitivity model similar to the hierarchical model with permitted ties from lower positions to all higher positions:

$$
\begin{array}{ccc}
0 & 1 & 1 \\
0 & 0 & 1 \\
0 & 0 & 0
\end{array}
\quad \text{or} \quad
\begin{array}{ccc}
0 & 0 & 0 \\
1 & 0 & 0 \\
1 & 1 & 0
\end{array}
$$

In these models, the 0s in an image matrix represent null blocks but the 1s can represent additional blocks besides the complete block. Any nonnull block in Section 7.1 (Table 7.1) can be considered here.[11]

One of these blockmodels or some others can be tested by the optimizational approach we have described.

---

11 The logic extends to future invented blocks, including the symmetric block introduced in Chapter 11.

Table 7.17. *Structural Equivalence Partition of Boy–Girl*
Liking Ties

		1	2	3	4	5	6	7	8	9	10	11
Boy 1	1	0	1	1	*0*	1	1	0	0	0	0	0
Boy 2	2	1	0	1	1	*0*	1	0	0	0	0	0
Boy 3	3	1	1	0	1	1	*0*	0	0	0	0	0
Boy 4	4	*0*	1	1	0	1	*0*	0	0	0	0	0
Boy 5	5	1	1	1	*0*	0	1	0	0	0	0	0
Boy 6	6	1	1	*0*	1	1	0	0	0	0	0	0
Girl 1	7	0	0	0	0	0	0	0	1	1	1	1
Girl 2	8	0	0	0	0	0	0	1	0	1	1	1
Girl 3	9	0	0	0	0	0	0	*0*	1	0	1	*0*
Girl 4	10	0	0	0	0	0	0	*0*	1	1	0	1
Girl 5	11	0	0	0	0	0	0	*0*	1	1	*0*	0

7.6 APPLICATIONS OF PRESPECIFIED BLOCKMODELS

We consider a variety of data sets with a view to exploring the ways in which prespecified models can be formulated and fitted. During this examination we also explore the use of generalized blocks. The first example is a very simple network for some boys and girls in a school classroom, and it can be explored with structural equivalence in mind. When considering the second example – a baboon grooming network – we use two of the generalized blocks. Yet another type of prespecified blockmodel will be introduced in Chapter 11.

7.6.1 Classroom liking ties for boys and girls

It is well known that the structure of liking relationships between boys and girls in classrooms is distinctive and varies with age. In general, boys like boys and girls like girls but, at young ages, there are liking ties between gender groups. This is followed by a period when liking relations within gender seems the rule. At a later time point, there is a reappearance of between-gender ties. The matrix in Table 7.17 resembles those in the middle period and is presented in its permuted and blocked form. Knowing this pattern of childhood choices and encountering this network for the first time, we find that a reasonable blockmodel based on structural equivalence is a cohesive subgroups model:

complete	null
null	complete

When this blockmodel model is fitted, we get the result shown in Table 7.17, where the ties inconsistent with structural equivalence are in italics. There are 12 inconsistencies contained with the diagonal blocks, and they are from those cases in which some boys do not choose some of the other boys and some girls do not choose some of the other girls.

This seems to be a large number of inconsistencies, and it is reasonable to (provisionally) view the blockmodel as not fitting the data well. It is possible to argue that seeking complete blocks on the diagonal is too stringent. The pattern of boys choosing boys and girls choosing girls is clear. To have complete blocks on the diagonal means that each girl has to choose each of the other girls and each boy has to choose each of the other boys. It is clear that some of them inside of a gender group are not friends. With this in mind, the diagonal blocks can specified as regular. With this change, the blockmodel becomes

regular	null
null	regular

Exactly the same partition as in Table 7.17 results in zero inconsistencies: each diagonal block is one covered whereas the off-diagonal blocks remain null. Clearly, this model does fit the data. The issue of inconsistencies and fitting blockmodels is discussed further in Chapter 12. We note here that the second model is not necessarily better than the first simply because it has fewer inconsistencies. Although there are no inconsistencies with the second model fitted here, one possible drawback with this model is that a regular block is ambiguous in the following sense. The constraint of a regular block is that it be one covered. This can be satisfied by a complete block through to a very sparse block with as few as one 1 in each row and column. It follows that the elimination of inconsistencies is not as dramatic as it seems.[12]

7.6.2   Baboon grooming networks

The network of grooming ties for a group of baboons was introduced in Chapter 1 (Section 1.4.4). The grooming was observed at two points in time. There are seven females (f_1–f_7) and five males (m_1–m_5) in the group at the first time point, T_1. Two baboons, one male and one female, were added to the group and were accepted before the second time point, T_2. In Chapter 1 only the network observed at the first point in time is presented and discussed. Table 1.10 presents the network at the first point in time and Table 7.18 at the second.

With the creation of a potentially new grooming network through the addition of the two new baboons, one obvious question arises: Did the structure change? This raises the broad goal of studying structural change in networks and whether generalized blockmodeling can be useful in studying such changes. This moves us

---

12 In part, it reflects the fact that, under structural equivalence, many more inconsistencies are possible than under regular equivalence (unless all 0s in a row or column that is not one covered are counted).

Table 7.18. The Four-Position Model Fitted to the Baboon Network at T_2

		3	10	11	14	1	4	6	8	5	12	13	2	7	9
f_2	3	.	.	.	.	.	1	1	.	.	1	*1*	.	.	.
f_6	10	.	.	.	.	.	1	1	1	.	.	.	.	.	.
f_7	11	.	.	.	.	.	.	.	*1*	.	.	.	.	.	.
f_8	14	.	.	.	.	*1*	.	*1*	1	1	.	.	.	.	.
f_1	1	.	.	.	*1*	.	1	.	*1*	1	.	.	1	*1*	.
f_3	4	1	1	.	.	1	.	.	.	1	1	.	.	.	.
f_4	6	1	1	.	*1*	.	.	.	.	.	1	*1*	.	.	.
f_5	8	.	1	*1*	*1*	*1*	.	.	.	.	.	.	.	1	1
m_2	5	.	.	.	*1*	1	1	.	.	.	.	.	.	.	.
m_5	12	1	.	.	.	.	1	1	.	.	.	.	.	.	.
m_6	13	*1*	.	.	.	.	.	*1*	.	.	.	.	.	.	.
m_1	2	.	.	.	.	1	.	.	.	.	.	.	.	.	.
m_3	7	.	.	.	.	*1*	.	.	1	.	.	.	.	.	.
m_4	9	.	.	.	.	.	.	.	1	.	.	.	.	.	.

null	col-regular	col-regular	null
row-regular	null	col-regular	col-regular
row-regular	row-regular	null	null
null	row-regular	null	null

to illustrate some general blockmodeling strategies. One is the use of substantive ideas to prespecify a blockmodel. A second is to use a blockmodel established at one point in time as a prespecified blockmodel for a second time point. A third strategy is to be flexible in the face of surprising results.

When we presented the baboon network for T_1 in Chapter 1, two blockmodels were considered. The first one was a simple two-position core–periphery model (see Table 1.10). Its proposed blockmodel structure is

regular or complete	column-regular
row-regular	null

This model fits the data at first time point exactly with a core that is regular. There are inconsistencies if the core is specified as complete. However, we can see from Table 1.10 that two gender groups each show internal variation. Therefore, a second blockmodel was proposed in which the diagonal blocks can be null, complete, or regular. Continuing the logic of the two-position model, above the diagonal (in the image matrix) we specified blocks as column-regular or null and, below the diagonal, we specified the blocks as row regular or null. Again, each cluster was constrained to be homogeneous with regard to gender. A fitted model[13] for T_1 is shown in Table 1.11 and the blockmodel (with two inconsistencies from the reciprocal tie between f_1 and f_7) for T_1 was

complete	col-regular	col-regular	null
row-regular	null	col-regular	null
row-regular	row-regular	null	null
null	row-regular	null	null

The interpretation of the baboon grooming network for T_1 is given in Section 1.4.4. At T_2, all ties involving the new members are new, and italics mark these *new* ties in Table 7.18. A further comparison of the two time points shows that 10 edges from T_1 do not survive at T_2 and there are three new edges among the original members. A plausible hypothesis for T_2 is that the new baboons were absorbed into the network without altering its structure. The four-position T_1 block-model becomes a prespecified model for T_2 and was fitted. The message from the printout was nasty, brutish, and short: It does not fit! There were 14 inconsistencies, an increase that seems too large to support a claim that the model fits. A visual inspection (plus noting the location of the inconsistencies) revealed that the females are divided into two subgroups, $\{f_2, f_6, f_7, f_8\}$ and $\{f_1, f_3, f_4, f_5\}$ with no pair of females from different groups grooming each other. Again, males do not groom each other. So, the prespecified model was recast as the old prespecified blockmodel with one change: the first diagonal block is now null. This model did fit with just four inconsistencies and is shown in the top panel of Table 7.18 with the prespecified image in the second panel.

Clearly, for both time points, there is much in common. All cells but one are identical. The one – very striking – difference is that there is a core of mutually linked females in the center at T_1, whereas at T_2 there is no such core. The two networks are drawn in Figure 7.7.[14]

We show two depictions of the whole network. Figure 7.8 contains the grooming ties for both time points. Both the T_1 and T_2 networks can be read from this figure. The solid lines represent the 14 edges present at T_1 and T_2. The 10 edges that cease by T_2 are represented by the light dotted lines, and those new edges are represented by the heavy dashed lines. All but three new edges involve the new members. At the level of individual baboons, there is both change and stability. Although it is straightforward to describe these changes baboon by baboon, it is also tedious to do so and adds little to our interpretation.

---

13   There is a second equally well-fitting blockmodel with f_4 relocated from the first cluster into the second.

14   Given these partitions, the internal structure of the blocks can also be examined.

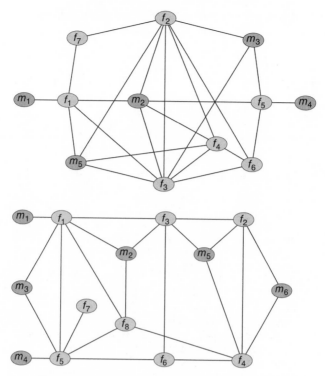

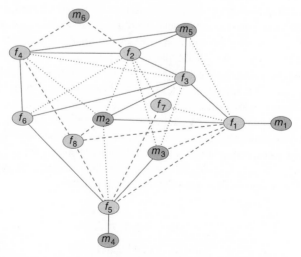

Figure 7.7. The baboon grooming network, T_1 and T_2.

Figure 7.8. The baboon grooming networks for both time points.

Table 7.19. Another Four-Position Model Fitted to the Baboon Network at T_2

		2	5	7	9	12	13	4	6	8	1	3	14	10	11
m_1	2	0	0	0	0	0	0	0	0	0	1	0	0	0	0
m_2	5	0	0	0	0	0	0	1	0	0	1	0	1	0	0
m_3	7	0	0	0	0	0	0	0	0	1	1	0	0	0	0
m_4	9	0	0	0	0	0	0	0	0	1	0	0	0	0	0
m_5	12	0	0	0	0	0	0	1	1	0	0	1	0	0	0
m_6	13	0	0	0	0	0	0	0	1	0	0	1	0	0	0
f_3	4	0	1	0	0	1	0	0	0	0	1	1	0	1	0
f_4	6	0	0	0	0	1	1	0	0	0	0	1	1	1	0
f_5	8	0	0	1	1	0	0	0	0	0	1	0	1	1	1
f_1	1	1	1	1	0	0	0	1	0	1	0	0	1	0	0
f_2	3	0	0	0	0	1	1	1	1	0	0	0	0	0	0
f_8	14	0	1	0	0	0	0	0	1	1	1	0	0	0	0
f_6	10	0	0	0	0	0	0	1	1	1	0	0	0	0	0
f_7	11	0	0	0	0	0	0	0	0	1	0	0	0	0	0

null	col-regular	col-regular	null
row-regular	null	col-regular	col-regular
row-regular	row-regular	null	null
null	row-regular	null	null

Because the blockmodel fitted in Table 1.12 had females in the first position, the prespecified blockmodel for Table 7.18 had the additional constraint that females had to be in the first position. Suppose we did not include this constraint, having recognized that, in addition to the null blocks among the males, there are null blocks among females. We get the partition shown in Table 7.19. There are two inconsistencies coming from the reciprocal tie between f_1 and f_8 in a block that was specified as null. This image provides a more differentiated view of the grooming behavior of the females while keeping the males in a single position.

Figure 7.9 presents another visual image of the baboon grooming network at the second time point. Its structure suggests a partition into three positions that is a completely constrained clustering model. The required partition for T_2 is then $\{f_1, f_2, f_3, f_4, f_5, f_8\}$, $\{f_6, f_7\}$, and $\{m_1, m_2, m_3, m_4, m_5, m_6\}$. Given the logic of the general hypothesized blockmodel, the blockmodel is

reg	cre	cre
rre	nul	nul
rre	nul	nul

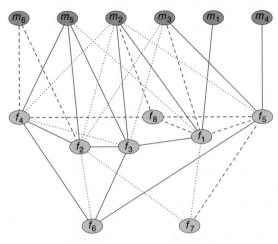

Figure 7.9. Distinguishing gender in the baboon grooming network.

This model fits exactly.[15] However, for T_1, this blockmodel fits with eight inconsistencies if f_6 and f_7 are specified as going together in a single cluster. If this constraint is not applied, then there is an exact model with the prespecified model for T_2: $\{f_1, f_2, f_3, f_4, f_5, f_6\}$, $\{f_7\}$, and $\{m_1, m_2, m_3, m_4, m_5\}$. It also does not fit. It appears that the structure among the female baboons did change between the two time points.

7.6.3 Multiple blockmodels and inconsistencies

We finish this section with some comments that are both supportive of generalized blockmodeling as an approach and reminders that there are some cautions regarding its use. First, it is possible to have multiple blockmodels of the same network. This was clear in our discussion of using optimization methods for fitting the so-called conventional blockmodels: talk of *the* (generalized) blockmodel for a network is misplaced. However, our discussion of the baboon network pushes this notion in the direction of thinking that there can be different fitted blockmodels that are complementary in their interpretations.[16]

Second, our experiences thus far in fitting generalized blockmodels suggest that it is always possible to fit such a model with few if any inconsistencies (with *some* ideal blockmodel). When our three-position generalized blockmodel for T_2 failed

15 There are two other partitions that also fit exactly: $\{f_1, f_2, f_3, f_4, f_5, f_6, f_8\}$, $\{f_7\}$, and $\{m_1, m_2, m_3, m_4, m_5, m_6\}$; and $\{f_1, f_2, f_3, f_4, f_5, f_7, f_8\}$, $\{f_6\}$, and $\{m_1, m_2, m_3, m_4, m_5, m_6\}$. These suggest that the blockmodel reported in the text is the most appropriate.

16 Of course, it may well be possible to fit multiple blockmodels that are not fully complementary with each other in their interpretations. This creates interesting substantive issues.

to fit for T_1, we gave some (inductive) thought to a three-position model for T_1. The following prespecified blockmodel fits without inconsistencies for T_1:

nul	cdo	nul
rdo	nul	cdo
nul	rdo	nul

We can look at this ad hoc model in two ways. We can reject it as a plausible blockmodel given the way we approached the baboon grooming network as a center–periphery model with regular, row-regular, and column-regular equivalences ideas in mind. Or we could begin considering row-dominance and column-dominance as ideas to think about. Of course, in general, choosing among alternative blockmodels is done within a substantive context. We do not advocate switching on any set of block types to see what happens, but we do remain open to the idea that we need to expand the number of block types and the ways we think in terms of them.

Third, because we use optimization methods, we emphasize the reduction of inconsistencies. However, we do not want to elevate the reduction of inconsistencies as the dominant goal in fitting generalized blockmodels. Rather, *given a prespecified* blockmodel, we must locate partitions with as few inconsistencies as possible. Comparing inconsistency counts across different blockmodel types solely to reduce inconsistencies is problematic. There are times when a fitted blockmodel with more inconsistencies is preferable to one with fewer inconsistencies if it makes substantive sense and the blockmodel with the few inconsistencies was established by varying block types just to get fewer inconsistencies.

Fourth, we note again that the regular block type is both flexible and weak. So many patterns of 0s and 1s in a regular block are consistent with its being one covered. If the goal is just to minimize the number of inconsistencies, using regular blocks is a tempting option, but it has two serious drawbacks. Consider a blockmodel that has a block with a specified complete block as its nearest ideal type. Now consider a second specified blockmodel that is identical to the first except that the complete block is replaced by a regular block in the specification. By definition, the first blockmodel with its complete block will have more inconsistencies than the second with the regular block (unless it fits exactly). It does not follow that the second blockmodel is preferable – all that changed was a change in a counting procedure. There is a related, more serious problem. When regular blocks are specified, it is common to get many equally well-fitting blockmodels that differ greatly from each other. This often precludes the selection of a small number of sensible fitted blockmodels. The baboon example had hints of this with a small number of equally well-fitting blockmodels. Fortunately, in this case, there were few of them and they differed little from each other, but, in general, regular (as well as row-regular and column-regular) blocks ought to be used with caution.

7.7 SOME BENEFITS OF THE OPTIMIZATION APPROACH

Given the specification of a blockmodel with the set of permitted block types and the specification of a criterion function as described, we solve the blockmodeling problem by using a local optimization procedure (a relocation algorithm) as described in Chapter 6 and in this chapter. There are clear benefits to using the optimization approach to blockmodeling. It enables us to do the following.

1. Exploratory blockmodeling: Given a network and set of block types, we can determine the blockmodel and the clustering (see Table 7.16, top row).
2. Confirmatory blockmodeling (model fitting): Given a network, a set of block types, and a prespecified blockmodel, we can determine those clusterings that minimize the criterion function or specify the clusterings and establish the block structure (Table 7.16, lower panel).
3. Evaluating the quality of a model, comparing different models, and analyzing the evolution of a network (see the Sampson 1968 data as analyzed by Doreian and Mrvar 1996, and in Chapter 10): Given a network, a set of block types, a prespecified blockmodel, and a clustering, we can compute the value of the corresponding criterion function (Table 7.16, last row).
4. Fitting a partial model: We can also analyze the residual block(s) later.
5. Considering different constraints on the model: These would be, for example, units x and y are of the same position, or positions of units x and y are not connected.

Although we have not written much about constraining blockmodels, we did use constraints in the baboon grooming network to ensure that females were clustered only with females and males were clustered only with males. Many other types of constraints on blockmodels are possible. We consider this topic in later chapters.

7.8 EXTENDING GENERALIZED BLOCKMODELING

Starting with new block types (and hence new blockmodel types) and allowing each block to have its own characterization means that the number of blockmodel types can be increased indefinitely. New block types can be defined formally or can have purely substantive foundations. We anticipate the creation of many new block types depending on the substantive problems being studied. The block types listed in Table 7.1 and Figure 7.1 are only one small set of possible options. Consider a signed relation in which the data values are 1, 0, and -1. Defining positive blocks as having either 0 or 1 as ties and negative blocks as having -1 or 0 as ties creates two new block types. Specifying a blockmodel type as having positive diagonal blocks and negative off-diagonal block brings the analysis of signed relations and structural balance within the generalized blockmodeling framework. We pursue this in Chapter 10 following the suggestions of Doreian and Mrvar (1996). Defining another new block type as symmetric and a ranked-clusters type of blockmodel means we can fit ranked-clusters blockmodels (Doreian, et al. 2000), which is a topic taken up in Chapter 11.

Given the generality of this optimizational approach, it also seems reasonable to extend the range of data structures approached in this fashion. We do this in Chapter 8 when we consider blockmodeling two-mode data. As noted earlier in Chapter 1, there are many areas of network analysis that do not feature social scientific examples. We believe that scholars working in these other fields will be able to define more new block types that are more appropriate for the problems that they study, and our hope is that generalized blockmodeling will be a useful tool in these other areas.

8

BLOCKMODELING TWO-MODE
NETWORK DATA

In developing a more general approach to blockmodeling, we have emphasized
the use of direct methods in an optimizational approach (Chapter 6) and the creation of an (indefinitely) expanding set of block types and the formulation of new
types of blockmodels (Chapter 7). We have confined our attention to one-mode
social network data in which a social relation(s) is defined over one set of social
actors. We have also stressed the generality of our methods and have suggested
that generalized blockmodeling could be applied to other data structures. In this
chapter we return to this idea and focus our attention on two-mode data. In Section 8.1 we define two-mode data and, in Section 8.2, we sketch some (but not
all) approaches that have been taken with data of this form. Section 8.3 contains
a brief proposal for extending generalized blockmodeling to two-mode data, and
Section 8.4 presents our formalization of blockmodeling for such data. Section 8.5
describes some applications of these new tools in different substantive contexts.

8.1 TWO-MODE NETWORK DATA

Two-mode data can be defined in terms of two sets of social network actors. As
Wasserman and Faust (1994:29–30) put it, "a two-mode network data set contains
measurements on which actors from one of the sets have ties to actors in the other
set." Pairs of network actor types and relations include the following: organizations
employing people and organizations of one type, such as corporations, sending resources, such as money, to organizations of a different type such as nonprofit
social service agencies (see Galaskiewicz 1985). For these examples, the formulation in terms of two sets of so-called actors works. However, two-mode data are
more general, and Wasserman and Faust (1994, Chapter 8) also discussed "affiliation networks" in which there is only one set of recognizable social actors. The
quintessential example of affiliation networks is the Deep South data, also known
as the Southern Women data, collected by Davis et al. (1941) for a set of women

attending social events over a nine-month period.[1] These data were described in Chapter 1. Another example is the Justices of the U.S. Supreme Court and the decisions they hand down (see Doreian and Fujimoto 2003) over some period of time. We use the term *units* for two-mode data rather than the term *actors*.

8.2   APPROACHES TO TWO-MODE NETWORK DATA

In a two-mode network, $\mathbf{N} = (\mathcal{U}_1, \mathcal{U}_2, R, w)$, there is one set of social units denoted by $\mathcal{U}_1 = \{u_1, u_2, \ldots, u_{n_1}\}$ with a second set of units denoted by $\mathcal{U}_2 = \{v_1, v_2, \ldots, v_{n_2}\}$ and $\mathcal{U}_1 \cap \mathcal{U}_2 = \emptyset$. The social relation $R \subseteq \mathcal{U}_1 \times \mathcal{U}_2$ is defined as one *between* the units in these two sets and is represented by the set of edges with initial vertices in the set $\mathcal{U}_1$ and terminal vertices in the set $\mathcal{U}_2$. The mapping $w : R \to \mathbb{R}$ is a weight. Examples of weighted two-mode networks are (Persons, Goods or Services, consumed, frequency) and (Countries, Countries, exported to, value). If no weight is defined, we can assume a constant weight: usually, $w(u, v) = 1$ for all uRv.

A wide variety of network analytic tools can be used to study the structure contained in two-mode data, and there are distinct ways of representing this type of data. One takes the form of using a *rectangular* $n_1 \times n_2$ matrix $\mathbf{A} = [a_{uv}]_{n_1 \times n_2}$ to represent the data for the two sets of units or vertices, $\mathcal{U}_1$ and $\mathcal{U}_2$:

$$a_{uv} = \begin{cases} w(u, v) & uRv \\ 0 & \text{otherwise.} \end{cases}$$

This (rectangular) matrix can be binary or valued. For most of the examples that follow, $\mathbf{A}$ has a binary form.

A two-mode network can be viewed also as an ordinary (one-mode) network on the vertex set $\mathcal{U}_1 \cup \mathcal{U}_2$ divided into two sets $\mathcal{U}_1$ and $\mathcal{U}_2$, where the arcs can only go from $\mathcal{U}_1$ to $\mathcal{U}_2$ – a bipartite directed graph. The corresponding network matrix has the form

$$\begin{bmatrix} \mathbf{0} & \mathbf{A} \\ \mathbf{0} & \mathbf{0} \end{bmatrix},$$

or, if we consider it as an undirected network (see Wasserman and Faust 1994, Section 8.3.2, where T denotes transposition), the form

$$\begin{bmatrix} \mathbf{0} & \mathbf{A} \\ \mathbf{A}^T & \mathbf{0} \end{bmatrix}.$$

Borgatti and Everett (1997:248) provided a pictorial representation of a bipartite graph for the Southern Women data set and advocated the inclusion of analyses of the bipartite matrix, in this form, in the analysis of two-mode data. Freeman (2003) also displayed the Southern Women data in this fashion.

---

1   Indeed, this data set has entered the literature not only as data but as a way of describing the nature of two-mode data.

One algebraic approach to two-mode data takes the form of exploring the "duality" of two-mode data (Breiger 1974) by constructing two-valued one-mode networks. The matrix $A_1 = AA^T$ is in the one-mode form for the actors in $\mathcal{U}_1$, and $A_2 = A^T A$ is in the one-mode form for the actors in $\mathcal{U}_2$. Analyses then are conducted by using these two one-mode representations.[2]

Atkin (1974) introduced Q-Analysis, an approach based on algebraic topology, as a way of delineating the structure of the dual simplicial complexes of A_1 and A_2. These tools were used by Doreian (1979) to analyze the structure of the Southern Women data considered below.[3] See Freeman (1980) for another example of using Q-Analysis for network data and Seidman (1981) for a related discussion in terms of hypergraphs. Everett and Borgatti (1993) also considered hypergraphs but with a view to using regular equivalence and coloring. Galois lattices provide another algebraic approach to two-mode data, one taken by Freeman and White (1994), who have applied these methods to the Southern Women data.

Once A_1 and A_2 have been constructed as one-mode matrices, all of the conventional techniques for analyzing one-mode data can be used. These include analyses in terms of reachability, connectivity, and other graph invariants. There are a variety of other approaches in the form of looking at eigenvalues[4] and eigenvectors for analyzing two-mode data. This includes correspondence analysis (Bonacich 1991, Borgatti and Everett 1997, and Roberts 2000). Freeman (1993) used a genetic algorithm to study the Southern Women data, and a statistical approach to these data, based on p^* models, can be taken (see Wasserman and Pattison 1996 and Skvoretz and Faust 1999). Our concern will be on blockmodeling two-mode data.

8.3 BLOCKMODELS FOR TWO-MODE NETWORK DATA

If we think of applying generalized blockmodeling tools, as described so far, to two-mode data, it follows that some adjustments to this set of techniques, as well as the thinking behind them, are required. Necessarily, the data come in the form of rectangular arrays rather than square arrays. This implies that the language of diagonal and off-diagonal blocks is no longer applicable. Further, for blockmodels applied to (the usual) square network data, the rows and columns are partitioned simultaneously in exactly the same way. However, for two-mode (rectangular) arrays, if partitioned, it is clear that the rows and columns cannot be partitioned in the same way. That is, the partitions of rows and columns are not identical. Of course, it makes no sense, conceptually and technically, to think of partitioning rows and columns of a rectangular array in an identical fashion.

2   Table 1.3 in Chapter 1 contains the Southern Women data. Denoting this as A, we display the matrix A_1 in Table 1.4.

3   However, his partitions of the actors and the social events has been superseded by other analyses and are suboptimal as descriptions of the structure of these data (Freeman 2003). These partitions will not be considered in this chapter.

4   This is not in the sense of eigenstructures preserved under isomorphism but rather in the sense of a data-reduction and representation strategy.

Recognizing that the row and column partitions may be different makes it possible to view one-mode network data in a different fashion by thinking of them as two-mode data in the following way. Consider the example of a journal-to-journal citation network and the application of blockmodeling tools. Doreian (1985) partitioned a set of psychology journals and a set of geography journals (Doreian 1988b) in terms of structural equivalence. Although the partitions had value, there is a sense in which such partitioning strategy for one-mode data is overly restricted. If there are so-called consumer journals (as the first set of units) and producer journals (as the second set of units), it makes sense to think of partitioning the rows and columns of such citation networks in different ways. We explore such a partitioning of a journal network in Section 8.5.5. Note that because the data come in the form of one-mode data, the diagonal elements of the data network are meaningful and relevant even if the term *diagonal block* for an image is no longer meaningful in the two-mode context.

We do not regard the use of partitioning tools for the above (Section 8.2) matrix representation of the bipartite graph (using $\mathbf{A}$, $\mathbf{A}^T$ and two null matrices) as a clean procedure. The reason is simple: It is possible to have mixtures of the two distinct types of actors in the same cluster. Indeed, exactly this happened with the Borgatti and Everett (1997) partition of the bipartite network in this form for the Southern Women data.

We establish some more simple notation given $\mathcal{U}_1 = \{u_1, u_2, \ldots, u_{n_1}\}$ and $\mathcal{U}_2 = \{v_1, v_2, \ldots, v_{n_2}\}$. Let k_1 be the number of clusters for actors in $\mathcal{U}_1$ and k_2 the number of clusters of actors in $\mathcal{U}_2$. Clearly, $1 \leq k_1 \leq n_1$ and $1 \leq k_2 \leq n_2$. Although it is possible to consider up to n_1 and n_2 for the number of clusters of the two sets of actors, the point of the blockmodeling effort is to use as few clusters as possible. We call the partition with k_1 and k_2 clusters a (k_1, k_2)-partition. Two strategies can be contrasted. One is exploratory and takes the form of specifying a set of values for k_1 and k_2 and searching the so-called fitting grid of values (over the ranges for k_1 and k_2). The second is confirmatory in the sense of prespecifying blockmodels in advance of an analysis. We consider both strategies in Section 8.5.

8.4 A FORMALIZATION OF BLOCKMODELING TWO-MODE DATA

The theoretical framework for two-mode blockmodeling is a simple extension of ordinary (one-mode) blockmodeling described in Sections 6.2 and 7.2.

The approach taken here is to extend the generalized blockmodeling formalization to two-clusterings. The main difference is that in blockmodeling of a two-mode network $\mathbf{N} = (\mathcal{U}_1, \mathcal{U}_2, R, w)$ we are trying to identify a two-clustering $\mathbf{C} = (\mathbf{C}_1, \mathbf{C}_2)$, where $\mathbf{C}_1$ is a partition of $\mathcal{U}_1$ and $\mathbf{C}_2$ is a partition of $\mathcal{U}_2$, such that they induce selected blocks. Again, we denote the set of all feasible two-clusterings with Φ.

The two-mode generalized blockmodeling problem is formulated as an optimization problem (Φ, P, min).

Determine the two-clustering $\mathbf{C}^* = (\mathbf{C}_1^*, \mathbf{C}_2^*) \in \Phi$ for which

$$P(\mathbf{C}^*) = \min_{\mathbf{C} \in \Phi} P(\mathbf{C}),$$

where Φ is the set of feasible two-clusterings and P is the criterion function.

The criterion function $P(\mathbf{C})$ is obtained in the same way as before (see Sections 6.2.1 and 7.2.3):

$$P(\mathbf{C}) = P((\mathbf{C}_1, \mathbf{C}_2)) = \sum_{C_u \in \mathbf{C}_1, C_v \in \mathbf{C}_2} \min_{B \in \mathcal{B}(C_u, C_v)} d(R(C_u, C_v), B).$$

Here $\mathcal{B}(C_u, C_v)$, $C_u \subseteq \mathcal{U}_1$ and $C_v \subseteq \mathcal{U}_2$, denotes the set of all ideal blocks corresponding to block $R(C_u, C_v)$, and the term $d(R(C_u, C_v), B)$ measures the difference (number of inconsistencies) between the empirical block $R(C_u, C_v)$ and the corresponding ideal block B. The function d has to be compatible with the selected type of equivalence.

The criterion function $P((\mathbf{C}_1, \mathbf{C}_2))$ is sensitive iff $P((\mathbf{C}_1, \mathbf{C}_2)) = 0 \Leftrightarrow$ the blockmodel determined by $(\mathbf{C}_1, \mathbf{C}_2)$ is exact.

The obtained optimization problem can be solved by local optimization. Once the partitions $(\mathbf{C}_1, \mathbf{C}_2)$ and types of blocks are determined, we can also compute the values of connections by using averaging rules.

We note that another (fully equivalent) approach is to treat the two-mode blockmodeling as an ordinary (one-mode) generalized blockmodeling problem on the (one-mode) network $\mathbf{N}' = (\mathcal{U}_1 \cup \mathcal{U}_2, R, w)$, where we add to the description of the set of feasible solutions (at least) the bipartition requirement (constraint)

$$\forall C \in \mathbf{C} \in \Phi : ((C \subseteq \mathcal{U}_1) \vee (C \subseteq \mathcal{U}_2)),$$

which does not allow a cluster C to contain units from both sets $\mathcal{U}_1$ and $\mathcal{U}_2$. However, we do not pursue this line of thought here.

8.5 BLOCKMODELS WITH EMPIRICAL DATA

We present examples of analyses of two-mode data in this section. They are ordered in terms of the kinds of blocks that are specified. We move from blockmodels based on structural and regular equivalence to generalized blockmodels. We consider both genuine two-mode (affiliation) data and one-mode data in which the rows and columns can be partitioned in different ways.

8.5.1 Supreme Court voting

Our first example comes from the simple preliminary study by Doreian and Fujimoto (2003) of the Supreme Court Justices and their votes on a set of 26 important decisions made during the 2000–2001 term. These data are presented in Table 8.1. The nine Justices (in the order of the year in which they joined the Supreme Court)

Table 8.1. Supreme Court Voting for 26 Important Decisions

Issue	Label	Br	Gi	So	St	OC	Ke	Re	Sc	Th
Presidential Election	PE	−	−	−	−	+	+	+	+	+
Criminal Law Cases										
Illegal Search 1	CL1	+	+	+	+	+	+	−	−	−
Illegal Search 2	CL2	+	+	+	+	+	+	−	−	−
Illegal Search 3	CL3	+	+	+	−	−	−	−	+	+
Seat Belts	CL4	−	−	+	−	−	+	+	+	+
Stay of Execution	CL5	+	+	+	+	+	+	−	−	−
Federal Authority Cases										
Federalism	FA1	−	−	−	−	+	+	+	+	+
Clean Air Action	FA2	+	+	+	+	+	+	+	+	+
Clean Water	FA3	−	−	−	−	+	+	+	+	+
Cannabis for Health	FA4	0	+	+	+	+	+	+	+	+
United Foods	FA5	−	−	+	+	−	+	+	+	+
NY Times Copyrights	FA6	−	+	+	−	+	+	+	+	+
Civil Rights Cases										
Voting Rights	CR1	+	+	+	+	+	−	−	−	−
Title VI Disabilities	CR2	−	−	−	−	+	+	+	+	+
PGA v. Handicapped Player	CR3	+	+	+	+	+	+	+	−	−
Immigration Law Cases										
Immigration Jurisdiction	Im1	+	+	+	+	−	+	−	−	−
Deporting Criminal Aliens	Im2	+	+	+	+	+	−	−	−	−
Detaining Criminal Aliens	Im3	+	+	+	+	−	+	−	−	−
Citizenship	Im4	−	−	−	+	−	+	+	+	+
Speech and Press Cases										
Legal Aid for Poor	SP1	+	+	+	+	−	+	−	−	−
Privacy	SP2	+	+	+	+	+	+	−	−	−
Free Speech	SP3	+	−	−	−	+	+	+	+	+
Campaign Finance	SP4	+	+	+	+	+	−	−	−	−
Tobacco Ads	SP5	−	−	−	−	+	+	+	+	+
Labor and Property Rights Cases										
Labor Rights	LPR1	−	−	−	−	+	+	+	+	+
Property Rights	LPR2	−	−	−	−	+	+	+	+	+

are Rehnquist (1972), Stevens (1975), O'Connor (1981), Scalia (1982), Kennedy (1988), Souter (1990), Thomas (1991), Ginsburg (1993), and Breyer (1994). The distribution of votes is arranged in terms of the substantive content of the decisions, as organized by Greenhouse (2001).

Each row of Table 8.1 represents a decision handed down by the Supreme Court in a single term.[5] On the left is a descriptive label for that decision; the second column has a corresponding brief label. A much fuller description of these cases can be found in Greenhouse (2001) and in Doreian and Fujimoto (2003). The substantive details of these cases are of secondary concern here. The columns correspond to the nine Justices, where the Justices are represented by a label: Breyer (Br), Ginsburg (Gi), Souter (So), Stevens (St), O'Connor (OC), Kennedy (Ke), Rehnquist (Re), Scalia (Sc), and Thomas (Th). In these data, a plus sign in the column of a Justice represents voting in the majority for that issue and a minus sign represents voting in the minority for that issue. The decisions range from the unanimous decision in the case involving the Clean Air Act to a quite large number of narrow 5–4 decisions. There is one case in which Breyer abstained because his brother had ruled on the case at a lower court level.

In the usual representation of such data, $\mathbf{A}$ is written with the actors (in this case the Justices) in the rows and the events (in this case the decisions) in the columns. Table 8.1 has been written as the transposed form for formatting reasons only. In terms of the analysis we have done, rows of $\mathbf{A}$ represent the Justices and the columns the events. Doreian and Fujimoto took note of the fact that these data can be viewed as signed two-mode data. They constructed a matrix $\mathbf{A}_p$ for majority voting where 1 represented a majority vote and 0 represented a vote that was not for the majority (i.e., either a vote against the decision or an abstention). Similarly, they constructed a matrix $\mathbf{A}_n$ for the negative votes for a decision, where 1 represented a vote in the minority and 0 represented either an abstention or a vote with the majority. Their analyses involved (for a focus on the Justices) $\mathbf{A}_p\mathbf{A}_p^T$ for majority voting, $\mathbf{A}_n\mathbf{A}_n^T$ for minority voting, and $\mathbf{A}_t$, where $\mathbf{A}_t = \mathbf{A}_p\mathbf{A}_p^T + \mathbf{A}_n\mathbf{A}_n^T$ for all voting. Their analyses were designed to explore the differing patterns of joint majority voting, joint minority voting, and joint overall voting patterns. They used a combination of tools including Q-Analysis and partitions based on structural equivalence for the generated one-mode matrices. As a result of these analyses, they reached the partition shown in Table 8.2. This matrix was constructed by looking at the partitions of the Justices and the partitions of the decisions (events) and was *not* the result of fitting a blockmodel explicitly. However, if we think of the blocks as either null blocks or complete blocks, a measure of fit is easy to construct. The 13 boldfaced entries marked in Table 8.2 are inconsistent with a blockmodel constructed in terms of structural equivalence. There are four clusters for the Justices and eight clusters for the decisions. This partition is the point of departure for exploring blockmodeling two-mode data for the set of affiliation

5 These are not the only decisions handed down by the Supreme Court in 2000–2001. They are the "important" decisions identified by Greenhouse (2001).

Table 8.2. A Partition of Supreme Court Voting

Issue	Br	Gi	So	St	OC	Ke	Re	Sc	Th
Presidential Election	.	.	.	.	1	1	1	1	1
Federalism	.	.	.	.	1	1	1	1	1
Labor Rights	.	.	.	.	1	1	1	1	1
Title VI Disabilities	.	.	.	.	1	1	1	1	1
Tobacco Ads	.	.	.	.	1	1	1	1	1
Clean Water	.	.	.	.	1	1	1	1	1
Property Rights	.	.	.	.	1	1	1	1	1
Free Speech	**1**	.	.	.	**1**	1	1	1	1
Citizenship	.	.	.	**1**	.	1	1	1	1
Seat Belts	.	.	**1**	.	.	1	1	1	1
United Foods	.	.	**1**	**1**	.	1	1	1	1
NY Times Copyrights	.	**1**	**1**	.	**1**	1	1	1	1
Illegal Search 3	1	1	1	**1**	.	.	**1**	1	1
Voting Rights	1	1	1	1	1	.	.	.	.
Campaign Finance	1	1	1	1	1	.	.	.	.
Deporting Criminal Aliens	1	1	1	1	1	.	.	.	.
Legal Aid for Poor	1	1	1	1	.	1	.	.	.
Detaining Criminal Aliens	1	1	1	1	.	1	.	.	.
Immigration Jurisdiction	1	1	1	1	.	1	.	.	.
Illegal Search 1	1	1	1	1	1	1	.	.	.
Illegal Search 2	1	1	1	1	1	1	.	.	.
Stay of Execution	1	1	1	1	1	1	.	.	.
Privacy	1	1	1	1	1	1	.	.	.
PGA v. Handicapped Player	1	1	1	1	1	1	**1**	.	.
Cannabis for Health	**0**	1	1	1	1	1	1	1	1
Clean Air Act	1	1	1	1	1	1	1	1	1

network data. It seems reasonable to consider $1 \leq k_1 \leq 4$ and $1 \leq k_2 \leq 8$ for partitioning the two-mode data given in Table 8.1.

For the Justices, two of the four clusters are {Breyer, Ginsburg, Souter, Stevens}, and {Rehnquist, Scalia, Thomas}, which can be viewed, respectively, as the liberal and conservative wings of the Supreme Court. The two singletons, O'Connor and Kennedy, are interpreted as Justices that form a bridge between the two wings. For the decisions, the top cluster in Table 8.2 is those decisions in which the conservative wing plus O'Connor and Kennedy won with a narrow 5–4 vote. The second cluster is one in which the majority of the inconsistencies with structural equivalence occur. These decisions all have Rehnquist, Scalia, Thomas, and Kennedy in the majority, where they are joined by at least one of the other Justices. (O'Connor joins them two times and Stevens joins them two times. Souter does so three times

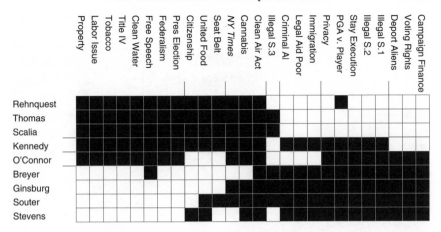

Figure 8.1. A (4,7) partition of the Supreme Court voting.

and both Breyer and Ginsburg join them once.) The singleton (Illegal Search 3) is a most improbable decision in which part of the conservative wing – perhaps its core – and some members of the liberal wing join in a yet another 5–4 decision. The next three clusters contain cases in which the liberal wing prevailed. The fourth cluster of Table 8.2 has the decisions in which it prevailed with O'Connor joining them. Next come the decisions in which this wing prevailed with Kennedy joining them, and the next cluster has the cases in which both O'Connor and Kennedy joined with the liberal wing. One case occupies the next cluster in which only Scalia and Thomas dissented. The last cluster has the two unanimous cases (allowing for Breyer's abstention).

The combination of Q-Analyses and blockmodeling the one-mode valued networks was a cumbersome procedure dictated by the absence of a clean way of partitioning the two-mode data directly. Here, we simply blockmodel the two-mode array directly.

Figure 8.1 shows the fitted blockmodel for structural equivalence in which four clusters were specified for the Justices and seven clusters were specified for the decisions. Although the format differs from Table 8.2, the content is readily interpreted and, in large measure, is consistent with that table. However, there are advantages to this partition that make it a better partition than the one obtained by means of Q-Analysis and blockmodeling the generated one-mode matrices. Figure 8.2 provides a pictorial representation of the partitioned two-mode Supreme Court data.

The partition of the justices in Figure 8.1 is identical to the partition reached by Doreian and Fujimoto. However, there are differences in the partitions of the decisions (events). First, there are seven clusters rather than eight, and second, the number of inconsistencies with structural equivalence has been reduced from 13 to 11. In addition to being slightly simpler and better fitting, there are some interpretational benefits. The large first cluster of decisions in which the conservative wing prevailed with both Kennedy and O'Connor joining them remains intact

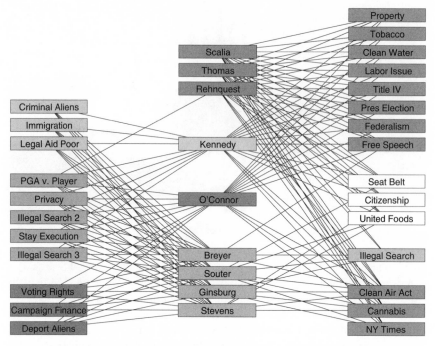

Figure 8.2. The Bipartite Supreme Court network with the (4,7)-partition.

but has the Free Speech Issue (SP3) located with them. Breyer's vote remains an inconsistency, but O'Connor's vote is no longer inconsistent with structural equivalence. This is one less inconsistency. The second cluster of Doreian and Fujimoto is further reduced by moving the *New York Times* case (FA6) to the cluster with the unanimous decisions. The same four inconsistencies (all involving one or two members of the liberal wing voting with the core of the conservative wing) remain, but the number of inconsistencies for FA6 is reduced by one when it is grouped with the Cannabis for Health case (FA4) and the Clean Air Act case (FA2). The highly unusual Illegal Search 3 case (CL3) is located as a singleton when the blockmodeling methods introduced here are used. The fourth and fifth clusters in Table 8.2 are both preserved. The sixth cluster of that table is also preserved with the PGA case (CR2) joining it in the partition shown in Figure 8.1. Having CR2 as a singleton in a cluster was unnecessary. Figure 8.2 is drawn to reflect the partition delineated in Figure 8.1.

It is clear that fitting a single blockmodel, constructed in terms of structural equivalence, to the two-mode data is a much more efficient procedure. It is important to note that a measure of fit was used during the fitting procedure and not computed at the end of an analysis. The clusters that are produced are homogenous – there is no mixing of the two types of social actors in them. Finally, together, the matrix display in Figure 8.1 and the picture of the bipartite graph in Figure 8.2

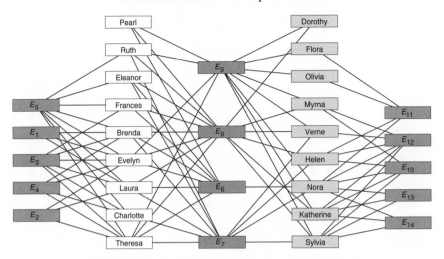

Figure 8.3. Southern Women Bipartite network: Version 1.

provide clean displays of the partitioned two-mode data. Of course, Figure 8.2 shows the bipartite graph, but it does so with the members of a cluster placed in close proximity to each other.

That a partition based on structural equivalence is sufficient to partition the Supreme Court data set is nice. However, in general, using just these two types of blocks will not be sufficient to blockmodel all two-mode data structures. We turn now to the consideration of other types of blockmodels for modeling two-mode data.

8.5.2 *The southern women event participation data*

Our second example is the Davis et al. (1941) Southern Women participating in social events data set. As Freeman (2003:41) noted, this data set "reappears whenever any network analyst wants to explore the utility of some new tool for analyzing data." We are no exception and will join the long line of analysts who have worked with these data. Our assessment of the utility of using blockmodeling tools with these two-mode data has been made much easier by Freeman's (2003) meta-analysis of 21 analyses of these data. To the extent that his analysis provides a consensual (induced) agreement regarding the "true structure" in these data, we have a criterion for assessing the adequacy of our own efforts.

Freeman is clear that the true structure of the Southern Women data on the participation in social events is one in which there are two subgroups. One is composed of {Evelyn, Laura, Theresa, Brenda, Charlotte, Frances, Eleanor, Pearl, Ruth} and the other has {Verne, Myra, Katherine, Sylvia, Nora, Helen, Dorothy, Olivia, Flora} as its members. We label these two subgroups of women as Group A and Group B. Consistent with that description, Figure 8.3 shows a picture of

Table 8.3. Sorted Participation Matrix

Actor	E_1	E_2	E_3	E_4	E_5	E_6	E_7	E_8	E_9	E_{10}	E_{11}	E_{12}	E_{13}	E_{14}
Evelyn	1	1	1	1	1	1	0	1	1	0	0	0	0	0
Laura	1	1	1	0	1	1	1	1	0	0	0	0	0	0
Theresa	0	1	1	1	1	1	1	1	1	0	0	0	0	0
Brenda	1	0	1	1	1	1	1	1	0	0	0	0	0	0
Charlotte	0	0	1	1	1	0	1	0	0	0	0	0	0	0
Frances	0	0	1	0	1	1	0	1	0	0	0	0	0	0
Eleanor	0	0	0	0	1	1	1	1	0	0	0	0	0	0
Pearl	0	0	0	0	0	1	0	1	1	0	0	0	0	0
Ruth	0	0	0	0	1	0	1	1	1	0	0	0	0	0
Verne	0	0	0	0	0	0	1	1	1	0	0	1	0	0
Myra	0	0	0	0	0	0	0	1	1	1	0	1	0	0
Katherine	0	0	0	0	0	0	0	1	1	1	0	1	1	1
Sylvia	0	0	0	0	0	0	1	1	1	1	0	1	1	1
Nora	0	0	0	0	0	1	1	0	1	1	1	1	1	1
Helen	0	0	0	0	0	0	1	1	0	1	1	1	0	0
Dorothy	0	0	0	0	0	0	0	1	1	0	0	0	0	0
Olivia	0	0	0	0	0	0	0	0	1	0	1	0	0	0
Flora	0	0	0	0	0	0	0	0	1	0	1	0	0	0

the bipartite graph with these two clusters of women. Freeman is silent about the corresponding partition of the set of events. We label the events E_j for $1 \leq j \leq 14$ for ease of presentation in this chapter. We have divided them into three clusters that almost have this form: events E_1–E_5 were events attended only by women of Group A; events E_6–E_9 were events attended by both groups of women; and events E_{10}–E_{14} were attended only by the women in Group B. Pearl and Dorothy appear to be exceptions because they each attend only events in the middle panel of Table 8.3. This partition is called the initial partition and is shown in pictorial form as Figure 8.3 to represent our point of departure for examining blockmodels of this two-mode data set. We note that in most of the partitioning reported below, the partition of the events into the three subsets of Table 8.3 was consistently reached.

At face value, given the partition structure shown in Table 8.3, there is little need to partition the events into more than three clusters if partitions are sought with structural equivalence in mind. The women can be split into two clusters given Table 8.3 or, anticipating two subgroups for each primary group, into four clusters. A summary of the event participation is provided in Table 8.4.

Table 8.4 makes it clear that there are events attended only by women from Group A and a set of events attended only by women from Group B. The partition shown in Table 8.3 has considerable appeal, but the location of Pearl in Group A and Dorothy in Group B can be seen as problematic.

Table 8.4. *Counts of Participation in Events*

Actor	E_1–E_5	E_6–E_9	E_{10}–E_{14}
Evelyn	5	3	0
Laura	4	3	0
Theresa	4	4	0
Brenda	4	3	0
Charlotte	3	1	0
Frances	2	2	0
Eleanor	1	3	0
Pearl	0	3	0
Ruth	1	4	0
Verne	0	3	1
Myra	0	2	2
Katherine	0	2	4
Sylvia	0	3	4
Nora	0	3	5
Helen	0	2	3
Dorothy	0	2	0
Olivia	0	1	1
Flora	0	1	1

Structural equivalence. We proved in Chapter 6 that, for partitioning one-mode data, the criterion for structural equivalence declines monotonically with the number of clusters (and the number of blocks). This result also holds for two-mode data and raises the same problem of making decisions regarding the number of clusters: Choose a partition that is too coarse and the criterion function will be large, or choose one that is too fine with a much smaller criterion function and gain little by way of having a simpler structure. We can approach blockmodeling these two-mode data inductively by specifying a structural equivalence model – permitting only null and complete blocks – and use the notion of a fitting grid described in Table 8.4. We get the results shown in Table 8.5, where the first number shows the value of the optimized criterion function and the second number gives the number of clusterings with the corresponding optimized values. Sometimes

Table 8.5. *Values in the Fitting Grid*

	Values of k_2	
k_1	2	3
2	63/3	53/many
3	50/2	40/many
4	50/many	37/1
5	50/many	37/1

there were many equally well-fitting partitions. The number of repetitions for these partitioning efforts was 50,000.

None of the clusterings whose values are given in Table 8.5 are satisfactory. One of the two clusterings for $k_1 = 2$ and $k_2 = 2$ gets the partition of the women correctly in terms of the truth described by Freeman. However, having just two clusters for the events dooms it to inadequacy. The two clusters for the events are E_1–E_8 and E_9–E_{14}. The second clustering with 63 as the value for the criterion function has the same partition for the events but clusters Pearl with the women in Group B. This minor difference is not unreasonable because a careful look at Pearl makes it clear that she could be equally well classified with Group A as Group B in that she attended none of the events unique to Group A nor the events unique to members of Group B. There are two (3,2)-partitions. One gets the partition of the women correct relative to the true structure, and one duplicates the grouping of Pearl with Group B. All of the partitions for $k_2 = 2$ have higher values of the criterion function. What is more important is that the clusterings of the events have little coherence relative to the structure depicted in Figure 8.3. Finally, the unique (3,3)-partition provides a partition of the women into {Katherine, Sylvia, Nora, Helen} and {Evelyn, Laura, Theresa, Brenda, Charlotte} with all of the remaining women in the third cluster. The first two clusters are the cores of the two groups, and the third cluster is simply composed of the noncore women. The partition of the events is {E_1–E_7}, {E_8, E_9}, and {E_{10}–E_{14}}. None of these partitions are truly satisfactory even though there are elements in them that have some appeal. The real problem with using structural equivalence is in the form of specifying only the permitted block types. We know more about the data structure than just the pair of permitted block types.

Using penalties in criterion functions. Apart from Section 6.2.2, we have assumed that inconsistencies between empirical blocks and their corresponding ideal blocks are weighted equally. Without a specific reason to weight inconsistencies differently, this seems entirely reasonable. We depart from this practice here and focus attention on the use of penalties in criterion functions. Again, the goal of considering such specifications is to allow ourselves to identify coherent social structure.

Specifying the presence of certain block types is fine as an initial step. An inspection of Table 8.3 suggests that one systematic aspect of these data is that there are subsets of events not attended by subsets of certain women. Some of the women identified as belonging to Group A never attend events associated exclusively with women of Group B, and vice versa. This suggests that null blocks have particular importance in these two-mode data. Thus, in addition to specifying that null blocks will occur, it is possible to heavily penalize 1s appearing in null blocks *wherever they occur*. For these Deep South two-mode data, this is a compelling reason to penalize 1s appearing in null blocks.

We also need to be clear about some of the consequences of using differential weights in criterion functions in order to penalize certain inconsistencies with an ideal block. The criterion function is now defined by both the inconsistencies

Table 8.6. *Counts of Participation in Events (Reordered)*

Actor	E_1-E_5	E_6-E_9	$E_{10}-E_{14}$
Evelyn	5	3	0
Laura	4	3	0
Theresa	4	4	0
Brenda	4	3	0
Charlotte	3	1	0
Frances	2	2	0
Eleanor	1	3	0
Ruth	1	4	0
Verne	0	3	1
Myra	0	2	2
Katherine	0	2	4
Sylvia	0	3	4
Nora	0	3	5
Helen	0	2	3
Olivia	0	1	1
Flora	0	1	1
Pearl	0	3	0
Dorothy	0	2	0

and the differential weights. Therefore, it need not be a simple count of inconsistencies. There can be a mixture of simple inconsistencies and heavily weighted inconsistencies. However, if the penalties are made very high, the penalties work to eliminate the penalized inconsistencies entirely. We have done this in the analyses that follow. The presence of 1s in null blocks was weighted at 100. This was intended to locate null blocks with zero inconsistencies. Of course, we get nothing for free, and the implication is that the counts of other types of inconsistencies will increase.

We specified first a two-mode blockmodel with two groups of women and three sets of events. We allowed 50,000 repetitions. Three equally well-fitting partitions were obtained, one of which is the partition shown in Table 8.3. The value of the criterion function is 73, the number of 0s in erstwhile complete blocks. We will comment on the other two equally well-fitting partitions shortly. Figure 8.3 was drawn to reflect this partition. Regarding the partition of the women, it is perfect according to Freeman (2003) following his meta-analysis of 21 prior attempts to delineate subgroups of women in the Deep South data.

Notwithstanding the label *perfect*, it is less than satisfactory in describing the partition of the women into subgroups. Slightly rearranging Table 8.4 gives Table 8.6. The striking feature of this table is that Pearl and Dorothy attend only events in the middle panel of Table 8.3. Neither woman attends those events associated exclusively with the women in Group A nor does she attend the events associated exclusively with Group B. Truly, they belong to neither A nor B. This

Table 8.7. The (3,3) Partition Fitted with a Heavy Null Block Penalty

Actor	E_1	E_2	E_3	E_4	E_5	E_6	E_7	E_8	E_9	E_{10}	E_{11}	E_{12}	E_{13}	E_{14}
Evelyn	1	1	1	1	1	1	0	1	1	0	0	0	0	0
Laura	1	1	1	0	1	1	1	1	0	0	0	0	0	0
Theresa	0	1	1	1	1	1	1	1	1	0	0	0	0	0
Brenda	1	0	1	1	1	1	1	1	0	0	0	0	0	0
Charlotte	0	0	1	1	1	0	1	0	0	0	0	0	0	0
Frances	0	0	1	0	1	1	0	1	0	0	0	0	0	0
Eleanor	0	0	0	0	1	1	1	1	0	0	0	0	0	0
Ruth	0	0	0	0	1	0	1	1	1	0	0	0	0	0
Verne	0	0	0	0	0	0	1	1	1	0	0	1	0	0
Myra	0	0	0	0	0	0	0	1	1	1	0	1	0	0
Katherine	0	0	0	0	0	0	0	1	1	1	0	1	1	1
Sylvia	0	0	0	0	0	0	1	1	1	1	0	1	1	1
Nora	0	0	0	0	0	1	1	0	1	1	1	1	1	1
Helen	0	0	0	0	0	0	1	1	0	1	1	1	0	0
Olivia	0	0	0	0	0	0	0	0	1	0	1	0	0	0
Flora	0	0	0	0	0	0	0	0	1	0	1	0	0	0
Pearl	0	0	0	0	0	1	0	1	1	0	0	0	0	0
Dorothy	0	0	0	0	0	0	0	1	1	0	0	0	0	0

suggests a partition into three sets of women and three sets of events. We anticipate that Pearl and Dorothy will be in a cluster by themselves and that there will be two more null blocks. Again, the null blocks are weighted heavily. The resulting partition is unique, with 63 as the value of the criterion function, and is shown in Table 8.7.

The partition shown in Table 8.7 is exactly the partition we anticipated. We note that the two additional partitions obtained with two clusters of women and three clusters of events depart simply from the partition shown in Table 8.3. In one, Pearl is joined with the women of Group B while leaving the rest of Group A intact. In the other, Dorothy joins the women of Group A while leaving the rest of Group B intact. The merit of this use of a penalty for the null block is that it is simple and direct. Moreover, it does not require any prespecification of clusters of location of block types. The downside is that it does not permit the delineation of subgroups. Figure 8.4 shows the redrawn sociogram to reflect the partition shown in Table 8.7.

We return to our earlier argument regarding the use of penalties in fitting block-models. In general, the direct fitting of a type of blockmodel – in this case a structural equivalence blockmodel – returns optimal partitions with fewer inconsistencies. With the imposition of penalties, in which some inconsistencies are weighted more – the nature of the criterion function has been changed through the use of weights. In general, they will increase relative to the optimized criterion functions through which all inconsistencies are weighted equally. For (2,3)-partitions, the optimized value of the criterion function for these data is 63 (inconsistencies), as shown in Table 8.5. The partition described in the Table 8.3 has 73 inconsistencies

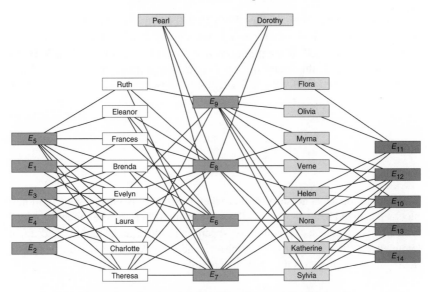

Figure 8.4. Southern Women Bipartite network: Version 2.

relative to a corresponding ideal blockmodel. This is not a surprise because we imposed additional constraints. For the (3,3)-partitions, the optimized value of the criterion function for structural equivalence is 40, whereas the value of the criterion function for the unique partition shown in Table 8.7 is 63. None of the unweighted structural equivalence partitions for the Deep South data provided adequate partitions relative to the truth described by Freeman (2003) for these data. In this way, they fail. The partitions returned by heavily weighting the inconsistencies in the null block are far superior because of their focus on an important part of the social structure. The so-called increase in the criterion function is a price we are willing to pay for getting this important part of the structure right.

Structural equivalence with prespecified null blocks. The problem of establishing or fitting a blockmodel to the Deep South can also be approached by means of prespecification. An inspection of Table 8.3 suggests the prespecification of the following blockmodel:

$$
\begin{array}{ccc}
\text{com} & \text{com} & \text{nul} \\
\text{nul} & \text{com} & \text{com}
\end{array}
$$

In addition to noting where null blocks should appear, we can add penalties to enforce their identification at those locations in a blockmodel. In this case, for these data, with null blocks identified as being especially important, we again specify a heavy penalty for inconsistencies in the form of 1s in these null blocks. Whereas our earlier use of penalties was done on an exploratory analysis, this use can be viewed as confirmatory. With 50,000 repetitions, this model was fitted with 73 inconsistencies – exactly the number identified above. There were also the two other equally well-fitting partitions that were identified in Table 8.5. Given the earlier analysis, this result does not come as a surprise. We can extend this further. An inspection of Table 8.7 suggests a prespecified model that could be "tested":

com	com	nul
nul	com	com
nul	com	nul

Again, it comes as no surprise that when this model is fitted – with 1s in null blocks penalized heavily – we get the same result as before. The model is unique with 63 inconsistencies. Of course, prespecifying a blockmodel requires additional knowledge, either substantive or empirical, and if this knowledge is not available, the inductive approach is the only one possible.

Regular equivalence with prespecified null blocks. As pleasing as the preceding partitions for the Deep South data are, there is one element that is less than pleasing: The specification of complete blocks seems too stringent. A more reasonable specification, if there is a Group A and events attended only by women of Group A, is that every such woman has to attend at least one such event and each such event has to be attended by at least one woman from Group A. This translates into specifying the (1,1) block as regular. Similarly, for Group B women, the (2,3) block ought to be regular. If there are events than women from both groups attend, then each woman attends at least one such event and each event is attended by at least one woman from each group. In short, both the (1,2) and (2,2) blocks are regular. Of course, the null blocks are specified as before. Knowing that Pearl and Dorothy attend only events in the middle panel of Table 8.3 suggests that requiring the (3,2) block to be regular is problematic. Instead, using a little bit of empirical knowledge, we specify this block as row-regular. The prespecified blockmodel is

reg	reg	nul
nul	reg	reg
nul	rrg	nul

Earlier, we commented that regular blocks are weak because many configurations can satisfy this form. Using an inductive approach and specifying only the three block types were useless because many blockmodels were returned that fit the data exactly. In addition, with this prespecified model, we knew in advance that just fitting it would lead to the same undesirable outcome. Again, the critical role of the null blocks can be used, and we added the same penalty to them as we did for structural equivalence. Using 50,000 repetitions, the prespecified blockmodel fitted exactly (with zero inconsistencies) and was unique. Furthermore, the partition was exactly the same as in Table 8.7. In terms of substance, this blockmodel is more appealing because specifying complete blocks is too stringent. Even so, if the important goal is to characterize structure, both structural and regular equivalence, with the use of appropriate penalties, led to the identification of the same unique partition of women and events.

It is interesting that both structural and regular equivalence (by means of specification of the permitted ideal blocks) led to the same identified structure. They are not the only block types that permit this. An inspection of Table 8.7 suggests yet another potential prespecified blockmodel that uses the row-dominant and column-dominant block types:

$$
\begin{array}{ccc}
\text{rdo} & \text{rdo} & \text{nul} \\
\text{nul} & \text{rdo} & \text{rdo} \\
\text{nul} & \text{cdo} & \text{nul}
\end{array}
$$

Again, 1s in the null block were heavily penalized and 50,000 repetitions employed. The unique outcome was the same partition as in Table 8.7 with a criterion function of 8. We emphasize, again, that the values of the criterion functions for these three prespecified blockmodels cannot be compared directly. The different blockmodels have different criterion functions. Just because the magnitudes of the criterion functions are 0, 8, and 63 tells us nothing as to which model is the better fit. Different inconsistencies are counted in different ways. Each specific empirical blockmodel was the unique best (optimal) blockmodel given the specific prespecified model.

8.5.3 *Journal-to-journal citation networks*

Journal networks are defined with journals as the vertices and have valued elements. These elements are counts of the number of times articles of one journal cite articles in another journal. The diagonal elements of these (one-mode) journal networks are counts of self-citation for the journals in the network. Such (valued) networks have been studied as one-mode networks and partitioned in terms of structural equivalence (see Doreian 1985, 1988b; Baker 1992). In these partitioning efforts, the rows and columns are clustered in the *same* way and the diagonal elements are ignored. These networks have also been studied as core–periphery structures (Borgatti and Everett 1999) in which, again, the rows and columns are clustered in the same way. At face value, these one-mode networks are better viewed as two-mode networks. When this is done, journals are seen as both consuming journals (in the rows as citing journals) and producing journals (in the columns as cited journals). And, consistent with the approach taken in this chapter, the rows and columns can be clustered in different ways. An additional advantage of viewing these citation networks as two-mode data is that the self-citation entries can be included as an integral part of the data even though, as noted in Section 8.3, diagonal blocks are meaningless in the two-mode view of journal citation networks. If journals vary in the extent to which they have articles citing other articles in the same journal, this becomes a source of useful information.

Viewing citation networks in this fashion allows us to examine the different roles that journals can perform as producers and consumers of knowledge. This can be approached as a simple form of hypothesis testing. If there is no difference between these roles, then the rows and columns, as an empirical matter, will be clustered in the same way. To the extent that rows and columns are clustered differently, we have evidence that journals function differently with regard to the production and consumption of disciplinary knowledge.

In approaching journal networks in this way, we had only some intuitions at the outset. We thought that there would be a core consumer position and a core producer position consistent with the idea of distinguishing cores from noncores. Further, to reflect coreness, the block corresponding to the two (producer and consumer) cores should be complete. Every core consumer journal will cite every core producer journal, and every core producer journal will be cited by every core consumer journal. Second, there will be noncore consumers and noncore producers that will vary in the extent to which they approximate a core and the extent to which they do not. A second level of consumer journals would occupy a position when the block defined by them and the core producer journals is regular. Put differently, for such a set of noncore consumer journals, each will cite at least one core producer journal and every core producer journal will be cited by at least one of the consumer journals at the second level. In a similar fashion, we thought there would be a second level of producer journals whose block with the core consumer journals would be regular. Third, weaker consumer and producer positions will have blocks, involving the core producer and core consumer journals, that would be row regular and column regular. Fourth, there will be null blocks to the extent that journals occupy different niches. There will be sets of consumer journals that never cite some of the producer journals, and there will sets of producer journals that are not cited by sets of consumer journals. Finally, we anticipated a need to allow for certain almost null blocks. We thought that some diagonal elements might cause some problems by appearing in erstwhile null blocks. If there are consumer journals that cite some of the core journals and then only themselves, these self-citation counts will appear in null blocks. This suggested the use of the row-function block type to allow a single nonzero element to appear in each row of such a null block. The specified model was

com	reg	cre	rre
reg	reg	nul	nul
reg	nul	rfn	nul
rre	rre	nul	rfn
cre	nul	nul	rfn

Table 8.8. *Journals in the Social Work Citation Network*

Title	Label
Administration in Social Work	ASW
British Journal of Social Work	BJSW
Child Abuse and Neglect	CAN
Child Care Quarterly	CCQ
Child Welfare	CW
Children and Youth Services Review	CYSR
Clinical Social Work Journal	CSWJ
Family Review	FR
Journal of Gerontological Social Work	JGSW
Journal of Social Policy	JSP
Journal of Social Work Education	JSWE
Public Welfare	PW
Social Case Work	SCW
Social Services Review	SSR
Social Work	SW
Social Work in Groups	SWG
Social Work Health Care	SWHC
Social Work Research and Abstracts	SWRA

A useful network for examining these ideas is the social work journal network reported by Baker (1992) and analyzed by Borgatti and Everett (1999). The included journals are listed in Table 8.8. We approach this network in a way that differs from the approach taken by Borgatti and Everett. First, the original data are not symmetric and, in contrast to Borgatti and Everett, we do not symmetrize them. This issue is particularly acute when the symmetrized elements are obtained from a zero element and a nonzero element. As a result, were these data symmetrized, there would be no distinction between production of, and consumption of, knowledge. A two-mode analysis of such a symmetrized citation network would yield the same partition of the rows and columns. Second, we leave out two of the journals included by Baker. One is the *Indian Journal of Social Work*, which really does not belong to the network.[6] It is linked weakly with only one other journal. Also eliminated was *Administration in Mental Health*, because it was linked weakly to one other journal. This leaves the 18 journals whose citation volumes are shown in Table 8.9.

Table 8.9 has rows and columns that have been permuted to reflect a partitioned structure with five consumer positions and four producer positions. There is a single inconsistency between the fitted blockmodel and the corresponding ideal blockmodel. An identifying label is supplied in the second column of this table. These labels are used also to label the columns. It is clear that the consuming

---

6 Consulting members of a social work faculty about these data, we found that all indicated the journal, regardless of its merits, is not visible in the United States and is seldom or never consulted.

Table 8.9. Journal Citation Matrix with the (5,4) Partition

	ID	a	c	f	d	m	e	g	h	i	j	k	l	n	o	b	p	q	r
CW	a	187	32	10	58	0	11	0	0	0	7	0	0	0	0	6	0	0	7
CYSR	b	70	8	14	28	0	0	0	0	5	12	0	0	0	5	26	0	0	6
SCW	c	17	149	36	124	8	21	8	6	18	6	8	6	0	0	0	6	0	0
SW	d	52	58	53	356	15	33	15	43	8	0	0	9	0	0	0	0	0	19
JSWE	e	0	18	16	58	9	104	0	7	16	0	0	0	0	0	0	0	0	0
SSR	f	17	30	105	106	7	9	0	0	25	0	0	0	0	0	0	0	0	0
SWG	g	0	9	7	40	0	9	41	9	0	0	0	0	0	0	0	0	0	0
SWHC	h	0	20	0	26	0	0	0	86	0	0	0	0	0	0	0	0	0	0
SWRA	i	8	8	39	44	0	24	0	0	40	0	0	0	0	0	0	0	0	0
CAN	j	9	6	0	8	0	0	0	0	0	109	0	0	0	0	0	0	0	0
CSWJ	k	0	47	20	45	0	0	0	0	0	0	40	0	0	0	0	0	0	0
FR	l	0	18	0	9	0	0	0	0	0	0	0	205	0	0	0	0	0	0
ASW	m	0	0	21	73	70	18	0	0	7	0	0	0	0	0	0	0	0	13
BJSW	n	0	0	0	19	0	13	0	0	0	0	0	0	95	0	0	0	0	0
CCQ	o	12	0	0	0	0	0	0	0	0	0	0	0	0	92	0	0	0	0
JGSW	p	0	16	0	18	0	0	0	0	0	0	0	0	0	0	0	9	0	0
JSP	q	0	0	7	0	0	0	0	0	0	0	0	0	0	0	0	0	35	0
PW	r	0	0	0	0	0	0	0	0	0	7	0	0	0	0	0	0	0	9

positions differ from the producing positions. The producer positions are

PJ_1	{CW, SCW, SSR, SW}
PJ_2	{ASW, JSWE, SWG, SWHC, SWRA}
PJ_3	{CAN, CSWJ, FR}
PJ_4	{BJSW, CCQ, CYSR, JGSW, JSP, PW}

and the consumer positions are

CJ_1	{CW, CYSR, SCW, SW}
CJ_2	{JSWE, SSR, SWG, SWHC, SWRA}
CJ_3	{CAN, CSWJ, FR}
CJ_4	{ASW, BJSW}
CJ_5	{CCQ, JGSW, JSP, PW}

Three journals (CW, SCW, and SW) belong to both of the core positions (PJ_1 and CJ_1). *Social Service Review* (SSR) is in PJ_1 but not CJ_1, whereas *Children and Youth Services Review* (CYSR) is a core consumer but is not a core producer. SSR does appear in the second consumer position. Four journals (JSWE, SWG, SWHC, SWRA) are common to the second producer position (PJ_2) and the second

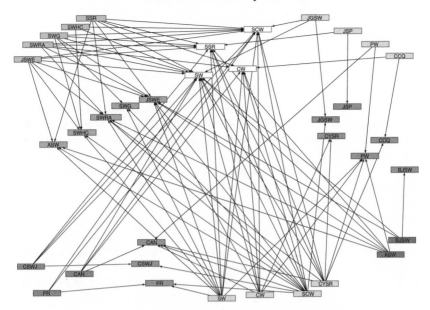

Figure 8.5. *Social Work* journal bipartite (5,4) network.

consumer position (CJ_2). Together, these most prominent journals vary in their roles as producers and consumers of social work knowledge. We note that the block defined by CJ_2 and PJ_2 is regular. This is also the case for the block defined by CJ_1 and PJ_2. The third producer position (PJ_3) and the third consumer position (CJ_3) share the same set of journals, namely, CAN, CSWJ, and FR. The block defined by CJ_3 and PC_1 is regular, as is the block defined by CJ_1 and PC_3 (although we only specified it as row regular). The block defined by CJ_3 and PJ_3 is a row-functional block. Apart from these block types, the blocks associated with these positions are null blocks. The block defined by CP_4 and CJ_1 is row-regular, whereas the block defined by CP_1 and CJ_5 is column-regular. Apart from these, the blocks for the last consumer and producer positions are null or row functional. The one inconsistency for the fitted blockmodel is the tie (whose value is 7) from PW to CAN.

There is an interesting contrast with the analysis of Borgatti and Everett (1999), who found a single core in a core–periphery structure. The core they established was {SSR, SCW, SW}. These three journals are in both our producer core and consumer core. In our analysis, the producer core includes CW whereas the core consumer includes CYSR. Analyzing these data with a two-mode blockmodeling approach provides a more differentiated view of the core.

Our primary concern here is to illustrate the process of prespecifying blockmodels and then fitting them. We are aware that the prespecified blockmodel for this particular network may not work for other journal networks. For example, if there are distinct subdisciplines, this will complicate the specification of blockmodels.

8.6 SUMMARY

This chapter extended the generalized blockmodeling approach to two-mode networks as a new data structure. The formalization and the computation of the criterion functions extends naturally. In addition, the application of the direct optimization methods extends in a straightforward fashion. The three examples that we used to illustrate these methods provide interesting interpretable structures. We used many of the new block types introduced in Chapter 7 in both exploratory and confirmatory modes. In Chapter 6 (Section 6.2.2), we introduced the idea of using weights in the form of penalties for certain kinds of departures from ideal blocks. Our attempts to fit blockmodels to two-mode data compelled our return to this strategy. Carefully selected penalties helped us delineate interesting structures cleanly. Chapter 11 presents a new block type and a new blockmodel structure, together with some new methods, for which differential weightings are particularly important. We have barely scraped the surface of using penalties in fitting blockmodels, and we anticipate an expanded role for them despite the complications they introduce. The use of differential weights as penalties requires additional social knowledge in the specification of these generalized blockmodels. We view this as an advantage because network analysts frequently know more about the structures being blockmodeled than a list of block types that might work.

9

SEMIRINGS AND LATTICES

In this chapter we elaborate some of the algebraic concepts introduced in Chapter 4 to provide foundations for a deeper understanding of signed networks and balance algorithms discussed in Chapter 10.

We continue to consider networks as graphs $\mathbf{G} = (\mathcal{V}, \mathcal{E}, \mathcal{A})$, where $\mathcal{E}$ is the set of edges and $\mathcal{A}$ is the set of arcs that link pairs of vertices from $\mathcal{V}$. As in Chapter 4, we use $\mathcal{L} = \mathcal{E} \cup \mathcal{A}$ for the set of lines in the graph, $\mathbf{G}$. These ties can be binary or valued. The lines form walks that, from Chapter 4, are finite sequences of alternating vertices and lines, $S = v_0, s_1, v_1, s_2, v_2, \ldots, s_k, v_k$, of a graph $\mathbf{G} = (\mathcal{V}, \mathcal{E}, \mathcal{A})$. Throughout this chapter we use either $\{v_i\}$ or $\{u, v, w, x, y, x, z\}$ to denote vertices.

9.1 WALKS, PATHS, AND ALGEBRAS

A variety of interesting problems stem from considering walks (or paths) in graphs and require special algebras for their solution. If the graph represents, for example, a communication network, one problem is whether or not pairs of actors are either unilaterally or mutually reachable. Let x, y, and z be three vertices in a graph. In a directed graph, y could be reachable from x, or x could be reachable from y, but not both (in which case the graph is unilaterally connected), or x and y could be mutually reachable.[1] If the graph is binary, we need to be able to determine if walks (or paths) exist between pairs of vertices, x and y, or not. To do this we need to determine if there are sequences of alternating vertices and lines that connect pairs of vertices. If a denotes the value of a line s_1 from x to y and b the value of a line, s_2 from y to z, we need to be able to combine a and b by some operation, denoted by a centered dot ($\cdot$), to provide a value for the path x, s_1, y, s_2, z. We can also write this sequence as $(x, y), (y, z)$, where (x, y) is s_1 and (y, z) is s_2. This value is denoted by $a \cdot b$. In a binary graph, the only values for a and b are

---

[1] In an undirected graph, only mutual reachability is relevant.

$\{0, 1\}$. If, for example, (x, y) and (y, z) exist, the values of a and b are both 1, and if $a \cdot b$ is the so-called minimum of a and b, then $a \cdot b$ is 1. This means that the two-step path from x to z through y exists. If (x, y) exists but (y, z) does not, then $a = 1$ and $b = 0$. It follows that $a \cdot b$ is 0, and this is interpreted as representing the absence of the two-step path from x to z through y. An algebra to keep track of this counting needs to have just two elements ($\{0, 1\}$) and a binary operation ($\cdot$) that is everywhere defined. If $A = \{0, 1\}$ and $(A, \cdot)$, where $\cdot$ has the Cayley table

$\cdot$	0	1
0	0	0
1	0	1

then A is a monoid $(a \cdot (b \cdot c) = (a \cdot b) \cdot c)$; see Section 3.4.[2] The general task of determining the reachability for all pairs of vertices is more complicated because all pairs of vertices must be considered as well as all possible walks (or paths, etc.) between them. Such a simple monoid will not suffice for this general task. However, it does point us in the direction of algebraic structures that will suffice for the more general task.

Another problem is that of determining the strength or level of a path (or a walk) between pairs of vertices in a valued graph. Suppose the value of the tie from x to y is 2 and the tie from y to z has strength 3. One question concerns the strength of the path between x and z. A natural specification is that it is the minimum value, that is, $a \cdot b = 2$. Suppose the potential values for the ties are $\{0, 1, 2, 3, 4\}$, which are ordered in the usual way, and the Cayley table for this binary operation (which is used in Section 9.3) is

$\cdot$	0	1	2	3	4
0	0	0	0	0	0
1	0	1	1	1	1
2	0	1	2	2	2
3	0	1	2	3	3
4	0	1	2	3	4

This, too, is a monoid with 4 as the neutral element, and this algebra allows us to think about combining lines between pairs of points in paths of length 2 to determine the strength of the path. This problem can be extended to considering all pairs of vertices and potential paths (or walks) between them. Again, such a simple structure is not sufficient for this task and a more general algebra is needed.

Yet another problem arises in a graph, where there can be multiple lines between pairs of vertices. Let the value of one line from x to y be a and the value of a second line be b. The task of determining the strongest line creates the need for a

2   Technically, this is also a Boolean algebra.

binary operation $+$ that assigns a value to $a + b$ given a and b. If we seek the most effective link, this could be the maximum value. Again, suppose that the values of ties can be $\{0, 1, 2, 3, 4\}$ and that they are ordered in the usual way. The addition table for $+$ is

$+$	0	1	2	3	4
0	0	1	2	3	4
1	1	1	2	3	4
2	2	2	2	3	4
3	3	3	3	3	4
4	4	4	4	4	4

This, again, defines a monoid. Its neutral element is 0 and we use it in Section 9.3. This kind of problem becomes more general if we want to compare alternative paths between x and z. We might want to determine the minimum value on each path and then select the maximum of these minimum values. This problem is studied in Doreian (1974). The kind of algebra for this general problem requires two binary operations.

A general set of such problems includes the following.

1. Determine the reachability for all pairs of vertices (and hence the connectivity of the graph).
2. Determine the shortest paths (geodesics) between all pairs of vertices (and hence the count of all paths between pairs of vertices).
3. Determine the longest paths between pairs of vertices (a task that is relevant in tracing paths in citation networks; see Hummon and Doreian 1990).
4. Determine, in a valued graph, paths that can carry the maximum flow (of, e.g., goods in a transportation network).
5. Determine the minimum guaranteed transmission flow in a valued graph between two vertices x and z (this is the maximum value of the minimum values across all paths between x and z).

An algebraic structure that is particularly important in tackling these types of problems is the semiring. It is not only the relevant algebraic structure for these tasks but also allows us to examine the partition structures of signed networks, which is a topic we consider in Chapter 10.

9.2 DISTRIBUTIVITY AND ABSORPTION

Here we consider a set A with two binary operations defined over it. First, we examine distributivity and absorption as two ways of connecting the two operations.

In the following we assume that, in the structure $(A, +, \cdot)$, the partial structures $(A, +)$ and $(A, \cdot)$ are groupoids and that the multiplication (dot sign) takes precedence over the addition (plus sign).

9.2.1   Distributivity

In general, in an algebraic structure $(A, +, \cdot)$, the operation $\cdot$ distributes over the operation $+$ if and only if

$$\forall a, b, c \in A : (((a + b) \cdot c = a \cdot c + b \cdot c) \wedge (a \cdot (b + c) = a \cdot b + a \cdot c)).$$

If only the first equality holds, it distributes from the right; if only the second equality holds, it distributes from the left.

Some examples of distributivity include these:

$$(a + b)c = ac + bc, \quad a, b, c \in \mathbb{R}$$
$$\min(a, b) + c = \min(a + c, b + c),$$
$$(A \cup B) \cap C = (A \cap C) \cup (B \cap C).$$

9.2.2   Absorption

In an algebraic structure $(A, +, \cdot)$ the absorption of $+$ for $\cdot$ holds if and only if

$$\forall a, b \in A : ((a + a \cdot b = a) \wedge (a + b \cdot a = a)).$$

If only the first equality holds, it is called absorption from the right; it is absorption from the left if only the second equality holds.

Two examples of absorption are

$$\min(a, a + b) = a, \quad a, b \in \mathbb{R}_0^+,$$
$$A \cup (A \cap B) = A.$$

Theorem 9.1   *Let in $(A, +, \cdot)$ the element $1 \in A$ be a neutral element for the multiplication $\cdot$ and the distributivity of $\cdot$ over $+$ hold. Then the absorption of $+$ for $\cdot$ holds if and only if 1 is the absorption element for addition $+$.*

9.3   VALUED GRAPHS

We consider social networks with valued ties where the values represent the strengths of the ties in networks. As noted in Section 9.1, two natural questions arise. First, given a path (or a walk) between pairs of the actors, is it possible to assign values to the paths given the strengths of the ties in the path? Second, given a set of paths (between two actors), is it possible to compare paths in terms of their values? Both questions can be answered in the affirmative, and we seek practical methods for assigning values to paths and then comparing paths in terms of their assigned values. We assume that these values for the ties are linearly ordered and, as a result, for all $a, b \in A$, the values of $\max(a, b)$ and $\min(a, b)$ exist. To motivate the discussion, we first consider the simple example of Figure 9.1 where the values,[3] g_{ij}, of the ties satisfy $0 \leq g_{ij} \leq 4$. Although tedious, it is straightforward

---

3 Anticipating the development in Section 9.3.2, we use g_{ij} as a notation for the set of values on the arcs (v_i, v_j).

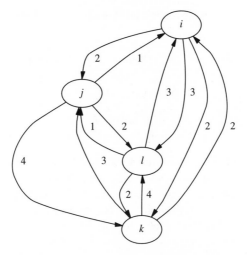

Figure 9.1. Simple valued graph with four vertices.

to list the paths (and walks and trails) between all pairs of vertices. For example, the paths[4] from v_i to v_j are

Path	Ties in Path	Minimum Value in Path
S_1	(v_i, v_j)	2
S_2	$(v_i, v_k), (v_k, v_j)$	2
S_3	$(v_i, v_l), (v_l, v_j)$	1
S_4	$(v_i, v_k), (v_k, v_l), (v_l, v_j)$	1
S_5	$(v_i, v_l), (v_l, v_k), (v_k, v_j)$	2

9.3.1 Assigning values to paths

If we envision support flowing over the network ties, one way of assigning values to the paths is to select the minimum value in the path so that the overall strength of the path is given by the strength of the weakest link in the path.[5] These values are shown on the right of the listing above. Given these path values, we can select the path(s) with the highest value as the best path(s) for the flow of support. For paths from v_i to v_j, there are three paths, $\{S_1, S_2, S_5\}$, each with the value of 2. This is the highest minimum level of support that can flow from v_i to v_j in the network shown in Figure 9.1.

The same procedure can be used to consider the flow of support from v_j to v_i. The paths from v_j to v_i are listed below and show that the highest level of support that can flow from v_j to v_i is 3 for the path S_9 of length 3. If attention is restricted

4 In this listing, we ignore walks such as $(v_i, v_j), (v_j, v_i), (v_i, v_j)$.
5 This can be viewed as the guaranteed minimum level of support that can flow along the path.

to paths of length 2, then the highest level of minimum support is 2.

Path	Ties in Path	Minimum Value in Path
S_6	(v_j, v_i)	1
S_7	$(v_j, v_k), (v_k, v_i)$	2
S_8	$(v_j, v_l), (v_l, v_i)$	2
S_9	$(v_j, v_k), (v_k, v_l), (v_l, v_i)$	3
S_{10}	$(v_j, v_l), (v_l, v_k), (v_k, v_i)$	2

Clearly, this is a tedious procedure when done in this fashion. Thus, we define an algebra, $(A, \cdot, +)$ with two operations, $\cdot$ and $+$. For $a, b \in A$, as in Section 9.1, we define the product, $\cdot$, as $a \cdot b = \min(a, b)$. The Cayley table for this multiplication was provided in Section 9.1. The sum of two elements is given by $a + b = \max(a, b)$. The Cayley table for this addition was also given in Section 9.1. We suppose that the range of values goes from 0 to some maximum value[6] – v for instance. These two binary operations have some simple properties.

1. Both $\cdot$ and $+$ are closed. For $a, b \in A$, $a \cdot b \in A$ (because both $a, b \in A$, $a \cdot b$ is either a or b). A similar argument holds for $+$.
2. The largest possible value, v, is the neutral element for the product $\cdot$, that is, $v \cdot a = a$, for all $a \in A$. The smallest element, 0, is the neutral element for $+$, that is, $0 + a = a$, for all $a \in A$.
3. Both binary operations are associative: $a \cdot (b \cdot c) = \min(a, \min(b, c)) = \min(a, b, c)$ and $(a \cdot b) \cdot c = \min(\min(a, b), c = \min(a, b, c)$. Similarly, $a + (b + c) = (a + b) + c = \max(a, b, c)$.
4. Both binary operations are commutative: $a \cdot b = b \cdot a = \min(a, b)$ and $a + b = b + a = \max(a, b)$.
5. Distributivity holds for $\cdot$ over $+$: $a \cdot (b + c) = \min(a, \max(b, c)) = \max(\min(a, b), \min(a, c)) = a \cdot b + a \cdot c$.
6. Absorption of $+$ over $\cdot$ holds: $a + (a \cdot b) = \max(a, \min(a, b))$. If $a \geq b$, then $a + (a \cdot b) = \max(a, b) = a$; and if $a < b$, then $a + (a \cdot b) = \max(a, a) = a$. Either way, $a + (a \cdot b) = a$.
7. Because (i) v is the neutral element for multiplication, (ii) distributivity of $\cdot$ over $+$ holds, and (iii) v is the absorption element for $+$, Theorem 9.1 implies that distributivity of $+$ over $\cdot$ holds also.[7]

9.3.2 Assessing paths in terms of their values

We return to the problem of tracking paths (or walks) and their levels. We let $G = [g_{ij}]$ be the matrix of values on the arcs (v_i, v_j) and consider two-step paths $(v_i, v_j), (v_j, v_k)$. Using the product $(\cdot)$ just defined, for a graph we can write the value of the two-step path as $g_{ij} \cdot g_{jk} = \min(g_{ij}, g_{jk})$. For example, the value of the path $(v_i, v_j)(v_j, v_k)$ in Figure 9.1 is $2 \cdot 4 = 2$ (with $g_{ij} = 2$ and $g_{jk} = 4$). Because the product, $\cdot$, is associative, it can be extended to a path of any length. For a path whose arcs have values $g_{ij_1}, g_{j_1 j_2}, \ldots, g_{j_r j_{r+1}}, \ldots, g_{j_{m-1} j_m}$, the element

---

6 In the example we are considering, $v = 4$.

7 In the following paragraphs, this property is not needed.

$(g_{ij_1} \cdot g_{j_1 j_2} \cdot \cdots \cdot g_{j_r j_{r+1}} \cdot \cdots \cdot g_{j_{m-1} j_m})$ is simply the minimum value on these arcs. This operation is defined for all paths and walks in the graph.

Suppose we have two paths of length 2 between v_i and v_k: $(v_i, v_{j_1}), (v_{j_1}, v_k)$ and $(v_i, v_{j_2}), (v_{j_2}, v_k)$. The value (given by the lowest value in the path) of the first path is $g_{ij_1} \cdot g_{j_1 k}$ and the value of the second is $g_{ij_2} \cdot g_{j_2 k}$. The value of the path with the highest value is $(g_{ij_1} \cdot g_{j_1 k} + g_{ij_2} \cdot g_{j_2 k})$, which will be the maximum of these values. In the simple example of Figure 9.1, the values of the five listed paths from v_j to v_i are 1, 2, 2, 3, and 2. The sum of these numbers is the maximum value (3) for the path labeled S_9. We can, of course, approach this by considering paths of a given length. If we restrict attention to paths of length 2, both S_2 and S_3 have a value of 2. Clearly the maximum of these is 2. For paths of length 3, the values of S_9 and S_{10} are, respectively, 3 and 2. The path with the maximum value is S_9. This idea extends to any number of two-step paths between pairs of points, to paths of any length up to $(n - 1)$ and walks of any length.

These ideas can be put into the context of matrices and used to locate those paths and walks in graphs with the highest values. For $G = [g_{ij}]$ as the adjacency matrix of a graph, we can define[8] an operation, $*$ giving $H = G * G$, where $H = [h_{ik}]$ with $h_{ik} = \Sigma_j (g_{ij} \cdot g_{jk})$.

The binary operation, $*$, for matrices of graphs satisfies certain properties. These include the following.

1. The operation $*$ is closed. For $G = [g_{ij}]$ and $M = [m_{ij}]$, and $Q = [q_{ij}]$ with $Q = G * M$, the elements of Q are $\Sigma_j (g_{ij} \cdot m_{jk})$. Because $\cdot$ is closed in the algebra $(A, \cdot, +)$, the operation $*$ is closed for the matrices whose elements come for A.
2. The operation $*$ is associative: $(G * M) * Q = G * (M * Q)$.
3. The operation $*$ is not commutative. Let G_1 and G_2 be two matrices whose elements come from A where G_1 is on the left and G_2 is on the right:

0	2	2	3		0	1	3	2
1	0	4	2		2	0	1	4
2	3	0	4		1	2	0	2
3	1	2	0		2	1	1	0

The values of the elements of $G_1 * G_2$ are on the left and those of $G_2 * G_1$ are on the right:

2	2	1	2		2	3	2	3
2	2	1	2		3	2	2	2
2	1	2	3		2	1	2	2
1	2	3	2		1	2	2	2

These matrices differ, and so, in general, $G_1 * G_2 \neq G_2 * G_1$.

Using these ideas, we can define $H_1 = G$, $H_2 = G * G$, and $H_3 = H_2 * G$. Table 9.1 has three panels that are labeled by these three matrices. On the left

8 Here, H is not meant as a subgraph of G.

Table 9.1. Values of Paths and Walks of Lengths 1, 2, and 3 for Figure 9.1

Vertex	H_1				H_2				H_3			
	v_i	v_j	v_k	v_l	v_i	v_j	v_k	v_l	v_i	v_j	v_k	v_l
v_i	0	2	2	3	3	2	2	2	2	2	2	2
v_j	1	0	4	2	2	3	2	4	3	2	2	2
v_k	2	3	0	4	3	4	3	2	2	2	3	3
v_l	3	1	2	0	2	2	2	3	2	2	2	2

are the valued ties (i.e., paths of length 1), in the middle are the maximum values (over the minimal values of paths) for the two-step paths between each pair of points, and on the right are maximum values for the three-step paths and walks. In the middle panel, the top left diagonal value of 3 comes from the two-cycle, (v_i, v_l), (v_l, v_i), for v_i and v_l. Similarly, the two-cycle, (v_j, v_k), (v_k, v_j), generates the value of 3 in the diagonal for v_j and for v_k. The path value of 4 from the middle panel of Table 9.1, for v_j and v_l, comes from the path (v_j, v_k), (v_k, v_l). Similarly, the only other path at level 4 in the graph is from v_k to v_i. Each of the values in the middle panel of Table 9.1 can be interpreted in this fashion – as is the case for the right-hand panel. The only new maximum value from the right-hand panel is 3 for the path (v_j, v_k), (v_k, v_l), (v_l, v_i).

The task of locating the maximum values of paths (or walks) between all pairs of vertices can be accomplished by defining another matrix operation. For two matrices, G and M, of the same order, we define $D = [d_{ij}] = G + M = [g_{ij} + m_{ij}]$, where "addition" is defined by the maximum value of $d_{ij} = \max(g_{ij}, m_{ij})$. It is straightforward to show the following.

1. The addition operation, $+$, is closed.
2. The neutral element for $+$ is the matrix of 0s.
3. The $+$ is associative: $(g_{ij} + m_{ij}) + p_{ij} = g_{ij} + (m_{ij} + p_{ij}) = \max(g_{ij}, m_{ij}, p_{ij})$. Hence, $(G + M) + P = G + (M + P) = G + M + P$.
4. The $+$ is commutative: $g_{ij} + m_{ij} = \max(g_{ij}, m_{ij}) = \max(m_{ij}, g_{ij}) = m_{ij} + g_{ij}$. It follows that $G + M = M + G$.

If we denote the matrix of values of the one-step paths by $G^1 = G$, the matrix of the values of the two-step paths by G^2 (i.e., $G * G = G^2$), and the matrix of three-step walks by $G^3 (= G * G * G)$, then the matrix for values for the strongest paths is $G^1 + G^2 + G^3$. Or, in general, the values of the strongest paths come from $\Sigma_r(G^r)$. For the simple example in Figure 9.1, these values are

Vertex	v_i	v_j	v_k	v_l
v_i	3	2	2	3
v_j	3	3	4	4
v_k	3	3	3	4
v_l	3	2	2	3

9.4 SEMIRINGS

If A is a nonempty set with two binary operations $+$ and $\cdot$, called addition and multiplication, where multiplication takes precedence over addition, then $(A, +, \cdot)$ is called a *semiring* if the following conditions all hold.

- $(A, +, 0)$ is an Abelian monoid with a neutral element (where, by convention, the neutral element is labeled 0 for $+$ and is often called a zero);
- $(A, \cdot, 1)$ is a monoid with a neutral element (where, by convention, the neutral element is labeled 1 for $\cdot$ and is often called a unit);
- The operations $\cdot$ and $+$ are connected by the distributive laws: for all $a, b, c \in A$, $a \cdot (b + c) = a \cdot b + a \cdot c$ and $(a + b) \cdot c = a \cdot c + b \cdot c$.

Further, a semiring $(A, +, \cdot)$ is said to be commutative if $(A, \cdot)$ is a commutative semigroup, and $(A, +, \cdot)$ is called a ring if $(A, +)$ is a commutative group.

An example of a semiring is the set of natural numbers under the usual addition $(+)$ and multiplication $(\cdot)$. In addition, the 0 is the neutral element for $+$ and 1 is the neutral element for $\cdot$. We denote this semiring by $(\mathbb{N}, +, \cdot, 0, 1)$. It is also known as the combinatorial semiring.

In Section 9.3.1 we introduced an algebra for computing the strengths of paths as the value of the weakest link in the path. Given two (or more) paths (or walks) between pairs of points, it is possible to select the maximum path strength. The binary operations introduced there, $\cdot = \min(a, b)$ and $+ = \max(a, b)$, $\forall a, b \in A$, also satisfy the conditions for a semiring. We call this semiring the *path values semiring*. Note that the neutral element for $\cdot$ is v, the maximum possible value for an arc or edge. This is also the absorption element for $\cdot$ in A. We denote this semiring by $(A, +, \cdot, 0, v)$. It can also be denoted by $(A, \max, \min, 0, v)$. Note also that this semiring is not a ring because the elements of A do not have inverse elements for $+$.

In Chapter 4, in discussing graphs, we introduced the notion of distances between vertices as the lengths of the geodesic (shortest) paths between pairs of vertices. The values for the lengths of paths for a binary graph come from $\mathbb{N}_0^+$ and can range from 0 (the distance of vertex from itself is zero) to ∞ (when there is no path between a pair of points). For a set of path lengths between a pair of vertices, the path distance is the smallest value of these lengths. Using min as the binary operation, we see that the neutral element is ∞ for min and 0 is the neutral element for $+$. This semiring is the *shortest paths semiring* and can be denoted by $(\mathbb{N}_0^+, \min, +, \infty, 0)$. Note that if the links on the paths are valued (as is the case if the values represent geographical distance), then $\mathbb{R}$ replaces $\mathbb{N}_0^+$ for this semiring.

Given a set, A, $\mathbf{Rel}(A, A)$ is the set of all binary relations on A, and with the binary operations $\cup$ and $\cap$ defined for sets, we have another semiring. The neutral element for $\cup$ is $\emptyset$ and the neutral element for $\cap$ is T, where $T = A \times A$. We denote this semiring by $(\mathbf{Rel}(A, A), \cup, \cap, \emptyset, T)$ and label it is the *relational semiring*.

In considering walks in graphs, we find that a problem arises when there are cycles in the graph. Cycles can be repeated indefinitely while traveling over walks.

As a result, there can be infinitely many links on walks, and this is a serious computational problem. One way of dealing with this problem is to define a complete semiring. A semiring $(A, +, \cdot, 0, 1)$ is complete iff the addition is also well defined for countable sets of elements, and the (generalized) commutativity, associativity (for addition), and distributivity also hold in this case.[9]

It is known that if the addition is idempotent, for every $a \in A : a + a = a$, the semiring over a finite set A is complete. Also needed for computational purposes is the idea of a closed semiring. In the context of relations, closure operations were introduced in Section 4.2.2. Motivation as an example of a closure in the context of semirings comes from considering an infinite sum: $a^\star = 1 + a + a^2 + \cdots$. This can be rewritten as $a^\star = 1 + a \cdot 1 + a \cdot a + \cdots = 1 + a \cdot (1 + a + a^2 + \cdots) = 1 + a \cdot a^\star$. Similarly, $a^\star = 1 + a^\star \cdot a$. A semiring, $(A, +, \cdot, ^\star, 0, 1)$, is defined as closed for a (unary) closure operation * iff it holds for every $a \in A$:

$$a^\star = 1 + a \cdot a^\star = 1 + a^\star \cdot a.$$

Different closures can exist over the same semiring.

A complete semiring is always closed for the closure defined by

$$a^\star = \sum_{k=0}^{\infty} a^k.$$

Henceforth, we use the term closure for the operation defined by this expression. In a closed semiring we can also define a strict closure $\bar{a}$ by

$$\bar{a} = a \cdot a^\star.$$

In the relational semiring, the closure is just a transitive and reflexive closure, $R^\star$, of a given relation R, and in the shortest paths semiring we have, since $a \geq 0$,

$$a^\star = \min(0, a, 2a, 3a, 4a, \ldots) = 0.$$

Suppose that for a given graph $G = (V, R)$, $R \subseteq V \times V$, and a semiring $(A, +, \cdot, 0, 1)$, a value function

$$d : R \to A$$

is given.

Using the results described in Section 9.3 for valued graphs, we can extend the value function d to walks and sets of walks[10] on G by the following.

- Let Z be a null walk in the vertex $v \in V$; then $d(\varepsilon_v) = 1$.
- Let $S = v_0, v_1, v_2, \ldots, v_{p-1}, v_p$ be a walk of length $p \geq 1$ on G; then

$$d(S) = d(v_0, v_1) \cdot d(v_1, v_2) \cdots d(v_{p-1}, v_p).$$

---

9   This is also the case for an infinite number of terms.
10   In this section, we use p to denote the length of a walk.

- For the empty set of walks Ø, we have $d(\emptyset) = 0$.
- Let $\mathcal{P} = \{S_1, S_2, \ldots\}$ be a set of walks on G; then

$$d(\mathcal{P}) = d(S_1) + d(S_2) + \cdots.$$

We denote by $\mathcal{P}_{uv}^p$ the set of all walks of length p from vertex u to vertex v, by $\mathcal{P}_{uv}^\star$ the set of all walks from vertex u to vertex v, and by $\overline{\mathcal{P}}_{uv}$ the set of all nontrivial (different from Z) walks from vertex u to vertex v.

The *value matrix* of a graph is a matrix $\mathbf{D}$ defined by

$$\mathbf{D}[u, v] = \begin{cases} d((u, v)) & (u, v) \in R \\ 0 & \text{otherwise} \end{cases}.$$

In the following we assume that in the semiring for every $a \in A$,

$$a \cdot 0 = 0 \cdot a = 0$$

holds and that the set of vertices $V = \{v_1, v_2, \ldots, v_n\}$ is finite. Then the addition and multiplication can be extended in the usual way to square matrices of order n, which themselves form a semiring.

A matrix semiring over a complete semiring is also complete and therefore closed for

$$\mathbf{D}^\star = \sum_{k=0}^{\infty} \mathbf{D}^k.$$

There are two well-known theorems (Aho et al. 1976, Carré 1979, Zimmermann 1981) connecting values of walks in graphs and their matrices.

Theorem 9.2 *Let $\mathbf{D}^p$ be the pth power of value matrix $\mathbf{D}$; then*

$$d(\mathcal{P}_{uv}^p) = \mathbf{D}^p[u, v].$$

Theorem 9.3 *Let $\mathbf{D}$ be a value matrix over complete semiring, $\mathbf{D}^\star$ its closure, and $\overline{\mathbf{D}}$ its strict closure matrix; then*

$$d(\mathcal{P}_{uv}^\star) = \mathbf{D}^\star[u, v] \qquad \text{and} \qquad d(\overline{\mathcal{P}}_{uv}) = \overline{\mathbf{D}}[u, v].$$

To compute the closure matrix $\mathbf{D}^\star$ of a given matrix $\mathbf{D}$ over a complete semiring $(A, +, \cdot, 0, 1, ^\star)$, we can use Fletcher's algorithm (Fletcher 1980):

```
C₀ := D;
for k := 1 to n do begin
        for i := 1 to n do for j := 1 to n do
            cₖ[i, j] := cₖ₋₁[i, j] + cₖ₋₁[i, k] · (cₖ₋₁[k, k])★ · cₖ₋₁[k, j];
        cₖ[k, k] := 1 + cₖ[k, k];
end;
D★ := Cₙ;
```

If we delete the statement $c_k[k, k] := 1 + c_k[k, k]$, we obtain the algorithm for computing the strict closure $\overline{\mathbf{D}}$.

If the addition, $+$, is idempotent, this algorithm allows us to compute the closure matrix in place (and we omit the subscripts in matrices $\mathbf{C}$).

Let us also define the symmetric, transitive, and reflexive closure of the value matrix by

$$\mathbf{D}^\bullet = (\mathbf{D} + \mathbf{D}^T)^\star,$$

where $\mathbf{D}^T$ denotes the transpose of matrix $\mathbf{D}$.

9.4.1   Some social network applications of semirings

There are several applications of semirings in social networks analysis. One is found in the semiring $(\{0, 1, 2, 3\}, \max, \min)$ and can be applied to determine the connectedness matrix (Harary et al. 1965:133). In a similar fashion, the semiring $(\{0, u, m\}, \max, \min)$, $0 < u < m$ (where 0 denotes no link, u denotes uniplex links, and m denotes multiplex links) can be used to analyze the connectivity of social networks (Doreian 1974).

The geodetic semiring. A third social network application semiring is founded in the concept of betweenness centrality (covered in Chapter 4, Section 4.7.1). Freeman (1977) introduced this centrality index for vertices (Freeman 1979, Gould 1987):

$$C_B(t) = \sum_u \sum_v \frac{n_{u,v}(t)}{n_{u,v}},$$

where $n_{u,v}$ is the number of geodesics from vertex u to vertex v, and $n_{u,v}(t)$ is the number of geodesics from u to v that contain vertex t. Freeman proposed the use of a method given in Harary et al. (1965:134–141) for computing $C_B(t)$.

Here, we present an alternative approach to computing $C_B(t)$. Suppose that we know a matrix

$$[(d_{u,v}, n_{u,v})],$$

where $d_{u,v}$ is the length of u–v geodesics and $n_{u,v}$ is the number of u–v geodesics. Then it is also easy to determine $n_{u,v}(t)$:

$$n_{u,v}(t) = \begin{cases} n_{u,t} \cdot n_{t,v} & d_{u,t} + d_{t,v} = d_{u,v} \\ 0 & \text{otherwise} \end{cases}.$$

The matrix $[(d_{u,v}, n_{u,v})]$ can be obtained by computing the closure of the relation matrix over the following geodetic semiring.

First we transform relation R to a matrix $\mathbf{R} = [(d, n)_{u,v}]$, which for entries has pairs defined by

$$(d, n)_{u,v} = \begin{cases} (1, 1) & (u, v) \in R \\ (\infty, 0) & (u, v) \notin R, \end{cases}$$

where d is the length of a shortest path and n is the number of shortest paths.

In the set $A = (\mathbb{R}_0^+ \cup \{\infty\}) \times (\mathbb{N} \cup \{\infty\})$, we define two operations: addition,

$$(a, i) \oplus (b, j) = (\min(a, b), \begin{cases} i & a < b \\ i + j & a = b \\ j & a > b \end{cases}),$$

and multiplication,

$$(a, i) \odot (b, j) = (a + b, i \cdot j).$$

It is easy to verify that $(A, \oplus, \odot)$ is indeed a semiring with zero $(\infty, 0)$ and identity $(0, 1)$. The verifications of semiring properties are straightforward (Batagelj 1994).

The semiring $(A, \oplus, \odot)$ is also complete and closed, with a closure

$$(a, i)^\star = \begin{cases} (0, \infty) & a = 0, i \neq 0 \\ (0, 1) & \text{otherwise} \end{cases}.$$

A semiring element (a, i) is *positive* iff $a > 0$. The set A^+ of all positive elements is closed for addition and multiplication. Note also that for positive elements the absorbtion property

$$(0, 1) \oplus (a, i) = (0, 1)$$

holds.

An algorithm and an example. Let $(d, c)_{u,v}$ be the entry of the strict closure $\overline{\mathbf{R}}$ of relation matrix $\mathbf{R}$ over the geodetic semiring. Then d equals the length of a shortest nontrivial u–v path (a geodesic or a shortest cycle), and c equals the number of different u–v geodesics.

Using this algorithm, for the graph represented in Figure 9.2 we obtained the strict geodetic closure presented in Table 9.2.

To adapt the Fletcher's algorithm for computing the strict geodetic closure, we have to consider some properties of geodetic semirings. By construction, all entries of the relation matrix $\mathbf{R}$ are positive. From the description of Fletcher's algorithm it also follows that the entry $c_{k-1}[k, k]$ in $(c_{k-1}[k, k])^\star$ is always positive. Therefore $(c_{k-1}[k, k])^\star = (0, 1)$ and we can omit it from the expression. A detailed analysis of the algorithm shows that we can compute the strict geodetic closure matrix in place; we omit the subscripts in matrices $\mathbf{C}$.

Representing the relation matrix $\mathbf{R}$ (and its geodetic closure) by two matrices, the shortest paths length matrix $\mathbf{D}$ and the geodetics count matrix $\mathbf{C}$, we obtain the

Table 9.2. Geodetic Closure for the Graph in Figure 9.2

	1	2	3	4	5	6	7	8
1	$(\infty, 0)$	$(1, 1)$	$(1, 1)$	$(2, 2)$	$(2, 2)$	$(3, 4)$	$(3, 4)$	$(4, 8)$
2	$(\infty, 0)$	$(4, 4)$	$(\infty, 0)$	$(1, 1)$	$(1, 1)$	$(2, 2)$	$(2, 2)$	$(3, 4)$
3	$(\infty, 0)$	$(4, 4)$	$(\infty, 0)$	$(1, 1)$	$(1, 1)$	$(2, 2)$	$(2, 2)$	$(3, 4)$
4	$(\infty, 0)$	$(3, 2)$	$(\infty, 0)$	$(4, 2)$	$(4, 2)$	$(1, 1)$	$(1, 1)$	$(2, 2)$
5	$(\infty, 0)$	$(3, 2)$	$(\infty, 0)$	$(4, 2)$	$(1, 1)$	$(1, 1)$	$(1, 1)$	$(2, 2)$
6	$(\infty, 0)$	$(2, 1)$	$(\infty, 0)$	$(3, 1)$	$(3, 1)$	$(4, 2)$	$(4, 2)$	$(1, 1)$
7	$(\infty, 0)$	$(2, 1)$	$(\infty, 0)$	$(3, 1)$	$(3, 1)$	$(4, 2)$	$(4, 2)$	$(1, 1)$
8	$(\infty, 0)$	$(1, 1)$	$(\infty, 0)$	$(2, 1)$	$(2, 1)$	$(3, 2)$	$(3, 2)$	$(4, 4)$

following adapted version of Fletcher's algorithm (in PASCAL) for computing the strict geodetic closure:

```
for k := 1 to n do begin
    for i := 1 to n do for j := 1 to n do begin
    dst := min(big, d[i, k] + d[k, j]);
    if d[i, j] ≥ dst then begin
        cnt := c[i, k] * c[k, j];
        if d[i, j] = dst then c[i, j] := c[i, j] + cnt
            else begin c[i, j] := cnt; d[i, j] := dst end;
        end;
    end;
end;
```

The constant *big* in the algorithm is a number representing infinity (∞).

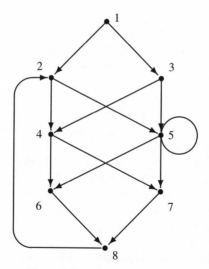

Figure 9.2. A directed graph.

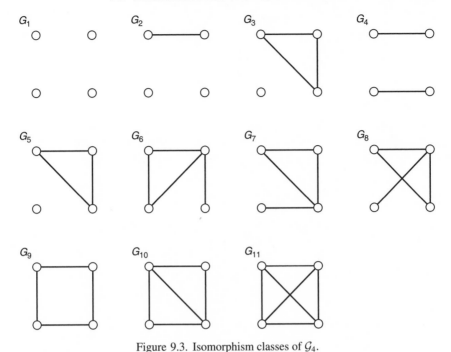

Figure 9.3. Isomorphism classes of $\mathcal{G}_4$.

9.5 SEMILATTICES AND LATTICES AS RELATIONS

We use a running illustrative example throughout this section on lattices and semi-lattices. Its elements are the set of isomorphism classes for the set of all undirected graphs, $\{G_i\} \in \mathcal{G}_n$, on n vertices. The isomorphism classes are shown in Figure 9.3 for $n = 4$ (we also use this example in Chapter 3). With a slight abuse of language, we will label an isomorphism class by the graph representing it in Figure 9.3. The number of graphs (isomorphism classes of graphs) in $\mathcal{G}_n$ is denoted by card($\mathcal{G}_n$), and for $n = 4$, card($\mathcal{G}_n$) = 11. The number of edges for these graphs ranges from 0 (for the null graph, N_n) to $n(n-1)/2$ (for the complete graph, K_n). We let $m_i = m(G_i)$ denote the number of edges in a graph, $G_i \in \mathcal{G}_n$, and use $e(G_i)$ to de-note the set of edges in G_i. A partial order[11] can be defined for $\mathcal{G}_n$, where $G_i \sqsubseteq G_j$ if $e(G_i) \subseteq e(G_j)$.

Figure 9.4 shows these graphs (as isomorphism classes of graphs) in relation to each other. Again, with a slight abuse of language, we will think in terms of adding an edge e to one graph, for instance $G_i \in \mathcal{G}_n$, to obtain a second graph, $G_j \in \mathcal{G}_n$, by means of the union $G_i \cup \{e\}$. In this construction, $m_j = (m_i + 1)$. Figure 9.4 is organized by levels, where the graphs in a level have the same number of edges. Reading up Figure 9.4, at any point, we see that a graph at one level is obtained from the graph below it by the addition on an edge if there is an arrow to it from

11 Orders are discussed in Chapter 4, Section 4.5.

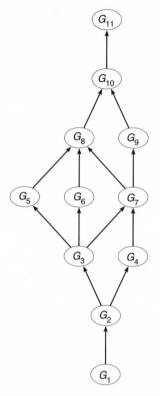

Figure 9.4. Lattice of isomorphism classes of $\mathcal{G}_4$.

the graph in the level below it. As an example, G_7 is gotten by the addition of one edge to G_3. It is also obtained from G_4 by the addition of an edge.

9.5.1   Bounds

Let $\sqsubseteq$ be a partial order on A. An element $b \in A$ is a lower bound of the set $B \subseteq A$ iff it holds $\forall x \in B : b \sqsubseteq x$, or equivalently $B \subseteq\uparrow (b)$. We say also that B is bounded from below.

An element $b \in A$ is a greatest lower bound of the set $B \subseteq A$ iff (see Figure 9.5)

- b is a lower bound, and
- if b' is also a lower bound, then $b' \sqsubseteq b$.

Theorem 9.4   *If it exists, a greatest lower bound of the set B is unique.*

Therefore we can introduce for the greatest lower bound of the set B a special notation $\sqsubseteq - \inf B$, or, when the relation $\sqsubseteq$ is apparent from the context, simply

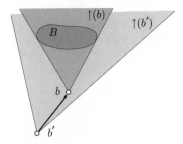

Figure 9.5. Illustration of the greatest lower bound.

inf B. When inf $B \in B$, we denote it also as min B. Therefore, min B satisfies these conditions:

- min $B \in B$;
- $B \subseteq \uparrow (\min B)$.

In the running example, any G_i is a lower bound of G_j in $\mathcal{G}_n$ if $e(G_i) \subset e(G_j)$, and, for certain pairs of graphs, G_i is an immediate lower bound if $G_i = G_j \setminus e$, where e is an edge in G_j. In $\mathcal{G}_4$, consider the two elements $\{G_5, G_7\}$ as an example B in Figure 9.5. The graph G_4 is not a lower bound for these elements. Although G_2 is a lower bound of these two elements, the greatest lower bound for the two selected elements is G_3 (i.e., B) and it is unique. The unique greatest lower bound of G_5 and G_9 in $\mathcal{G}_4$ is G_2.

In a similar fashion, we also introduce the notions of upper bound and least upper bound of the set $B \subseteq A$ for the partial order $\sqsubseteq$. The set $B \subseteq A$ is bounded if it is bounded from below and from above. Any G_j is an upper bound of $G_i \in \mathcal{G}_n$ if $e(G_i) \subset e(G_j)$. The set $\{G_5, G_6, G_7\}$ is bounded (with G_8 as the least upper bound and G_3 as the greatest lower bound).

In addition, the least upper bound of B is, when it exists, unique. We denote it by $\sqsubseteq - \sup B$.

9.5.2 Semilattices and lattices

A partially ordered set $(A, \sqsubseteq)$ is a sup-semilattice iff for each two-element set $\{a, b\} \subseteq A$ its least upper bound $\sup\{a, b\}$ exists (see Figure 9.6). In other words, when for each pair $a, b \in A, c \in A$ exists such that

$$(a \sqsubseteq c) \wedge (b \sqsubseteq c) \wedge \forall x \in A : ((a \sqsubseteq x) \wedge (b \sqsubseteq x) \Rightarrow c \sqsubseteq x).$$

Therefore in the $\uparrow (a) \cap \uparrow (b)$ the least element exists. We denote it by $\sup\{a, b\}$, and it holds:

$$\sup\{a, b\} = \min(\uparrow (a) \cap \uparrow (b)).$$

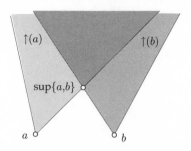

Figure 9.6. An illustration of a semilattice.

We can look on $\sup\{a, b\}$ as a binary operation that assigns an element from the semilattice to the given pair of elements. In this case, we introduce another notation:

$$a \sqcup b \equiv \sup\{a, b\}.$$

In a similar fashion, we could also define an inf-semilattice. Alternatively we can say $(A, \sqsubseteq)$ is a $\sqsubseteq$ – inf-semilattice iff $(A, \sqsubseteq^{-1})$ is a $\sqsubseteq^{-1}$ – sup-semilattice. Then

$$a \sqcup b \equiv \sqsubseteq - \inf\{a, b\} = \sqsubseteq^{-1} - \sup\{a, b\}.$$

In the running example, suppose that a restriction is imposed that the maximum degree of a vertex is 2. This would eliminate $\{G_6, G_8, G_{10}, G_{11}\}$ as elements of the set. In the resulting structure, G_5 and G_7 do not have a least upper bound. Or, in the language of Figure 9.6, with $G_5 = a$ and $G_7 = b$, $\sup\{a, b\}$ does not exist. Suppose, instead, that a restriction was imposed that isolates are not permitted. In Figure 9.4, this would eliminate $\{G_1, G_2, G_3, G_5\}$ as elements of the set. The resulting structure is an example of a semilattice in which G_6 and G_4 do not have a greatest lower bound. Note that both semilattices differ from the semilattice shown in Figure 3.7.

Remark: In the literature, instead of the symbols $\sqcup$ (join) and $\sqcap$ (meet), the symbols $\vee$ and $\wedge$ or $\cup$ and $\cap$ are often used. ☐

Not all partially ordered sets are semilattices. See Figure 9.7, where, for both partially ordered sets, there is no least common upper bound for the elements depicted at the top of the partial orders in the figure and no least common bound for the elements depicted at the bottom of these partial orders.

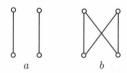

Figure 9.7. Two partially ordered sets that are not semilattices.

Since every inf-semilattice is also a sup-semilattice, in the following our discussion is limited to sup-semilattices.

Theorem 9.5   *In a* sup-*semilattice* $(A, \sqsubseteq)$*, it holds:*

$$\uparrow (x) \cap \uparrow (y) = \uparrow (x \sqcup y).$$

Theorem 9.6   *If* $(A, \sqsubseteq)$ *is a* sup-*semilattice, then* sup B *exists for every finite subset* $B \subseteq A$ *and it holds:*

$$\sup\{B \cup \{a\}\} = \sup\{\sup B, a\}.$$

A sup-semilattice $(A, \sqsubseteq)$ is complete iff sup B exists for every nonempty set $B \subseteq A$.

The connection between the operation $\sqcup$ and relation $\sqsubseteq$ is given by the following theorem.

Theorem 9.7   *In a* sup-*semilattice* $(A, \sqsubseteq)$*, it holds:*

$$a \sqcup b = b \quad \text{iff} \quad a \sqsubseteq b.$$

The last part from the definition of a semilattice can be expressed also.

Theorem 9.8   *In a* sup-*semilattice* $(A, \sqsubseteq)$*, it holds:*

$$\forall d \in A : ((a \sqsubseteq d) \wedge (b \sqsubseteq d) \Rightarrow a \sqcup b \sqsubseteq d).$$

Theorem 9.9   *In a* sup-*semilattice* $(A, \sqsubseteq)$*, the following all hold:*
a. $a \sqsubseteq b \Longrightarrow a \sqcup c \sqsubseteq b \sqcup c,$
b. $a \sqcup a = a,$
c. $a \sqcup b = b \sqcup a,$
d. $a \sqcup (b \sqcup c) = (a \sqcup b) \sqcup c.$

A partially ordered set $(A, \sqsubseteq)$ is a lattice iff $(A, \sqsubseteq)$ and $(A, \sqsubseteq^{-1})$ are semilattices of the same type, or equivalently, when it is a sup- and inf-semilattice. A lattice is complete iff both semilattices are complete.

In the running example, the set $\mathcal{G}_n$ of all edge graphs on n vertices is a lattice. Therefore, in a lattice both operations $\sqcup$ and $\sqcap$ are defined (see Figure 9.8).

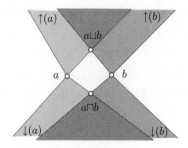

Figure 9.8. An illustration of a lattice.

Theorem 9.10 *In a lattice $(A, \sqsubseteq)$ the absorption laws*

$$a \sqcup (a \sqcap b) = a \qquad \text{and} \qquad a \sqcap (a \sqcup b) = a$$

hold, and we have

$$a \sqcap b = a \Leftrightarrow a \sqcup b = b.$$

Example 9.1 *Equivalence relations.* The set $(\mathbf{Eqv}(A), \subseteq)$, where $\subseteq$ is the ordinary set inclusion, is a lattice. Let $R_1, R_2 \in \mathbf{Eqv}(A)$; then

$$R_1 \sqcap R_2 = R_1 \cap R_2 \qquad \text{and} \qquad R_1 \sqcup R_2 = \overline{(R_1 \cup R_2)}. \qquad \square$$

In proving that a given partially ordered set is a lattice, we find that the following theorem is often useful.

Theorem 9.11 *Let a partially ordered set $(A, \sqsubseteq)$ satisfy these conditions:*

- *For every nonempty set $B \subseteq A$, its greatest lower bound $\inf B \in A$ exists:*

$$\forall B \subseteq A : (B \neq \emptyset \Rightarrow \exists a \in A : a = \inf B).$$

- *For every subset $B \subseteq A$, its upper bound in A exists:*

$$\forall B \subseteq A \exists a \in A \forall b \in B : b \sqsubseteq a.$$

Then $(A, \sqsubseteq)$ is a lattice.

In the case when the set A is finite, this theorem reduces to the following.

Theorem 9.12 *Let a partially ordered set $(A, \sqsubseteq)$ over a finite set A be*

a. *an inf-semilattice with the largest element 1, or*
b. *a sup-semilattice with the least element 0;*

then it is also a lattice.

This theorem was used by Borgatti and Everett (1989) to prove that all regular partitions of a network form a lattice.

9.6　ALGEBRAIC VIEW ON LATTICES

As we know, in a lattice $(A, \sqsubseteq)$ the structures $(A, \sqcup)$ and $(A, \sqcap)$ are (algebraic) semilattices and both absorption laws hold. We can also prove the opposite.

Theorem 9.13 *Let an algebraic structure $(A, \sqcup, \sqcap)$ satisfy these conditions: $(A, \sqcup)$ and $(A, \sqcap)$ are semilattices and both absorption laws hold. Then, for the relation $\sqsubseteq$ defined by*

$$a \sqsubseteq b \equiv a \sqcup b = b,$$

$(A, \sqsubseteq)$ is a lattice.

For these reasons we also call the algebraic structure $(A, \sqcup, \sqcap)$, which satisfies the conditions from the theorem, an (algebraic) lattice.

Let us repeat. $(A, \sqcup, \sqcap)$ is a lattice iff

$$a \sqcup a = a, \qquad\qquad a \sqcap a = a,$$
$$a \sqcup b = b \sqcup a, \qquad\qquad a \sqcap b = b \sqcap a,$$
$$(a \sqcup b) \sqcup c = a \sqcup (b \sqcup c), \qquad (a \sqcap b) \sqcap c = a \sqcap (b \sqcap c),$$
$$a \sqcup (a \sqcap b) = a, \qquad\qquad a \sqcap (a \sqcup b) = a.$$

The properties of operations $\sqcap$ and $\sqcup$ appear symmetrically in the definition of a lattice. Therefore, if in the proof of the statement $\Phi(\sqcap, \sqcup)$ we everywhere interchange both operations, we get the proof of the statement $\Phi(\sqcup, \sqcap)$. In a lattice a *duality* principle holds: If in a lattice the statement $\Phi(\sqcap, \sqcup)$ holds, then the statement $\Phi(\sqcup, \sqcap)$ also holds.

A mapping $h:A \to B$ is a *homomorphism* of a lattice $L = (A, \sqcup, \sqcap)$ in a lattice $M = (B, \triangledown, \triangle)$ iff

$$h(a \sqcup b) = h(a) \triangledown h(b) \qquad \text{in} \qquad h(a \sqcap b) = h(a) \triangle h(b).$$

9.6.1 Types of lattices

A lattice is *bounded* if it posses the largest element 1 and the least element 0,

$$\forall a \in A : a \sqsubseteq 1 \qquad \text{in} \qquad \forall a \in A : 0 \sqsubseteq a,$$

or, equivalently,

$$1 \sqcup a = 1 \qquad \text{in} \qquad a \sqcup 0 = a,$$

$$1 \sqcap a = a \qquad \text{in} \qquad a \sqcap 0 = 0.$$

We know from the partial orders the following.

Theorem 9.14 *Every finite lattice is bounded.*

If in a lattice the statement $\Phi(\sqcap, \sqcup, 0, 1)$ holds, then the statement $\Phi(\sqcup, \sqcap, 1, 0)$ also holds.

In a bounded lattice $(A, \sqcup, \sqcap, 0, 1)$ we call a complement of element $a \in A$ an element $b \in A$, which satisfies these conditions:

$$a \sqcap b = 0 \qquad \text{and} \qquad a \sqcup b = 1.$$

In general, each element can have one, several (left-hand side of Figure 9.9), or (right-hand side of Figure 9.9) complements. A bounded lattice in which every element has at least one complement is called a complemented lattice.

A lattice $(B, \triangledown, \triangle)$ is a sublattice of a lattice $(A, \sqcup, \sqcap)$ iff $B \subseteq A$, $\triangledown = \sqcup|_B$, and $\triangle = \sqcap|_B$.

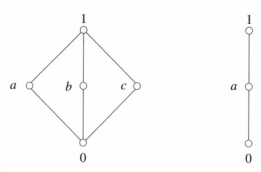

Figure 9.9. Complements.

Example 9.2   A lattice in Figure 9.10(b) is not a sublattice of a lattice in Figure 9.10(a), but the lattice in Figure 9.10(c) is.   □

A lattice is modular iff

$$\forall a, b, c \in A : (a \sqsubseteq c \Rightarrow a \sqcup (b \sqcap c) = (a \sqcup b) \sqcap c),$$

and it is distributive iff both distributivity laws hold:

$$a \sqcap (b \sqcup c) = (a \sqcap b) \sqcup (a \sqcap c),$$
$$a \sqcup (b \sqcap c) = (a \sqcup b) \sqcap (a \sqcup c).$$

It is possible to prove that one distributivity implies the other.

Theorem 9.15   *A lattice is modular iff it does not contain a sublattice isomorphic to the left lattice in Figure 9.11; it is distributive iff it does not contain a sublattice isomorphic to one of the lattices in Figure 9.11.*

Therefore, every distributive lattice is modular.

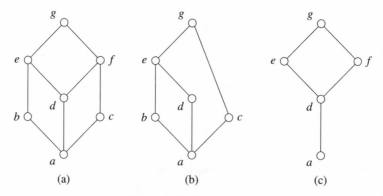

Figure 9.10. Sublattices.

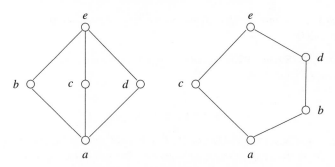

Figure 9.11. Nondistributive lattices.

Theorem 9.16 *In a bounded distributive lattice, every element has at most one complement.*

A complemented distributive lattice is a form of a Boolean algebra. In this Boolean algebra, every element $a \in A$ has a unique complement $\bar{a} \in A$. Therefore, the mapping⁻ : $A \to A$ is a unary operation. In proving equalities in Boolean algebras, the following property is quite useful.

Theorem 9.17 *Let, for elements $a, b \in A$ in Boolean algebra, $a \sqcap b = 0$ and $a \sqcup b = 1$ hold. Then $b = \bar{a}$.*

Theorem 9.18 *In Boolean algebra, the De Morgan laws hold:*

$$\overline{a \sqcap b} = \bar{a} \sqcup \bar{b} \qquad \text{and} \qquad \overline{a \sqcup b} = \bar{a} \sqcap \bar{b}.$$

9.6.2 Representations

Element $a \in A$ is irreducible *(for $\sqcup$)* iff

$$x \sqcup y = a \Rightarrow (x = a) \vee (y = a).$$

In a lattice bounded from below, we call the immediate successors of the element 0 *atoms*. Element 0 and atoms are irreducible.

Theorem 9.19 *In a lattice in which all chains are finite, every element can be expressed as a join of a finite number of irreducible elements.*

An expression of element a as a join of a finite number of irreducible elements is nonredundant iff a is not equal to the join of any of its proper subsets.

Theorem 9.20 *In a distributive lattice with finite chains, for every element there exists a unique (up to ordering) nonredundant expression as a join of a finite number of irreducible elements.*

Theorem 9.21   *Nonreducible elements of a type of Boolean algebra are exactly its atoms and* 0.

Theorem 9.22 (Stone 1973)   *Boolean algebra is isomorphic to the set algebra of its atoms* $(\mathcal{P}(A), \cup, \cap)$.

9.7   CONCLUSION

Semirings, semilattices, and lattices are flexible and general algebraic structures. We use them in the chapter when we consider structural balance theory.

10

BALANCE THEORY AND BLOCKMODELING SIGNED NETWORKS

In our discussion of blockmodeling in Chapter 6, we presented definitions of equivalences used within conventional blockmodeling. We identified the permitted ideal block types for structural and regular equivalence and outlined an optimizational approach to establish blockmodels according to specified equivalences. Each criterion function measures the inconsistency between the set of empirical blocks and a set of ideal blocks, and we sought partitions by using direct local optimization procedures. In Chapter 7, we suggested *starting* with patterns of ideal blocks defined for the image matrix with an expanded set of block types. In this chapter, we continue in this spirit by defining some new block types after considering essential elements of structural balance theory.

Our focus shifts to signed networks, a network data type introduced in Chapter 1, with the intent of bringing them inside the generalized blockmodeling framework. It is important to note that this is *not* an attempt to apply structural equivalence ideas to signed data. In fact, *structural equivalence is singularly inappropriate for analyzing signed networks*. In certain signed networks (graphs), there are partitioned structures with a distinctive balanced pattern. We construct a criterion function that measures inconsistencies between empirical structures and balanced structures and use the relocation clustering procedure with a criterion function defined for structural balance to partition signed networks.

Section 10.1 outlines the key idea of structural balance theory as proposed by Heider (1946), and Section 10.2 provides a specification of signed networks. The idea of exact k-balanced networks is defined and conditions for exact k-balance are provided. Section 10.3 draws on materials on semirings from Chapter 9 and provides conditions for determining whether or not a signed network is balanced. These form the foundation for algorithms identifying exact k-balanced partitions of them in terms of structural balance. In most cases, however, empirical signed networks are not exactly balanced and methods are needed for partitioning them in ways that are as *close as possible* to exactly balanced partitions. Such a partitioning approach is outlined in Section 10.4. Some exactly k-balanced networks are considered in Section 10.5, and some structures that are not k-balanced are considered in Section 10.6.

In Section 10.7 we return to the BWR data and focus on the signed data they contain. Section 10.8 contains an analysis of a signed network from a Bales-type experimental group. As a part of our narrative, we show that structural equivalence ideas are not useful for signed networks. Section 10.9 deals with through time balance processes with which we look at the Sampson monastery (SM) data and the Newcomb fraternity (NF) data. Both of these data sets were introduced in Chapter 2.

10.1   STRUCTURAL BALANCE THEORY

One of the most successful areas in social psychology, both substantively and technically, has been structural balance theory. Heider (1946, 1958) has been credited with the first *systematic* statement within this approach to interpersonal relations (Taylor 1970). For his version of balance theory, there are three objects: a focal person, p, another actor, o, and a nonperson object, x. The nonperson object can be "a situation, event, an idea or a thing" (Heider 1946:107). This permits great flexibility. There are sentiment relations between p and o and unit relations between both p and o and the nonperson object x. Together, these form the *pox* triple. This theoretical unit can have any of the structures shown in Figure 10.1. By convention, solid lines represent positive ties and dashed lines represent negative ties. In the first structure, p has a positive tie with o and both p and o have a positive tie with x. Intuitively, the situation is balanced. Similarly, p likes o in the second network and they both have a negative view of x. Again the network is balanced. In the third triple, p dislikes both o and x knows that o has a favorable view of x. Again the triple is balanced as is the last triple in the top panel.

Dropping to the second panel of Figure 10.1, we see that the first triple shows p liking o, but the two disagree about x. Intuitively, this is imbalanced and a source of strain. In the second triple depicted in this row, p likes both o and x but knows that o dislikes x – another imbalanced configuration. The remaining triples in the bottom panel can be read in the same way. All of the structures in the top panel of Figure 10.1 are defined as balanced, while all of the triples in the lower panel are taken as imbalanced.[1]

Heider's basic idea is that people prefer balanced configurations to those that are imbalanced, and they experience strain and tension when they are in any of the imbalanced structures of Figure 10.1. In contrast, balanced states are viewed as both comfortable and stable. Strain in an imbalanced triple is assumed to lead to

---

1   Anticipating that one of the formalized statements of balance theory that allows the x to be another person, for instance q, some of the structures in Figure 10.1 can be put into language about friends and enemies (Rapoport 1963). The first in the top row represents "a friend (q) of a friend (o) is a friend (of p)." The second structure in that row represents "an enemy (q) of a friend (o) is an enemy (of p)." For the third, "a friend (q) of an enemy (o) is an enemy (of p)." Finally, the last network of the top row represents the idea that an "enemy (q) of an enemy (o) is a friend (of p)."

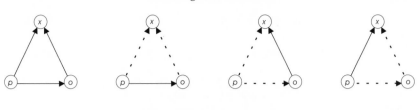

Four Balanced Triadic Configurations

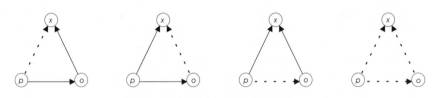

Four Imbalanced Triadic Configurations

Figure 10.1. Balanced and imbalanced signed triads.

efforts by individuals, in such a triple, to make changes that move the triple toward balance. Of course, because people are involved in multiple triples, changes in one triple that move it toward balance may make another triple imbalanced.

Ideas of strain and tension are also present in Newcomb's (1961) formulation of structural balance.[2] For Newcomb, the object x can also be another person, and it can be the rest of the group (to which p and o both belong). In Heider's approach, the ties are present or not (i.e., they are binary), whereas for Newcomb the ties can have magnitude. We consider both versions in this chapter. There are other variants of balance theory, but regardless of the formulation, they all share the feature in which strain generates forces that move structures from imbalance toward balance. For a review, see Taylor (1970) or Forsyth (1990). Partitioning social networks can be seen as an analytic descriptive (inductive) activity as well as a (deductive) activity for testing hypotheses about structures by means of prespecified models. With structural balance theory, time is critical because it is a theory about change. As a result, examining a series of signed networks for a specific social group is crucial if the hypothesis of movement toward balance is to be tested. We think that generalized blockmodeling is a useful tool for doing this.

10.2 SIGNED NETWORKS

Cartwright and Harary (1956) generalized structural balance theory by using signed networks (graphs). In this generalization, the difference between sentiment relations and unit relations is ignored.

2 The *pox* triple terminology comes from his work (although the term *triad* is used there).

A *signed* network is an ordered pair, $(\mathbf{G}, \sigma)$ for which the following are true.

1. $\mathbf{G} = (\mathcal{U}, \mathcal{A})$ is a digraph, without loops, having a set of units (vertices) $\mathcal{U}$ and a set of arcs $\mathcal{A} \subseteq \mathcal{U} \times \mathcal{U}$.
2. $\sigma : \mathcal{A} \rightarrow \{p, n\}$ is a sign function. The arcs with the sign p are positive whereas the arcs with the sign n are negative. Equivalently, and consistent with most diagrams of signed networks, $\sigma : \mathcal{A} \rightarrow \{+1, -1\}$.

As shorthand notation, we denote such a network by $(\mathcal{U}, \mathcal{A}, \sigma)$. For a social network, v_i is an actor and an ordered pair $(v_i, v_j) \in \mathcal{A}$ is a tie from the actor v_i to the actor v_j if $v_i, v_j \in \mathcal{U}$. For the *pox* triples of Heider and of Newcomb, $p, o, x \in \mathcal{U}$ whereas the ties are elements of $\mathcal{A}$. In the Cartwright and Harary formulation, the networks can have any size and are not restricted to triples.

When the network contains undirected lines, these edges can be reexpressed by replacing each edge e by a pair of opposite arcs both signed with the sign of the edge e. The modified directed graph contains only arcs.

Walks, paths, cycles, and semiwalks are defined for signed networks in the same way as for unsigned graphs. The additional concept that is added is their sign. The *sign* of a (semi)walk is the product of the signs of the lines they contain. The corresponding semigroup operation (see Section 3.4) is obvious:

$\cdot$	n	p
n	p	n
p	n	p

The (semi)walk on the signed network is *positive* iff it contains an even number of negative arcs; otherwise it is *negative*.

All of the triples (semicycles) in the upper panel of Figure 10.1 are positive, whereas all of the triples in the bottom panel have negative signs. By definition, a semicycle is balanced if its sign is positive and imbalanced if its sign is negative.

Our point of departure for a partitioning procedure is the structural balance theory of Cartwright and Harary (1956; also see Harary et al. 1965; Davis 1967; Doreian 1970; Cartwright and Harary 1968, 1979; Riley 1969; Roberts 1976:75–77).

A signed network (G, σ) is balanced if and only if the set of units $\mathcal{U}$ can be partitioned into two subsets (clusters) so that every positive arc joins units of the same subset and every negative arc joins units of different subsets.

The balanced signed networks are characterized by the following theorem (Harary et al. 1965; Davis 1967; Riley 1969; Roberts 1976; Chartrand 1985).

Theorem 10.1   *A signed network* $(\mathbf{G}, \sigma)$ *is balanced if and only if every closed semiwalk is positive.*

We refer to the clusters from such partitions as plus-sets.[3] The preceding structure theorem specifies only two plus-sets. Davis (1967) observed that human groups can split into more than two mutually antagonistic subgroups and sought the conditions under which this would occur. In essence, he found those conditions by reconsidering the last triple of the bottom panel of Figure 10.1. At best, "the enemy of an enemy is an enemy" seems ambiguous as a candidate for imbalance. What if it were defined as balanced?

Following Roberts (1976:75–77), we specify that a signed network $(\mathbf{G}, \sigma)$ is partitionable iff the set of $\mathcal{U}$ can be partitioned into subsets, called clusters or plus-sets, so that every positive arc joins units of the same subset and every negative arc joins units of different subsets.

With this reformulation, the Cartwright and Harary structure theorem generalizes (see Davis 1967:181)[4] to the following theorem (Harary et al. 1965; Davis 1967; Riley 1969; Roberts 1976; Chartrand 1985).

Theorem 10.2 *A signed network $(\mathbf{G}, \sigma)$ is exactly partitionable into two or more plus-sets if and only if it contains no closed semiwalk with exactly one negative line.*

We use k-balance to refer to an exact partition into k plus-sets according to the structure theorems, and we describe such graphs as k-balanced.

10.3   PARTITIONING SIGNED NETWORKS AND SEMIRINGS

In this section we show how the structure theorems of Section 10.2 are reflected in a matrix algebra over appropriately defined semirings (also see the discussion of semirings in Chapter 9).

To construct a semiring corresponding to the balance problem, we take the set A with four elements (Cartwright and Harary 1956; Doreian 1970):

$0 =$ no walk;

$n =$ all walks are negative;

$p =$ all walks are positive;

$a =$ at least one positive and at least one negative walk.

It is easy to produce the Cayley tables (see Sections 3.4, 9.1, and 9.3.1) for the balance semiring (see Table 10.1). The balance semiring is an idempotent closed semiring with zero 0s and unit p.

---

3   The term comes from Davis (1967).
4   Davis used the term *clusterable* for partitions into more than two plus-sets to distinguish it from the balance theorem partition into just two plus-sets. Given our general usage of clustering, we prefer to use the term (k-balance) *partitionable*, where k is the number of plus-sets.

Table 10.1. Balance Semiring

+	0	n	p	a		$\cdot$	0	n	p	a		x	x^*
0	0	n	p	a		0	0	0	0	0		0	p
n	n	n	a	a		n	0	p	n	a		n	a
p	p	a	p	a		p	0	n	p	a		p	p
a	a	a	a	a		a	0	a	a	a		a	a

For construction of the partition semiring corresponding to the partitionability problem, we need the set A with five elements (Batagelj 1994):

$0 =$ no walk;

$n =$ at least one walk with exactly one negative arc, and no walk with only positive arcs;

$p =$ at least one walk with only positive arcs, and no walk with exactly one negative arc;

$a =$ at least one walk with only positive arcs, and at least one walk with exactly one negative arc;

$q =$ each walk has at least two negative arcs.

The Cayley tables for this partition semiring are given in Table 10.2. The partition semiring is an idempotent closed semiring with zero 0s and unit p. On the basis of Theorems 10.1 and 10.2, we have the following.

Theorem 10.3 *A signed network (G, σ) is balanced iff the diagonal of its balance-closure matrix $\mathbf{D}_B^\bullet$ contains only elements with value p.*

Theorem 10.4 *A signed network (G, σ) is partitionable iff the diagonal of its partition-closure matrix $\mathbf{D}_P^\bullet$ contains only elements with value p.*

The balance-closure matrix of a balanced signed network contains no element with value a since in this case the corresponding diagonal elements should also have value a. Similarly, the partition-closure matrix of a partitionable signed network contains no element with value a.

A cluster is a maximal set of vertices with equal lines in matrix $\mathbf{D}^\bullet$.

In the balance closure of a balanced signed network and in the partition closure of a partitionable signed network, all the entries between vertices of two clusters

Table 10.2. Partition Semiring

+	0	n	p	a	q		$\cdot$	0	n	p	a	q		x	x^*
0	0	n	p	a	q		0	0	0	0	0	0		0	p
n	n	n	a	a	n		n	0	q	n	n	q		n	a
p	p	a	p	a	p		p	0	n	p	a	q		p	p
a	a	a	a	a	a		a	0	n	a	a	q		a	a
q	q	n	p	a	q		q	0	q	q	q	q		q	p

have the same value. The value of entries between vertices of the same cluster is p.

In both cases, different partitions of the set of vertices correspond to the (nonequivalent) colorings of the graph with clusters as vertices in which there is an edge between two vertices iff the entries between the corresponding clusters in matrix $\mathbf{D}^\bullet$ have value n.

There is another way to test the partitionability of a given signed network. Let R be a relation describing adjacency in graph $\mathbf{G}$. We denote the set of all positive arcs by R^+ and the set of all negative arcs by R^-.

Theorem 10.5 *A signed network (G, σ) is partitionable iff $(R^+)^\bullet \cap R^- = \emptyset$, where the closure $\bullet$ is computed in the semiring $(\{0, 1\}, \vee, \wedge, 0, 1)$.*

This form of Theorem 10.2 has considerable value because the intersection $(R^+)^\bullet \cap R^-$ consists of those arcs that prevent the signed network (G, σ) from being partitionable.

10.3.1 Examples

Example 10.1 In Figure 10.2, we show a network from Chartrand (1985:181) together with its signed matrix. The positive edges are represented by solid lines and the negative edges are represented by dotted lines.

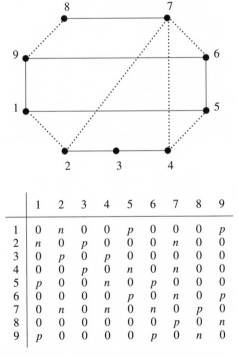

	1	2	3	4	5	6	7	8	9
1	0	n	0	0	p	0	0	0	p
2	n	0	p	0	0	0	n	0	0
3	0	p	0	p	0	0	0	0	0
4	0	0	p	0	n	0	n	0	0
5	p	0	0	n	0	p	0	0	0
6	0	0	0	0	p	0	n	0	p
7	0	n	0	n	0	n	0	p	0
8	0	0	0	0	0	0	p	0	n
9	p	0	0	0	0	p	0	n	0

Figure 10.2. A graph example from Chartrand.

Table 10.3. Chartrand's Example – Closures

	1	2	3	4	5	6	7	8	9	1	2	3	4	5	6	7	8	9
1	*a*	*a*	*a*	*a*	*a*	*a*	*a*	*a*	*a*	**p**	*n*	*n*	*n*	**p**	**p**	*n*	*n*	**p**
2	*a*	*a*	*a*	*a*	*a*	*a*	*a*	*a*	*a*	*n*	**p**	**p**	**p**	*n*	*n*	*n*	*n*	*n*
3	*a*	*a*	*a*	*a*	*a*	*a*	*a*	*a*	*a*	*n*	**p**	**p**	**p**	*n*	*n*	*n*	*n*	*n*
4	*a*	*a*	*a*	*a*	*a*	*a*	*a*	*a*	*a*	*n*	**p**	**p**	**p**	*n*	*n*	*n*	*n*	*n*
5	*a*	*a*	*a*	*a*	*a*	*a*	*a*	*a*	*a*	**p**	*n*	*n*	*n*	**p**	**p**	*n*	*n*	**p**
6	*a*	*a*	*a*	*a*	*a*	*a*	*a*	*a*	*a*	**p**	*n*	*n*	*n*	**p**	**p**	*n*	*n*	**p**
7	*a*	*a*	*a*	*a*	*a*	*a*	*a*	*a*	*a*	*n*	*n*	*n*	*n*	*n*	*n*	**p**	**p**	*n*
8	*a*	*a*	*a*	*a*	*a*	*a*	*a*	*a*	*a*	*n*	*n*	*n*	*n*	*n*	*n*	**p**	**p**	*n*
9	*a*	*a*	*a*	*a*	*a*	*a*	*a*	*a*	*a*	**p**	*n*	*n*	*n*	**p**	**p**	*n*	*n*	**p**

On the left-hand side of Table 10.3, the corresponding balance closure is given, and it is clear that the network is not balanced for $k = 2$. However, from the partition closure on the right-hand side of Table 10.3, it is clear that the network is partitionable into three clusters:

$$C_1 = \{1, 5, 6, 9\}, \qquad C_2 = \{2, 3, 4\}, \qquad C_3 = \{7, 8\}. \quad \square$$

Example 10.2 The signed network from Roberts (1976:77, Exercise 16) is presented in Figure 10.3, and its value matrix on the left-hand side of Table 10.4. In this case the balance closure and the partition closure are equal (right-hand side of Table 10.4). The corresponding partition is

$$C_1 = \{v, x, y\}, \qquad C_2 = \{u, w, z\}. \quad \square$$

10.4 A PARTITIONING ALGORITHM FOR SIGNED NETWORKS

Empirically, most signed structures are not exactly k-balanced, and we seek partitions as close to k-balance as possible. Our goal is to partition signed networks in order to create or establish a generalized blockmodel. The discussion of balanced networks makes clear the nature of the blocks to expect in balanced networks.

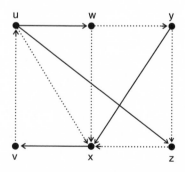

Figure 10.3. An example from Roberts.

Table 10.4. *The Value Matrix and Its Closure for Roberts's Example*

	u	v	w	x	y	z		u	v	w	x	y	z
u	0	0	p	n	0	p	u	**p**	n	**p**	n	n	**p**
v	n	0	0	0	0	0	v	n	**p**	n	**p**	**p**	n
w	0	0	0	n	n	0	w	**p**	n	**p**	n	n	**p**
x	0	p	0	0	0	0	x	n	**p**	n	**p**	**p**	n
y	0	0	0	p	0	n	y	n	**p**	n	**p**	**p**	n
z	0	0	0	n	0	0	z	**p**	n	**p**	n	n	**p**

Some blocks have only 0 or 1 and other blocks have only 0 and −1. Of course, if the ties are valued, then one type of block has only 0 and positive values and the other type has only 0 and negative values. The plus-sets (clusters) identify the positive blocks, and these blocks will be located on the main diagonal of the blockmodel. Ties between units in different plus-sets identify the negative blocks, and they will be off-diagonal blocks. This provides the shape of the blockmodel of an exactly k-balanced network: There will be k positive blocks on the diagonal and $k(k − 1)$ off-diagonal negative blocks. We note that, although some blocks can be null empirically, they are not specified as such at the outset.

The statement of balance theory, in both the Heider and Newcomb versions, is cast in terms of structures moving toward balance. The strain or tension of imbalanced structures acts as a force that moves those structures toward balance. This is a substantive hypothesis, and to make it testable it is necessary to have a measure of imbalance. Two classes of measures have been proposed (Harary et al. 1965:346–353). The first stays close to the initial definition of balance in terms of cycles: Imbalance is measured by the ratio of the number of imbalanced cycles to the total number of cycles in the network.[5]

The second class of imbalance measures rests on the structure theorems. Every negative tie within a plus-set and every positive tie between plus-sets is inconsistent with balance. So, one measure of imbalance is the number of ties whose signs must be changed in order to make the network balanced. A collection of lines is a negation-minimal set if the negation of all of them results in a balanced network but the negation of any proper subset of these lines does not do so (Harary et al. 1965:349). A second imbalance measure is the deletion-minimal sets of lines whose removal leads to balance, but the deletion of any of its proper subsets does not do so. Harary et al. (1965:350) proved that any deletion-minimal set of lines is also a negation-minimal set (and vice versa). For the rest of this chapter we use the size of the deletion-minimal set as the measure of imbalance[6] for a network.

5 This measure can be modified with a restriction on the length of the cycles included in the proportion. Long cycles, for example, can be excluded. Less radical is the notion of weighting them less in constructing this kind of measure.

6 Numerically, the line-negation and line-deletion measures of imbalance are identical. The algorithm of Doreian and Mrvar (1996) discussed below simply identifies those arcs that are inconsistent with

Doreian and Mrvar (1996) proposed a partitioning procedure for signed networks we consider here. As in earlier chapters, we state the problem in terms of wanting to determine the clustering $\mathbf{C}^*$ for which

$$P(\mathbf{C}^*) = \min_{\mathbf{C} \in \Phi} P(\mathbf{C}),$$

where $\mathbf{C}$ is a clustering of a given *set of units* $\mathcal{U}$, Φ is the set of all possible clusterings, and $P : \Phi \to \mathbb{R}$ is a criterion function.

The criterion function can be defined in terms of either the original structure theorem (Theorem 10.1) or the modified version (Theorem 10.2). Let $\mathcal{N}$ be the total number of negative ties within plus-sets and let $\mathcal{P}$ be the total number of positive ties between plus-sets. The criterion function is defined as

$$P(\mathbf{C}) = \mathcal{N} + \mathcal{P}.$$

In this formulation, the two types of inconsistencies[7] are treated as equally important: The criterion function is simply the count of all inconsistencies regardless of their type. A slightly more general criterion function is

$$P(\mathbf{C}) = \alpha \mathcal{N} + (1 - \alpha)\mathcal{P},$$

where $0 \leq \alpha \leq 1$. With $\alpha = 0.5$, the two inconsistencies are equally weighted. For $0 \leq \alpha < 0.5$, positive inconsistencies are more important, and for $0.5 < \alpha \leq 1$, the negative inconsistencies are considered as more consequential.

The criterion function is then minimized by the relocation algorithm described earlier (see Section 4.4.3). We have to repeat the procedure many times (e.g., 1,000 times) because it is a local optimization procedure.

10.5   EXACTLY k-BALANCED STRUCTURES

Consider the constructed network shown in Figure 10.4. It contains 10 positive ties and 12 negative ties. From the way we have drawn the network, it is clear that there is a partition into four plus-sets with no inconsistencies. This implies that the criterion function for this partition will be zero.

It is useful to consider this in the context of examining all partitions ($1 \leq k \leq n$) and noting those with a minimum value of the criterion function for each value of k. For this simple network, the number of plus-sets can vary from 1 to 12. The distribution of the number of plus-sets (clusters) together with the values

---

balance. For such arcs, one can construct a balanced network either by deleting these ties or negating them. Empirically, the overwhelming number of tie changes take the form of being deleted rather than negated (Doreian 2002).

7   Throughout our discussion, we use the term *inconsistency* to refer to inconsistencies with regard to (perfect) balance, and we do not refer to these inconsistencies as errors. Positive inconsistencies are positive ties between plus-sets, and negative inconsistencies are negative ties within plus-sets.

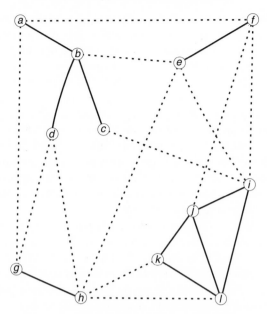

Figure 10.4. A constructed k-balanced network.

of the criterion function and the number of different partitions for each number of plus-sets is

Number of plus-sets	1	2	3	4	5	6	7	8	9	10	11	12
Criterion function	12	2	1	0	1	2	3	4	6	8	9	10
Number of partitions	1	2	4	1	4	5	2	1	3	11	1	1

Clearly, with all of the vertices of the network in a single cluster (plus-set), all of the negative ties will be counted as inconsistencies. So the one-cluster partition has 12 inconsistencies. Similarly, at the other extreme, if every vertex is a singleton (in its own cluster), then all of the positive ties will be counted as inconsistencies. The value of the criterion function is 10. Between these extremes, the shape of the criterion function with the number of plus-sets is very suggestive. Let k be the number of plus-sets in a partition with $1 \leq k \leq n$. Partitions with k and $k + 1$ plus-sets are said to be adjacent.

Theorem 10.6 *For any signed network, $(\mathbf{G}, \sigma)$, there will be a unique lowest value of the criterion function. This value will occur for partitions with a single number of plus-sets or for adjacent partitions.*[8]

8 This proof was kindly provided by Martin Everett.

Proof: Let the criterion function $P(\mathbf{C})$ be denoted by f. We first consider the case in which $f = 0$. Suppose there is a largest value of k (which we denote by q) for which f is zero. Let $\mathbf{G}^q$ be the network that contains as vertices the plus-sets and the negative lines between these plus-sets. By this construction, $\mathbf{G}^q$ has only negative lines. If $\mathbf{G}^q$ is complete, then the value of q is the unique value of k for partitions of $\mathbf{G}$ without inconsistencies. If $\mathbf{G}^q$ is not complete, then there are vertices on the network that are not directly connected. If we merge these vertices (equivalently the two clusters from $\mathbf{G}$ that they represent), we have a network with $(q - 1)$ vertices. If this network is complete, the process stops. If not, continue to merge plus-sets in the same fashion. The process stops when there are no nonadjacent clusters (vertices) in some $\mathbf{G}^{q-r}$ after r steps. If it did not, then the network obtained by placing positive lines between elements of the merged clusters would contradict the uniqueness of the complete $\mathbf{G}^q$ network.

Now consider the case in which f has a nonzero minimum, m for instance, for some number of clusters, k. The value of m is the number of lines inconsistent with balance. Denote the set of these lines by $\mathcal{A}_m$. Delete these ties from $\mathbf{G}$ and form a new network, $\mathbf{G}'$. Then for the network $\mathbf{G}'$ the criterion function is zero and we can use the construction above. If a pair of merged clusters contains negative lines, this makes no difference for the minimum value of f. Positive internal links are also irrelevant with regard to f. The set $\mathcal{A}_m$ may contain positive lines between clusters, but placing these clusters together would lower the criterion function below m for the $k - 1$ clusters. This contradicts the condition in which m is a minimum. It follows that the minimum value of the criterion function must be in a consecutive range of values for k. $\square$

10.5.1   An empirical example

Young (1971) provides an account of life in the village of Kaluana in the New Guinea Highlands. The vertices in Figure 10.5 represent clans or major clan segments. They are as follows: 1, Mulina I; 2, Mulina II; 3, Ainaona; 4, Malabuabua; 5, Foloyai; 6, Lulauvile I; 7, Lulavile II; 8, Nouneya; and 9, Iwaoyana. The positive and negative lines represent friend–enemy relations. This structure is not balanced

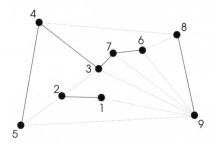

Figure 10.5. An empirical signed network of clans with three plus-sets.

with two plus-sets, but it is exactly partitionable into three plus-sets of clans. The two subclan segments of Mulina form one plus-set. Another plus-set is made up of Nouneya and Iwaoyana. The remaining clans go into the third plus-set. All pairs of the plus-sets have negative ties between them.

10.6   STRUCTURES THAT ARE NOT *k*-BALANCED

Many signed networks are not *k*-balanced: they are not partitionable in a way that conforms exactly with either of the structure theorems, and the value of the earlier defined criterion function is not zero.

10.6.1   A constructed example

This is illustrated by the network (Roberts 1976:73) in Figure 10.6. For all numbers of plus-sets (values of *k*) there are no partitions without inconsistencies. The number of plus-sets and partition information follow:

Number of plus-sets (*k*)	1	2	3	4	5	6	7
Criterion function	4	2	2	2	3	4	5
Number of partitions	1	6	12	4	8	5	1

Note that for $2 \leq k \leq 4$ there are adjacent partitions in the sense of Theorem 10.6.

10.6.2   An empirical example

An empirical example illustrating this kind of a structure also comes from New Guinea. Read (1954) provided an extensive discussion of some of the cultures in the Central Highlands of New Guinea. In particular, he discussed a set of political ties and oppositions between the Gahuku–Gama subtribes that are distributed in part of this region. "Similar in their ecology, the groups of populations also reveal a widespread uniformity of culture and structure" (Read 1954:21). He indicated that their relations are seldom peaceable for long. "Warfare ... occurs between

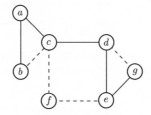

Figure 10.6. A signed network that is not *k*-balanced.

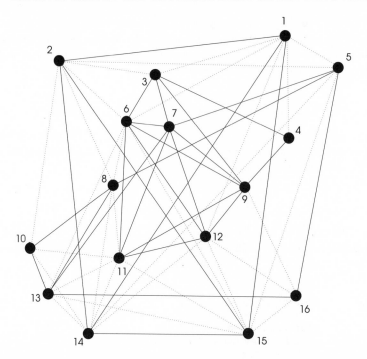

Figure 10.7. The signed alliance structure for subtribes of the Gahuku–Gama.

traditional enemies: it carries on indefinitely and is never concluded" (1954:12). Indeed, in Read's account, "warfare ... is that activity which characterizes the tribes of the Gahuku–Gama as a whole and which differentiates them from groups in other socio-geographic regions" (1954:39). "Local subdivisions are indicated by the names of the principal subtribes" (1954:36), which have "an ascertainable reality to every adult." These subtribes are territorially exclusive and linked through the constraints imposed by geographical space. Frequently, "[t]raditional enemies were separated by only a few miles. Scattered raids and organized, concerted attacks were constantly expected." Moreover, "[t]he aim of each group was not only to kill its enemies but also to destroy their villages, gardens, and livestock, and to deprive them of any means of support, for only thus could they safeguard their own integrity" (1954:22). Starting at any point in geographic space, "the continuum of social ties spreads outwards uniting some groups in a common bond on the one hand and opposing them to a different combination of groups on the other" (1954:38).

These subtribes have an institutionalized form of warfare, termed *Rova*, which "is conceived of as something that continues indefinitely, something that is never lost" (1954:40).[9]

---

9   This is distinguished from *Hina*, a form of fighting that is an "accepted form of redress" that is controlled by rules and is expected to be terminated amicably.

Table 10.5. Partitioned Matrix for the Gahuka–Gama Subtribes

	1	2	14	15	3	4	6	7	9	11	12	5	8	10	13	16
1	.	1	1	1	−1	−1	−1	.	.	.	−1	−1	.	.	.	.
2	1	.	1	1	−1	.	−1	.	.	.	.	−1	−1	−1	.	.
14	1	1	.	1	.	.	.	.	.	−1	−1	−1	−1	−1	−1	.
15	1	1	1	.	.	.	−1	.	.	−1	−1	−1	.	.	−1	−1
3	−1	−1	.	.	.	1	1	1	1	.	.	.	.	.	.	.
4	−1	.	.	.	1	.	.	.	1	.	.	.	.	.	.	.
6	−1	−1	.	−1	1	.	.	1	1	1	1.	−1	.	−1	.	.
7	.	.	.	.	1	.	1	.	1	1	1	1	.	.	1	.
9	.	.	.	.	1	1	1	1	.	1	1	.	.	.	.	−1
11	.	.	−1	−1	.	.	1	1	1	.	1	.	−1	−1	−1	.
12	−1	.	−1	−1	.	.	1	1	1	1	.	.	.	.	.	−1
5	−1	−1	−1	−1	.	.	.	1	.	.	.	.	1	.	.	1
8	.	−1	−1	.	.	.	−1	.	.	−1	.	1	.	1	1	.
10	.	−1	−1	.	.	.	.	.	.	−1	.	.	1	.	1	.
13	.	.	−1	−1	.	.	−1	1	.	−1	.	1	1	.	.	1
16	.	.	.	−1	.	.	.	.	−1	.	−1	1	.	.	1	.

Figure 10.7 displays the pattern of alliances and oppositions described by Read. Of some interest is the fact that these locations are in a broad correspondence with the actual locations of the clans in geographical space. The names of the 16 subtribes are as follows:

1	Gavave	2	Kotuni	3	Ove	4	Alikadzuha
5	Nagamiza	6	Gahuku	7	Masilakidzuha	8	Notohana
9	Ukudzuha	10	Kohika	11	Gehamo	12	Asarodzuha
13	Uheto	14	Nagamidzuha	15	Gama	16	Seu've

If this form of violence is so institutionalized, and if a general pattern of oppositions and alliances is expected to continue indefinitely, it seems that this will be a stable arrangement.[10] The balance theory argument suggests that balanced networks are stable. Consistent with this, the structure of the ties in Figure 10.7 should be balanced or be close to k-balance for some value of k. Read noted that there is an element of expediency in some of the alliances: They are both made and broken. At any point in time, alliance shifts introduce some imbalance to an extant structure. This suggests that the structure of ties will be close to balance rather than be balanced exactly. Table 10.5 shows the partitioned structure of the alliance and enemy ties reported by Read. The partition that is closest to

---

10 We surmise that the near-balanced aarangement, as a whole, is stable. Consistent with Read's account, some ties will change while the macrostructure remains stable.

being a k-balanced one has three clusters (where the value of the criterion function is 2)[11]:

$$\{1, 2, 14, 15\}, \{3, 4, 6, 7, 9, 11, 12\}, \{5, 8, 10, 13, 16\}.$$

For structural balance ($k = 2$), the value of the criterion function is 7. For $k = 3$ there is a unique partition into three plus-sets with a value of the criterion function of only 2. This partition is very close to being a 3-balanced one and is the best-fitting partition. Some features of the partition are noteworthy. *All* of the inconsistencies are associated with the Masilakidzuha subtribe (actor 7 in Table 10.5). Read's account described universal warfare across a culturally homogeneous set of tribes and subtribes. If they are all warlike, then this subtribe is quite remarkable because it has only positive relations with other subtribes. This suggests one of two things. Either this subtribe is very different (and we have identified it) or there are errors in Read's data (and we have located the source of the errors). In either event, the partitioning tool in terms of balance theory is useful. If the former is the case, one post hoc intuition is that because this subtribe is in the geographic center of the Gahuka–Gama region, it has to live in some harmony with all of the subtribes surrounding it.

One of the plus-sets is made up of four subtribes that form two spatially dispersed pairs. The Kotuni and Gavave subtribes are at the top of the network shown in Figure 10.7, whereas the Nagamidzuha and Gama subtribes are at the bottom of the figure. A second plus-set is composed of the Notchana, Kohika, and Uheto subtribes (lower left), the Nagamiza subtribe (top right), and the Seu've subtribe (bottom right). Members of this set of subtribes are also geographically dispersed. In the middle of the network (and the geographic region) are the remaining seven subtribes. They share no negative ties among themselves and are mutually hostile with all of the subtribes on the periphery of the network (and region). The figure clearly shows the three plus-sets and the unusual nature of the Nagamidzuha subtribe.

10.7   ANOTHER LOOK AT THE BANK WIRING ROOM DATA

The BWR data come in the form of multiple relations defined over the 14 actors in the room,[12] and we look at the positive and negative affect ties from the BWR in this section. Schwartz and Sprinzen (1984) examined these ties in terms of blockmodeling and proposed a new methodology for partitioning actors by considering structurally weak ties and using the algebra of relations as an integral part of the partitioning. "Structurally strong ties conform to or are reinforced by the pattern of interaction in the group and . . . structurally weak ties are not reinforced by a pattern of interaction in a group" (1984:107). Given our focus on structural balance in this chapter, we anticipate that structurally weak ties are either positive ties between plus-sets or negative ties within them.

---

11   In this case the criterion function was defined with $\alpha = 0.5$.
12   The data are described in Section 2.1.2.

Schwartz and Sprinzen (1984) identified "two distinct closely-knit groups and a group of outsiders who exchange hostility among themselves and with each of the closely-knit groups." They also demonstrated that the use of CONCOR will not lead to the identification of this structure because of the presence of structurally weak links. Their procedure is rather complex, and it would be nice if a simpler procedure could be used fruitfully. We believe that the partitioning approach to balance does this.

Rather than use the stacked positive and negative relational ties, we appeal directly to structural balance ideas and construct a single matrix of the two ties (positive and negative). If structural balance processes operated within this group, we would expect a partitioned structure consistent with either of the structure theorems. From the account from either Homans (1950) or Schwartz and Sprinzen (1984), the partition will be into more than two plus-sets. For a partition into six plus-sets, we see there is an exact 6-balance structure. The partition is shown in Table 10.6. Using the labeling of the units from Chapter 2, we see that the exact partition is

$$\{I_1, W_1, W_3, W_4, W_7, W_8, W_9, S_1, S_4\}, \{I_3\}, \{W_2\}, \{W_5\}, \{W_6\}, \{S_2\}.$$

All of the negative ties involve the singletons. They are indeed a set of actors exchanging mutual hostility with each other and with many of the other actors. To gain additional insights, we can seek a partition into seven plus-sets. Of course, the value of the criterion function must be more than 0 because, if we do this, we will have a positive tie between plus-sets. When this partition is sought, we get the

Table 10.6. The Exact 6-Balance Partition of the BWR Affect Data

	I_1	W_1	W_3	W_4	W_7	W_8	W_9	S_1	S_3	I_3	W_2	W_5	W_6	S_2
I_1	.	.	1	.	.	.	.	.	.	−1	−1	.	.	.
W_1	.	.	1	1	.	.	.	1	.	.	.	.	.	.
W_3	1	1	.	1	.	.	.	1	.	.	.	.	.	.
W_4	.	1	1	.	.	.	.	1	.	.	.	−1	.	.
W_7	.	.	.	.	.	1	1	1	.	−1	−1	−1	−1	.
W_8	.	.	.	.	1	.	1	.	1	−1	−1	−1	.	.
W_9	.	.	.	.	1	1	.	.	1	−1	−1	−1	.	.
S_1	.	1	1	1	1	.	.	.	.	.	.	−1	.	.
S_3	.	.	.	.	.	1	1	.	.	−1	.	.	.	.
I_3	−1	.	.	.	−1	−1	−1	.	−1	.	.	−1	−1	.
W_2	−1	.	.	.	−1	−1	−1	.	.	.	.	.	.	.
W_5	.	.	.	−1	−1	−1	−1	−1	.	−1	.	.	−1	−1
W_6	.	.	.	.	−1	.	.	.	.	−1	.	−1	.	.
S_2	.	.	.	.	.	.	.	.	.	.	.	−1	.	.

Table 10.7. Partition of the BWR Affect Data into Seven Clusters

	I_1	W_1	W_3	W_4	S_1	I_3	W_2	W_5	W_6	W_7	W_8	W_9	S_3	S_2
I_1	.	.	1	.	.	-1	-1	.	.	.	.	.	.	.
W_1	.	.	1	1	1	.	.	.	.	.	.	.	.	.
W_3	1	1	.	1	1	.	.	.	.	.	.	.	.	.
W_4	.	1	1	.	1	.	.	-1	.	.	.	.	.	.
S_1	.	1	1	1	.	.	.	-1	.	1	.	.	.	.
I_3	-1	.	.	.	.	.	.	-1	-1	-1	-1	-1	-1	.
W_2	-1	.	.	.	.	.	.	.	.	-1	-1	-1	.	.
W_5	.	.	.	-1	-1	-1	.	.	-1	-1	-1	-1	.	-1
W_6	.	.	.	.	.	-1	.	-1	.	-1	.	.	.	.
W_7	.	.	.	.	1	-1	-1	-1	-1	.	1	1	.	.
W_8	.	.	.	.	.	-1	-1	-1	.	1	.	1	1	.
W_9	.	.	.	.	.	-1	-1	-1	.	1	1	.	1	.
S_3	.	.	.	.	.	-1	.	.	.	.	1	1	.	.
S_2	.	.	.	.	.	.	.	-1	.	.	.	.	.	.

results shown in Table 10.7. The clusters are

$$\{I_1, W_1, W_3, W_4, S_1\},\ \{I_3\},\ \{W_2\},\ \{W_5\},\ \{W_6\},\ \{W_7, W_8, W_9, S_4\},\ \{S_2\}.$$

Not only do we get the two closely knit subgroups identified elsewhere with this procedure, but we identify the same structurally weak ties between S_1 and W_7. We note also that if we separate the five actors having all of the negative ties and partition the remaining nine actors by using only their positive ties, we get exactly the same partition.

10.8 BALANCE AND IMBALANCE IN A BALES GROUP

We now consider data reported by Schwartz and Sprinzen (1984), whose original source is Bales (1970). These data were generated in a small group dynamics study. After 13 weeks of interaction, the group participants provided ratings of their relations with the other members of the group on three dimensions: positive affect (liking), negative affect (disliking), and similarity. Schwartz and Sprinzen recoded the ratings on all three dimensions into binary matrices. The two affect matrices are presented in Table 10.8.

For this analysis, we ignore the similarity relation. We use the same argument concerning these data as we did for the BRW affect data. If structural balance is the theoretical concern, it is best viewed not as a conventional blockmodeling problem but as a structural balance partitioning problem. Approached in this way, there

Table 10.8. Two Affect Matrices for the Bales Group

		Like (Positive Affect Ties)
A	0	0	0	0	0	0	0	0	0	0	1	0	0	0	0	1	0	0	0	0
B	0	0	0	0	0	1	0	0	1	0	0	0	0	0	1	0	0	0	1	0
C	1	0	0	0	0	0	1	0	1	1	0	0	0	0	1	0	0	0	0	0
D	0	0	0	0	0	0	0	0	0	0	1	0	0	0	0	0	0	0	0	0
E	0	0	0	0	0	0	1	0	1	0	0	0	1	0	0	0	0	0	0	0
F	0	0	0	0	0	0	0	0	0	0	0	0	0	0	0	0	0	0	0	0
G	1	0	0	0	0	0	0	0	1	1	1	0	0	1	1	0	0	0	0	1
H	0	0	0	0	1	0	1	0	1	1	0	0	0	0	0	0	0	0	0	0
I	1	0	0	0	0	0	0	1	0	0	1	0	0	0	0	0	0	0	1	0
J	0	0	0	0	0	0	0	0	0	0	0	1	0	0	1	0	0	0	0	0
K	0	0	0	0	0	0	0	0	0	1	0	0	0	0	1	0	0	0	0	0
L	0	1	0	0	1	0	0	0	0	0	0	0	0	0	0	1	0	0	0	0
M	0	0	0	0	0	0	0	0	0	0	1	0	0	0	0	0	0	0	0	0
N	0	0	0	0	0	0	1	0	0	0	0	0	0	0	0	0	0	0	0	0
O	1	0	0	0	0	0	0	0	0	1	1	0	0	0	0	0	0	0	0	0
P	0	0	0	0	0	0	0	0	0	1	0	0	0	0	0	0	1	0	1	0
Q	1	0	0	0	0	0	0	0	0	1	0	0	0	0	1	1	0	0	0	0
R	0	0	0	1	0	0	0	0	0	1	0	0	0	0	0	0	0	0	0	1
S	0	0	0	0	0	0	0	0	0	0	0	0	0	0	0	1	0	0	0	0
T	0	0	0	0	0	0	0	0	0	1	0	0	0	0	0	0	0	1	0	0
		Dislike (Negative Affect Ties)
A	0	0	0	0	0	1	0	0	0	0	0	0	0	0	0	0	0	1	0	0
B	0	0	0	0	0	0	0	0	0	0	0	0	0	0	0	0	0	0	0	0
C	0	0	0	0	0	0	0	0	0	0	0	0	0	0	0	1	0	1	0	0
D	0	0	0	0	0	1	0	1	0	0	0	0	0	0	1	0	0	0	0	0
E	0	0	0	0	0	0	0	0	0	0	0	0	0	0	0	0	0	0	0	0
F	0	0	0	0	0	0	0	0	0	0	0	0	0	0	0	0	0	0	0	0
G	0	0	0	0	0	0	0	0	0	0	0	0	0	0	0	0	0	1	0	0
H	1	0	0	0	0	1	0	0	0	0	0	0	0	0	0	1	0	1	0	0
I	0	0	0	0	0	0	0	0	0	0	0	0	0	0	0	0	1	1	0	0
J	0	1	0	0	0	0	0	0	0	0	0	0	0	0	0	0	0	0	0	0
K	0	0	0	0	0	0	0	0	0	0	0	0	0	0	0	0	1	0	0	0
L	0	0	0	0	0	0	0	0	0	0	0	0	0	0	0	0	0	0	0	0
M	0	0	1	0	0	1	1	0	0	0	0	0	0	0	0	0	0	1	0	0
N	0	0	0	0	0	1	0	0	0	0	0	0	0	0	0	0	0	1	0	0
O	0	0	0	0	0	0	0	0	0	0	0	0	0	0	0	0	0	0	0	0
P	0	0	0	0	0	0	0	0	0	0	0	0	0	0	0	0	0	1	0	0
Q	0	1	0	0	0	0	0	0	0	0	0	1	1	0	0	0	0	0	0	0
R	0	0	0	0	0	0	0	0	0	0	1	0	0	0	0	0	0	0	0	0
S	0	0	0	0	0	0	0	0	0	0	0	0	1	0	0	0	0	0	0	0
T	0	0	0	0	0	0	0	0	0	0	0	0	1	0	0	0	0	0	0	0

Table 10.9. Unique Partition of the Bales Group for Balance Theory ($k = 2$)

	A	B	C	E	G	H	I	J	K	L	N	O	P	Q	S	T	D	F	M	R
A	.	.	1	.	1	−1	1	.	1	1	.	1	1	1	.	.	.	−1	.	−1
B	.	.	1	.	1	.	1	−1	.	1	.	1	1	−1	1	.	.	.	.	.
C	1	.	.	.	1	.	1	1	.	1	.	1	−1	.	1	.	.	−1	.	1
E	−1	.	1	1	1	.	1	1	1	1	1	1	1	.	.	1	.	1	−1	−1
G	−1	.	1	1	.	.	1	1	1	.	.	1	1	1	1	.	.	−1	−1	1
H	−1	.	.	.	.	.	1	.	.	.	.	.	.	.	.	.	−1	−1	−1	−1
I	.	−1	1	1	1	.	.	1	1	1	1	1	1	.	.	.	1	.	.	1
J	.	−1	1	1	1	.	1	.	1	.	.	1	1	.	1	.	1	.	1	1
K	1	1	1	.	1	.	1	1	.	1	.	1	1	.	.	.	.	.	.	−1
L	1	1	1	.	1	.	1	1	1	.	.	1	1	1	.	.	.	.	.	.
N	.	1	.	.	.	.	1	1	.	.	.	1	.	.	.	.	.	−1	−1	.
O	1	1	.	.	1	.	1	1	1	1	.	.	.	−1	.	.	−1	.	.	.
P	1	−1	−1	.	1	−1	1	1	.	.	.	.	.	1	.	.	.	1	.	1
Q	1	.	.	.	.	.	−1	1	.	−1	.	1	1	.	.	.	1	.	1	.
S	1	1	.	.	.	.	1	1	.	.	.	1	1	.	.	.	.	.	−1	1
T	.	.	.	1	1	.	1	.	.	.	.	.	.	.	.	.	.	.	.	1
D	−1	.	.	.	.	−1	1	1	.	.	−1	−1	.	.	.	−1	.	−1	.	1
F	−1	1	−1	1	−1	−1	.	.	.	.	1	.	.	−1	−1	−1	−1	.	−1	.
M	.	.	−1	.	−1	−1	1	1	1	.	−1	.	.	.	.	.	.	−1	.	−1
R	−1	.	1	.	1	−1	−1	1	−1	.	−1	.	−1	−1	.	−1	−1	−1	−1	.

is a unique partition into two plus-sets for the original formulation of structural balance with 16 inconsistencies. The unique partition with two plus-sets is shown in Table 10.9. The two clusters are these:

$$\{A, B, C, E, G, H, I, J, K, L, N, O, P, Q, S, T\}, \{D, F, M, R\}.$$

When the value of k is above 2, the unique partition (for $k = 4$) shown in Table 10.10 results. The smaller plus-set for the balance theory partition has been broken up into two singletons and a dyad as a result of the presence of negative affect ties among them. This structure is very similar to the structure of the BWR data in the previous section with one large subgroup and a smaller set of actors that singly or in pairs are the target of negative affect ties.

Schwartz and Sprinzen (1984) reported the results of a structural equivalence analysis using CONCOR. The four-cluster partition is

$$\{A, J, K, O, Q, T\}, \{F, P, R, S\}, \{B, D, M\}, \{C, E, G, H, I, L, N\},$$

whereas the two-cluster partition is an aggregation of these clusters:

$$\{A, F, J, K, O, P, Q, R, S, T\}, \{B, C, D, E, G, H, I, L, M, N\}.$$

These partitions seem much less in accord with structural balance ideas. For structural balance ($k = 2$), the optimal partition reported in Table 10.9, the value of the criterion function is 8.5 (with 17 ties inconsistent with structural balance and $\alpha = 0.5$). For the Schwartz and Sprinzen partition, the value of the criterion function is 14 (i.e., there are 28 ties inconsistent with structural balance and $\alpha = 0.5$). For $k = 4$, there is again a difference between the two partitions. For the structural equivalence partition, the value of the criterion function is 15.5 (with 31 ties inconsistent with 4-balance and $\alpha = 0.5$), whereas the partition of Table 10.10 has a criterion function value of 7 (with only 14 ties inconsistent with 4-balance and $\alpha = 0.5$). Further, we note that if we search for a partition directly with three clusters using the generalized partitioning approach, we get four partitions, each with 14 inconsistencies. The partitions are similar to the four-cluster partition reported above. From the perspective of structural balance, the basic problem with the Schwartz and Sprinzen partitions is that they do not fit well with the structural balance concepts. This argument concerns structural equivalence as a concept and not the particular algorithm used. When we stack the two separate affect matrices and partition the group members into three clusters by using the direct local optimization algorithm with the structural equivalence criterion function (as described in Chapter 6), we fare even less well. We get four partitions with the same value of the criterion function. When these partitions are imposed on the joint affect matrix, the inconsistencies are 20.5, 22.5, 23, and 24. These inconsistencies are well above even the count of inconsistencies for the Schwartz and Sprinzen partition. In short, structural equivalence partitions into two and four clusters using the methods of Chapter 6 fare badly.

The basic point we want to make, using this example, is that *structural equivalence is not appropriate for data of this type*. For affect signed data, it is more

Table 10.10. General Partition of the Bales Group into Four Plus-Sets

	A	B	C	E	G	H	I	J	K	L	N	O	P	Q	S	T	D	R	F	M
A	·	·	1	·	−1	−1	−1	·	1	1	·	1	1	1	1	·	·	−1	−1	·
B	·	·	·	·	1	−1	−1	−1	1	1	·	1	−1	−1	1	·	·	·	1	−1
C	1	·	·	·	1	1	1	·	·	1	1	1	·	·	·	·	·	1	·	−1
E	−1	·	1	·	1	1	1	1	·	1	·	1	−1	·	·	1	·	·	·	·
G	−1	1	1	1	·	1	1	1	1	1	1	1	−1	−1	·	1	·	1	·	−1
H	−1	·	−1	1	1	·	·	1	·	1	1	1	·	1	·	·	−1	−1	−1	·
I	·	1	·	1	1	·	·	1	·	·	1	1	1	·	1	1	·	−1	·	1
J	1	1	1	·	1	1	1	·	1	1	1	·	1	−1	1	·	1	1	·	·
K	·	1	·	1	·	1	·	·	·	1	·	1	1	1	·	·	1	−1	·	1
L	·	1	−1	·	1	·	·	1	·	·	1	·	·	·	1	·	·	·	−1	·
N	·	·	1	1	1	·	·	·	1	1	·	1	·	1	·	1	−1	·	·	1
O	·	·	·	·	1	·	·	·	1	·	1	·	1	1	·	·	·	·	·	−1
P	−1	−1	−1	·	1	−1	−1	−1	1	−1	·	1	1	1	1	·	−1	1	·	−1
Q	1	−1	·	·	·	·	·	1	·	1	·	·	1	·	·	·	−1	1	−1	−1
S	1	1	·	·	1	·	·	·	·	·	·	·	·	·	·	·	·	·	−1	−1
T	·	·	·	·	1	·	1	1	1	·	1	1	·	·	·	·	1	1	·	−1
D	·	·	−1	·	·	−1	·	1	1	·	−1	1	1	·	·	1	·	1	·	·
R	−1	−1	−1	·	1	−1	−1	1	−1	·	−1	·	−1	·	·	1	1	·	·	−1
F	−1	1	·	1	·	−1	·	·	·	−1	−1	·	·	·	·	·	−1	·	·	−1
M	·	−1	−1	1	−1	·	1	1	1	·	·	−1	−1	−1	−1	−1	·	−1	−1	·

appropriate to use a partitioning procedure that is constructed directly on the relevant theory. In this case, it is structural balance theory. Additionally, for data of this sort, stacking separate positive and negative affect matrices is not a fruitful step in analyzing signed affect relations. For partitioning a network, it is necessary to select the partitioning tool with care. In general, this is an issue concerning substance and not technique.

10.9 THROUGH-TIME BALANCE PROCESSES

The anthropological examples of Sections 10.5.1 and 10.6.2 share some common characteristics. The signed networks are defined for institutional units and are stable. One was defined for clans and clan segments, whereas the other was defined for subtribes. At an institutional level, it seems reasonable that there is greater stability of social relations simply because they are institutionalized. Human societies do not institutionalize transitory phenomena. There may be some minor local shifts, but they do not change the overall partitioned structure of the network. It follows that it is reasonable to analyze these ties as *the network* – one that has evolved over a long period of time and is stable.

If the structural balance hypothesis is correct, then balancing processes occur through time such that the structures that they generate move toward balance through time. Ties (positive, negative, or null) can remain stable or change depending on the forces acting on them. In terms of change, positive ties can change to either null or negative, but the latter type of change is less likely in the short term; negative ties can change to become null or positive, but the extreme shift is again less likely; and null ties can change to be either positive or negative. Doreian et al. (1996), using some of the NF (Newcomb 1961) data, found that the proportion of stable dyadic ties increased through time until a maximum was reached in the 12th week (of a 15-week observation period). What was more important was that there was movement toward k-balance throughout the study period.

If the substantive balance theory hypothesis is correct, the two structure theorems imply movement toward certain partitioned forms: a set of plus-sets having only positive lines within them with only negative ties between them. With imbalance, there are ties that are inconsistent with an ideal structure implied by the structures theorem. Consistent with our clustering approach, we view them as inconsistencies.[13] Most often, prior to an analysis, we know neither the plus-sets nor the number of inconsistencies in the signed network. These are established during the analysis by varying the number of plus-sets and selecting those partitions with the minimum number of inconsistencies.

However, if we consider the initial focus of structural balance, it is clear that, although there are tendencies toward balance, there is no reason to expect that a network of human actors, selected at an arbitrary point of time, will be balanced

---

13 Substantively, it may be more useful to view them as departures from balance and see these ties as subject to the forces moving signed structures toward balance.

Table 10.11. Measures of Imbalance
through Time for Various Partitions
$(\alpha = 0.5)$

k	T_2	T_3	T_4
1	48.5	48.0	47.0
2	21.5	16.0	12.5
3	17.5	11.0	10.5
4	19.0	13.5	12.5
5	20.5	16.0	15.0

and stable. It is not sensible to look for the group structure without knowing where the network is located in its through-time trajectory. Doreian et al. (1996) showed that the structure of ties in the classic NF (Newcomb 1961) data does move toward k-balance through a 15-week period. We consider this example later, but for now we observe that at any point in time such movement would be missed if "the" network was defined only for one point in time. The statement of the fundamental structural balance hypothesis compels us to examine the structure of signed ties through time. This seems a much harder task.

10.9.1   The Sampson data

The affect data from Sampson (1968)[14] provide a useful source for examining structural balance through time. (See Doreian and Mrvar 1996 for a more complete description and use of these data.) Sampson described a polarization process for a group of postulants and novices of the New England monastery, one that operated through time. Sampson described the partition of the trainee monks into three subgroups. One group was the Young Turks, made up of Gregory, John Bosco, Mark, Winfrid, Hugh, Boniface, and Albert. A second subgroup was the Loyal Opposition and was composed of Peter, Bonaventure, Berthold, Victor, Ambrose, Romuald, Louis, and Amand. These groups were opposed to each other on a variety of fundamental issues. The remaining three individuals – Basil, Simplicius, and Elias – were the Outcasts. This partition is exactly the one reported by Breiger et al. (1975) with standard blockmodeling procedures. We consider the partitions reported by Doreian and Mrvar (1996) that were established with the partitioning methods described in Sections 10.3 and 10.4.

Sampson reported data for these actors for three periods in time. Each actor was asked to name the three other actors he liked the most and the three he disliked the most. The ties {3, 2, 1} are the labels for the positive ties and {−3, −2, −1} denote the negative ties. Table 10.11 reports the values of the criterion function for

---

14 The SM data are described in Section 2.1.1.

Table 10.12. Partition of Sampson Monks at T_2, T_3, and T_4

		1	2	7	12	14	15	16	3	13	17	18	4	5	6	8	9	10	11
									T_2										
John Bosco	1	.	.	-1	.	1	.	.	2	.	.	.	.	3	-2	.	.	-3	.
Gregory	2	3	.	2	.	1	.	.	.	-3	-2	.	.	.	.	.	.	-1	.
Mark	7	.	2	.	.	.	.	3	.	.	.	.	-3	-1	-2	1	.	.	.
Winfrid	12	3	2	.	.	1	.	.	-1	.	.	.	-3	.	.	.	.	.	-2
Hugh	14	3	.	.	2	.	2	.	.	-3	-1	.	.	.	.	-2	.	.	1
Boniface	15	3	2	.	.	1	.	.	-2	-3	-1	-1	.	.	.	.	.	.	.
Albert	16	1	2	3	.	.	.	.	.	-1	-3	-2	.	.	.	.	.	.	.
Basil	3	2	3	.	.	.	.	.	.	.	1	.	-1	.	.	-3	-2	.	.
Amand	13	.	-3	1	-1	.	.	.	.	.	.	3	.	2	-2	.	.	.	.
Elias	17	.	.	.	.	.	.	.	3	2	.	1	-3	-2	.	.	.	.	-1
Simplicius	18	2	3	1	.	.	.	-1	.	.	.	.	-3	.	-2	.	.	.	.
Peter	4	.	.	-3	.	.	.	.	-2	.	.	-1	.	3	1	.	.	2	.
Bonaventure	5	.	.	.	.	.	.	.	.	1	.	.	3	.	.	.	.	.	2
Berthold	6	1	.	-3	-2	.	.	.	.	.	.	.	3	.	.	-1	2	.	.
Victor	8	3	2	.	.	-2	.	.	-3	.	-1	.	.	.	.	.	1	.	.
Ambrose	9	.	.	.	.	.	.	1	-3	.	-2	-1	.	2	.	3	.	.	.
Romuald	10	.	.	.	.	2	.	.	.	.	.	.	3	.	.	1	.	.	.
Louis	11	.	.	.	.	2	.	.	-1	-3	-2	.	.	3	.	1	.	.	.
									T_3										
		1	2	7	12	14	15	16	3	13	17	18	4	5	6	8	9	10	11
John Bosco	1	.	2	.	.	.	.	.	.	.	.	.	-2	1	.	3	.	-3	-1
Gregory	2	3	.	1	2	.	1	.	.	-1	.	.	-3	.	.	-2	.	.	.
Mark	7	1	2	.	.	.	.	3	.	.	.	.	-3	.	-2	-1	.	.	.
Winfrid	12	3	1	.	.	2	.	.	-3	.	-1	.	.	.	.	-2	.	.	.
Hugh	14	3	1	.	1	.	2	.	.	.	-1	.	-3	.	.	.	.	-2	.
Boniface	15	2	3	.	.	1	.	.	-2	-3	-1	.	.	1	.	.	.	-1	.
Albert	16	.	2	3	1	.	.	.	-1	.	-2	.	-3	.	.	.	.	.	.
Basil	3	3	-1	.	.	.	.	.	.	.	1	2	.	.	-2	-3	.	.	.
Amand	13	.	-3	1	-1	.	.	.	.	.	.	3	.	2	-2	.	.	.	.
Elias	17	.	1	.	.	.	.	.	2	.	.	3	-2	.	-1	.	.	.	-3
Simplicius	18	.	1	.	.	.	.	.	.	.	2	3	-3	.	-2	.	.	.	-1
Peter	4	-2	-3	.	.	.	.	.	.	.	.	.	.	3	2	.	.	.	1
Bonaventure	5	2	.	.	.	.	.	.	.	.	.	.	3	.	.	.	.	.	1
Berthold	6	1	.	.	-2	.	.	.	-3	.	.	.	3	.	.	-1	2	.	.
Victor	8	-2	-3	.	.	.	.	.	-1	.	.	.	3	.	1	.	.	2	.
Ambrose	9	.	.	.	2	.	.	.	-3	.	-2	-1	.	1	.	3	.	.	.
Romuald	10	.	.	.	.	.	.	.	.	2	.	.	3	1	.	.	.	.	.
Louis	11	-1	-3	.	.	.	.	1	-2	.	.	.	2	3	.	.	.	.	.
									T_4										
		1	2	7	12	14	15	16	3	13	17	18	4	5	6	8	9	10	11
John Bosco	1	.	-2	-3	1	2	.	.	3	.	.	.	.	.	.	.	.	-1	.
Gregory	2	3	.	1	2	.	.	.	.	-1	.	.	-3	.	.	-2	.	.	.
Mark	7	.	3	.	1	.	.	2	.	.	.	.	-3	.	-2	-1	.	.	.
Winfrid	12	3	2	1	.	.	.	.	.	.	.	.	.	.	.	.	.	.	.
Hugh	14	3	.	.	1	.	2	.	.	.	-1	.	-3	.	.	-2	.	.	.
Boniface	15	.	3	1	2	.	.	.	-2	-3	.	.	-1	.	.	.	.	.	.
Albert	16	.	3	2	.	.	1	.	-1	.	-2	.	-3	.	.	.	.	.	.

(continued)

Table 10.12 (*continued*)

		1	2	7	12	14	15	16	3	13	17	18	4	5	6	8	9	10	11
											T_4								
Basil	3	3	−2	.	.	.	.	−1	.	2	1	2	−3	.	−2	.	.	.	.
Amand	13	.	−3	1	−1	.	.	.	.	.	.	3	.	2	−2	.	.	.	.
Elias	17	.	1	.	.	.	.	.	2	.	.	3	−1	.	−3	−2	.	.	.
Simplicius	18	.	1	.	.	.	.	.	2	.	3	.	−1	.	.	−3	.	−2	.
Peter	4	−2	−3	.	.	−1	.	.	.	.	.	.	.	3	1	.	.	.	2
Bonaventure	5	.	.	.	.	.	.	.	.	.	.	.	3	.	.	.	1	.	2
Berthold	6	.	−1	−2	.	.	.	.	−3	.	−2	.	3	1	.	.	2	.	.
Victor	8	.	−3	.	.	−1	.	.	−2	.	.	.	3	.	2	.	1	.	.
Ambrose	9	.	.	.	2	.	.	.	−3	.	−2	−1	.	1	.	3	.	.	.
Romuald	10	.	.	.	.	.	.	.	.	2	.	.	3	1	.	.	1	.	.
Louis	11	−1	−3	.	.	.	1	.	−2	.	.	.	.	2	.	3	.	.	.

partitions having one to five clusters. Partitions consistent with structural balance (into two plus-sets) show a consistent drop through time of the criterion function. The same is true for generalized balance ($k > 2$). The lowest values of the criterion function are those for a partition into three plus-sets. Table 10.11 shows strong support for the fundamental structural balance hypothesis. This group evolved through time toward a balanced form.

Table 10.11 shows the best partitions into three plus-sets and the ties for T_2, T_3, and T_4. The clusters are exactly those identified at T_2. The partition reported here is close to the partition reported by Sampson. The one departure from his characterization is the inclusion of Amand among the Outcasts rather than with the Loyal Opposition. Doreian and Mrvar (1996) argued that there are grounds for preferring this partition. At an election, Amand nominated Basil, one of the Outcasts, as a candidate and voted for him. Also note the positive tie, at all three time points, from Amand to Simplicius, another Outcast member. Additionally, Amand receives a positive tie from Elias (the third member of the Outcasts identified by Sampson) at T_2, one from Simplicius at T_3, and one from Basil at T_4. Amand sends a positive tie to Mark (one of the Young Turks) and one to Bonaventure (a member of the Loyal Opposition) at all time points. Although he sent two negative ties to members of the Young Turks, he also sent one to a member of the Loyal Opposition. This pattern of ties is not consistent with the idea of Amand's belonging to the Loyal Opposition, and it seems reasonable to see him as a member of the Outcasts. We note that two of the analyses of White et al. (1976), as listed in Chapter 2, have Amand grouped with the Outcasts.

10.9.2   The Newcomb data

The substantive balance theory hypothesis claims that signed networks move toward balance through time. From Table 10.11 it is clear that the SM data do move toward balance regardless of the value k. However, three time points may be too few for a resounding declaration of support for the balance theory hypothesis.[15]

Doreian et al. (1996) used the NF (Newcomb 1961) data to examine k balance through 15 time periods.[16] They reported through-time trajectories for the measure of imbalance for the structural balance ($k = 2$) and for the more general case of k-balance for $k > 2$. Overall, the trajectories declined through time. This was seen most clearly when $k > 2$ and the trajectories were smoothed.[17] This trajectory was consistent with structural balance ideas.

As was the case with blockmodeling in Chapter 6, there may be more than one partition with the same value of the criterion function. At the beginning of the study period, there were two partitions into three clusters with an imbalance measure of 8.5:

$$\{A, F, H, M\}, \{B, D, G, J, N, P\}, \{C, E, I, K, L, O, Q\},$$
$$\{A, F, H, M\}, \{B, D, G, N, P\}, \{C, E, I, J, K, L, O, Q\}.$$

These partitions have three subgroups and differ only in the location of J, and they are shown in Table 10.13.

At time T_7, the partition structure of the Newcomb actors has changed to one in which there is a large subgroup with all but four of the actors. The remaining two subgroups are dyads whose members receive most of the negative ties. This partition is shown in the top panel of Table 10.14. At the last time point, the partition is the same but the measure of imbalance has declined (to 6.0). Between T_7 and T_{15} the partition structure changes slightly but the essential structure is the same – a large subgroup with the four so-called disliked actors appearing either as dyads or singletons. In essence this is the same outcome as reported by Doreian et al. (1996).

Some caution is needed in interpreting the results of Doreian et al. (1996). Subsequently, Doreian and Krackhardt (2001) presented an additional reanalysis of these data by taking triples $\{p, o, q\}$ and examining the extent to which the pretransitive conditions given by the signs of $p \to o$ and $o \to q$ were completed in ways that were consistent with balance theory in terms of the sign of $p \to q$. They examined the through-time counts of each of the triples of Figure 10.1. A simple interpretation of structural balance theory and the expectation that imbalance declines through time is that the frequency of balanced triples would increase and the frequency of the imbalanced triples would decrease. Labeling the triples of Figure 10.1 by using the signs (p or n) of the ties in the triples where the first tie is $p \to o$, the second tie is $o \to q$, and the third tie is $p \to q$, they found that the balanced ppp and pnn triples did behave according to balance theory by becoming more frequent. They also found that the imbalanced ppn and pnp

---

15 In addition, the data were collected retrospectively.
16 The NF data are reported as ranks with each actor ranking the other 16 actors. Doreian et al. (1996) recoded the top four ranks as $+1$, the last three as 1, and all of the middle ranks as 0.
17 The smoothing was done by using the lowest methods proposed by Cleveland (1985).

Table 10.13. Two Partitions into Three Clusters of the Newcomb Actors at T_1

		First Partition at T_1															
	A	F	H	M	B	D	G	J	N	P	C	E	I	K	L	O	Q
A	.	.	.	1	.	.	.	−1	.	.	.	.	−1	1	.	.	1
F	.	.	1	1	.	1	.	−1	.	.	.	−1	.	.	.	.	.
H	.	1	.	.	.	.	.	1	−1	.	−1	.	.	1	.	.	.
M	1	1	.	.	−1	.	.	.	.	.	−1	.	.	.	.	1	.
B	.	.	.	.	.	1	1	.	.	1	−1	.	.	−1	.	.	.
D	.	.	−1	.	1	.	1	.	.	.	−1	.	.	.	.	.	1
G	−1	.	.	.	.	1	.	.	.	.	.	−1	.	.	1	.	1
J	1	.	.	.	−1	.	1	.	.	.	.	.	.	−1	.	1	.
N	.	.	−1	−1	.	.	1	1	.	.	.	.	1	.	.	.	.
P	.	−1	.	.	.	1	.	.	.	.	−1	.	1	1	.	.	.
C	.	.	−1	−1	.	.	.	.	.	.	.	.	.	1	1	.	1
E	.	−1	.	.	.	.	.	.	−1	.	.	.	.	1	1	.	1
I	.	.	−1	.	−1	.	.	.	.	.	.	.	.	1	1	.	1
K	.	.	−1	.	.	.	.	.	−1	.	.	.	1	.	1	.	1
L	−1	.	.	−1	.	.	.	.	.	.	1	.	.	1	.	.	1
O	−1	.	.	.	.	.	.	1	−1	.	.	1	.	1	.	.	.
Q	.	.	.	.	−1	1	.	.	−1	.	.	.	1	.	1	.	.

		Second Partition at T_1															
	A	F	H	M	B	D	G	N	P	C	E	I	J	K	L	O	Q
A	.	.	.	1	.	.	.	.	.	.	.	−1	−1	1	.	.	1
F	.	.	1	1	.	1	.	.	.	.	−1	.	−1	.	.	.	.
H	.	1	.	.	.	.	.	−1	.	−1	.	.	1	1	.	.	.
M	1	1	.	.	−1	.	.	.	.	−1	.	.	.	.	.	1	.
B	.	.	.	.	.	1	1	.	1	−1	.	.	.	−1	.	.	.
D	.	.	−1	.	1	.	1	.	.	−1	.	.	.	.	.	.	1
G	−1	.	.	.	.	1	.	.	.	.	−1	.	.	.	1	.	1
N	.	.	−1	−1	.	.	1	.	.	.	.	1	1	.	.	.	.
P	.	−1	.	.	.	1	.	.	.	−1	.	1	.	1	.	.	.
C	.	.	−1	−1	.	.	.	.	.	.	.	.	.	1	1	.	1
E	.	−1	.	.	.	.	.	−1	.	.	.	.	.	1	1	.	1
I	.	.	−1	.	−1	.	.	.	.	.	.	.	.	1	1	.	1
J	1	.	.	.	−1	.	1	.	.	.	.	.	.	−1	.	1	.
K	.	.	−1	.	.	.	.	−1	.	.	.	1	.	.	1	.	1
L	−1	.	.	−1	.	.	.	.	.	1	.	.	.	1	.	.	1
O	−1	.	.	.	.	.	.	−1	.	.	1	.	1	1	.	.	.
Q	.	.	.	.	−1	1	.	−1	.	.	.	1	.	.	1	.	.

Table 10.14. *Partitions of the Newcomb Actors at T_7 and T_{15}*

Partition at T_7

	A	B	D	E	F	G	H	I	K	L	M	N	Q	C	J	O	P
A	.	.	.	.	.	.	.	.	.	.	1	1	1	−1	−1	.	.
B	1	.	1	.	.	.	.	.	.	1	.	.	.	.	−1	−1	.
D	.	1	.	.	.	.	.	1	.	.	.	.	1	−1	.	−1	.
E	.	.	.	.	.	.	.	1	.	.	1	.	1	−1	−1	.	.
F	1	.	.	.	.	.	1	1	.	.	.	.	.	.	−1	.	−1
G	.	.	1	.	.	.	1	.	.	1	.	.	.	.	−1	.	−1
H	.	.	1	.	1	.	.	.	.	.	.	1	.	−1	.	.	−1
I	.	.	.	1	1	.	.	.	.	.	.	.	1	−1	−1	.	.
K	.	.	.	.	.	.	.	1	.	1	.	.	1	.	−1	.	−1
L	.	1	.	−1	−1	1	.	1	.	.	.	.	.	.	.	.	.
M	1	.	.	.	1	.	1	.	.	.	.	.	.	.	−1	.	−1
N	1	.	.	.	.	.	1	.	1	.	.	.	.	.	−1	−1	.
Q	.	.	1	1	.	.	.	1	.	.	.	−1	.	.	−1	.	.
C	.	.	.	.	.	1	.	.	.	1	.	.	1	.	.	−1	−1
J	.	.	.	.	.	1	.	.	.	1	−1	.	1	.	.	.	−1
O	.	.	.	.	.	.	.	1	.	1	.	.	.	−1	−1	.	1
P	−1	.	1	.	.	.	.	.	.	1	−1	.	1	.	.	.	.

Partition at T_{15}

	A	B	D	E	F	G	H	I	K	L	M	N	Q	C	J	O	P
A	.	.	.	.	.	.	.	.	.	.	1	1	1	−1	−1	.	.
B	.	.	1	1	.	.	.	.	.	.	.	.	1	.	−1	.	−1
D	.	.	.	1	1	.	.	.	.	.	.	.	1	−1	−1	.	.
E	.	.	1	.	.	.	.	1	.	.	1	.	.	.	.	−1	−1
F	.	.	1	.	.	.	1	1	.	.	.	.	.	.	−1	.	−1
G	.	.	.	.	.	.	.	.	1	1	.	.	1	.	−1	.	−1
H	1	.	1	.	.	.	.	.	.	.	1	.	.	−1	.	.	−1
I	.	.	1	.	1	.	.	.	.	.	.	.	1	.	−1	.	−1
K	.	1	.	.	.	.	.	.	.	1	.	.	1	.	−1	.	−1
L	.	1	.	.	.	1	.	1	.	.	.	.	.	.	−1	−1	.
M	1	.	.	.	.	1	1	.	.	.	.	.	.	.	−1	.	−1
N	.	.	.	−1	1	.	.	1	1	.	.	.	.	−1	.	.	.
Q	.	1	1	.	.	.	.	1	.	.	.	.	.	.	−1	.	−1
C	.	.	.	.	1	.	.	.	.	1	.	−1	1	.	.	.	−1
J	1	.	.	.	.	1	.	.	.	1	−1	.	.	.	.	.	−1
O	.	.	1	−1	.	.	.	.	−1	.	.	.	1	.	.	.	1
P	.	.	1	.	.	.	−1	1	.	1	.	.	.	−1	.	.	.

triples did become less frequent. All of this supports balance theory. However, they also found that the balanced *npn* and *nnp* triples became less frequent, thereby contradicting the expectation based on structural balance theory. Making matters worse, the imbalanced *npp* triple became more frequent. In addition, the *nnn* triple also became more frequent. The latter can be interpreted in two ways: In terms of $(k = 2)$-balance, this is more contradictory evidence regarding balance, but in terms of $(k > 2)$-balance, this trajectory provides some additional support.

In expressing their results, Doreian and Krackhardt (2001) concluded that *the implicit single mechanism of balance theory is better replaced by a set of multiple mechanisms* and that not all of the balance theoretic hypotheses regarding them will receive empirical support. Characterizing the trajectories that increase or decrease can be done in two ways. First, the trajectories not increasing in frequency all have the first tie in the triple, $p \rightarrow o$, with a negative sign. Balance theory might not work if that first tie were negative – a result anticipated by Newcomb (1968). Second, the triples increasing in frequency all have the second two ties with the same sign. What is seen as a decrease in imbalance may be a function of differential popularity and unpopularity. Complicating matters further is that structures and types of actors coevolve. In the NF data, actor J did not start out by being disliked. However, at the end of Newcomb's study, this actor was universally disliked. Between them, actors C, J, O, and P receive a huge number of negative ties. As the structure evolved through the structures shown in Table 10.13 and Table 10.14, actors like J became disliked whereas actors like Q remained liked and actors like D became more liked. Looking at the details of the tie changes, Doreian (2002) saw that there were many changes in the ties that did not alter the measures of imbalance. Not all of the change that occurs in signed networks is driven by structural balance forces.

10.10   BLOCKMODELING AND SIGNED NETWORKS

Throughout this chapter we have presented ways in which signed networks can be partitioned by the use of blockmodeling methods in ways that are consistent with, and attuned to, the basic substantive ideas of balance theory. Two types of blocks were defined and a blockmodel was specified. Positive blocks have only positive or null ties and are expected to be diagonal blocks in a blockmodel. Negative blocks have negative or null ties and are expected to be off-diagonal blocks. With the efficient algorithm proposed by Doreian and Mrvar (1996), obtaining blockmodels of signed networks that minimize the number of inconsistencies with balance can be located in a straightforward fashion. Applying these blockmodels in a through-time context is also consistent with the underlying intuitions that human signed networks tend toward balance through time. Although this becomes rather complicated in the details, the relevant point here is that partitioning signed networks by blockmodeling methods is a straightforward task. It also permits the pursuit of interesting substantive phenomena in a theoretically informed fashion.

We note that, thus far, most of the partitioning efforts for signed networks have taken an inductive form. It may make sense to think of a deductive approach through prespecification for signed networks. However, we suspect that the role of prespecification may be less general for signed networks than for unsigned networks. As formulated, the specification of a blockmodel type is complete in the sense that all blocks are specified as positive or negative and their locations are known. However, the analysis of the SM data suggests that it is possible to take the partition of the actors at T_2 as a prespecified blockmodel for subsequent time points. In such an analysis, the prespecification would be limited to specifying the number of clusters and which actors belonged to which clusters. A weaker form of prespecification could involve just the number of clusters. For the NF data, a plausible (early) prespecification would specify three subgroups for subsequent time points. It would be validated up to the point in time when the group was restructured into one large group of actors and the singletons and dyads that were the object of most of the negative ties. As noted, null blocks can occur. Moreover, they can occur on the main diagonal or off it. The simulations of Hummon and Doreian (2003) suggest that there may be some opportunities for specifying null blocks for larger systems of actors.

11

SYMMETRIC–ACYCLIC BLOCKMODELS

Here we introduce a new type of permitted diagonal block and a new type of block-model, respectively labeled the symmetric block and the acyclic blockmodel. The idea behind these two objects comes from a consideration of the idea of a ranked-clusters model from Davis and Leinhardt (1972), which we discussed in Chapter 1. We examine the form of these models and approach them with the perspective of specified blockmodeling. As a consequence, we do not consider the distribution of triads. Instead of considering permitted and forbidden triads, we focus on allowed and not allowed blocks. Operationally, this focuses on allowed and not allowed ties within blocks according to the type of block. The symmetric–acyclic blockmodel was introduced informally in Chapter 1 (Section 1.4.3). We note that the symmetric–acyclic blockmodel and the symmetric–acyclic decomposition are used in conjunction with each other. They share the same conceptual foundations but differ in the formal details of their execution for a given network.

11.1 BLOCKS FOR DIRECTED GRAPHS AND ACYCLIC GRAPHS

The networks considered here have directed ties so that the appropriate tools for representing these structures are directed graphs.

The model shown in Figure 1.4 is an example of an acyclic directed graph, and the ideal ranked-clusters model is acyclic. The distinction between mutual and asymmetric ties is critical, for these ties are distributed in a systematic fashion. Actors within subgroups are linked only by mutual ties, whereas asymmetric ties are directed only up. Thus, asymmetric ties within levels and down levels, as well as mutual ties between levels, are excluded. It is useful to distinguish the two important properties, and hence inconsistencies, for the ranked-clusters model. Asymmetric ties within clusters violate the *symmetry requirement*, whereas the ties down between the ranked clusters violate the *acyclic requirement*.

11.2 TWO CONSTRUCTED EXAMPLES

Consider the blocked structure (permuted relational matrix) shown in Table 1.9 that was constructed to be consistent with the acyclic structure shown in Figure 1.4. There are five positions in the blockmodel. All of the blocks above the diagonal are null blocks. If we followed the Davis and Leinhardt (1972) narrative exactly, all of the diagonal blocks would be cliques – as is the case for the second and fourth positions. It seems unreasonable to expect complete diagonal blocks, and we now propose the additional block type. Having units within a cluster linked by mutual ties is one of the crucial features of the Davis and Leinhardt model. The specification that all pairs are linked this way can be relaxed. The new block type reflects these ideas by allowing some of the diagonal blocks to contain zeros – but only if they are symmetric within this block type. The first, third, and last diagonal blocks in Table 1.9 have this feature. This becomes a 10th type of ideal block – one that can be added to those from Table 7.1.

The permuted matrix in Table 11.1 shows another relation constructed (modified) from that in Table 1.9. Some ties have been deleted and some added in ways that result in a relation inconsistent with the ranked-clusters model. Specifically,

Table 11.1. A Fitted Ranked-Clusters Blockmodel

a	.11..	...	....	.....	**1** ....
b	1.111	...	....	**1**	.....
c	11.11	...	....	.....	.....
d	*1* 11.1	...	....	.....	.....
e	.111.	...	....	.....	.....
f	11.11	.1 *1*	....	.....	.....
g	.111.	1.1	....	.....	.....
h	11.11	.1.	....	**.1** ...	.....
i	1.111	...	.111	.....	**.1** ...
j	11111	...	1...	.....	.....
k	111.1	...	1..1	.....	.....
l	.111.	...	1.1.	.....	.....
m	.111.	.1.	....	.1111	.....
n	11..1	1..	....	1.111	.....
o	1.11.	1.1	....	11.11	.....
p	.11.1	.1.	....	111.1	.....
q	.1.11	.1.	....	1111.	.....
r	.1...	...	111.	.....	.11.*1*
s	11..1	...	1111	.....	1..1*1*
t	1.11.	...	1.1.	.....	1..11
u	111.1	...	11.1	.....	.11.1
v	11.11	...	.111	.....	..11.

$(a, d), (h, f), (v, r)$, and (v, r) were removed. These changes now mean that (d, a), $(f, h), (r, v)$, and (s, v) are unreciprocated ties. Four ties – $(a, r), (b, m), (h, n)$, and (i, s) – have been added. There are now two kinds of blocks that are not allowed in an ideal ranked-clusters model: (i) diagonal blocks with asymmetric ties and (ii) nonzero blocks above the diagonal. Recall from Chapter 7 that all deviations are sensitive when

$$\delta(X, Y; T) = 0 \Leftrightarrow T(R(X, Y)).$$

The criterion function for a ranked-clusters model is simply a count of the number of contributions to δ. Every tie above the diagonal in the permuted and blocked relation will be counted as will all unreciprocated ties in diagonal blocks. Given the fundamental importance of ranking, ties above the diagonal can be weighted more heavily in the computation of the criterion function.

Table 11.1 shows the partition of the constructed data when a ranked-clusters model with five positions has been fitted. By virtue of the nature of the inconsistencies with ranked clusters, no zero can be an inconsistency. The four italicized 1s in the diagonal blocks contribute to the criterion function as do the four bolded 1s in the blocks above the diagonal.

11.3 ESTABLISHING SYMMETRIC–ACYCLIC DECOMPOSITIONS OF NETWORKS

The problem of establishing a partition of units in a network in terms of a ranked-clusters model can be treated in different ways. First, we assume the ideal structure in the measured network, which means that there are k symmetric clusters with the asymmetric ties in a single direction between them. In this case, the symmetric–acyclic decomposition discussed in this section reveals the structure. When the structure is not ideal, there are at least two possible algorithms in addition to the prespecified blockmodeling approach. The first involves deleting arcs.[1] The second is the iteration of the symmetric–acyclic decomposition, which, unlike the arc deletion method, is much more efficient. Both of the additional methods are motivated by Theorem 11.1. After presenting the mathematical ideas, we apply the methods to three examples: (i) a classroom network with boys and girls, (ii) a reanalysis of the Student Government data, and (iii) an analysis of the Ragusan family marriage network.

11.3.1   Ideal structures

A relation $R \subseteq \mathcal{U} \times \mathcal{U}$ has a *symmetric–acyclic decomposition* (S, Q) if and only if there exist relations $S, Q \subseteq \mathcal{U} \times \mathcal{U}$ such that

---

1 This is not very promising because it is computationally very complex.

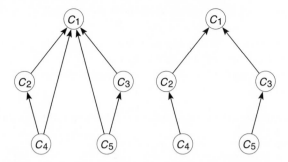

Figure 11.1. A three-level acyclic graph and its Hasse graph.

- S is symmetric, $S = S^{-1}$,
- Q is acyclic, $\overline{Q} \cap I = \emptyset$, and
- $S \cup Q = R$ and $\overline{S} \cap \overline{Q} = \emptyset$ both hold.

$I = \{(x, x) : x \in \mathcal{U}\}$ is the identity relation and $\overline{R}$ denotes transitive closure of relation R.

Theorem 11.1 *If a relation $R \subseteq \mathcal{U} \times \mathcal{U}$ has a symmetric–acyclic decomposition (S, Q), then*

$$S = R \cap R^{-1} \qquad and \qquad Q = R \setminus S.$$

The reflexive and transitive closure S^* of relation S is an equivalence relation equal to the strong connectivity relation in $(\mathcal{U}, R)$. Let $\mathcal{U}'$ denote the factor set $\mathcal{U}/S^*$. The relation $\sqsubset$ defined by

$$X \sqsubset Y \equiv \exists x \in X \exists y \in Y : x Q y$$

is acyclic on $\mathcal{U}'$.

We say that a clustering $\mathbf{C} = \{C_1, \ldots, C_k\}$ over the relation R is a *symmetric-acyclic* clustering iff

- all subgraphs induced by clusters from $\mathbf{C}$ contain only bidirectional arcs (edges); and
- the remaining graph (without these subgraphs) is acyclic.

If the relation shown in Table 11.1 had 0s instead of the italicized 1s and 0s instead of the bolded 1s, it would have a symmetric–acyclic decomposition. As such, it is an ideal model, and we confine attention to it in this section. The ideal model for the relation in Table 1.9 is drawn in Figure 11.1 (on the left) with five positions: $C_1 = \{a, b, c, d, e\}$, $C_2 = \{f, g, h\}$, $C_3 = \{i, j, k, l\}$, $C_4 = \{m, n, o, p, q\}$, and $C_5 = \{r, s, t, u, v\}$.

The cover relation $\sqsubset\!\!\cdot$, an analogue to the Hasse relation of an order, can also be defined for an acyclic relation $\sqsubset$ by

$$\sqsubset\!\!\cdot \ = \sqsubset \ \setminus \ \sqsubset * \overline{\sqsubset}.$$

The operation $*$ denotes the product of relations $R_1 * R_2 = \{(x, y) : \exists z : (x R_1 z \wedge z R_2 y)\}$.

We obtain $\sqsubset$ from $\sqsubseteq$ by deleting each arc (x, y) with the property that there exists a path with a length of at least 2 from x to y.

Using the Hasse graph $\mathbf{H} = (\mathcal{U}', \sqsubset)$, we can describe the set Σ of all acyclic clusterings with symmetric clusters over R:

- the minimum number of clusters is equal to $1 + d$, where d is the length of the longest path in $\mathbf{H}$;
- the maximum number of clusters is equal to card $\mathcal{U}'$;
- card $\Sigma = 1$ iff $\mathbf{H}$ is a path;
- each k-clustering (partition into k clusters) is determined by a k-set (a set with k elements) of "compatible independent" vertices of $\mathbf{H}$.

Two vertices $u, v \in \mathcal{U}'$ are *independent* if and only if they are not connected by a path in $\mathbf{H}$. A pair of sets $X, Y \subset \mathcal{U}'$ is *compatible* if and only if

$$\neg \exists x_1, x_2 \in X \, \exists y_1, y_2 \in Y : (x_1 \sqsubset y_1 \wedge y_2 \sqsubset x_2).$$

All pairs of sets in a k-set have to be compatible. The clusters are unions of the sets corresponding to vertices from the sets of a k-set. We note that, as a special case, an asymmetric tie down a ranked-clusters model leads to an incompatibility.

For the example shown in Table 11.1, the graph on the right side of Figure 11.1 is its Hasse graph. To obtain the Hasse graph $\mathbf{H}$, two arcs (C_4, C_1), given the path $C_4 C_2 C_1$, and (C_5, C_2), given the path $C_5 C_3 C_1$, have to be deleted. The longest path in $\mathbf{H}$ has length 2, and therefore the number of levels is three. From $\mathbf{H}$ we see that the following symmetric–acyclic clusterings (where only compatible clusters can be grouped together) exist:

$$\mathbf{C}_1^3 = \{C_1, C_2 \cup C_3, C_4 \cup C_5\},$$
$$\mathbf{C}_1^4 = \{C_1, C_2, C_3, C_4 \cup C_5\},$$
$$\mathbf{C}_2^4 = \{C_1, C_2 \cup C_3, C_4, C_5\},$$
$$\mathbf{C}_3^4 = \{C_1, C_2 \cup C_5, C_3, C_4\},$$
$$\mathbf{C}_4^4 = \{C_1, C_2, C_3 \cup C_4, C_5\},$$
$$\mathbf{C}_1^5 = \{C_1, C_2, C_3, C_4, C_5\}.$$

We can introduce, in Σ, an operation

$$\mathbf{C}_1 \sqcap \mathbf{C}_2 \equiv \{C_1 \cap C_2 : C_1 \in \mathbf{C}_1, C_2 \in \mathbf{C}_2\} \setminus \{\emptyset\}.$$

For example,

$$\mathbf{C}_1^4 \sqcap \mathbf{C}_3^4 = \mathbf{C}_1^5.$$

It is easy to verify that $(\Sigma, \sqcap)$ is a semilattice (associative, commutative, idempotent, with an absorption element).

The semilattice of clusterings for our example is presented in Figure 11.2.

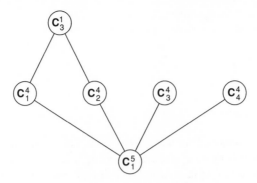

Figure 11.2. Semilattice.

11.3.2 Relations without a symmetric–acyclic decomposition

There are several possible approaches to networks that do not have an exact ranked-clusters structure (and so are not ideal).

The symmetric–acyclic decomposition (S, Q) described in the previous section can be improved by setting

$$S = R \cap R^{-1} \quad \text{and} \quad Q = R \setminus \overline{S},$$

where $\overline{S}$ replaces S in the definition of Q. In the ideal case this still produces the asymmetric–acyclic decomposition, but in the nonideal case it removes all asymmetric inconsistencies from diagonal blocks.

Deleting arcs. This procedure provides useful information even though R has no symmetric–acyclic decomposition. The set

$$\Delta = \overline{S} \cap (R \setminus S)$$

gives us asymmetric arcs inside the otherwise symmetric classes of $\mathcal{U}$. For Table 10.1, Δ identifies exactly the asymmetric ties within the diagonal blocks. If the only violations of the symmetric–acyclic assumption concerned symmetry, the analysis would be complete. In the example, Q is not acyclic and we have to delete some arcs to make it acyclic. Here, the bolded 1s above the diagonal would be located and deleted, leaving an exact model (with the violations noted). In general, however, the identification of the smallest number of violations of acyclicity is not an easy problem.

Iteration of the symmetric–acyclic decomposition. We can also iterate the preceding decomposition procedure until we obtain a graph without edges.

Let $\mathcal{U}_0 := \mathcal{U}$, $R_0 := R$ and set $i := 0$. Then repeat the following steps.

1. Determine the symmetric part of R_i (the edges):

$$S_i := (R_i \cap R_i^{-1}) \setminus I_{\mathcal{U}_i}.$$

2. If no edge exists, $S_i = \emptyset$, stop iterating.
3. Shrink symmetric components, producing a new reduced graph $(\mathcal{U}_{i+1}, R_{i+1})$, determined by

$$\mathcal{U}_{i+1} := \mathcal{U}_i / S_i^*,$$
$$R_{i+1} := \{(X, Y) : \exists x \in X \exists y \in Y : xRy\}.$$

4. Increase the counter of steps $i := i + 1$.

The clusterings obtained are nested (and form a hierarchy) and all clusters are strongly connected. If the final clustering is not acyclic, we introduce an additional step in which the graph is factorized according to strong connectivity. The final graph is the condensation of the original network (Harary et al. 1965).

Blockmodels for ranked-clusters models. In this case the specified blockmodel is acyclic with symmetric diagonal blocks. An example of a clustering into three-cluster symmetric–acyclic types of models can be specified in the following way:

sym	nul	nul
nul, one	sym	nul
nul, one	nul, one	sym

In the concrete analyses, we usually also add the subtypes nul and one to the symmetric part of the diagonal (see the definition in Chapter 1, Section 1.4.3.).

In much of our discussion thus far, all inconsistencies are alike in the sense that they contribute in the same fashion to the total number of inconsistencies. Given the ranked-clusters model, it is possible to argue that some inconsistencies are more consequential than others. (Compare our discussion in Chapter 8, where 1s in null blocks were seen as more consequential for blockmodeling the Deep South data.) Following this logic, asymmetric ties down from a higher to a lower level are the most serious. The computed criterion function can include having a higher penalty for these ties (e.g., 100). Asymmetric ties within clusters seem the next most important type of inconsistency. The modification to the criterion function can have a milder penalty for these ties (e.g., 10). Finally, inconsistencies in the blocks below the main diagonal can be specified as minor (e.g., 1). Therefore, the penalty matrix for the previous example can be the following one:

10	100	100
1	10	100
1	1	10

Table 11.2. Ranked-Clusters Model for Boys

23-Jacque	. 1 1 1	. . . . .	. . . .
28-Jack	1 . 1 1	. . . . .	. . . .
29-Wolf	1 1 . 1	. . . . .	. . . .
33-Nero	1 1 1 .	. . . . .	. . . .
25-Guy	1 . . .	. 1 1 . .	. . . .
26-Davan	. 1 . .	1 . 1 . .	. . . .
27-Dalti	1 . . .	1 1 . . .	. . . .
30-Joe	. 1 1 1	. . . . .	. . . .
34-Mick	. 1 1 1	. . . . .	. . . .
24-Lionel	. . . .	. . . 1 .	. . . .
31-Frank	. 1 . .	 1	. . 1 .
32-Marc	. 1 . .	 1	. 1 . .
35-Peter	. 1 1 .	1	. . . .

11.4 LIKING TIES FOR CHILDREN IN A CLASSROOM

We next consider a network taken from Jennings (1948) and listed in Table 11.4. There are boys and girls in the classroom and, consistent with the literature on these networks, it is reasonable (tentatively) to examine the boys and girls separately before examining the whole network. In addition to the prespecifications of the ranked-clusters model, the next diagonal blocks were prespecified as null or regular.

The ranked-clusters model obtained by the blockmodeling approach for the boys with $k = 3$ is provided in Table 11.2.[2] There are no inconsistencies with the acyclic requirement and none with the symmetry requirement. Although there are errors in the below diagonal blocks, they are inconsistencies with the specification regular blocks or null blocks. Thus, they are of secondary interest (in relation to ranked clusters). However, they are not irrelevant, for they can be considered in constructing the ties between the blocks. From the strict specification of null and regular blocks, only the regular blocks define a between-clusters tie in the blockmodel. This gives the model on the left in Figure 11.3. If just the presence of some 1s in these below diagonal blocks is considered, the model on the right of Figure 11.3 results.

The three positions of the model are as follows: *A* with Jacque, Jack, Wolf, and Nero; *B* with Guy, Davan, Dalti, Joe, and Mick; and *C* with Lionel, Frank, Marc, and Peter. The model is clearly acyclic and has symmetric diagonal blocks.

The corresponding partition for the girls is found in Table 11.3. Here also are no inconsistencies with the acyclic requirement. However, in contrast to the boys, there are inconsistencies with the symmetry requirement inside diagonal clusters.

2   The numbering of the units comes from the whole network with boys and girls.

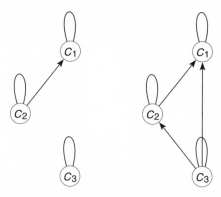

Figure 11.3. Two images of the ranked-clusters model for the boys.

Eleven inconsistencies within the large first block are present as well as one in the diagonal block for the second cluster. The remaining inconsistencies below the diagonal are due to departures from the null or regular block specification.

The three positions are as follows: A_1 contains Lily through Rea; B_1 contains Edith, Lorine, Lucia, and Sylvia; and C_1 has Edna through July. Invoking the strict interpretation of the below diagonal specification, we see that the image of this

Table 11.3. Ranked-Clusters Model for the Girls

3-Lily	. . . . . . 1 1 . *1* . . .	. . . .	. . . . .
6-Carmen	. . 1 *1* . . . . . *1* . . .	. . . .	. . . . .
8-Ethel	. 1 . *1* . . . . . *1* . . .	. . . .	. . . . .
12-Lisa	. . . . 1 . . *1* . 1 . . .	. . . .	. . . . .
13-Nina	. . . 1 . 1 . . . 1 . . .	. . . .	. . . . .
14-Thela	. . . *1* 1 . . . . 1 . . .	. . . .	. . . . .
15-Clara	1 . . . . . . 11	. . . .	. . . . .
16-Janice	1 . . . . . 1 . 1	. . . .	. . . . .
17-Pat	. . . . . . 11 . . . *1* .	. . . .	. . . . .
18-Alice	. . . 11 1	. . . .	. . . . .
19-Angel	. . . . *1* . 1 1	. . . .	. . . . .
20-Teresa	. *1* . . . . 1 . 1	. . . .	. . . . .
21-Rea	. . . . *1* 1 1 .	. . . .	. . . . .
7-Edith	1 . . . . . . 1	. *1* . .	. . . . .
9-Lorine	. . . . 1 1 . . . 1 . . .	. . . .	. . . . .
11-Lucia	. . . 1 1 . . . . 1 . . .	. . . .	. . . . .
22-Sylvia	*1*	. . . .	. . . .
1-Edna	. . . . . . 11	. . . .	. 1 . . .
2-Paula	. . . . . . 11	. . . .	1 . . . .
4-Claire	. 1 . . . . 11	. . . .	. . . . .
5-Ella	. 1 . . . . 1	1 . . .	. . . . .
10-July	. . . . 1	. 1 1 .	. . . . .

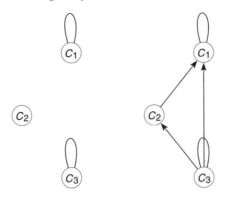

Figure 11.4. Two images of the ranked clusters model for the girls.

ranked-clusters model is on the left of Figure 11.4. The three positions are isolates with one having a null diagonal block. With the looser interpretation, the image on the right of Figure 11.4 results – one that is identical to the corresponding model for the boys (except for the absence of a reflexive loop at C_2).

Table 11.4 contains the whole network (boys and girls together) with the obtained blocks between the double lines. All of the inconsistencies with the ranked-clusters model come from the girl network. Position A_2 has four boys (Jacque, Jack, Wolf, and Nero). Position B_2 has the same girls from the large block, A_1, of Table 11.4 together with five boys (Guy through Mick). Position C_2 has the remaining girls (Edna through Sylvia) and four boys (Lionel through Peter). Figure 11.5 contains two possible images for this network. On the left is the image with the strict interpretation of regular blocks, and the less restricted image is on the right. Again, these images are acyclic with reflexive diagonal blocks.

The partition of the boys in Table 11.2 is reproduced exactly in Table 11.4. However, the partition for the girls differs slightly from that in Table 11.3. The large position A_1 (Lily through Rea) is reproduced and the two other clusters, B_1 and C_1, of Table 11.3 are merged into C_2 in the partition shown in Table 11.4. The single lines in Table 11.4 mark the separation by gender within the clusters and clearly show how the separate gender-based partitions fold into the partition of the whole network.

Both the boys and girls have structures with three positions, and so there appears to be parallel ranked systems for the girls and boys. There are suggestive patterns in Table 11.4 that stem from distinguishing boys and girls. Some of the blocks of Table 11.4 are separated into null parts and quite densely populated parts. However, the impulse to act on this and propose a five-clusters model has to be resisted, for this would depart from the ranked-clusters nature of the separate systems for boys and girls. These parallel systems are linked with some ties between boys and girls. However, there are so few between-gender ties that they do not compromise the separate within-gender analyses.

Table 11.4. Ranked-Clusters Model for the Boys and Girls

23-Jacque	.1 1 1	....	.....	....	....
28-Jack	1 .1 1	....	.....	....	....
29-Wolf	1 1 .1	....	.....	....	....
33-Nero	1 1 1 .	....	.....	....	....
3-Lily	....	......1 1 .1 ...	.....	....	....
6-Carmen	....	..1 1 .....1 ...	.....	....	....
8-Ethel	....	.1 .1 .....1 ...	.....	....	....
12-Lisa	....	....1 ..1 .1 ...	.....	....	....
13-Nina	....	...1 .1 ...1 ...	.....	....	....
14-Thela	....	...1 1 ....1 ...	.....	....	....
15-Clara	....	1 ......1 1	.....	....	....
16-Janice	....	1 .....1 .1	.....	....	....
17-Pat	....	......1 1 ...1 .	.....	....	....
18-Alice	....	...1 1 1	.....	....	....
19-Angel	....	.........1 .1 1	.....	....	....
20-Teresa	....	.1 ....1 .1	.....	....	....
21-Rea	....	.........1 1 1 .	.....	....	....
25-Guy	1 ...	....	.1 1 ..	....	....
26-Davan	.1 ..	....	1 .1 ..	....	....
27-Dalti	1 ...	....	1 1 ...	....	....
30-Joe	.1 1 1	....	.....	....	....
34-Mick	.1 1 1	....	.....	....	....
1-Edna	....	......1 1	.....	.1	....
2-Paula	....	......1 1	.....	1	....
4-Claire	....	.1 ....1 1	.....	....	....
5-Ella	....	.1 ....1	.....	....1	....
7-Edith	....	1 .....1	.....	.....1 ...	....
9-Lorine	....	....1 1 ...1 ...	.....	....	....
10-July	....	....1	.....	.....1 .1 .	....
11-Lucia	....	...1 1 ....1 ...	.....	....	....
22-Sylvia	1 1 ..	1	.....	....	....
24-Lionel	....	........1 1 ...	...1 .	....	....
31-Frank	.1 ..	....	1	....	..1 .
32-Marc	.1 ..	....	1	....	.1 ..
35-Peter	.1 1 .	....	1	....	....

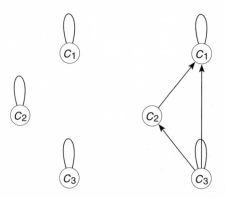

Figure 11.5. Two images of the ranked-clusters model for the full network.

11.5 THE STUDENT GOVERNMENT EXAMPLE

We next use the prespecified blockmodeling approach and return to the communications among 12 members and advisors of the Student Government (SG) at the University in Ljubljana (Hlebec 1993). The SG data set is described in detail in Section 2.2.3. The communication flow among actors was measured by several survey questions. Here, we use the recall relation: With which of the members and advisors do you (most often) discuss SG matters? The relational matrix presented in Table 2.18 (top, left matrix) contains the data used here.

11.5.1 A hypothesized blockmodel

The intuitively, so-called obvious, hypothesized structure of the SG network, which specifies a hierarchy with three levels at which each advisor communicates at least to one minister and the ministers to the Prime Minister, is presented in Figure 11.6. The hypothetical model is acyclic. From the graph on the right side of Figure 11.6 we can see that there are four ties that do not satisfy the hierarchical structure. These are (PM, M_7), (M_7, A_3), (M_6, A_1), and (M_6, A_3). These inconsistencies strongly question the obvious hierarchical structure of the SG network. Therefore, a less restricted hierarchical model is required.

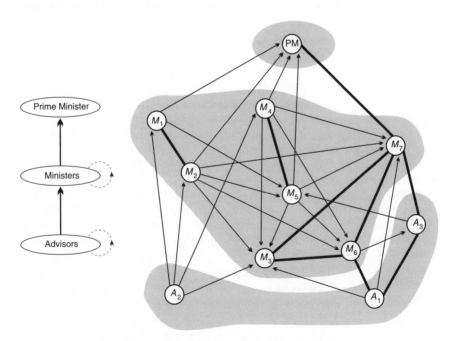

Figure 11.6. SG – hypothetical blockmodel.

11.5.2   A second hypothesized blockmodel

First, decomposition with respect to strong connectivity was performed. Three levels were obtained with the following clusters of the SG members:

$$\mathbf{C} = \{\{PM, M_3, M_4, M_5, M_6, M_7, A_1, A_3\}, \{M_1, M_2\}, \{A_2\}\}\}.$$

The internal structure of the second cluster is complete, and the structure of the first cluster is regular. The first cluster is the largest with two symmetric sub-clusters

$$\{PM, M_3, M_6, M_7, A_1, A_3\}, \{M_4, M_5\}$$

that are not hierarchically connected because of the tie $\{A_3, M_5\}$.

According to these results, the assumed prespecified blockmodel is a hierarchical structure with three clusters having the following block types allowed in each cell of the image matrix:

	1	2	3
1	{nul, reg, com}	{nul}	{nul}
2	{cre, rre}	{nul, reg, com}	{nul}
3	{cre, rre}	{cre, rre}	{nul, reg, com}

With the use of the optimizational approach, the following model was obtained:

π	1	2	3
1	reg	nul	nul
2	rre	com	nul
3	rre	rre	nul

The three resulting clusters are the same $\mathbf{C}$. The model has a perfect fit (zero inconsistencies). This solution is also presented in Figure 11.7.

The hierarchical structure obtained shows that there is a strongly connected core group in the SG with a mixed composition. Besides the Prime Minister, there are five ministers and also two advisors. Also the optimal solution into four clusters splits the first cluster into the same two symmetrical subclusters with one backward error $\{A_3, M_5\}$ and three asymmetric errors in the first (sub)cluster: $\{A_1, M_3\}$, $\{A_1, M_7\}$, and $\{M_6, A_3\}$. The second group is peripheral and consists of two ministers who consult the first group if they have some problems in the governmental work. They also communicate with each other. The other peripheral member is advisor 2, who is located alone in a cluster and asks both ministers of the second cluster, and one of the first cluster, for help.

We have shown that there is a hierarchical communication structure in the SG network, but it is not the one that would be expected with the Prime Minister on the top, ministers on the second position, and advisors on the bottom. The location

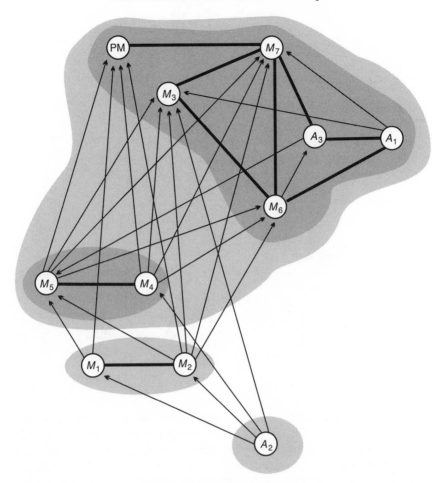

Figure 11.7. SG – final clustering.

of A_1 and A_3 is especially interesting, for they are in the top-ranked cluster in the established ranked-clusters model.

11.6 A RETURN TO THE CLASSROOM EXAMPLE

Given the nature of the boys network – perfect conformity with the ranked-clusters structure – the symmetric–acyclic decomposition located this structure exactly. For the girls, the iterated decomposition also provides useful information. At this point, we need to tie the use of the specific names of the girls to labels that we use in Figure 11.8 and Figure 11.9. In Table 11.4 the name of each girl has a number. We use this number to construct labels in the following fashion. Edna (1-Edna) is represented by g_1, Paula (2-Paula) is represented by g_2, and so on; Sylvia

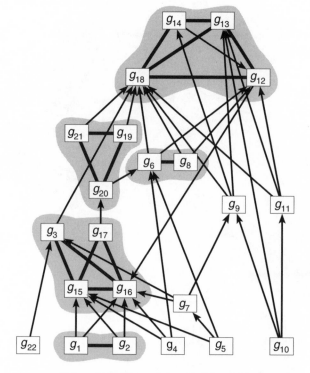

Figure 11.8. Network for all of the girls.

(22-Sylvia) is represented by g_{22}. In fitting a ranked-clusters model, we sought one as finely grained as possible. To do this, we split up the clusters so that each diagonal block had only girls involved in symmetric ties. In essence, we returned to a specification close to Davis and Leinhardt's ranked-clusters model. As a result, there are many singleton clusters. The internal structure of the large cluster for the girls is a part of Figure 11.8 with four clusters of those girls in shaded regions. There are 13 girls in the large cluster. Four subsets of girls from the large cluster are linked internally through symmetric ties: G_1 has {Lisa (g_{12}), Nina (g_{13}), Thela (g_{14}), Alice (g_{18})}; G_2 has {Carmen (g_6), Ethel (g_8)}; G_4 has {Angel (g_{19}), Theresa (g_{20}), Rea (g_{21})}; and G_4 has {Lily (g_3), Clara (g_{15}), Janice (g_{16}), Pat (g_{17})}. The one violation of the symmetry condition is the tie from Thela (g_{14}) to Lisa (g_{12}). Outside the large cluster of girls, there is a symmetric tie between Edna (g_1) and Paula (g_2). When these fine-grained symmetric clusters are shrunk to a new unit in the next iteration, the resulting ranked-clusters structure is as shown in Figure 11.9.

11.7 MARRIAGE NETWORK OF THE RAGUSAN NOBLE FAMILIES

We consider the binarized marriage network for the second period (18th and 19th centuries). As a point of departure, Batagelj (1996b) found the partition shown in

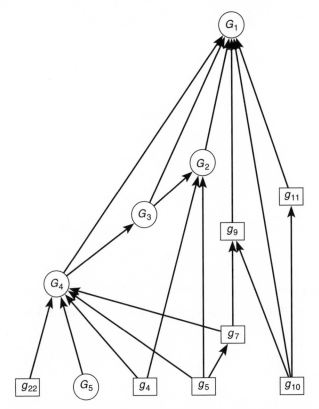

Figure 11.9. Fine-grained ranked-clusters structure of the girl network.

Chapter 2 (Section 2.2.6). Here, we establish the symmetric–acyclic decomposition of this network.

11.7.1   *Network decomposition*

Acyclic decomposition with respect to strong connectivity yielded three levels (see Figure 11.10). In the first and the third level, only single families are present. The middle level consists of a cluster C with several families. The men from the families of the first level choose wives from the families of the second level, and the men from the second level choose wives from the families of the third level. It is worth noting that five families are sources in the network, providing husbands to the large middle cluster of families, among which husbands (and wives) circulate. These families are transmitters, and there are two families that are sinks.

The internal structure of the second cluster (the middle level in Figure 11.10) can be revealed by the iteration of the symmetric–acyclic decomposition method.

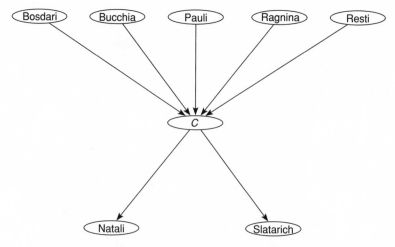

Figure 11.10. Acyclic model of Ragusan families.

The symmetric components of the middle cluster C are as follows:

$C_1 = \{$Bona, Bonda, Caboga, Cerva, Goze, Gradi, Menze, Sorgo, Zamagna$\}$,

$C_2 = \{$Ghetaldi, Saraca$\}$,

$C_3 = \{$Basilio$\}$,

$C_4 = \{$Georgi$\}$,

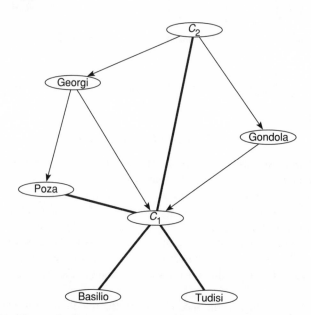

Figure 11.11. The graph of seven first-order symmetric components of the middle cluster.

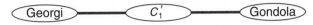

Figure 11.12. The graph of three second-order symmetric components of the middle cluster.

$C_5 = \{\text{Gondola}\}$,
$C_6 = \{\text{Poza}\}$,
$C_7 = \{\text{Tudisi}\}$.

The graph of the seven (first-order) symmetric components (clusters) of the cluster C is presented in Figure 11.11. This reduced graph has three (second-order) symmetric components:

$$C_1' = \{C_1, C_2, C_3, C_6, C_7\},$$
$$C_2' = \{\text{Georgi}\},$$
$$C_3' = \{\text{Gondola}\}.$$

Their reduced graph (see Figure 11.12) is a single symmetric component. All three steps of the hierarchical decomposition can be seen in Figure 11.13.

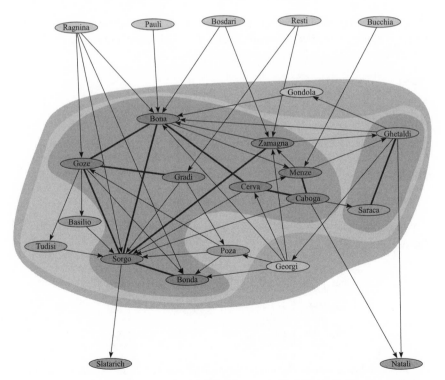

Figure 11.13. Acyclic–symmetric decomposition of Ragusan families network.

11.7.2   *Blockmodeling approach*

On the basis of the three-level network decomposition, we can assume two block-models. The first one is

nul, reg, sym	nul	nul
cre, rre	nul, reg, sym	nul
cre, rre	cre, rre	nul, reg, sym

The second prespecified model is similar to the first one. The only difference is that the "reg" type is excluded from the diagonal elements (this model has more precisely defined blocks in the lower triangle than in the general case):

nul, sym	nul	nul
cre, rre	nul, sym	nul
cre, rre	cre, rre	nul, sym

Only the second model is an symmetric–acyclic one. The penalties in each cell were assumed in accordance with Section 11.3.2. For both models the same clustering of families was obtained (compare Figure 11.13).

Cluster 1:

    Natali   Slatarich

Cluster 2:

Basilio	Bona	Bonda	Caboga	Cerva	Georgi	Ghetaldi	Gondola
Goze	Gradi	Menze	Poza	Saraca	Sorgo	Tudisi	Zamagna

Cluster 3:

    Bosdari   Bucchia   Pauli   Ragnina   Resti

The permuted original relational matrix for this clustering is given in Table 11.5. The obtained models are

nul	nul	nul
cre	reg	nul
nul	rre	nul

and

nul	nul	nul
cre	sym	nul
nul	rre	nul

The first one has no inconsistencies; the second one has 28 inconsistencies in the middle diagonal block. These inconsistencies are produced by nonsymmetric ties.

Table 11.5. Permuted Ragusan Families Marriage Network, 18th and 19th Centuries

		14	20	1	3	7	10	12	19	22	23	2	8	9	6	13	11	16	21	4	5	15	17	18
Natali	14	.	.	.	.	.	.	.	.	.	.	.	.	.	.	.	.	.	.	.	.	.	.	.
Slatarich	20	.	.	.	.	.	.	.	.	.	.	.	.	.	.	.	.	.	.	.	.	.	.	.
Basilio	1	.	.	.	.	.	.	.	.	.	.	.	.	.	.	.	.	.	1	.	.	.	.	.
Bonda	3	.	.	.	.	.	.	.	.	.	.	.	.	.	.	.	.	.	2	.	.	.	.	.
Cerva	7	.	.	.	.	.	.	.	.	.	.	1	.	.	1	1	.	.	1	.	.	.	.	.
Gondola	10	.	.	.	.	.	.	.	.	.	.	1	.	.	.	.	.	.	.	.	.	.	.	.
Gradi	12	.	.	.	.	.	.	.	.	.	.	.	.	.	1	.	1	.	3	.	.	.	.	.
Saraca	19	.	.	.	.	.	.	.	.	.	.	.	.	1	.	.	.	.	1	.	.	.	.	.
Tudisi	22	.	.	.	.	.	.	.	.	.	.	.	.	.	.	.	.	.	1	.	.	.	.	.
Zamagna	23	.	.	.	.	.	.	.	.	.	1	1	.	2	.	.	.	.	1	.	.	.	.	.
Bona	2	.	.	.	2	1	.	.	.	.	1	.	.	.	.	2	2	.	.	.	.	.	.	.
Georgi	8	.	.	.	.	1	1	.	.	.	.	1	1	.	.	.	.	4	.	.	.	.	.	.
Ghetaldi	9	.	.	.	.	.	1	.	1	.	.	1	.	.	.	.	.	.	1	.	.	.	.	.
Caboga	6	.	.	.	.	1	.	.	1	.	.	.	.	.	.	.	.	.	.	.	.	.	.	.
Menze	13	.	.	1	.	.	.	.	.	.	.	.	.	1	1	.	.	.	.	.	.	.	.	.
Goze	11	.	.	1	1	.	2	2	.	1	.	2	.	.	.	.	2	1	2	.	.	.	.	.
Poza	16	.	.	2	2	.	.	.	.	1	.	.	.	.	.	.	1	1	1	.	.	.	.	.
Sorgo	21	.	1	1	1	.	.	.	.	.	1	2	.	.	.	.	1	.	1	.	.	.	.	.
Bosdari	4	.	.	.	.	.	.	.	.	.	1	1	.	.	.	.	.	.	.	.	.	.	.	.
Bucchia	5	.	.	.	.	.	.	.	.	.	.	.	.	.	.	1	.	.	.	.	.	.	.	.
Pauli	15	.	.	.	1	.	.	.	.	.	.	1	.	.	.	.	1	.	.	.	.	.	.	.
Ragnina	17	.	.	.	.	.	.	.	.	.	.	1	.	.	.	.	1	.	1	.	.	.	.	.
Resti	18	.	.	.	.	.	.	1	.	.	1	.	.	.	.	.	.	.	.	.	.	.	.	.

For the clusterings with larger numbers of clusters (four, five or six), the solutions for the first model have no inconsistencies. All obtained clusterings have the same second cluster. There are some splits, as we can expect from the theory of decomposition, of the first or the third cluster.

When the structure inside the cluster in one of the levels of the symmetric–acyclic decomposition is not clearly symmetric, some other types of the structure can be tested by applying the blockmodeling approach to this cluster separately. In this case an appropriate model should be specified. Because the iterative decomposition is based on the symmetric components of the diagonal clusters, the blockmodeling approach is more appropriate to search for other types of structures also (e.g., center–periphery structure).

Using blockmodeling on the subgraph induced by the cluster C, we obtained the following results.

The symmetric clusters model {nul} on the out diagonal and {com, sym} on the diagonal with penalty 1 gives for seven clusters the same clustering as was obtained at the first step of the iterative procedure.

The center–periphery model, {nul, one} with penalty 1 on the out diagonal, {com} with penalty 10 on the diagonal, and {nul} with penalty 100 as the first diagonal element, gives the following four clusters of C: periphery – Basilio, Bonda, Cerva, Gondola, Gradi, Saraca, Tudisi, Zamagna; Center 1 – Caboga, Menze; Center 2 – Bona, Georgi, Ghetaldi; Center 3 – Goze, Poza, Sorgo. These are also considered in the ordering of the second cluster in Table 11.5.

11.8 DISCUSSION

These analyses can all be located within the domain of blockmodeling insofar as they were designed to partition social networks. However, several procedural conclusions can be drawn from these analyses and are worth stressing. On the blockmodeling side, we emphasize that the analyses were done with generalized blockmodeling and that prespecified blockmodels were used. Their use produces new major departures from conventional blockmodeling. Further, the symmetric–acyclic decomposition is a new method that forces analysts to look *inside* the blocks of a blockmodel. The structure of the network inside a block can have substantive and empirical value. With the specification of the ranked-clusters model, and networks that do not fit exactly, attention has to be paid to asymmetric ties within diagonal blocks and the ties that violate the acyclic specification.

Finally, we note that the symmetric–acyclic decomposition method has its origins firmly in substance. It was a consideration of the ranked-clusters model that led us to formulate both the new block type and the decomposition itself. This seems very appropriate because the initial formulation of blockmodeling was also grounded in theoretical concerns and is a reminder that substance is likely to be the source of the most useful new block types.

12

EXTENDING GENERALIZED
BLOCKMODELING

In our concluding chapter, we step back from the details of specific analyses and examine the overall framework within which these analyses were conducted. In Chapter 6, we distinguished conventional and generalized blockmodeling and stressed fundamental differences between the two approaches. Chapters 6–11 contain a variety of blockmodels fitted with the generalized blockmodeling framework. Here, we pursue some of the implications stemming from the use of generalized blockmodeling methods.

12.1 BLOCK TYPES

One key feature in the development of generalized blockmodeling is the translation of equivalence ideas into a corresponding set of ideal block types. For structural equivalence, the two ideal block types are null and complete. For regular equivalence we added the regular (one-covered) block type. Empirically, rather than focus on types of equivalence per se, we focused on the block types. This has the benefit, realized in the materials in Chapters 6–11, of permitting a potentially unending way of generalizing blockmodels and motivates the title for this book. Once we are free to specify additional block types, we are freed from having to conform to one or two particular definitions of equivalence. As a result, we are able to specify new types of blockmodels based on the new block types. The expansion of block types and blockmodel types can proceed both on substantive and technical foundations.

In the initial presentation of new block types in Chapter 7, row-regular blocks and column-regular blocks are natural generalizations of regular blocks that were useful block types for the TI example and the baboon grooming network. The row-function and column-function blocks were blocks that were specified more on technical grounds. However, they had great utility in blockmodeling the journal citation network described in Chapter 8. Both row-dominant and column-dominant blocks were also specified on technical grounds but have obvious substantive utility, as shown in the analysis of the TI and SG networks in Chapter 7. We envision other block types' being created on technical grounds and being useful for substantive purposes.

Given that the major purpose of blockmodeling social scientific data is substantive, we think that substantive ideas will be particularly fruitful in specifying new block types. Indeed, in Chapter 10 we used ideas from structural balance theory to specify the positive and negative blocks given the basic structure theorems. This in turn allowed us to specify a blockmodel having the positive blocks on the main diagonal and negative blocks elsewhere. In Chapter 11, the idea of viewing small social systems as systems of ranked clusters led us to formulate the symmetric block and a blockmodel with an asymmetric block structure in one direction or the other (but not both). We believe there are many block types that can be formulated and found to have uses in the understanding of social network structures. The nine block types in Table 7.1, the signed blocks of Chapter 10, and the symmetric block introduced in Chapter 11 are, we think, only the beginning of constructing catalogues of block types that can be used as ideal blocks for partitioning social networks. As other substantive domains are examined, including those from outside the social sciences, we anticipate the creation of more block types appropriate for those domains.

12.2   BLOCK TYPES AND CRITERION FUNCTIONS

As described throughout Chapters 6–11, the formulation of block types sets up the comparison between an empirical block and a corresponding ideal (permitted) block. For every block type defined in this book, we provided a measure of the extent to which an empirical block deviates from the ideal block. In most cases this measure is a count of the inconsistencies between the two blocks, but, in some situations, it may be a weighted count of inconsistencies. We called this the block inconsistency. Further, the block inconsistencies for a blockmodel can be combined into an overall measure of the total inconsistency between an empirical blockmodel and the nearest ideal blockmodel. This total inconsistency is the criterion function for fitting the blockmodel, and many examples were provided throughout Chapters 6–11. For each specified blockmodel, we use optimization methods to minimize an appropriate criterion function and so establish the best fitting blockmodel(s). This notion is at the core of what we have described as the direct approach to fitting a blockmodel. In contrast to the indirect methods of conventional blockmodeling in which some measure of (dis)similarity is used in conjunction with some clustering algorithm, the direct approach uses the network data rather than some transformed version of them.

There are three advantages stemming from the use of direct methods within the optimization approach of generalized blockmodeling. One is that, to the extent that the block types have substantive meaning, the criterion function reflects substantive concerns. Second, the optimization methods seek the best partitions – in the sense of having the smallest values of the criterion function – for the blockmodel. Third, this criterion function is built directly into the fitting procedure and provides a measure of fit for the blockmodel.

In earlier presentations on blockmodeling (Batagelj et al. 1992, 1998; Doreian et al. 1994; Ferligoj, Batagelj, and Doreian 1994), we argued that these direct methods are preferable to the indirect methods for an additional reason: They produce partitions with fewer inconsistencies (or no more inconsistencies) than conventional blockmodeling for structural or regular equivalence. Once we move into generalized blockmodeling, direct methods have obvious appeal and indirect methods do not exist for most of the generalized blockmodels that we have fitted. Even if they did exist, we suspect that, as with structural and regular equivalence, they would return inferior fitting blockmodels.

12.3 USING SUBSTANTIVE AND EMPIRICAL KNOWLEDGE

In Chapter 7, we distinguished different approaches to fitting blockmodels. Common to them all is the notion that there are clusters (of units) and a set of permitted block types. If that is all we know, then we have to use the exploratory approach: Specify the permitted block types, be inductive, and establish blockmodels. Some empirical blockmodel(s) will be returned with blocks in which the total inconsistency between the empirical blockmodel and the corresponding ideal blockmodel will be minimized for a selected criterion function. The fitted blockmodel(s) can be interpreted.

12.3.1 Prespecification

However, we believe that, more often than not, network analysts know more than just the possible permitted block types. They may also know the location of the block types in the blockmodel. To specify *where* block types are located is to pre-specify the blockmodel. In the extreme, every block type is specified by location, but this can be relaxed to specifying only some of the locations of block types. We think that prespecification is particularly important because it is a part of a confirmatory – or deductive – blockmodeling effort. By putting social knowledge into the prespecification of a blockmodel, we are able to test that blockmodel and the knowledge that went into its prespecification. We return to this idea in Section 12.5.

We note that some of the new types of blockmodels have much prespecification built into them. For example, the blockmodels based on structural balance theory have positive blocks on the diagonal and negative blocks off the diagonal. The ranked-clusters blockmodel has symmetric or null blocks on the diagonal and null blocks either above or below the diagonal (but not both). Of course, a blockmodel based on, for instance, structural equivalence is not likely to have these automatic prespecified features. Even so, all prespecified block models have the feature of being tested as a basic part of the fitting procedure.

12.3.2   Constraints

Prespecifying a blockmodel says something about its structure in terms of the locations of block types, and even an inductive model specifying only the block types is stating something about the presence of block types. Using constraints is an additional way of importing substantive knowledge into a blockmodeling effort. For the baboon grooming network, we specified that males must be clustered with males, females with females, and that males and females cannot be clustered together because of the clear differences based on gender in the grooming behavior of the baboons. This is an example of imposing a constraint. Of course, we could have proceeded by fitting a blockmodel to these grooming data and then discarding all partitions where there are some clusters with males and females in them. We have two reservations about such a procedure. First, it does not use the social knowledge that we have. Second, as a practical matter, it seems inefficient.

An additional form of imposing a constraint is to state that certain units must not be in the same cluster. For the political actor network described in Chapter 6, there were two political rivals around whom coalitions appeared to have formed. It is possible to constrain the blockmodeling by ensuring that, whatever clusters are returned, these two actors could not be in the same cluster. Similarly, it is possible to select a pair (or a subset) of actors and impose the constraint that they must belong to the same cluster. The most extreme form of this kind of constraint is to specify the composition of every cluster.

12.3.3   Imposing penalties

In addition to prespecifying a blockmodel or constraining a blockmodel, we can use our social knowledge in a different way by imposing penalties to be used in the fitting process. This was illustrated in Chapter 8, where we fitted a blockmodel to the Deep South two-mode data. We wanted null blocks to appear, given their obvious importance in the attendance patterns of the women in this human group. We imposed a very heavy penalty on 1s appearing in null blocks to ensure that null blocks were truly null and not approximately null. For fitting the ranked-clusters model discussed in Chapter 11, the nonnull blocks on one side of the diagonal were penalized heavily.

We emphasize the following: The point of imposing penalties is to ensure that the structural features we think, or know, are in the data are reflected in the blockmodel fitted. If the resulting blockmodel fits, we have some confirmation that the structural features are there. Of course, if the model does not fit, it suggests that the structural features that we think were there are probably not in the data.

12.4   THE MAGNITUDES OF CRITERION FUNCTIONS

One of the benefits of using the direct approach, and its optimization procedures, is that a measure of the extent to which a blockmodel departs from an ideal blockmodel is built into the procedure. Put differently, we have a measure of fit for blockmodeling, which is a tremendous benefit. We have advocated its use and continue to do so here. However, we recognize that, although this is a great benefit, it is also a source of serious problems, some of which we discuss below.

If we are concerned with a specific type of equivalence such as structural equivalence, then the use of a sound measure of fit is very useful for distinguishing models that are fitted to data with the specific equivalence in mind. On the basis of a criterion function, a count of the number of 0s in one blocks and 1s in zero blocks has much to recommend it. In Chapter 6 (Section 6.7) we presented an analysis of an interorganizational network. The structural equivalence partition gotten by using indirect methods had 79 inconsistencies. Our analysis, done within the direct approach, located four partitions with only 57 inconsistencies. Clearly, these four partitions are better than the one reported that used indirect methods. However, we are not able to conclude that the entire partition really is one consistent with structural equivalence. A total of 57 inconsistencies might be too high (or not) for such a conclusion.[1] As a result, we see a need for measures that allow us to conclude whether or not a blockmodel really fits the data, regardless of how the model was established.

The algorithms that support the types of generalized blockmodeling we describe share many features. One is that in a specific analysis of a network, the number of positions (clusters) is specified in advance. Doing this is useful because it forces an analyst to specify the number of positions (and hence blocks). Such a specification demands considerable theoretical and empirical knowledge, all of which is a part of prespecifying models. Of course, things are different when blockmodeling is used inductively. It may well be the case that we need to learn the correct number of clusters. It is possible first to specify two clusters and then do the analysis, then specify three clusters, and so on. Choosing the partition(s) with the fewest inconsistencies seems a reasonable action, but this also seems atheoretic. In the case of structural equivalence, for any network, we know that there is one partition with the fewest (zero) inconsistencies: the one in which each unit is in its own cluster. Selecting this partition, with its guaranteed lowest inconsistency score of 0, is nonsensical given the objectives of blockmodeling. Given a specified blockmodel, it is appropriate to minimize the number of inconsistencies with a corresponding ideal blockmodel.

We need to be extremely cautious when discussions, and empirical procedures, involve different types of blockmodels. One point is brutally simple: The meaning of the idea of inconsistency changes depending on which ideal block types and blockmodels are considered. In Chapter 7 (Section 7.2) we display an array and observe that if only the predicates complete and null are allowed, the array in blockmodel form has six inconsistencies. Adding the predicate regular and reexamining

---

1   Although a proportional reduction in error measure could be constructed, for example, $(79 - 57)/79 = 0.28$, we do not know if normalizing from an error count from an indirect solution is appropriate for this (new) task. We suspect that this is not the case.

the blocks leads to zero inconsistencies. We then modified the example by changing a 1 to a 0 in such a fashion that one column was not one covered. This meant
that there were inconsistencies even with the predicate regular. However, this time
adding the predicate row-regular created a blockmodel with zero inconsistencies.
Are the blockmodels without zero inconsistencies better than those with inconsistencies? No, we cannot conclude this because the inconsistencies are different
when different block types are considered. In short, comparisons of the number of
inconsistencies for evaluating the fit of a blockmodel within a given type of blockmodel are appropriate. Such comparisons across different block types and blockmodel types are so fraught with hazard that they are best avoided. The three (3,3)-
blockmodels fitted to the Deep South Data in Chapter 8 with the heavy penalty of
1s in null blocks are instructive. One used null blocks and complete blocks having
63 inconsistencies with the corresponding ideal blockmodel. A second used null
blocks, regular blocks, and a row-regular block with zero inconsistencies. The
third used null blocks, row-dominant blocks, and column-dominant blocks with a
total of eight inconsistencies. The clusters were identical for all three blockmodels.
As we noted in Chapter 8, the total inconsistency measures provide no basis for
deciding which, if any, blockmodel is the better model of the structure in the data.
If such a decision has to be rendered, it rests on what went into the prespecification.
In short, it depends on substance.

To view generalized blockmodeling, at least as we have constructed it, as a
mindless search for the model(s) with the smallest number of errors – regardless
of the nature of the errors – is a mistake.[2] We do *not* counsel the minimization of
the criterion function as an end in itself because we can even offer a guarantee: Any
network can be fitted with some combination of predicates with zero or almost
zero inconsistencies. The trouble is that figuring out the substantive meaning of
such a (blindly established) partition seems an activity with a very low probability
of achieving success.[3] We think that the starting point of specifying blockmodels
has to be based substantively in order for it to be fruitful. Focusing on minimizing
inconsistencies alone has no value – unless it is done within a well-specified
blockmodel.

12.5   THE GENERALIZED BLOCKMODELING FRAMEWORK

The generalized blockmodeling framework is very flexible and permits a wide variety of choices. Having options on block types, constructing criterion functions,
having options with regard to prespecifying blockmodels, being able to include
constraints, and having the chance to impose penalties on parts of blockmodels
create enormous flexibility. Although this flexibility completely transforms the
blockmodeling enterprise, it also imposes a rather large substantive burden on

2 Because many network analysts look askance at the statistical analysis of attribute data, the following
   parallel may help make the point. In regression analysis, experts argue that the goal is never to
   maximize the explained variance regardless of what is stuck in an equation as regressor.
3 Continuing the regression comparison, we say that this is a bit like throwing all sorts of variables –
   including residuals! – into a regression.

those choosing to work within this framework. At a minimum, priorities concerning the relative importance of particular block types can be specified. In considering this, we find that the relations between block types described in Chapter 7 have value. Both the complete and symmetric block types are special cases of the complete block type. The complete block is a special case of a regular block. In turn, the regular block is a special case of both the row-regular and column-regular block types. It seems that with the most general block types, it is easier to find some partition that fits – so much so that many equally well-fitting partitions are likely. This has been our experience with the regular block types and suggests that it is more fruitful to try and fit stringent (less general) block types before attempting to fit the general block types. One reason why the inconsistency measures tend to be higher for blockmodels based on structural equivalence is that the complete block is very stringent. If some combination of stringent and less stringent blocks is included in a blockmodel specification, priority is best given to the stringent block types. For example, we did this in fitting a blockmodel to the Deep South data in Chapter 8 by putting a heavy penalty on 1s in null blocks. One possible compromise here is to specify densities for blocks.

It is clear that specifying (generalized) blockmodels is primarily (perhaps always) a substantive matter. This is one reason why we are especially excited by the materials in Section 7.4, where we deal with prespecified models. Even so, the ugly problem mentioned in Section 12.4 rears its head here: Exactly what should the criterion function be for us to conclude that a prespecified blockmodel actually fits? For the ranked-clusters model fitted for the boys in a classroom (Table 7.17), we are on solid ground: there are no inconsistencies. For the girls, however, the foundations are less firm, for there are inconsistencies in that fitted model. Again, we have no definitive statement concerning thresholds below which blockmodels can be seen as fitting the data and above which they do not. Establishing such thresholds is a future direction for further work.

This issue becomes more complicated when the idea of penalty functions is considered. For most of the models and modeling procedures we discuss, we have placed limited emphasis on giving different weights to different types of inconsistencies: each type contributed equally. In the balance theoretic partitioning described in Chapter 10, there were two types of inconsistencies: negative ties within plus-sets and positive ties between them. For our analyses, these ties contributed equally to the criterion function. Empirically, when weighting them equally, we found that the overwhelming majority of partitions had fewer negative ties within plus-sets than positive ties between them. This we treated as an intuitively appealing and plausible finding.[4] However, there is nothing in the procedure to prevent unequal weighting of these two types of inconsistencies. The implications of using differential weights in fitting generalized blockmodels is a topic for further research.

---

4 Had we specified the two kinds of inconsistencies differently at the outset, it is not clear that we would have gotten this result.

For the ranked-clusters models there were also two types of inconsistencies: violations of the acyclic requirement and violations of the asymmetry requirement. In some of the analyses that we described, these inconsistencies were weighted unequally. In some contexts, the symmetry requirement is more important, and in others it can be the acyclic requirement. For the different contexts, the weights should be unequal. In principle, the application of different penalties will lead to different partitions. At face value, this appears to be disturbing: It suggests anything is possible and that by the selection of penalties any desired partition can be obtained. Such arguments place the emphasis in the wrong place. Having to consider penalties is simply another way in which analysts are compelled to use knowledge and to be explicit about the models they propose.

12.6 COMPOSITION OF BLOCKS

It seems that in most of the empirical uses of blockmodels, including some of our own, attention is focused on establishing the blockmodel, constructing the image, and then interpreting this image in some fashion.[5] Once the blocks are summarized (see Chapter 7, Section 7.2), their internal composition is of limited interest.

This connects with our discussion of moving from a partition to a substantive characterization of the equivalence underlying the partition in the following way. In seeking such an equivalence, we need to be clear as to what is meant by the term itself. By definition, units in equivalence classes of equivalence relations are equivalent. In the ideal blocks consistent with structural equivalence, the meaning is the following: Units located in a position are all equivalent in the sense that the units are identically connected to the rest of the network. For regular equivalence, units in a position need not be identically connected to the rest of the network, but they are linked in equivalent ways to equivalent others. In short, for both of these equivalences, the traditional notion that the members of a position are similar to each other holds.

The idea of equivalence, as a sociological concept, is generalized also when we move to generalized blockmodeling. Consider row-dominant and column-dominant block types. Suppose the social relation is "controls." Actors from the row cluster of a row-dominant block share the property that at least one of them can control all actors in the column cluster. (This is similar to a group saying "we are rich because one of us can afford to pay for whatever we want.") The idea of actors being similar in the sense of structural equivalence has to be modified. To do this, it is necessary to make the distinction between equivalent and similar. Under structural equivalence and regular equivalence, actors that are equivalent are also similar. This need not be the case for other interesting equivalences. If we stay within the structural equivalence framework, it seems strange that units in a cluster for a row-dominant block are equivalent because one or more rows (under row dominance) or columns (under column dominance) most likely will be very

---

5   This can range from a straightforward description to the use of role algebras.

different from other members of the block. Such units are equivalent, but they need not be similar under the row-dominant predicate.

In the balance theoretic partitioning of Chapter 10, the nature of the ideal blocks pointed to the distribution of positive and negative ties. Given a set of actors in a plus-set, there are no negative ties among them in the ideal block. This is a statement about the block and less a statement about the actors. In contrast to the sense of structural equivalence, members of a plus-set under a balance partition need not be equivalent to each other. Their equivalence, under the balance partition, is one of sending their positive ties to others in the same subgroup and sending their negative ties, if any, elsewhere. Such negative ties can be directed to very different actors in other subgroups. There may be additional patterning of the positive ties *inside* the plus-set that is worth pursuing. In the BWR example, this is clearly the case in Table 10.7. The one large plus-set in that table is made up of two quite distinct and cohesive subgroups.[6]

The structure within blocks is an important property. If there are negative ties within a diagonal block, their identification and location helps us understand the structure and some of its dynamics. Certainly, noticing patterns in the off-diagonal blocks is equally important. In Figure 10.7, for subtribes in Highland New Guinea, there were positive ties between plus-sets that are inconsistent with perfect balance. On closer inspection, all involve a single subtribe (Masilakidzuha) and are clear in Table 10.5. In the signed networks the pattern of between-block ties shows the concentration of negative ties on a small number of group members.

The need to look inside blocks seems more important for the symmetric–acyclic decomposition of a network. The overall goal of this type of analysis is to establish a ranked-clusters model with very specific properties. Units belong to positions that are partially ordered in an acyclic graph. As noted in Chapter 11, there are two types of departures from an ideal ranked-clusters model. One concerns ties down the (otherwise) ranked clusters, which violates the acyclic property of a ranked-clusters blockmodel. The other concerns the presence of asymmetric ties within a position, which violates the symmetry property. Locating the structural characteristic inside a (diagonal) block is important and, again, is an instance of there being useful structural information inside a block.

Of course, a close examination of the internal structure of a diagonal block is possible within the indirect approach. Our point is that such examinations are compelled by the direct approach with its attention to ideal block types and gauging the departures of an empirically established blockmodel from one or more ideal blocks.

12.7 MULTIPLE FITTED BLOCKMODELS

When reading the conventional blockmodeling literature, we have formed the impression that the there is a strong tendency to think in terms of *the* blockmodel

---

6 Also see Tables 10.6 and 10.7 and the narratives around these tables.

fitting the data. Partitions are reached, reported, and interpreted. Working within the generalized blockmodeling framework has persuaded us that the idea that there is one blockmodel fitting the data is far too limited. In one respect, this is a trivial observation stemming from the fact that the reallocation algorithm, as we use it, frequently leads to more than one equally well-fitting blockmodel (given a set of block types and number of clusters). It is also possible that partitions with different numbers of clusters fit equally well. There is no way to distinguish between different equally well-fitting partitions in terms of the criterion function used in the fitting procedure. Such blockmodels have to be distinguished on other grounds.

The partition of the SAR mission network in Chapter 6 had three equally well-fitting partitions. They had considerable consistency, and the difference may have more to do with measurement error. In such cases, a compromise partition can be established. More interesting are equally well-fitting partitions that differ considerably. For the partition of the SM data at the third time point, there was a second partition. Instances like this force network analysts to think more critically about their theories and their understandings of the data analyzed. In this context, we also note that partitions established within the generalized blockmodeling framework need not be nested – in marked contrast to the hierarchical methods used within conventional blockmodeling. Again, interpreting nonnested, equally well-fitting partitions is a challenge for analysts to think further about the conjunction of substance and data.

In a nonmethodological fashion, generalized blockmodeling permits multiple, different partitions of the same network based on different specifications of block types and blockmodels. For example, we have multiple partitions of the TI data in Chapters 6 and 7. This is also the case for the SG data. We believe, very strongly, that it is important not to choose among these different partitions. They need to be interpreted together for the differing insights they confer on network data where different generalized blockmodels fit. The different block types for the partition of the Deep South data point to the same conclusion: Use the different blockmodels so that they complement each other.

12.8   MULTIPLE RELATIONS

For the most part, we have remained silent about multiple relations. Here we consider them only briefly and with the intent of pointing to future work. In the conventional blockmodeling approach, multiple relations have been considered and even advocated for constructing blockmodels. Incorporating them into a blockmodel is straightforward through the device of stacking the relations, computing some (dis)similarity over the stacked relations, and clustering the (dis)similarity measures.

In principle, multiple relations can be included in the generalized blockmodeling approach, albeit with a little more difficulty than in the indirect approach. We are also cautious about the ways in which multiple relations can be included. If the relations are essentially the same, problems seem minor. The multiple relations could be combined in the sense of constructing a latent relation from the sets of measured relations. If the relations are very different, then we see many more problems in bringing them into the generalized blockmodeling framework and treating them in the same fashion. In fact, if the relations are quite different, we see no point in treating them in essentially the same fashion. Stacking markedly different relations in the indirect approach seems a guarantee for generating confusion. Unknown differences will be buried within the (dis)similarity measures.

If multiple relations are considered within the generalized blockmodeling framework, it seems better to examine the relations carefully before proceeding. At a minimum, it would seem foolish to expect the same block types to fit both relations. For example, if it is the case that informal interaction patterns in an organization are conditioned by the formal hierarchy, then the hierarchy and the informal relations, even with the same clusters, could be structured quite differently. Using the imagery of the hypothetical hierarchy in Chapter 1, we see that the actors could be partitioned in terms of regular equivalence to get the hierarchical structure. If the informal structure occurs largely within levels, then the partition of that structure could be made in terms of structural equivalence. Trying to fit the same block types to both structures would obscure these differences.

Some of the analyses in earlier chapters may be instructive. The baboon network considered in Chapter 7 had grooming relations at two time points. Given the similarities and the differences in the two structures at the two points in time, the outcome of a joint analysis of the two relations is not clear to us. Using the complete, regular, row-regular, column-regular, and null blocks, we obtained a partition for the first time point. A reasonable hypothesis is that, with the introduction of the two new baboons, the structure is unchanged. To test that hypothesis, we could fit the Time 1 blockmodel structure to the data for the second time point. In one sense, that model did have the same structure in 15 of the 16 blocks. However, for one block location, what was a complete block at the first time point was a null block at the second point in time. Of additional interest is that the baboons present at both time points rotated among the positions. Put differently, although the positions and the structure largely remained intact, the clusters differed substantially. Any analysis that tried to impose the same clustering of the baboons for both time points would obscure this critical difference.

For the NF data considered in Chapter 10, the early structure of three (reasonably sized) clusters persisted for a few weeks. The structure of the signed structure, as a balance theoretic blockmodel, for one time point could serve as a hypothesis for the structure at the next time point and fitted to the data for the later time point. For a while, the blockmodel would still fit. However, with the structural change to one large subgroup with some much disliked singletons and a dyad, such a hypothesis would fail. Considering all of the time points simultaneously would mask this. Of course, we cannot rule out the possibility that other interesting structural features could be delineated, but the general point we want to make is that if multiple relations are considered, it seems best to look at the structures separately but in the light of each other. At a minimum, seeking partitions using the same block types for all relations is problematic.

12.9 OTHER NETWORKS AND NETWORK TYPES

All of the examples we have used throughout this book have drawn upon network examples in the social sciences, yet the range of networks is much broader. Kolchanov et al. (2000) provided a definition of gene networks and described the construction of a vast GeneNet system as a bipartite network. Their work also included a discussion of "equivalent components" of gene networks that appears to use concepts very consistent with regular equivalence. We know that there are cell networks of molecules connected by biochemical reactions. In the realm of biology, food webs have been studied extensively with a close focus on systems of predator–prey relationships. Although who eats what among species in an ecological system can be viewed as a social network of sorts, few social network analysts have studied them. An exception is provided by Luczkovich et al. (2003), who used regular equivalence as a foundation for partitioning food webs and delineating trophic levels. Included in this work is the idea of graph coloring (Borgatti and Everett 1990; Everett and Borgatti 1994, 2002), which has obvious systematic connections with equivalence concepts and blockmodeling. Ecological systems can be viewed as networks of species through which critical chemicals flow. Finally, King (1993) provided a wide variety of applications of graph theory and topology within inorganic chemistry. This list, although truncated, makes it clear that there are many areas besides social networks in which network thinking and ideas can be used fruitfully.

Although items created by applications of human technology can also be seen as social, they are also hardware systems. The electrical power grid of a nation is a network – and the grid failure in the United States in August 2003 provided a powerful reminder of this societal interconnectedness. As noted implicitly in Chapter 1, transportation systems are, in essence, networks linking locations in geographical space with the purpose of moving materials, information, and people between locations. Wilson and Watkins (1990) presented a map of (part of) the London Underground Transport system as an example of such a network. Comparisons of different subways systems, such as the London Underground with the Paris Metro, could use generalized blockmodeling techniques to depict their fundamental structures. Foulds (1992) presented other examples of networks that are based in engineering. These include electrical circuits (Electrical Engineering), facilities layout (Industrial Engineering), and the design of traffic systems (Civil Engineering).

Still more fields that use network ideas include linguistics, computer science, ecology, and economics. Such uses need not be consistent. The kinds of network representation of social relations and natural resources used by economists are dramatically different from the networks studied by ecologists. Much of the contemporary debate concerning the environment can be framed in terms of these competing paradigms. See Brown (2001) for the implications of this radical disjunction and the need to reconcile the paradigms in some fashion.

The Internet serves as a frequently analyzed network, and there have been attempts to study its structural properties. Broder et al. (2000) provided an analysis of Web network data having roughly 200 million pages and 1.5 billion links and produced by a Web crawl. The broad structure they depict – with a central core having about 56 strongly connected vertices; an "in" part of about 44 million weakly connected vertices that sends ties to the core but receives none from the core; a an "out" part, also weakly connected with about 44 million vertices, that receives ties from the core but sends none to the core; tendrils that receive ties from the in part but not linked in any way to the core; tendrils that send ties to the out part alone; so-called tubes of connections from the in part to the out part that bypass the core completely; and a set of smaller isolated components – has a shape readily described by a blockmodel.

Albert and Barabasi (2002) reviewed the developments in the field of complex networks, describing a wide range of systems in nature and society (e.g., networks of chemicals connected by chemical reactions and networks of routers and computers connected by physical links). Through empirical studies, models, and analytical approaches, they learned that real networks are far from random and that they display generic organizing principles shared by rather different systems. Albert and Barabasi (2002) also uncovered some generic topological and dynamic principles. They concluded that, in the future, new concepts, ideas, and analytical tools should be developed to understand these complex networks. We believe that the proposed generalized blockmodeling approach can be used in this direction. Barabasi and his collegues (e.g., Barabasi 2003; Barabasi and Bonabeau 2003) discussed "scale-free networks" that exhibit a property known as a power law. If we let a vertex in a network have k lines, the distribution of k follows a power law for which the probability of a vertex being connected to k other vertices is $1/k^r$, where r is parameter in the range of 2 to 3 for many networks. According to Barabasi and Bonabeau (2003), Web pages form a scale-free network, and they report researchers finding some social networks that are scale free. These include people linked by e-mail, scientific citations of papers, and collaborations among scientists. Such networks are characterized by the presence of a few vertices with very high degree (called hubs) that dominate the network. There are different explanations of the origins of the power law, such as preferential attachment and modularization. Examples of networks that are not scale free include the U.S. power grid and interstate highway system. Some hierarchical clusterings of scale-free networks have been reported by Watts and Strogatz (1998) and suggest that clustering principles are useful for these networks. Given that blockmodeling provides a set of clustering tools for partitioning networks into clusters, generalized blockmodeling may have some utility in this realm also. Partitions of networks that are not scale free are likely to be quite different and suggest that different block types and blockmodels may be needed for these two broad network types.

Indeed, a more general point can be made. If, as we anticipate, it is possible to apply generalized blockmodeling methods to network data from many other substantive realms, we have no doubt that other block types will have to be defined and used. Although it is appealing to think that the presence of hubs in scale-free networks can translate into the presence of column-dominant and row-dominant block types, we suspect that other block types will be required. One promising avenue for future work is the creation of new block types and, with them, new types of blockmodels.

12.10   NETWORK SIZE AND VALUED GRAPHS

Thinking about networks of the size of the Web and electrical transmission systems raises the issue of network size. The optimizational tools described in this book are computer intensive, and most of the problems that have been tackled are NP hard (Brucker 1978; Roberts and Sheng 2001). Although the concepts elaborated for generalized blockmodeling have completely general applicability, their application is constrained by computational limits. The procedures that are described in this book are implemented in a program for network analysis and visualization, PAJEK, developed by Batagelj and Mrvar (2003), which is a suite of algorithms for large networks; de Nooy et al. (2004) provide an extensive introduction to PAJEK and include a chapter on role systems that describes many blockmodeling procedures. Even so, existing algorithms do impose limits on the size of networks that can be studied by means of generalized blockmodeling methods. Advances in algorithmic solutions will be required to expand the size of networks studied within the direct approach. For some specific blockmodels, such as symmetric–acyclic ones, efficient algorithms also exist for (very) large networks.

A second problem that we have skated around is the use of valued graphs. For binary networks, the presence or absence of ties is a qualitative difference that is exploited in the blockmodeling methods we propose. However, once we start working with valued networks, there is now a quantitative difference that has to be considered in addition to just the presence or absence of ties. Most of the computational procedures employed in this book rest only on the qualitative procedures. This could have raised a problem with the social work journal network considered in Chapter 8 but for the presence of so many 0s in the actual data. Had there been many entries in, say, the range 1–5, these would not have been recognized as different from the values in the 100s in that network. This suggests the need to move in one of two directions. One is to find a principled method to recode small values to 0s and then use the tools that we have currently. The other is to seek a more sophisticated way of dealing with valued data. In this direction, Nowicki and Snijders (2001) proposed a statistical approach to a posteriori blockmodeling for valued digraphs. The proposed probability model assumes that the vertices of the digraph are partitioned into several unobserved (latent) classes and that the probability of a relationship between two vertices depends only on the classes to which they belong. Their estimation procedure (a Bayesian estimator based on Gibbs sampling) is implemented into the program BLOCKS.

We see the need to deal with large network sizes and the need to take into account the valued nature of valued ties as the two most pressing constraints on a wider use of generalized blockmodeling methods. Even so, we regard generalized blockmodeling as a highly flexible framework for delineating the structure of networks in a variety of fruitful ways. We end by extending an invitation to others to explore the creation of new block types, new blockmodels, and new algorithms, and to examine the use of these methods in other disciplines.

BIBLIOGRAPHY

Aho, A. V., Hopcroft, J. E, & Ullman, J. D. (1976). *The Design and Analysis of Computer Algorithms*. Reading, MA: Addison-Wesley.

Alba, R. D. (1973). A graph-theoretic definition of a sociometric clique. *Journal of Mathematical Sociology, 3*, 113–126.

Albert, R., & Barabasi, A.-L. (2002). Statistical mechanics of complex networks. *Reviews of Modern Physics, 74*, 47–97.

Appel, K., & Haken, W. (1977a). Every planar map is four-colourable. Part I: Discharging. *Illinois Journal of Mathematics, 21*, 429–490.

Appel, K., & Haken, W. (1977b). Every planar map is four-colourable. Part II: Reducibility. *Illinois Journal of Mathematics, 21*, 491–567.

Arabie, P., Boorman, S. A., & Levitt, P. R. (1978). Constructiong blockmodels: How and why. *Journal of Mathematical Psychology, 17*, 21–63.

Atkin, R. H. (1974). *Mathematical Structure in Human Affairs*. London: Heinemann Educational.

Baker, D. R. (1992). A structural analysis of the social work journal network: 1985–1986. *Journal of Social Service Research, 15*, 153–167.

Bales, R. F. (1970). *Personality and Interpersonal Behavior*. New York: Holt, Rinehart & Winston.

Barabasi, A.-L. (2003). *Linked*. Cambridge: PLUME.

Barabasi, A.-L., & Bonabeau, E. (2003). Scale-free networks. *Scientific American*, May, 60–69.

Barbut, M., & Monjardet, B. (1970). *Ordre et classification, algebre et combinatoire, tome I et II*. Paris: Hachette Universite.

Batagelj, V. (1989). Similarity measures between structured objects. In Graovac, A. (Ed.), *Studies in Physical and Theoretical Chemistry*, (vol. 63, pp. 25–40). Amsterdam: Elsevier.

Batagelj, V. (1991a). Dissimilarities between structured objects – fragments. In Diday, E., & Lechevallier, Y. (Eds.), *Proceedings of the Conference Symbolic-Numeric Data Analysis and Learning* (pp. 255–262). New York: Nova Science.

Batagelj, V. (1991b). *STRAN – STRucture ANalysis*. Department of Mathematics, Faculty for Mathematics and Physics, University of Ljubljana, Slovenia.

Batagelj, V. (1993). Centrality in social networks. In Ferligoj, A., & Kramberger, A. (Eds.), *Developments in Statistics and Methodology* (pp. 129–138). Ljubljana, Slovenia: FDV.

Bibliography

Batagelj, V. (1994). Semirings for social network analysis. *Journal of Mathematical Sociology, 19*, 53–68.

Batagelj, V. (1996a). *MODEL 2 – Program for Generalized Pre-Specified Blockmodeling.* Department of Mathematics, Faculty for Mathematics and Physics, University of Ljubljana, Solvenia.

Batagelj, V. (1996b). Ragusan families marriage networks. In Ferligoj, A., & Kramberger, A. (Eds.), *Developments in Data Analysis* (pp. 217–228). Ljubljana, Slovenia: FDV.

Batagelj, V. (1997). Notes on blockmodeling. *Social Networks, 19*, 143–155.

Batagelj, V., & Bren, M. (1995). Comparing similarity measures. *Journal of Classification, 12*, 73–90.

Batagelj, V., Doreian, P., & Ferligoj, A. (1992). An optimizational approach to regular equivalence. *Social Networks, 14*, 121–135.

Batagelj, V., & Ferligoj, A. (1990). Agglomerative hierarchical multicriteria clustering using decision rules. In Momirović, K., & Mildner, V. (Eds.), *Proceedings of COMPSTAT'90* (pp. 15–20). Heidelberg: Physica-Verlag.

Batagelj, V., & Ferligoj, A. (1998). Constrained clustering problems. In Rizzi, A., Vichi, M., & Bock, H. H. (Eds.), *Advances in Data Science and Classification* (pp. 137–144). Berlin: Springer-Verlag.

Batagelj, V., & Ferligoj, A. (2000). Clustering relational data. In Gaul, W., Opitz, O., & Schader, M. (Eds.), *Data Analysis* (pp. 3–16). New York: Springer-Verlag.

Batagelj, V., Ferligoj, A., & Doreian, P. (1992). Direct and indirect methods for structural equivalence. *Social Networks, 14*, 63–90.

Batagelj, V., Ferligoj, A., & Doreian, P. (1998). Fitting pre-specified blockmodels. In Hayashi, C., Ohsumi, N., Yajima, K., Tanaka, Y., Bock, H. H., & Baba, Y. (Eds.), *Data Science, Classification, and Related Methods* (pp. 199–206). Tokyo: Springer-Verlag.

Batagelj, V., & Mrvar, A. (1998). Pajek – program for large network analysis. *Connections, 21* (2), 47–57.

Batagelj, V., & Mrvar, A. (2003). Pajek – analysis and visualisation of large networks. In Junger, M., & Mutzel, P. (Eds.), *Graph Drawing Software Book*. Berlin: Springer-Verlag.

Berge, C. (1985). *Graphs*. Amsterdam: North-Holland.

Berkowitz, S. D. (1982). *An Introduction to Structural Analysis: The Network Approach to Social Research*. Toronto: Butterworths.

Bernard, H. R., & Killworth, P. D. (1977). Informant accuracy in social network data II. *Human Communications Research, 4*, 3–18.

Bernard, H. R., Killworth, P. D., Kronenfeld, D., & Sailer, L. (1985). On the validity of retrospective data: The problem of informant accuracy. *Annual Review of Anthropology, 13*, 495–517.

Bernard, H. R., Killworth, P. D., & Sailer, L. (1982). Informant accuracy in social network data V: An experimental attempt to predict actual communication from recall data. *Social Science Research, 11*, 30–66.

Blumenthal, L. M. (1953). *Theory and Applications of Distance Geometry*. London: Oxford University Press.

Bolland, J. M. (1988). Sorting out centrality: An analysis of the performance of four centrality models in real and simulated networks. *Social Networks, 10*, 233–253.

Bonacich, P. (1971). Factoring and weighting approaches to status scores and clique identification. *Journal of Mathematical Sociology, 2*, 113–120.

Bonacich, P. (1979). The 'common structure semigroup' a replacement for the Boorman and White 'joint reduction', *American Journal of Sociology, 86*, 159–166.

Bonacich, P. (1991). Simultaneous group and individual centralities. *Social Networks, 13*, 155–168.

Borgatti, S. P. (1989). Regular Equivalence in Graphs, Hypergraphs and Matrices, Ph.D. Dissertation, University of California, Irvine.

Borgatti, S. P., & Everett, M. G. (1989). The class of all regular equivalences: Algebraic structure and computation. *Social Networks*, *11*, 65–88.

Borgatti, S. P., & Everett, M. G. (1990). Role colouring a graph. *Mathematical Social Science*, *21*, 183–188.

Borgatti, S. P., & Everett, M. G. (1992a). Notations of positions in social network analysis. In Marsden, P. V. (Ed.), *Sociological Methodology* (pp. 1–35). San Francisco: Jossey-Bass.

Borgatti, S. P., & Everett, M. G. (1992b). Regular blockmodels of multiway, multimode matrices. *Social Networks*, *14*, 91–120.

Borgatti, S. P., & Everett, M. G. (1997). Network analysis of 2-mode data. *Social Networks*, *19*, 243–269.

Borgatti, S. P., & Everett, M. G. (1999). Models of core/periphery structures. *Social Networks*, *21*, 375–395.

Borgatti, S. P., Everett, M. G., & Freeman, L. C. (1998). *UCINET VI Network Analysis Software*. Cambridge: Analytic Technologies.

Boyd, J. P. (1969). The algebra of group kinship. *Journal of Mathematical Psychology*, *6*, 139–167.

Boyd, J. P. (1991). *Social Semigroups. A Unified Theory of Scaling and Blockmodelling as Applied to Social Networks*. Fairfax, VA: George Mason University Press.

Boyle, R. (1969). Algebraic systems for normal and hierarchical sociograms. *Sociometry*, *32*, 91–111.

Breiger, R. L. (1974). The duality of persons and groups. *Social Forces*, *53*, 181–190.

Breiger, R. L., Boorman, S. A., & Arabie, P. (1975). An algorithm for clustering relational data with applications to social network analysis and comparison to multidimensional scaling. *Journal of Mathematical Psychology*, *12*, 328–383.

Breiger, R. L., & Pattison, P. E. (1986). Cumulated social roles: The duality of persons and their algebras. *Social Networks*, *8*, 215–256.

Brigham, R. C., & Dutton, R. D. (1985). A compilation of relations between graph invariants. *Networks*, *15*, 73–107.

Brigham, R. C., & Dutton, R. D. (1991). Supplement I. *Networks*, *21*, 421–455.

Broder, R., Kumar, R., Maghoul, F., Raghaven, P., & Stata, R. (2000). Graph structure in the web. In *Proceedings of the 9th International World Wide Web Conference on Computer Networks* (pp. 247–256). Amesterdam: North Holland. Available at http://www9.org/w9cdrom/160/160.html.

Brown, L. R. (2001). *Eco-Economy: Building and Economy for the Earth*. New York: W. W. Norton.

Brucker, P. (1978). On the complexity of clustering problems. In Henn, R., Korte, B., & Oettli, W. (Eds.), *Optimization and Operations Research*. Berlin: Springer-Verlag.

Burkard, R. E., Cuninghame-Greene, R. A., & Zimmermann, U. (Eds.). (1984). *Algebraic and Combinatorial Methods in Operations Research*. Annals of Discrete Mathematics, No. 19. Amsterdam: North-Holland.

Burt, R. S. (1976). Positions in networks. *Social Forces*, *55*, 93–122.

Burt, R. S. (1977a). Positions in multiple networks I: A general conception of stratification and prestige in a system of actors cast as a social topology. *Social Forces*, *56*, 106–131.

Burt, R. S. (1977b). Positions in multiple networks II: Stratification and prestige among elite decision-makers in the community of Altneustadt. *Social Forces*, *56*, 551–575.

Burt, R. S. (1986). A cautionary note. *Social Networks*, *8*, 205–211.

Burt, R. S. (1988). Some properties of structural equivalence, measures derived from sociometric choice data. *Social Networks*, *10*, 1–28.

Burt, R. S. (1990). Detecting role equivalence. *Social Networks*, *12*, 83–97.

Burt, R. S., & Minor, M. J. (1983). *Applied Network Analysis*. Beverly Hills, CA: Sage.

Carré, B. (1979). *Graphs and Networks*. Oxford: Clarendon.

Carrington, P. J., Heil, G. H., & Berkowitz, S. D. (1980). A goodness-of-fit index for blockmodels. *Social Networks*, 2, 219–234.

Cartwright, D., & Harary, F. (1956). Structural balance: A generalization of Heider's theory. *Psychological Review*, 63, 277–292.

Cartwright, D., & Harary, F. (1968). On the coloring of signed graphs. *Elemente der Mathematik*, 23, 85–89.

Cartwright, D., & Harary, F. (1979). Balance and clusterability: An overview. In Holland, P., & Leinhardt, S. (Eds.), *Perspectives on Social Network Research* (pp. 25–50). New York: Academic.

Chankong, V., & Haimes, Y. Y. (1983). *Multiobjective Decision Making*. New York: North-Holland.

Chartrand, G. (1985). *Introductory Graph Theory*. New York: Dover.

Chartrand, G., & Oellerman, O. (1992). *Applied and Algorithmic Graph Theory*, New York: McGraw-Hill.

Cleveland, W. S. (1985). *The Elements of Graphing Data*. Belmont, CA: Wadsworth.

Clifford, H. T., & Stephenson, W. (1975). *An Introduction to Numerical Classification*. New York: Academic.

Cohen, I. (1985). *Revolution in Science*. Cambridge, MA: Belknap.

Conte, S., & de Boor, C. (1981). *Elementary Numerical Analysis* (3rd ed.). Singapore: McGraw-Hill.

Czekanowski, J. (1913). *Zarys metod statystycznek*. Warsaw: E. Wendego.

Davey, B. A., & Priestley, H. A. (1990). *Introduction to Lattices and Order*. Cambridge: Cambridge University Press.

Davis, A., Gardner, B., & Gardner, M. R. (1941). *Deep South*. Chicago: University of Chicago Press.

Davis, J. A. (1967). Clustering and structural balance in graphs. *Human Relations*, 20, 181–187.

Davis, J. A., & Leinhardt, S. (1972). The structure of positive interpersonal relations in small groups. In Berger, J. (Ed.), *Sociological Theories in Progress* (vol. 2, pp. 218–251). Boston: Houghton Mifflin.

Day, W. H. E. (1986). Foreword: Comparison and consensus of classifications. *Journal of Classification*, 3, 183–185.

de Nooy, W., Mrvar, A., & Batagelj, V. (2004). *Exploratory Social Network Analysis with Pajek*. Cambridge: Cambridge University Press.

DeSarbo, W. S., & Mahajan, V. (1984). Constrained classification: The use of a priori information in cluster analysis. *Psychometrika*, 49, 187–215.

Diday, E. (1974). Optimization in nonhierarchical clustering. *Pattern Recognition*, 6, 17–33.

Dolan, A., & Aldous, J. (1993). *Networks and Algorithms: An Introductory Approach*. Chichester, England: Wiley.

Doreian, P. (1970). *Mathematics and the Study of Social Relations*. London: Weidenfeld and Nicolson.

Doreian, P. (1974). On the connectivity of social networks. *Journal of Mathematical Sociology*, 3, 245–258.

Doreian, P. (1979). On delineation of small group structure. In Hudson, H. C. (Ed.), *Classifying Social Data* (pp. 215–230). San Francisco: Jossey-Bass.

Doreian, P. (1985). Structural equivalence in a psychology journal network. *Journal of the American Society for Information Science*, 36, 411–417.

Doreian, P. (1988a). Equivalence in a social network. *Journal of Mathematical Sociology*, 13, 243–282.

Doreian, P. (1988b). Testing structural equivalence in a network of geographical journals. *Journal of the American Society for Information Science*, 39, 79–85.

Doreian, P. (1995). Social network analysis as a scientific revolution: Thinking in circles or genuine progress? In Everett, M. G., & Rennolls, K. (Eds.), *Methodology; Proceedings of the International Conference on Social Networks* (vol. 1, pp. 1–21). London: Greenwich University Press.

Doreian, P. (2002). Event sequences as generators of social network evolution. *Social Networks, 24*, 93–119.

Doreian, P., & Albert, L. H. (1989). Partitioning political actor networks: Some quantitative tools for analyzing qualitative networks. *Journal of Quantitative Anthropology, 1*, 279–291.

Doreian, P., Batagelj, V., & Ferligoj, A. (1994). Partitioning networks based on generalized concepts of equivalence. *Journal of Mathematical Sociology, 19*, 1–27.

Doreian, P., Batagelj, V., & Ferligoj, A. (2000). Symmetric-Acyclic Decomposition of Networks. *Journal of Classification, 17*, 3–28.

Doreian, P., & Fararo, T. J. (1985). Structural equivalence in a journal network. *Journal of the American Society for Information Science, 36*, 28–37.

Doreian, P., & Fujimoto, K. (2003). Structures of Supreme Court voting. *Connections, 25*(3).

Doreian, P., Kapuscinski, R., Krackhardt, D., & Szczypula, J. (1996). A brief history of balance through time. *Journal of Mathematical Sociology, 21*, 113–131.

Doreian, P., & Krackhardt, D. (2001). Pre-transitive mechanisms for signed networks. *Journal of Mathematical Sociology, 25*, 43–67.

Doreian, P., & Mrvar, A. (1996). A partitioning approach to structural balance. *Social Networks, 18*, 149–168.

Doreian, P., & Stokman, F. (Eds.) (1997). *Evolution of Social Networks*. New York: Gordon & Breach.

Doreian, P., & Woodard, K. L. (1992). Fixed list versus snowball selection of social networks. *Social Science Research, 21*, 216–233.

Doreian, P., & Woodard, K. L. (1994). Defining and locating cores and boundaries of social networks. *Social Networks, 16*, 267–293.

Drabek, T. E., Tamminga, H. L., Kilijanek, T. S., & Adams, C. R. (1981). *Managing Multiorganizational Emergency Responses*. Boulder: University of Colorado, Institute of Behavioral Science.

Dunbar, R., & Dunbar, P. (1975). Social dynamics of Gelada baboons. *Contributions to Primatology, 6*, 1–57.

Erdös, P. (1959). Graph Theory and Probability. *Canadian Journal of Mathematics, 11*, 34–38.

Erdös, P. (1961). Graph Theory and Probability II. *Canadian Journal of Mathematics, 13*, 346–352.

Everett, M. G. (1982). A graph theoretic blocking procedure for social networks. *Social Networks, 4*, 147–167.

Everett, M. G., & Borgatti, S. P. (1988). Calculating role similarities: An algorithm that helps determine the orbits of a graph. *Social Networks, 10*, 71–91.

Everett, M. G., & Borgatti, S. P. (1993). An extension of regular colouring of graphs to digraphs, networks and hypergraphs. *Social Networks, 15*, 237–254.

Everett, M. G., & Borgatti, S. P. (1994). Regular equivalence: General theory. *Journal of Mathematical Sociology, 19*, 29–52.

Everett, M. G., & Borgatti, S. P. (2002). Computing regular equivalence: Practical and theoretical issues. In Mrvar, A., & Ferligoj, A. (Eds.), *Developments in Statistics* (pp. 31–42). Ljubljana, Slovenia: FDV.

Everitt, B. (1974). *Cluster Analysis*. London: Heinemann Educational.

Fabič-Petrač, I., Jerman-Blažič, B., & Batagelj, V. (1991). Study of computation, relatedness and activity prediction of topological indices. *Journal of Mathematical Chemistry, 8*, 121–134.

Faust, K. (1988). Comparison of methods for positional analysis: Structural and general equivalences. *Social Networks, 10,* 313–341.

Faust, K., & Romney, A. K. (1985). Does structure find structure? A critique of Burt's use of distance as a measure of structural equivalence. *Social Networks, 7,* 77–103.

Faust, K., & Wasserman, S. (1992). Blockmodels: Interpretation and evaluation. *Social Networks, 14,* 5–61.

Ferligoj, A. (1986). Clustering with constraining variables. *Journal of Mathematical Sociology, 12,* 299–313.

Ferligoj, A., & Batagelj, V. (1982). Clustering with relational constraint. *Psychometrika, 47,* 413–426.

Ferligoj, A., & Batagelj, V. (1983). Some types of clustering with relational constraint. *Psychometrika, 48,* 541–552.

Ferligoj, A., & Batagelj, V. (1992). Direct multicriteria clustering algorithms. *Journal of Classification, 9,* 43–61.

Ferligoj, A., Batagelj, V., & Doreian, P. (1994). On connecting network analysis and cluster analysis. In Fischer, G. H., & Laming, D. (Eds.), *Contributions to Mathematical Psychology, Psychometrics, and Methodology* (pp. 329–344). New York: Springer-Verlag.

Ferligoj, A., Doreian, P., & Batagelj, V. (1996). Optimizational approach to blockmodeling. *Journal of Computing and Information Technology, 4,* 225–233.

Ferligoj, A., & Hlebec, V. (1999). Evaluation of social network measurement instruments. *Social Networks, 21,* 111–130.

Ferligoj, A., & Lapajne, Z. (1986). Razvrščanje srednješolskih programov v skupine. *Sodobna pedagogika, 38,* 27–37.

Fiksel, J. (1980). Dynamic evolution in societal networks. *Journal of Mathematical Sociology, 7,* 27–46.

Fine, G. A. (1987). *With the Boys: Little League Baseball and Preadolescent Culture.* Chicago: University of Chicago Press.

Fletcher, J. G. (1980). A more general algorithm for computing closed semiring costs between vertices of a directed graph. *Communications of the Association for Computing Machinery, 23,* 350–351.

Florek, K. et al. (1951). Sur la liaison et la division des points d'un ensemble fini. *Colloquium Mathematicum, 2,* 282–285.

Forsyth, D. R. (1990). *Group Dynamics.* Belmont, MA: Brooks-Cole.

Foulds, L. R. (1984). *Combinatorial Optimization for Undergraduates.* New York: Springer-Verlag.

Foulds, L. R. (1992). *Graph Theory Applications.* New York: Springer-Verlag.

Freeman, L. C. (1977). A set of measures of centrality based on betweenness. *Sociometry, 40,* 35–41.

Freeman, L. C. (1979). Centrality in social networks: Conceptual clarification. *Social Networks, 1,* 215–239.

Freeman, L. C. (1980). Q-analysis and the structure of friendship networks. *International Journal of Man-Machine Studies, 12,* 367–378.

Freeman, L. C. (1992). The sociological conception of "group": An empirical test of two models. *American Journal of Sociology, 98,* 152–166.

Freeman, L. C. (2003). Finding social groups: A meta-analysis of the southern women data. In Breiger, R., Carley, K., & Pattison, P. (Eds.), *Dynamic Social Network Modeling and Analysis: Workshop Summary and Papers* (pp. 39–77). Washington, DC: National Academy Press.

Freeman, L. C., Borgatti, S. P., & White, D. R. (1991). Centrality in valued graphs: A measure of betweenness based on network flow. *Social Networks, 13,* 141–154.

Freeman, L. C., & White, D. R. (1994). Using Galois lattices to present network data. In Marsden, P. (Ed.), *Sociological Methodology* (pp. 127–146). Cambridge: Blackwell.

French, S. (1986). *Decision Theory – An Introduction to Mathematics of Rationality.* New York: Wiley.

Galaskiewicz, J. (1985). *Social Organization of an Urban Grants Economy.* New York: Academic.

Gatrell, A. C., & Smith, A. (1984). Networks of relations among a set of geographical journals. *Professional Geographer, 36,* 300–307.

Gordon, A. D. (1973). Classification in the presence of constraints. *Biometrics, 2,* 821–827.

Gordon, A. D. (1980). Methods of constrained classification. In Tomassone, R. (Ed.), *Analyse de Donnee Informatique.* Le Chesnay, France: INRIA.

Gordon, A. D. (1981). *Classification.* London: Chapman & Hall.

Gordon, A. D. (1987). Classification and assignment in soil science. *Soil Use and Management, 3,* 3–8.

Gordon, A. D. (1996). A survey of constrained classification. *Computational Statistics & Data Analysis, 21,* 17–29.

Gould, R. V. (1987). Measures of betweenness in non-symmetric networks. *Social Networks, 9,* 277–282.

Gower, J. C. (1967). A comparison of some methods of cluster analysis. *Biometrics, 23,* 623–638.

Gower, J. C., & Legendre, P. (1986). Metric and Euclidean properties of dissimilarity coefficients. *Journal of Classification, 3,* 5–48.

Greenhouse, L. (2001). In year of Florida vote, Supreme Court did much other work. *New York Times,* Monday, July 2.

Hage, P., & Harary, F. (1983). *Structural Models in Anthropology.* Cambridge: Cambridge University Press.

Hanani, U. (1979). *Multicriteria Dynamic Clustering.* Rapport de Recherche No. 358. Rocquencourt, France: INRIA.

Hansen, P., Jaumard, B., & Sanlaville, E. (1993). Partitioning problems in cluster analysis: A review of mathematical programming approaches. Invited paper presented at IFCS'93, Paris.

Harary, F. (1953). On the notion of balance in signed graphs. *Michigan Mathematical Journal, 2,* 143–146.

Harary, F. (1972). *Graph Theory.* Reading, MA: Addison-Wesley.

Harary, F., Norman, R. Z., & Cartwright, D. (1965). *Structural Models: An Introduction to the Theory of Directed Graphs.* New York: Wiley.

Hartigan, J. A. (1975). *Cluster Algorithms.* New York: Wiley.

Heider, F. (1946). Attitudes and cognitive organization. *Journal of Psychology, 21,* 107–112.

Heider, F. (1958). *The Psychology of Interpersonal Relations.* New York: Wiley.

Heil, G. H., & White, H. C. (1976). An algorithm for finding simultaneous homomorphic correspondences between graphs and their image graphs. *Behavioral Science, 21,* 26–35.

Historijski archiv u Dubrovniku (Historic Archive of Dubrovnik), Littere et Commissiones Levantis, vol. xxx, fol. 100–101, Commissio Reverendissimi Episcopi Stagnensis Profecturi Romam, 5. March 1566 (Transcription published in Krivošić, S: Stanovništo Dubrovnika i domografske Promjene u prošlosti, JAZU, Dabrovnik, 1999, 189–190.)

Hlebec, V. (1993). Recall versus recognition: Comparison of two alternative procedures for collecting social network data. In Ferligoj, A., & Kramberger, A. (Eds.), *Developments in Statistics and Methodology* (pp. 121–128). Ljubljana, Slovenia: FDV.

Hlebec, V., & Ferligoj, A. (2001). Respondent mood and the instability of survey network measurements. *Social Networks, 23,* 125–139.

Hlebec, V., & Ferligoj, A. (2002). Reliability of social network measurement instruments. *Field Methods, 14,* 288–306.

Hoivik, T., & Gleditsch, N. P. (1975). Structural parameters of graphs: A theoretical investigation. In Blalock, H., Aganbegian, A., Borodkin, F. M., Boudon, R., & Cappechi, V. (Eds.), *Quantitative Sociology* (pp. 203–223). New York: Academic.

Homans, G. C. (1950). *The Human Group*. New York: Harcourt, Brace & World.

Homenjuk, V. V. (1983). *Elementi teorii mnogocelevoj optimizacii*. Moscow: Nauka.

Hrbacek, K., & Jech, T. (1978). *Introduction to Set Theory*. New York: Marcell–Dekker.

Hubálek, Z. (1982). Coefficients of association and similarity, based on binary (presence–absence) data: An evaluation. *Biological Review*, *57*, 669–689.

Hummell, H., & Sodeur, W. (1987). Strukturbeschreibung von positionen in sozialen beziehungsnetzen. In Pappi, F. U. (Ed.), *Methoden der Netzwerkanalyse*. Munich: Oldenburg.

Hummon, N. P., & Carley, K. (1993). Social networks as normal science. *Social Networks*, *15*, 71–106.

Hummon, N. P., & Doreian, P. (1989). Connectivity in a citation network: The development of DNA theory. *Social Networks*, *11*, 39–63.

Hummon, N. P., & Doreian, P. (1990). Computational methods for social network analysis. *Social Networks*, *12*, 273–288.

Hummon, N. P., & Doreian, P. (2003). Some dynamics of social balance processes: Bringing Heider back into balance theory. *Social Networks*, *25*, 17–49.

Hummon, N. P., Doreian, P., & Freeman, L. C. (1990). Analyzing the structure of the centrality–productivity literature created between 1948 and 1979. *Knowledge: Creation, Diffusion, Utilization*, *11*, 459–480.

Jaccard, P. (1908). Nouvelles recherches sur la distribution florale. *Bulletin de la Societe Vaudoise des Sciences Naturelles*, *44*, 223–270.

Janowitz, X. (1978). An order theoretic model for cluster analysis. *SIAM Journal on Applied Mathematics*, *34*, 55–72.

Jennings, H. H. (1948). *Sociometry in Group Relations: A Manual for Teachers*. Westport, CT: Glenwood.

Karp, R. M. (1972). Reducibility among combinatorial problems. In Miller, R. E., & Thatcher, J. W. (Eds.), *Complexity of Computer Computations* (pp. 85–103). New York: Plenum.

Killworth, P. D., & Bernard, H. R. (1978). Reverse small world experiment. *Social Networks*, *1*, 159–192.

Killworth, P. D., & Bernard, H. R. (1979). Informant accuracy in social network data III: A comparison of triadic structure in behavioral and cognitive data. *Social Networks*, *2*, 10–46.

King, R. B. (1993). *Applications of Graph Theory and Topology in Inorganic Cluster and Coordination Chemistry*. Boca Raton, FL: CRC.

Klenk, V. (1989). *Understanding Symbolic Logic*. Englewood Cliffs, NJ: Prentice-Hall.

Knoke, D., & Kuklinski, J. H. (1982). *Network Analysis*. Beverly Hills, CA: Sage.

Kolchanov, N. A., Anan'ko, F. A., Podkolodnaya, E. V., Ignat'eva, T. N., Goryachkovskaya, T., & Stepanenko, I. L. (2000). Gene networks. *Molecular Biology (USSR)*, *34*, 449–460.

Krivošić, S. (1990). *Stanovništvo Dubrovnika i demografske promjene u prošlosti*. Dubrovnik, Yugoslavia: Zavod za povjesne znanosti JAZU u Dubrovniku.

Kulczynski, S. (1927). Die pflanzenassoziationen der pieninen. *Bulletin International de l'Academie Polonaise des Sciences et des Lettres*, Serie B, Suppl. II, 57–203.

Lance, G. N., & Williams, W. T. (1966). Computer programs for hierarchical polythetic classification ("similarity analyses"). *Computer Journal*, *9*, 60–64.

Lance, G. N., & Williams, W. T. (1967). Mixed-data classificatory programs. I. Agglomerative systems. *Australian Computer Journal*, *1*, 15–20.

Lapajne, Z. (1984). *Proces izbire poklica 1980–1982*. Ljubljana, Slovenia: Center za razvoj univerze.

Laumann, E. O., Marsden, P. V., & Prensky, D. (1983). The boundary specification problem in network analysis. In Burt, R. S., & Minor, M. J. (Eds.), *Applied Network Analysis: A Methodological Introduction* (pp. 18–34). Beverly Hills, CA: Sage.

Lebart, L. (1978). Programme d' agregation avec contraintes (cah contiguite). *Les Cahiers d'Analyse des Donnes, 3*, 275–287.

Lefkovitch, L. P. (1980). Conditional clustering. *Biometrics, 36*, 43–58.

Legendre, P. (1987). Constrained clustering. In Legendre, P., & Legendre, L. (Eds.), *Developments in Numerical Ecology* (pp. 289–307). Berlin: Springer-Verlag.

Lidl, R., & Pilz, G. (1984). *Applied Abstract Algebra*. New York: Springer-Verlag.

Lorr, M. (1983). *Cluster Analysis for Social Scientists*. San Francisco: Jossey-Bass.

Lorrain, F., & White, H. C. (1971). Structural equivalence of individuals in social networks. *Journal of Mathematical Sociology, 1*, 49–80.

Lovász, L. (1968). On Chromatic number of Finite Set Systems. *Acta Mathematica Academy of Sciences Hungary, 19*, 59–67.

Luce, R. D. (1950). Connectivity and generalized cliques in sociometric group structure. *Psychometrika, 15*, 159–190.

Luce, R. D., & Perry, A. D. (1949). A method of matrix analysis of group structure. *Psychometrika, 14*, 95–116.

Luczkovich, J. J., Borgatti, S. P., Johnson, J. C., & Everett, M. G. (2003). Defining and measuring trophic role similarity in food webs using regular equivalence. *Journal of Theoretical Biology, 220*, 303–321.

MacCrimmon, K. R. (1973). An overview of multiple objective decision making. In Cochrane, J. L., & Zeleny, M. (Eds.), *Multiple Criteria Decision Making*. Columbia: University of South Carolina Press.

MacQueen, J. B. (1967). Some methods of classification and analysis of multivariate observations. In *Proceedings of the 5th Berkeley Symposium, 1*, 281–297.

Mahalanobis, P. C. (1936). On the generalized distance in statistics. *Proceedings of the National Institute of Sciences of India, 2*, 49–55.

Mandel, M. J. (1983). Local roles and social networks. *American Sociological Review, 48*, 376–386.

Marsden, P. V. (1990). Network data and measurement. *Annual Review of Sociology, 16*, 435–463.

McQuitty, L. L. (1960). Hierarchical linkage analysis for the isolation of types. *Educational and Psychological Measurement, 20*, 55–67.

McQuitty, L. L. (1966). Similarity analysis by reciprocal pairs for discrete and continuous data. *Educational and Psychological Measurement, 26*, 825–831.

McQuitty, L. L. (1967). Expansion of similarity analysis by reciprocal pairs for discrete and continuous data. *Educational and Psychological Measurement, 27*, 253–255.

McQuitty, L. L. (1968). Multiple clusters, types, and dimensions from iterative intercolumnar correlational analysis. *Multivariate Behavioral Research, 3*, 465–477.

Milgram, S. (1967). The small world problem. *Psychology Today, 22*, 61–67.

Mojena, R. (1977). Hierarchical grouping methods and stopping rules: An evaluation. *Computer Journal, 20*, 359–363.

Mokken, R. J. (1979). Cliques, clubs and clans. *Quality and Quantity, 13*, 161–173.

Moon, J., & Moser, L. (1965). On cliques in graphs. *Israel Journal of Mathematics, 3*, 23–28.

Moreno, J. L. (1934). *Who Shall Survive?: Foundations of Sociometry, Group Psychotherapy, and Sociodrama*. Washington, DC: Nervous and Mental Disease Publishing.

Murtagh, F. (1985). A survey of algorithms for contiguity-constrained clustering and related problems. *Computer Journal, 28*, 82–88.

Nakao, K., & Romney, A. K. (1993). Longitudinal approach to subgroup formation: Reanalysis of Newcomb's fraternity data. *Social Networks, 15*, 109–131.

Newcomb, T. M. (1961). *The Acquaintance Process*. New York: Holt, Rinehart & Winston.

Newcomb, T. M. (1968). Interpersonal balance. In Abelson, R., Aronson, E., McGuire, W., Newcomb, T., Rosenberg, M., & Tannenbaum, O. (Eds.), *Theories of Cognitive Consistency: A Source Book* (pp. 28–51). Chicago: Rand McNally.

Nordlie, P. (1958). *A Longitudinal Study of Interpersonal Attraction in a Natural Group Setting*. Ph.D. thesis. Ann Arbor: University of Michigan.

Nowicki, K., & Snijders, T. A. B. (2001). Estimation and prediction for stochastic block-structures. *Journal of the American Statistical Association, 96*, 1077–1087.

Olsen, M. E. (1968). *The Process of Social Organization*. New York: Holt, Rinehart & Winston.

Panning, W. H. (1982). Fitting blockmodels to data. *Social Networks, 4*, 81–101.

Pattison, P. E. (1988). Network models; some comments on papers in this special issue. *Social Networks, 10*, 383–411.

Pattison, P. E. (1993). *Algebraic Models for Social Networks*. Cambridge: Cambridge University Press.

Pearson, K. (1926). On the coefficient of racial likeness. *Biometrika, 18*, 105–117.

Perruchet, C. (1983). Constrained agglomerative hierarchical classification. *Pattern Recognition, 16*, 213–217.

Podinovskij, V. V., & Nogin, V. D. (1982). *Pareto-optimalnye rešenija mnogokriterialnyh zadač*. Moscow: Nauka.

Preparata, F. P., & Yeh, R. T. (1973). *Introduction to Discrete Structures for Computer Science and Engineering*. Reading, MA: Addison-Wesley.

Press, W., Flannery, B., Teukolsky, S., & Vetterling, W. (1986). *Numerical Recipes: The Art of Scientific Computing*. Cambridge: Cambridge University Press.

Price, D. S. (1965). Networks of scientific papers. *Science, 149*, 510–515.

Rapoport, A. (1957). A contribution to the theory of random and biased nets. *Bulletin of Mathematical Biophysics, 19*, 257–271.

Rapoport, A. (1963). Mathematical models of social interaction. In Luce, R. D., Bush, R., & Galanter, E. (Eds.), *Handbook of Mathematical Psychology* (pp. 493–579). New York: Wiley.

Read, K. E. (1954). Cultures of the central highlands, New Guinea. *Southwestern Journal of Anthropology, 10*, 1–43.

Riley, J. E. (1969). An application of graph theory to social psychology. In Chartrand, G., & Kapoor, S. F. (Eds.), *The Many Facets of Graph Theory*. Number 110 in Lecture Notes in Mathematics (pp. 275–280). Berlin: Springer-Verlag.

Roberts, F. S. (1976). *Discrete Mathematical Models with Applications to Social, Biological, and Environmental Problems*. Englewood Cliffs, NJ: Prentice-Hall.

Roberts, F. S., & Sheng, L. (2001). How hard is it to determine if a graph has a 2-role assignment? *Networks, 37*, 67–73.

Roberts, J. M. (2000). Correspondence analysis of two-mode network data. *Social Networks, 22*, 65–72.

Roethlisberger, F. J., & Dickson, W. J. (1939). *Management and the Worker*. Cambridge, MA: Harvard University Press.

Rogers, D. J., & Tanimoto, T. T. (1960). A computer program for classifying plants. *Science, 132*, 1115–1118.

Rogers, E. M. (1987). Progress, problems and prospects for network reserach: Investigating relationships in the age of electronic communication technologies. *Social Networks, 9*, 285–310.

Russell, F. F., & Rao, T. R. (1940). On habitat and association of species of anopheline larvae in south-eastern madras. *Journal of the Malaria Institute of India, 3*, 153–178.

Sabidussi, G. (1966). The centrality index of a graph. *Psychometrika, 31*, 581–603.

Sailer, L. D. (1978). Structural equivalence: Meaning and definition, computation and application. *Social Networks, 1*, 73–90.

Salancik, G. R. (1986). An index of subgroup influence in dependency networks. *Administrative Science Quarterly, 31*, 194–211.

Sampson, S. F. (1968). *A Novitiate in a Period of Change: An Experimental and Case Study of Social Relationships*. Ph.D. thesis. Ithaca, NY: Cornell University.

Schreider, J. A. (1975). *Equality, Resemblance and Order*. Mosow: Mir.

Schwartz, J. E., & Sprinzen, M. (1984). Structures of connectivity. *Social Networks, 6*, 103–140.

Scott, J. (1991). *Social Network Analysis: A Handbook*. London: Sage.

Seidman, S. (1981). Structures induced by collection of subsets. *Mathematical Social Sciences, 1*, 381–396.

Seidman, S. B. (1983). Network structure and minimum degree. *Social Networks, 5*, 269–287.

Seidman, S. B., & Foster, B. L. (1978). A graph-theoretic generalization of the clique concept. *Journal of Mathematical Sociology, 6*, 139–154.

Skvoretz, J., & Faust, K. (1999). Logit models for affiliation networks. *Sociological Methodology, 29*, 253–280.

Sneath, P. H. A. (1957). Some thoughts on bacterial classification. *Journal of General Microbiology, 17*, 184–200.

Sokal, R. R., & Michener, C. D. (1958). A statistical method for evaluating systematic relationships. *University of Kansas Science Bulletin, 38*, 1409–1438.

Sokal, R. R., & Sneath, P. H. A. (1963). *Principles of Numerical Taxonomy*. San Francisco: Freeman.

Stephenson, K., & Zelen, M. (1989). Rethinking centrality: Methods and examples. *Social Networks, 11*, 1–37.

Stoll, R. R. (1961). *Set Theory and Logic*. San Francisco: Freeman.

Stone, H. S. (1973). *Discrete Mathematical Structures and Their Applications*. Chicago: Science Research Associates.

Sudman, S. (1985). Experiments in the measurement of the size of social networks. *Social Networks, 7*, 127–151.

Sudman, S. (1988). Experiments in measuring neighbor and relative social networks. *Social Networks, 10*, 93–108.

Taylor, H. F. (1970). *Balance in Small Groups*. New York: Van Nostrand Reinhold.

Wall, R. (1972). *Introduction to Mathematical Linguistics*. Englewood Cliffs, NJ: Prentice-Hall.

Wallerstein, I. (1974). *The Modern World System: Capitalist Agriculture and the Origins of the European World-Economy in the Sixteenth Century*. New York: Academic.

Ward, J. H. (1963). Hierarchical grouping to optimize an objective function. *Journal of the American Statistical Association, 58*, 236–244.

Wasserman, S., & Faust, K. (1994). *Social Network Analysis: Methods and Applications*. Cambridge: Cambridge University Press.

Wasserman, S., & Pattison, P. (1996). Logit models and logistic regressions for social networks: An introduction to Markov random graphs and p^*. *Psychometrika, 60*, 401–425.

Watts, D. J., & Strogatz, S. H. (1998). Collective dynamics of "small-world" networks. *Nature, 393*, 440–442.

Wellman, B. (1988). Structural analysis: From method and methaphor to theory and substance. In Wellman, B., & Berkowitz, S. D. (Eds.), *Social Structures: A Network Approach* (pp. 19–61). Cambridge: Cambridge University Press.

Wellman, B., & Berkowitz, S. D. (Eds.). (1988). *Social Structures: A Network Approach*. Cambridge: Cambridge University Press.

White, D. R., & Reitz, K. P. (1983). Graph and semigroup homomorphisms on networks of relations. *Social Networks, 5*, 193–234.

White, H. C., Boorman, S. A., & Breiger, R. L. (1976). Social structure from multiple networks. I. blockmodels of roles and positions. *American Journal of Sociology, 81,* 730–779.

Whitney, H. (1932). Congruent graphs and the connectivity of graphs. *American Journal of Mathematics, 54,* 150–168.

Wilson, R. J., & Watkins, J. J. (1990). *Graphs: An Introductory Approach.* New York: Wiley.

Winship, C. (1974). *Thoughts about roles and relations. Part I: Theoretical considerations.* Unpublished manuscript. Cambridge, MA: Harvard University.

Winship, C. (1988). Thoughts about roles and relations: An old document revised. *Social Networks, 10,* 209–231.

Winship, C., & Mandel, M. (1983). Roles and positions: A critique and extension of the blockmodeling approach. In Leinhardt, S. (Ed.), *Sociological Methodology 1983–1984* (pp. 314–344). San Francisco: Jossey-Bass.

Young, M. W. (1971). *Fighting with Food.* Cambridge: Cambridge University Press.

Zeleny, M. (1974). The theory of the displaced ideal. In Zeleny, M. (Ed.), *Multiple Criteria Decision Making* (pp. 153–206). New York: Springer-Verlag.

Zimmermann, U. (1981). *Linear and Combinatorial Optimization in Ordered Algebraic Structures.* Number 10 in Annals of Discrete Mathematics. Amsterdam: North-Holland.

AUTHOR INDEX

SUBJECT INDEX

Other Books in the Series
(*Continued from p. iii*)